VEGETARIAN

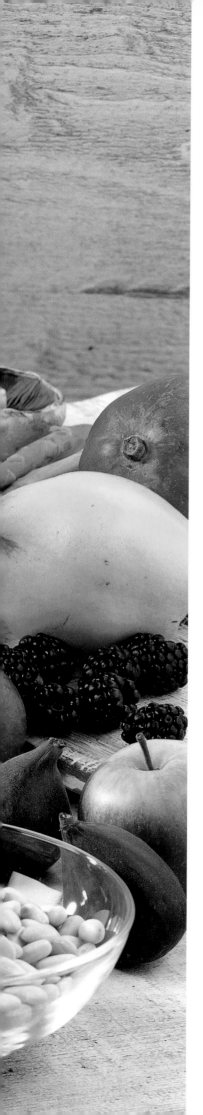

VEGETARIAN

a cook's guide to the sensational world of
vegetarian cooking with 500 recipes

Edited by Valerie Ferguson

LORENZ BOOKS

First published in 2001 by Lorenz Books
© Anness Publishing Limited 2001

Lorenz Books is an imprint of Anness Publishing Limited, Hermes House
88–89 Blackfriars Road, London SE1 8HA
www.lorenzbooks.com

Published in the USA by Lorenz Books
Anness Publishing Inc.
27 West 20th Street, New York
NY10011

This edition distributed in Canada by Raincoast Books
9050 Shaughnessy Street, Vancouver
British Columbia V6P 6E5

A CIP catalogue record for this book is available from the British Library.

Publisher: Joanna Lorenz
Managing Editor: Helen Sudell
Editor: Valerie Ferguson
Designer: Carole Perks
Editorial Reader: Richard McGinlay
Production Controller: Steve Lang

Recipes contributed by:
Catherine Atkinson, Alex Barker, Michelle Berriedale-Johnson, Angela Boggiano, Kathy Brown,
Carla Capalbo, Kit Chan, Jacqueline Clark, Carole Clements, Trish Davies, Roz Denny, Patrizia Diemling, Matthew Drennan,
Sarah Edmonds, Rafi Fernandez, Christine France, Silvano Franco, Shirley Gill,
Nicola Graimes, Rosamund Grant, Carole Handslip, Rebekah Hassan, Deh-Ta Hsuing, Shehzad Husain, Christine Ingram,
Judy Jackson, Manisha Kanani, Sheila Kimberley, Sara Lewis, Patricia Lousada,
Lesley Mackley, Sue Maggs, Kathy Man, Sally Mansfield, Norma Miller, Sallie Morris, Annie Nichols,
Maggie Pannell, Katherine Richmond, Jennie Shapter, Anne Sheasby, Liz Trigg, Hilaire Walden,
Laura Washburn, Steven Wheeler, Elizabeth Wolf-Cohen, Jeni Wright.

Photography:
William Adams-Lingwood, Karl Adamson, Edward Allwright, Steve Baxter, Nicki Dowey,
James Duncan, John Freeman, Ian Garlick, Michelle Garrett, John Heseltine, Amanda Heywood,
Ferguson Hill, Janine Hosegood, David Jordan, Dave King, Don Last, Patrick McLeavey,
Michael Michaels, Steve Moss, Thomas Odulate, Simon Smith, Sam Stowell, Polly Wreford.

3 5 7 9 10 8 6 4 2

Notes
For all recipes, quantities are given in both metric
and imperial measures and, where appropriate, measures are
also given in standard cups and spoons. Follow one set, but
not a mixture, because they are not interchangeable.

Standard spoon and cup measures are level.
1 tsp = 5ml, 1 tbsp = 15ml, 1 cup = 250ml/8fl oz

Australian standard tablespoons are 20ml. Australian readers
should use 3 tsp in place of 1 tbsp for measuring small quantities of cornflour, salt, etc.
Medium eggs are used unless otherwise stated.

Contents

Introduction

Some of the most exciting and innovative food available today is vegetarian. Glorious colours and enticing flavours epitomize this type of cooking, and when you consider the superb

soups, starters, snacks, salads and main courses that make up green cuisine, it seems inconceivable that vegetarian food could ever have been considered dull or unappetizing.

When it comes to vegetarian cooking, the pleasure starts long before the cook reaches the kitchen. What could be more sensual than stooping to pick fresh herbs, bruising them between the fingers and releasing those wonderful scents? Or meandering through a

market, filling a basket with dark purple aubergines, fat red tomatoes, glossy peppers, tiny radishes or creamy bulbs of fennel with their feathery fronds? Shopping for spices is another delight, as is discovering a new type of oil or vinegar, or a supplier of superb fresh pasta.

Vegetarian food has come a long way from the dreary days when it had a reputation for being brown and beany. It may once have been marginalized, but today it is very definitely mainstream. Visit any good restaurant, especially at lunchtime, and many of the most delectable items on offer will be meatless. Chargrilled slices of aubergine or courgette, layered with goat's cheese and served with a rich tomato sauce, pasta with pesto and pine nuts, puff pastry boxes filled with

baby vegetables, asparagus risotto – such delicious dishes aren't on the menu because they are vegetarian, but because they are what people really love to eat.

The good news is that you don't have to go to a restaurant to taste treats like these. There are more than five hundred wonderful vegetarian dishes in this collection, each one as appealing to the eye as the palate. Many of the dishes will naturally promote good health, but

that's a bonus, not a basic requirement. You'll find the frivolous and indulgent as well as the sane and sensible, so if you start a meal with cocktails and naughty nibbles, you can pick a prudent main course, such as the Harvest Vegetable & Lentil Casserole or the Spinach & Hazelnut Lasagne from the Low-fat Vegetarian chapter. A balanced diet is not difficult to achieve. Try to eat plenty of fruit and vegetables, pulses, nuts, seeds, rice, bread, pasta and potatoes, with some dairy food or non-dairy alternatives. Keep fats, sweets and high-calorie/low-nutrient foods to the

minimum. (There are no recipes for puddings or cakes in this book, so that's a start!)

With so many recipes to choose from, special-occasion cooking need never be a nightmare. There's a whole chapter devoted to dishes you will want to serve to friends, such as Celeriac & Blue Cheese Roulade; Courgette Fritters with Pistou; Mushroom, Nut & Prune Jalousie, or Parsnip & Pecan Gougères. If you prefer to theme the evening, choose dishes from China,

India, Greece or Morocco, or seek some inspiration in the Hot & Spicy chapter.

It is likely that as many non-vegetarians as vegetarians will enjoy this book. Some of the former will adapt the recipes to include prawns, perhaps, or strips of chicken, and some may use chicken stock instead of the vegetable stock featured. This is fine, but it is important to stress that if you are a carnivore cooking for a vegetarian, it is essential to follow the recipes scrupulously, avoiding not only the obvious things, such as meat, poultry and fish, but also any products that may contain derivatives of these foods, such as fish sauce or Worcestershire sauce (of which there are vegetarian versions). Guidance on ingredients is given in the pages that follow.

A number of the recipes feature cheese. We haven't stipulated vegetarian cheeses, assuming that committed vegetarians will choose varieties they feel able to use, while vegans will opt for recipes that exclude dairy products entirely. Although specific cheeses are listed in ingredients, it is almost always possible to substitute alternatives, just so long as you match like with like. A vegetarian Cheddar won't give you the same results as Parmesan, for instance, but the results will be perfectly acceptable.

Vegetarian Ingredients

The cardinal rule when shopping for vegetarian ingredients is to choose the freshest possible produce, buying little and often. For dried goods, find a supplier with a healthy turnover, so stocks don't have time to get stale. Keep a constant lookout for new and exciting products. Vegetarian food is a growth market, and the range of available foods is constantly increasing. Once the preserve of the health food shop, vegetarian ingredients are now stocked in every supermarket, and the demand for organic produce, and products made from organic ingredients, is huge.

Vegetables & Fruit

Buy the bulk of your produce from local growers, if possible, balancing home-grown vegetables and fruit with exotic imports. Some supermarkets support local growers, including organic ones, so look out for labels that state the provenance of the produce. Several organic farms offer box schemes, where you opt to buy a box of vegetables and/or fruit every week. What goes into the box depends on what is being harvested at the time, and because everything is picked to order, it is beautifully fresh. This is a great way of buying greens such as spinach or Swiss chard. Farmer's markets are excellent sources of fruit and vegetables, as are allotment shops, where growers sell their surplus. If you live in the country, look out for roadside stalls. Gardeners often grow vegetables not generally available in the shops, such as the more unusual types of squash, and sell them at very reasonable prices. Pick-your-own vegetable farms aren't as common as those offering pick-your-own fruit, but corn on the cob is sometimes sold that way. Don't forget essential aromatics such as fresh garlic and root ginger.

tomatoes

winter squash

Swiss chard

garlic

apples

aubergines

Herbs & Spices

The most satisfying way to obtain herbs is from your own garden. You don't need acres of space as even a window-box or a few pots on the patio will yield a generous harvest. Obvious candidates are mint and parsley, preferably the flat leaf variety, but you should also aim to grow thyme, basil, sage and oregano or marjoram. If you possibly can, add coriander, chives, chervil, tarragon, rosemary and bay, all of which feature in this book. Alternatively, buy herbs from the supermarket, but use them as soon as possible after purchase. Dried herbs lose their potency quite quickly, so buy small amounts at a time, keep them in a cool, dry place (out of direct sunlight) and replace them as soon as they start to go stale.

For the best flavour, buy whole spices and seeds, and grind them as needed in a spice mill or coffee grinder kept for the purpose. Dry-frying spices before grinding intensifies their flavour. Essential spices include cardamom pods, cumin and coriander seeds, cinnamon sticks, nutmeg, dried chillies and chilli powder, cayenne, paprika, Chinese five-spice powder, garam masala, saffron, turmeric and curry powder.

flat leaf parsley

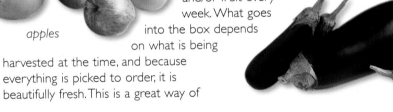

cinnamon

basil

coriander seeds and leaves

chives and bay leaves

Clockwise from top: celery seeds, chilli powder, chilli flakes and cayenne

Grains, Pasta & Pulses

The dried versions of these easy-to-use ingredients are store-cupboard staples. Rice is invaluable to the vegetarian cook, both as a base for vegetable stews and sautés and for stuffed vegetables. In addition to regular white and brown long grain rice, try basmati, which has a wonderful fragrance and flavour. Rinse it well before use and, if there is time, soak it in the water used for the final rinse. For risotto you will need a short grain rice such as arborio, carnaroli or Vialone Nano. Bulgur wheat has already been partially prepared, so needs only a brief soaking before use. It is the basis for tabbouleh, and also tastes good in pilaffs and bakes. Another great grain that needs very little preparation is couscous, which is made from coarse semolina.

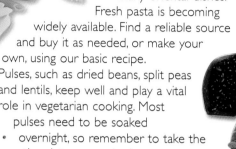
rice

Dried pasta comes in an astonishing array of shapes. Some of the more unusual types are introduced in recipes in this book, but you can always substitute whatever you have in the cupboard. Dried egg noodles are essential for many oriental dishes.

Fresh pasta is becoming widely available. Find a reliable source and buy it as needed, or make your own, using our basic recipe.

dried pasta

lentils

Pulses, such as dried beans, split peas and lentils, keep well and play a vital role in vegetarian cooking. Most pulses need to be soaked overnight, so remember to take the time into account when you are planning your menu.

dried beans

From the Fridge & Freezer

Dairy products provide lacto-vegetarians (those who eat dairy produce) with valuable protein, calcium and vitamins B_{12}, A and D, but can be high in fat. Like eggs, they should be eaten in moderation. Look out for vegetarian versions of your favourite cheeses (produced with vegetable rennet). Yogurt, crème fraîche and fromage frais are also very useful, as is beancurd (tofu), a protein-rich food made from soya beans. Various forms are available, from soft silken tofu to a firm type which can be cubed and sautéed. Tempeh is similar to beancurd, but has a nuttier taste.

Keep filo pastry, shortcrust and puff pastry in the freezer, but allow plenty of time for slow thawing. Nuts will also store well in the freezer.

Parmesan cheese

beancurd (tofu)

soured cream and crème fraîche

From the Larder

If your store cupboard is well stocked, spur-of-the-moment meals will never be a problem. In addition to pasta, pulses and grains, dry goods should include different types of flour, easy-blend dried yeast, polenta and oatmeal, and you'll also want a small supply of nuts. Don't buy these in bulk, as nuts become rancid if stored for too long. Dried mushrooms are useful, as are sun-dried tomatoes and peppers, but you may prefer to buy the ones that come packed in oil in jars. Also in jars, look for pesto (both green and red), tahini, peanut butter, capers and olives.

mixed nuts

canned beans

Useful sauces include passata (puréed tomatoes), creamed horseradish, soy sauce in various strengths, black bean sauce and the vegetarian versions of oyster sauce and Worcestershire sauce. You'll need various vinegars, including balsamic and rice vinegar, and oils, especially olive oil, sunflower oil, sesame oil, groundnut oil and walnut oil. For low-fat cooking, a light oil spray is useful.

Cans take up quite a lot of space, but it is well worth keeping a stock of favourites, such as canned tomatoes, kidney beans, borlotti beans, flageolets and chick-peas, plus sweetcorn kernels, artichoke hearts and bamboo shoots. Canned coconut milk comes in handy for vegetable curries and some soups.

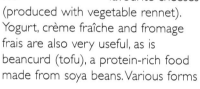

wine vinegar

Techniques

Even the simplest tasks in the kitchen can take longer than necessary if you don't know a few useful techniques and short cuts. Below are some step-by-step instructions for preparing a variety of ingredients that will save time and help to improve the presentation of the final dishes. No special equipment is required for most of them, just a sharp knife.

Chopping Onions

1 Cut a peeled onion in half lengthways and place one half, cut side down, on a board. Slice it vertically several times.

2 Make two horizontal cuts in from the stalk end towards the root, but not through it. Holding the onion by the root end, cut it crossways to form even diced pieces.

Cutting Vegetable Matchsticks

1 Peel firm vegetables and cut in 5cm/2in lengths. Cut these into 3mm/⅛in slices.

2 Stack the slices and cut them neatly lengthways into matchstick strips.

Peeling & Chopping Tomatoes

1 Cut a cross in the blossom end of each tomato. Put them in a heatproof bowl and pour over boiling water.

2 Leave for 30 seconds, until the skins wrinkle and start to peel back from the crosses. Drain, peel off the skin and chop the flesh neatly.

Chopping Herbs

1 Remove any thick stalks and discard. Pile the herbs on a board and chop them finely, first in one direction, then the other, using a sharp knife or a mezzaluna (half-moon herb chopper), which you use in a see-saw motion.

Blanching Vegetables

1 Bring a pan of water to the boil. Using a wire basket, if possible, lower the vegetables into the water and bring it back to the boil.

2 Cook for 1–2 minutes, then drain the vegetables and cool them quickly under cold running water or by dipping them in a bowl of iced water. Drain well.

Roasting & Peeling Peppers

1 Leave the peppers whole or cut them in half and scrape out the cores and seeds. Place them on a grill rack under medium heat, turning them occasionally, until the skins are evenly blistered and charred but not too burnt, as this will make the flesh taste bitter.

2 Seal the peppers in a plastic bag or place them in a bowl and cover them with several sheets of kitchen paper. When the steam has softened them, peel off the skins. Remove the bitter seeds if necessary, working over a bowl to catch any juices. The juices can be used in a salad dressing.

Crushing Garlic

1 Break off a clove of garlic and smash it firmly with the flat side of the blade of a cook's knife. Pick off all the papery skin.

2 Chop the clove roughly, sprinkle over a little table salt, then use the flat side of the knife blade to work the salt into the garlic until it is reduced to a fine paste.

Preparing Chillies

1 Wearing rubber gloves if possible, halve the chilli lengthways. Leave the seeds inside or scrape them out and discard them.

2 Slice or chop the chilli finely. Wash the knife, board and your hands (if not gloved) in hot soapy water, as chillies contain a substance that burns sensitive skin. Never rub your eyes or touch your lips after handling chillies.

Preparing Fresh Root Ginger

1 Using a vegetable peeler or a small knife, peel the skin off a piece of fresh root ginger. Cut the ginger in thin slices.

2 Place each slice on a board. Cut it into thin strips and use, or turn the strips around and chop them finely. Ginger can also be grated, in which case it need not be peeled.

Preparing Lemon Grass

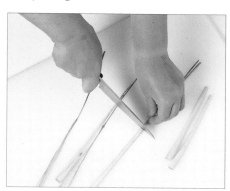

1 Discard any tough outer layers from the lemon grass stem, then cut off the end and trim the top, leaving a piece 10cm/4in long.

2 Split this in half lengthways, then chop very finely. If the bulb is particularly fresh, it can be thinly sliced. Whole stems can be used for flavouring and removed before serving.

Crushing Spices

1 Dry-fry whole spices in a frying pan, then put them in a mortar and grind them with a pestle to make a smooth powder.

2 Alternatively, grind them in a spice mill or a coffee grinder kept specifically for the purpose. Use a pastry brush to remove all the ground spice from the inside of the grinder.

Preparing Pulses

1 Rinse well, pick out any small stones, then put the pulses in a bowl with plenty of cold water. Soak for 4–8 hours.

2 Drain the pulses, rinse them under cold water and drain them again. Tip them into a pan. Add plenty of cold water but no salt. Bring to the boil, boil hard for 10 minutes, then simmer until tender. Drain and season.

Lentils do not need to be soaked, although soaking will shorten the cooking time. Red lentils become very soft when cooked and are ideal for purées. Green or brown lentils are firmer and retain more texture. The finest flavoured are Puy lentils.

Basic Recipes

The recipes in this book are largely complete in themselves, but there are a few basics that crop up again and again, such as vegetable stock, tomato sauce, flavoured oils, and doughs for pizzas and pastas. You can, of course, substitute bought ingredients, such as sauces, ready-made pasta and pizza bases, but do make your own if you have time as they taste great.

Pizza Dough
Makes 1 x 25–30cm/10–12in round pizza base

175g/6oz/1½ cups white bread flour
1.5ml/¼ tsp salt
5ml/1 tsp easy-blend dried yeast
120–150ml/4–5fl oz/½–⅔ cup
*   lukewarm water*

1 Sift the flour and salt into a mixing bowl and stir in the yeast. Add the water and mix to a soft dough. Knead on a lightly floured surface for 10 minutes, until smooth and elastic. Return to the clean bowl, cover with lightly oiled clear film and leave in a warm place for about 1 hour, or until the dough has doubled.

2 Knock back the dough, knead it for 2 minutes, then roll it out to a 25–30cm/10–12in round. Place on a greased baking sheet and knock up the edges. Top and bake as suggested in recipes.

Cook's Tip
Mix and knead the dough in a food processor, if you prefer, but transfer it to a bowl for rising.

Pasta Dough
Serves 6

300g/11oz/2¾ cups Italian Tipo 00 flour or
*   white bread flour*
5ml/1 tsp salt
3 eggs, beaten

1 Put the flour and salt in a food processor fitted with the metal blade. Pour in one egg, cover and pulse to mix on maximum speed. Add the remaining eggs through the feeder tube and mix briefly to form a dough.

2 Knead the dough on a clean surface for 5 minutes if you are shaping it in a pasta machine; 10 minutes if shaping by hand. The dough should be very smooth and elastic. Wrap it in clear film and let it rest for 15–20 minutes before rolling it and cutting it into shapes.

Making Pasta Dough by Hand

1 Mound the flour on a work surface, make a well in the centre and add the eggs and salt. Mix with your hands or a fork, gradually incorporating the surrounding flour until a rough dough forms. Knead as in the main recipe.

Tomato Sauce
Makes about 350ml/12fl oz/1½ cups

15ml/1 tbsp olive oil
1 onion, finely chopped
1 garlic clove, crushed
400g/14oz can chopped tomatoes
15ml/1 tbsp tomato purée
15ml/1 tbsp chopped fresh mixed herbs
*   (parsley, thyme, oregano, basil)*
pinch of granulated sugar
salt and ground black pepper

1 Heat the oil in a pan and fry the onion and garlic gently until softened. Stir in the tomatoes, tomato purée, herbs and sugar, with salt and pepper to taste.

2 Simmer, uncovered, for 15–20 minutes, stirring occasionally, until the mixture has reduced and is thick. Use at once or cool, cover and store in the fridge.

Cook's Tip
Use this tomato sauce on pizzas or pasta. It is excellent in lasagne, and also tastes good with vegetables. Spoon it over cooked cauliflower, top with grated cheese and grill until bubbly.

Vegetable Stock
Makes about 2.4 litres/4 pints

2 large onions, roughly chopped
2 leeks, sliced
3 garlic cloves, crushed
3 carrots, roughly chopped
4 celery sticks, sliced
a large strip of pared lemon rind
12 fresh parsley stalks
a few fresh thyme leaves
2 bay leaves
2.4 litres/4 pints water

1 Put the onions, leeks, crushed garlic cloves, carrots and celery slices in a large saucepan. Add the strip of pared lemon rind, with the parsley, thyme and bay leaves. Pour in the water and bring to the boil. Skim off the foam that rises to the surface.

2 Lower the heat and simmer, uncovered, for 30 minutes. Strain the stock, season it to taste and leave it to cool. Cover and keep in the fridge for up to 5 days, or freeze for up to 1 month.

Cook's Tip
To save freezer space, boil vegetable stock down to concentrate it to about half the original quantity and then freeze in ice cube trays. When defrosting add an equal amount of water.

French Dressing
Makes about 120ml/4fl oz/ ½ cup

90ml/6 tbsp olive oil or a mixture of olive and
   sunflower oils
15ml/1 tbsp white wine vinegar
5ml/1 tsp French mustard
pinch of granulated sugar
salt and ground black pepper

1 Place the oil and vinegar in a screw-top jar. Add the mustard and sugar.

2 Close the lid tightly and shake well. Season to taste.

Mayonnaise
Makes about 350ml/12fl oz/1½ cups

2 egg yolks
15ml/1 tbsp Dijon mustard
30ml/2 tbsp lemon juice or white wine vinegar
300ml/ ½ pint/1¼ cups oil (vegetable, corn or
   light olive)
salt and ground black pepper

1 Put the egg yolks, mustard, half the lemon juice or vinegar and a pinch of salt in a blender or food processor and process for 10 seconds to mix. With the motor running, add the oil through the funnel in the lid, drop by drop at first and then in a steady stream, processing constantly until the mayonnaise is thick and creamy. Taste and sharpen with the remaining juice or vinegar, if you like, and season to taste.

Chilli Oil
Makes about 150ml/ ¼ pint/ ⅔ cup

150ml/ ¼ pint/ ⅔ cup olive oil
10ml/2 tsp tomato purée
15ml/1 tbsp dried red chilli flakes

1 Heat the oil in a pan. When it is very hot, but not smoking, stir in the tomato purée and chilli flakes. Leave to cool.

2 Pour into a small jar or bottle. Cover well and store in the fridge for up to 2 months (the longer you keep it the hotter it gets).

Garlic Oil
Makes about 120ml/4fl oz/ ½ cup

3–4 garlic cloves
120ml/4fl oz/ ½ cup olive oil

1 Peel the garlic cloves and put them into a small jar or bottle. Pour in the oil, cover securely and store in the fridge for up to 1 month.

Chilled Tomato & Sweet Pepper Soup

Roasted red peppers give this chilled soup a sweet and slightly smoky flavour that is delicious with sun-ripened tomatoes.

Serves 4
2 red peppers, halved and seeded
45ml/3 tbsp olive oil
1 onion, finely chopped
2 garlic cloves, crushed
675g/1¹/₂lb ripe well-
    flavoured tomatoes
150ml/ ¹/₄ pint/ ²/₃ cup red wine
600ml/1 pint/2¹/₂ cups
    vegetable stock
salt and ground black pepper
snipped fresh chives,
    to garnish

For the croûtons
2 slices day-old white bread,
    crusts removed
60ml/4 tbsp olive oil

1 Place the pepper halves, skin side up, on a grill rack and grill until the skins have charred. Transfer to a bowl and cover with crumpled kitchen paper. Leave to cool slightly.

2 Heat the oil in a large pan. Add the onion and garlic and cook until soft. Meanwhile, remove the skin from the peppers and roughly chop them. Cut the tomatoes into chunks.

3 Add the peppers and tomatoes to the pan, then cover and cook gently for 10 minutes. Pour in the wine and cook for 5 minutes more, then add the stock. Season well and continue to simmer for 20 minutes.

4 To make the croûtons, cut the bread into cubes. Heat the oil in a small frying pan, add the bread cubes and fry until golden. Drain on kitchen paper. When cold, store in an airtight box.

5 Process the soup in a blender or food processor until smooth. Pour into a clean glass or ceramic bowl and leave to cool thoroughly before chilling in the fridge for at least 3 hours. Serve the soup in chilled bowls, topped with the croûtons and garnished with snipped chives.

Gazpacho

Tomatoes, cucumber and peppers form the basis of this classic chilled soup.

Serves 4
2 slices day-old white bread
600ml/1 pint/2¹/₂ cups
    chilled water
1kg/2¹/₄ lb tomatoes
1 cucumber
1 red pepper, halved, seeded
    and chopped
1 fresh green chilli, seeded
    and chopped
2 garlic cloves, chopped
30ml/2 tbsp extra virgin olive oil
juice of 1 lime and 1 lemon
a few drops of Tabasco sauce
salt and ground black pepper
a handful of fresh basil leaves,
    to garnish
ice cubes and Avocado Salsa
    (optional), to serve

For the garlic croûtons
2 slices day-old white bread,
    crusts removed
1 garlic clove, halved
15ml/1 tbsp olive oil

1 Soak the bread in 150ml/ ¹/₄ pint/ ²/₃ cup of the chilled water for 5 minutes. Meanwhile, place the tomatoes in a bowl and pour over boiling water to cover. Leave for 30 seconds, then drain, peel, seed and chop the flesh.

2 Peel the cucumber thinly, then cut it in half lengthways and scoop out the seeds with a teaspoon. Discard the seeds and chop the flesh.

3 Place the soaked bread, tomatoes, cucumber, red pepper, chilli, garlic, olive oil, lime juice, lemon juice and Tabasco sauce in a food processor or blender, with the remaining chilled water. Process until thoroughly combined but still chunky. Pour the soup into a bowl, season to taste with salt and pepper and chill in the fridge for 2–3 hours.

4 Make the croûtons. Rub the surface of the bread slices with the cut garlic clove. Cube the bread and toss with the olive oil until evenly coated. Heat a large non-stick frying pan and fry the croûtons over a medium heat until crisp and golden. Drain on kitchen paper.

5 Ladle the soup into bowls and add two ice cubes to each portion. Garnish with the basil. Top with the avocado salsa, if using, and hand the croûtons separately.

Avocado Salsa

Serve a spoonful of this tasty salsa on top of each portion of Gazpacho, or enjoy it on its own, with crisps or French bread.

Serves 4
1 ripe avocado
5ml/1 tsp lemon juice
2.5cm/1in piece cucumber, diced
¹/₂ fresh red chilli, finely chopped

1 Cut the avocado in half, remove the stone, then peel. Dice the flesh and put it in a bowl. Toss immediately with the lemon juice to prevent it from browning.
2 Mix the avocado with the diced cucumber and finely chopped chilli. Serve as soon as possible.

Chilled Almond Soup

Unless you want to spend time pounding the ingredients for this refreshing Spanish soup by hand, a food processor is an essential kitchen tool.

Serves 6
4 slices day-old fresh white bread, crusts removed
750ml/1¼ pints/3 cups chilled water
115g/4oz/1 cup blanched almonds
2 garlic cloves, sliced
75ml/5 tbsp olive oil
25ml/5 tsp sherry vinegar
salt and ground black pepper
toasted flaked almonds and skinned seedless grapes, to garnish

1 Break the bread into a bowl and pour over 150ml/ ¼ pint/ ⅔ cup of the chilled water. Leave for 5 minutes.

2 Put the almonds and garlic in a blender or food processor and process until very finely ground. Add the soaked white bread and process until smooth.

3 With the motor running, gradually add the oil through the lid or feeder tube until the mixture forms a smooth paste. Add the sherry vinegar and remaining chilled water and process until smooth and thoroughly combined.

4 Scrape the mixture into a bowl and season with salt and pepper, adding a little more water if the soup is very thick. Chill in the fridge for at least 3 hours.

5 Ladle the soup into chilled bowls and scatter with the toasted almonds and skinned grapes.

Cook's Tip
To blanch almonds, put the kernels in a bowl, pour over boiling water and leave for about 5 minutes. Drain, then rub off the skins with the palms of your hands.

Cold Cucumber & Yogurt Soup with Walnuts

Walnuts make an interesting addition to this refreshing cold soup.

Serves 5–6
1 cucumber
4 garlic cloves, peeled
2.5ml/ ½ tsp salt
75g/3oz/ ¾ cup walnut pieces
40g/1 ½ oz day-old white bread, torn into pieces
30ml/2 tbsp walnut oil
400ml/14fl oz/1⅔ cups natural yogurt
120ml/4fl oz/ ½ cup chilled still mineral water
5–10ml/1–2 tsp lemon juice

For the garnish
40g/1 ½ oz/scant ½ cup walnuts, coarsely chopped
25ml/5 tsp olive oil
fresh dill sprigs

1 Cut the cucumber in half lengthways. Peel one half. Dice both halves, so that you have a mixture of peeled and unpeeled pieces of cucumber. Set aside.

2 Crush the garlic and salt together in a mortar with a pestle. Add the walnuts and crush them into the mixture, then work in the bread. When the mixture is smooth, gradually add the walnut oil, using the pestle to ensure that the mixture is thoroughly combined.

3 Scrape the mixture into a large bowl. Beat in the yogurt and diced cucumber, then beat in the mineral water and lemon juice to taste. Chill the soup if time permits.

4 Pour the soup into chilled soup bowls. Sprinkle the coarsely chopped walnuts on top, then drizzle a little olive oil over the nuts. Complete the garnish with the fresh dill.

Cook's Tip
If you prefer your soup smooth, process it in a food processor or blender to a purée before serving.

Chilled Leek & Potato Soup

This creamy-smooth soup is served with a tangy yogurt topping that beautifully complements its subtle, but distinctive flavour.

Serves 4
25g/1oz/2 tbsp butter
15ml/1 tbsp vegetable oil
1 small onion, chopped

3 leeks, sliced
2 medium floury potatoes, diced
about 600ml/1 pint/2½ cups
    vegetable stock
about 300ml/ ½ pint/
    1¼ cups milk
45ml/3 tbsp single cream
salt and ground black pepper
60ml/4 tbsp natural yogurt and
    fried chopped leeks, to serve

1 Heat the butter and oil in a large, heavy-based pan and add the onion, leeks and potatoes. Cover and cook over a low heat, stirring occasionally, for 15 minutes, until the vegetables have softened and the onion is golden.

2 Stir in the stock and milk. Bring to the boil, lower the heat, cover and simmer for 10 minutes.

3 Allow to cool slightly, then process the mixture, in batches if necessary, in a blender or a food processor to a purée. Pour the soup into a bowl, stir in the cream and season generously with salt and pepper.

4 Set the soup aside to cool, then cover and chill in the fridge for 3–4 hours. You may need to add a little extra milk or cold vegetable stock to thin the soup before serving, as it will thicken slightly as it cools.

5 Ladle the soup into chilled soup bowls and top each portion with a spoonful of yogurt and a sprinkling of fried leeks.

> **Cook's Tip**
> *You will need one or two thin young leeks for the garnish. Clean them, then slice them into rounds. Fry them in a mixture of butter and olive oil until they are crisp-tender.*

Chilled Coconut Soup

Refreshing, cooling and not too filling, this soup makes an excellent summer starter, but it could also be served after a spicy curry, to refresh the palate.

Serves 6
1.2 litres/2 pints/5 cups milk
225g/8oz/2⅔ cups unsweetened
    desiccated coconut

400ml/14fl oz/1⅔ cups coconut
    milk from a can or carton
400ml/14fl oz/1⅔ cups
    vegetable stock
200ml/7fl oz/scant 1 cup
    double cream
2.5ml/ ½ tsp salt
2.5ml/ ½ tsp ground
    white pepper
5ml/1 tsp caster sugar
small bunch of fresh coriander

1 Bring the milk to the boil in a large saucepan. Stir in the coconut, lower the heat and simmer, stirring occasionally, for 30 minutes. Spoon the mixture into a food processor and process until smooth. This may take a while – up to 5 minutes – so pause frequently and scrape down the sides of the bowl.

2 Rinse the pan to remove any traces of coconut, pour in the processed mixture and add the coconut milk. Stir in the stock, cream, salt, pepper and sugar. Bring to the boil, stirring occasionally, then lower the heat and cook for 10 minutes.

3 Reserve a few coriander leaves for the garnish, then chop the rest finely and stir them into the soup. Pour the soup into a large bowl, let it cool, then cover and chill in the fridge.

4 Just before serving, taste the soup and adjust the seasoning, as chilling will have altered the taste. Serve in chilled bowls, garnished with the reserved coriander leaves.

> **Cook's Tips**
> • *Avoid using sweetened desiccated coconut, which would spoil the flavour of this soup.*
> • *Use a tasty vegetable stock, boiling it down if necessary to concentrate the flavour.*

French Onion Soup

This classic French soup is popular the world over. It is always served with a slightly chewy topping of melted Gruyère cheese.

Serves 4
50g/2oz/ ¼ cup butter
2 onions, about 250g/9oz total
   weight, sliced
10ml/2 tsp plain flour
1 litre/1 ¾ pints/4 cups
   vegetable stock
60ml/4 tbsp dry white wine or
   30ml/2 tbsp dry sherry
4 slices crusty white bread
150g/5oz/1 ¼ cups grated
   Gruyère or Emmenthal cheese
salt and ground black pepper

1 Melt the butter in a large, heavy-based saucepan. Add the sliced onions and cook over a moderately low heat, stirring occasionally, for about 12 minutes, or until lightly browned. Stir in the flour and continue to cook, stirring constantly, until the flour turns a sandy colour.

2 Pour in the stock and wine or sherry, then bring to the boil, stirring constantly. Season to taste with salt and pepper, cover and simmer for 15 minutes.

3 Spread out the slices of bread in a grill pan and toast them lightly. Divide the grated cheese among them. Return to the grill and heat until the cheese is bubbling. Place the cheese toasts in four warmed, heatproof bowls.

4 Using a slotted spoon, scoop out the onions from the soup and divide them equally among the heated bowls. Pour over the soup and serve immediately.

Cook's Tips
• *To give the soup a good colour, make sure the onions are lightly browned before you add the stock.*
• *Grated mature Cheddar cheese can be substituted for Gruyère or Emmenthal, but neither the flavour nor the texture will be strictly authentic.*

Cream of Courgette Soup

The joys of this soup are its delicate colour, creamy texture and subtle taste.

Serves 4–6
30ml/2 tbsp olive oil
15g/ ½ oz/1 tbsp butter
1 medium onion, roughly chopped
900g/2lb courgettes, trimmed
   and sliced
5ml/1 tsp dried oregano
about 600ml/1 pint/2 ½ cups
   vegetable stock
115g/4oz dolcelatte cheese, rind
   removed, diced
300ml/ ½ pint/1 ¼ cups
   single cream
salt and ground black pepper
fresh oregano and extra
   dolcelatte, to garnish

1 Heat the oil and butter in a large saucepan until foaming. Add the onion and cook gently, stirring frequently, for about 5 minutes, until softened but not brown.

2 Add the sliced courgettes and dried oregano and season with salt and pepper to taste. Cook over a medium heat, stirring frequently, for 10 minutes.

3 Pour in the stock and bring to the boil, stirring constantly. Lower the heat and partially cover the pan. Simmer gently, stirring occasionally, for about 30 minutes. Stir in the diced dolcelatte until melted.

4 Pour the mixture into a blender or food processor. Process until smooth, then press through a sieve into a clean pan.

5 Add two-thirds of the cream. Stir over a low heat until hot, but not boiling. Check the consistency and add more stock if the soup is too thick. Taste for seasoning, then pour into heated bowls. Swirl in the remaining cream. Garnish with fresh oregano and extra cheese and serve immediately.

Cook's Tip
There are vegetarian versions of a wide·variety of cheeses. Look for them in large supermarkets or health food stores.

Pear & Watercress Soup

Pears and Stilton are classic companions, although they are seldom served in soup. Try this sophisticated starter – it is delicious!

Serves 6
1 bunch watercress
4 medium pears, peeled and sliced
900ml/1½ pints/3¾ cups
   vegetable stock
120ml/4fl oz/½ cup
   double cream
juice of 1 lime
salt and ground black pepper

For the Stilton croûtons
25g/1oz/2 tbsp butter
15ml/1 tbsp olive oil
3 slices day-old white bread,
   crusts removed, cubed
115g/4oz Stilton cheese

1 Reserve about one-third of the watercress leaves. Place the rest of the watercress leaves and the stalks in a large pan and add the pears and stock. Bring to the boil, then lower the heat and simmer for 15–20 minutes.

2 Allow the mixture to cool slightly, then pour it into a food processor. Add most of the reserved watercress leaves, reserving some for garnishing, and blend until smooth.

3 Scrape the mixture into the clean pan and stir in the cream and lime juice. Season to taste with salt and pepper.

4 Make the croûtons. Melt the butter and oil and fry the bread cubes until golden brown. Drain on kitchen paper, then spread out in a shallow heatproof dish. Crumble the Stilton on top and heat under a hot grill until bubbling.

5 Meanwhile, reheat the soup gently, stirring constantly. Pour it into heated bowls. Divide the croûtons and remaining watercress among the bowls and serve immediately.

> **Cook's Tip**
> Watercress does not keep well, so use it within a day of purchase. Otherwise, the leaves will wilt and turn yellow.

Asparagus Soup

Home-made asparagus soup has a delicate flavour, quite unlike that from a can. Use young asparagus, which is tender and easy to blend.

Serves 4
450g/1lb young asparagus
40g/1½ oz/3 tbsp butter
6 shallots, sliced
15g/½ oz/2 tbsp plain flour
600ml/1 pint/2½ cups
   vegetable stock
15ml/1 tbsp lemon juice
250ml/8fl oz/1 cup milk
120ml/4fl oz/½ cup
   single cream
salt and ground black pepper
10ml/2 tsp chopped fresh chervil,
   to garnish

1 Trim the stalks of the asparagus if necessary. Cut 4cm/1½ in off the tops of half the asparagus and set aside for a garnish. Slice the remaining asparagus.

2 Melt 25g/1oz/2 tbsp of the butter in a large, heavy-based saucepan. Add the sliced shallots and fry over a low heat, stirring occasionally, for 2–3 minutes, until softened and translucent but not brown.

3 Add the sliced asparagus and fry over a gentle heat for about 1 minute. Stir in the flour and cook, stirring constantly, for 1 minute. Stir in the stock and lemon juice and season to taste with salt and pepper. Bring to the boil, then lower the heat and simmer, partially covered, for 15–20 minutes, until the asparagus is very tender.

4 Cool the soup slightly, then process the mixture with the milk in a blender or food processor until smooth. Press the purée through a sieve into a clean pan.

5 Melt the remaining butter in a frying pan over a low heat. Add the reserved asparagus tips and fry gently for 3–4 minutes, until softened.

6 Heat the soup gently for 3–4 minutes. Stir in the cream and the fried asparagus tips. Ladle into heated bowls, sprinkle with the chopped fresh chervil and serve immediately.

Tomato & Fresh Basil Soup

This is the perfect choice for late summer, when fresh tomatoes are at their most flavoursome and sweet.

Serves 4–6
15ml/1 tbsp olive oil
25g/1oz/2 tbsp butter
1 medium onion, finely chopped
900g/2lb ripe Italian plum tomatoes, roughly chopped
1 garlic clove, roughly chopped
about 750ml/1¼ pints/3 cups vegetable stock
120ml/4fl oz/½ cup dry white wine
30ml/2 tbsp sun-dried tomato paste
30ml/2 tbsp shredded fresh basil, plus a few whole leaves, to garnish
150ml/¼ pint/⅔ cup double cream
salt and ground black pepper

1 Heat the oil and butter in a large, heavy-based saucepan. Add the chopped onion and cook over a low heat, stirring occasionally, for about 5 minutes, until softened and translucent but not browned.

2 Stir in the chopped tomatoes and garlic, then add the stock, white wine and sun-dried tomato paste, with salt and pepper to taste. Bring to the boil, then lower the heat, half-cover the pan and simmer gently for 20 minutes, stirring occasionally.

3 Process the soup with the shredded basil in a blender or food processor, then press through a sieve into a clean pan.

4 Stir in the double cream and heat through, stirring. Do not allow the soup to approach boiling point. Check the consistency and flavour. Add more stock and seasoning if necessary. Pour into heated bowls and garnish with whole basil leaves. Serve at once.

> **Variation**
> The soup can also be served chilled. Pour it into a container after sieving, cool, then chill in the fridge for at least 4 hours. Serve in chilled bowls.

Garlic & Coriander Soup

This simple soup should be made with the best ingredients – plump garlic, fresh coriander, high-quality crusty country bread and extra virgin olive oil.

Serves 6
25g/1oz/1 cup fresh coriander, leaves and stalks chopped separately
1.5 litres/2½ pints/6¼ cups vegetable stock
5–6 plump garlic cloves, peeled
6 eggs
3 slices day-old white bread, crusts removed and torn into bite-size pieces
90ml/6 tbsp extra virgin olive oil, plus extra to serve
salt and ground black pepper

1 Place the coriander stalks in a saucepan. Add the stock and bring to the boil over a medium heat. Lower the heat and simmer for 10 minutes. Cool slightly, then process the mixture in a blender or food processor. Press through a sieve into the clean pan. Heat gently.

2 Crush the garlic with 5ml/1 tsp salt, then stir in 120ml/4fl oz/½ cup of the hot coriander stock. Return the mixture to the pan.

3 Bring the soup to the boil and season to taste with salt and pepper. Leave over a low heat. Poach the eggs.

4 Divide the pieces of bread among six soup plates or bowls and drizzle the olive oil over it. Stir the chopped coriander leaves into the soup, then ladle it over the bread. Stir each portion once, then add a poached egg to each bowl. Serve immediately, offering more olive oil at the table so that it can be drizzled over the soup to taste.

> **Cook's Tip**
> The olive oil is traditionally used to moisten the bread and flavour the soup, but you can use less than the recommended quantity if you prefer.

Wild Mushroom Soup

Dried porcini mushrooms have an intense flavour, so a small quantity is sufficient to give this soup a truly superb taste.

Serves 4
25g/1oz/1 cups dried
    porcini mushrooms
250ml/8fl oz/1 cup warm water
30ml/2 tbsp olive oil
15g/ 1/2 oz/1 tbsp butter
2 leeks, thinly sliced

2 shallots, roughly chopped
1 garlic clove, roughly chopped
225g/8oz/3 cups fresh
    wild mushrooms
about 1.2 litres/2 pints/5 cups
    vegetable stock
2.5ml/ 1/2 tsp dried thyme
150ml/ 1/4 pint/ 2/3 cup
    double cream
salt and ground black pepper
fresh thyme sprigs, to garnish

1 Soak the dried porcini in the warm water for 20–30 minutes. Lift out of the liquid and squeeze out as much of the liquid as possible. Strain all the liquid and reserve. Chop the mushrooms.

2 Heat the oil and butter in a large pan and cook the leeks, shallots and garlic gently for about 5 minutes, stirring frequently.

3 Slice the fresh mushrooms and add them to the pan. Stir over a medium heat until they begin to soften, then pour in the stock and bring to the boil. Add the porcini, soaking liquid and dried thyme and season to taste. Lower the heat, half-cover the pan and simmer gently for 30 minutes, stirring occasionally.

4 Process three-quarters of the soup in a blender or food processor until smooth. Return it to the pan, stir in the cream and heat through. Add more stock if the soup is too thick. Taste for seasoning. Serve hot, garnished with the thyme sprigs.

> **Cook's Tip**
> *Look out for packets of fresh mixed wild mushrooms in the supermarket. Use them on the day of purchase, if possible, as they don't keep well.*

Borsch

Beetroot is the main ingredient of this classic Russian soup, which is also very popular throughout Eastern Europe.

Serves 4–6
40g/1 1/2 oz/3 tbsp butter
2 onions, sliced
900g/2lb raw beetroot, peeled
    and cut into thick batons
2 carrots, cut into thick batons
2 celery sticks, cut into
    thick batons

2 garlic cloves, crushed
4 tomatoes, peeled, seeded
    and chopped
bouquet garni
4 whole peppercorns
1.2 litres/2 pints/5 cups
    vegetable stock
150ml/ 1/4 pint/ 2/3 cup beetroot
    kvas (see Cook's Tip) or the
    liquid from pickled beetroot
salt and ground black pepper
soured cream and snipped fresh
    chives, to garnish

1 Melt the butter in a large pan and cook the onions over a low heat for 5 minutes, stirring occasionally.

2 Add the beetroot, carrots and celery and cook for 5 minutes more, stirring occasionally.

3 Stir in the garlic and chopped tomatoes and continue to cook, stirring, for 2 minutes more.

4 Add the bouquet garni, peppercorns and stock. Bring to the boil, lower the heat, cover and simmer for 1 1/4 hours, until all the vegetables are tender. Discard the bouquet garni. Stir in the beetroot kvas and season to taste. Bring to the boil. Ladle into bowls and serve with soured cream sprinkled with chives.

> **Cook's Tip**
> *Beetroot kvas, fermented beetroot juice, adds an intense colour and a slight tartness. If unavailable, peel and grate 1 beetroot, add 150ml/ 1/4 pint/ 2/3 cup vegetable stock and 10ml/2 tsp lemon juice. Bring to the boil, cover and remove from the heat. Leave for 30 minutes. Strain before using.*

Pea, Leek & Broccoli Soup

A delicious and nutritious soup, ideal for a family supper to warm those chilly winter evenings.

Serves 4–6

1 onion, chopped
225g/8oz/2 cups sliced leeks
225g/8oz unpeeled
  potatoes, diced
900ml/1½ pints/3¾ cups
  vegetable stock
1 bay leaf
225g/8oz/2 cups broccoli florets
175g/6oz/1½ cups frozen peas
30–45ml/2–3 tbsp chopped
  fresh parsley
salt and ground black pepper
fresh parsley leaves, to garnish

1 Put the onion, leeks, potatoes, stock and bay leaf in a large, heavy-based saucepan and mix together well. Cover and bring to the boil over a medium heat. Lower the heat and simmer, stirring frequently, for 10 minutes.

2 Add the broccoli and peas, cover and return to the boil. Lower the heat and simmer, stirring occasionally, for a further 10 minutes.

3 Set aside to cool slightly. Remove and discard the bay leaf. Process the soup in a blender or food processor, in batches if necessary, until a smooth purée.

4 Add the parsley, season to taste with salt and pepper and process again briefly. Return to the saucepan and reheat gently until piping hot. Ladle into heated soup bowls and garnish with parsley leaves. Serve immediately.

> **Variations**
> • If you prefer, cut the vegetables finely and leave the cooked soup chunky rather than puréeing it.
> • The potatoes can be peeled before cooking, but the soup will contain less fibre and fewer nutrients.
> • Substitute frozen or drained, canned sweetcorn kernels for the frozen peas.

Spiced Indian Cauliflower Soup

Light and tasty, this creamy, mildly spicy soup makes a wonderfully warming first course. It would also make a delicious light lunch with some Indian bread.

Serves 4–6

1 large potato, diced
1 small cauliflower, chopped
1 onion, chopped
15ml/1 tbsp sunflower oil
45ml/3 tbsp water
1 garlic clove, crushed
15ml/1 tbsp grated fresh
  root ginger
10ml/2 tsp ground turmeric
5ml/1 tsp cumin seeds
5ml/1 tsp black mustard seeds
10ml/2 tsp ground coriander
1 litre/1¾ pints/4 cups
  vegetable stock
300ml/½ pint/1¼ cups
  natural yogurt
salt and ground black pepper
fresh coriander or parsley sprigs,
  to garnish

1 Put the potato, cauliflower and onion into a large, heavy-based saucepan with the oil and water. Cook over a medium heat until hot and bubbling, then cover and lower the heat. Continue cooking the mixture for about 10 minutes.

2 Add the garlic, ginger, turmeric, cumin seeds, mustard seeds and ground coriander. Stir well and cook for 2 minutes more, stirring occasionally.

3 Pour in the stock and season to taste with salt and pepper. Bring to the boil, then lower the heat, cover and simmer for about 20 minutes.

4 Stir in the yogurt and adjust the seasoning, if necessary. Ladle the soup into heated bowls, garnish with fresh coriander or parsley sprigs and serve immediately.

> **Variation**
> This soup is equally delicious chilled. After simmering, let it cool, then stir in the yogurt. Chill in the fridge for 4–6 hours before serving in chilled bowls.

Roasted Vegetable Soup

Roasting the vegetables gives this winter soup a wonderful depth of flavour.

Serves 6
60ml/4 tbsp olive oil
1 small butternut squash, peeled, seeded and cubed
2 carrots, cut into thick rounds
1 large parsnip, cubed
1 small swede, cubed
2 leeks, thickly sliced
1 onion, quartered
3 bay leaves
4 fresh thyme sprigs, plus extra to garnish
3 fresh rosemary sprigs
1.2 litres/2 pints/5 cups vegetable stock
salt and ground black pepper
soured cream, to serve

1 Preheat the oven to 200°C/400°F/Gas 6. Put the olive oil into a large bowl. Add the vegetables and toss until well coated.

2 Spread out the vegetables in a single layer on one large or two small baking sheets. Tuck the bay leaves and thyme and rosemary sprigs among the vegetables.

3 Roast the vegetables for about 50 minutes, until tender, turning them occasionally to make sure that they brown evenly. Remove from the oven, discard the herbs and transfer the vegetables to a large saucepan.

4 Pour the stock into the pan and bring to the boil. Lower the heat, season to taste with salt and pepper, then simmer for 10 minutes. Transfer the soup to a food processor or blender and process for a few minutes until thick and smooth.

5 Return the soup to the pan and heat through. Season well. Serve in heated bowls, adding a swirl of soured cream to each portion. Garnish with the extra thyme sprigs.

> **Cook's Tip**
> A hand-held blender makes short work of puréeing the soup and saves washing up.

Spicy Peanut Soup

When you serve a lot of soups, it is good to have some more unusual recipes in your repertoire. This one comes from Africa, and it tastes delicious.

Serves 6
30ml/2 tbsp vegetable oil
1 large onion, finely chopped
2 garlic cloves, crushed
5ml/1 tsp mild chilli powder
2 red peppers, seeded and finely chopped
225g/8oz carrots, finely chopped
225g/8oz potatoes, finely chopped
3 celery sticks, sliced
900ml/1½ pints/3¾ cups vegetable stock
90ml/6 tbsp crunchy peanut butter
115g/4oz/⅔ cup sweetcorn kernels
salt and ground black pepper
roughly chopped unsalted roasted peanuts, to garnish

1 Heat the oil in a large, heavy-based pan. Add the onion and garlic and cook, stirring occasionally, for about 3 minutes, until softened and translucent. Stir in the chilli powder and cook for 1 minute more.

2 Add the peppers, carrots, potatoes and celery. Stir well, then cook for 4 minutes more, stirring occasionally.

3 Add the stock, peanut butter and sweetcorn and stir well until thoroughly combined.

4 Season to taste with salt and pepper. Bring to the boil, lower the heat, cover and simmer for about 20 minutes, or until the vegetables are tender. Adjust the seasoning, if necessary. Ladle the soup into heated bowls, sprinkle with the chopped peanuts and serve immediately.

> **Cook's Tip**
> Different brands of chilli powder vary in strength, so it is best to use it with caution to begin with. Some varieties also include added ingredients, which may not go with your recipe.

Butternut Squash Soup

The rich golden colour, creamy texture and mild curry flavour combine to make this soup a winter winner with all the family.

Serves 6
1 butternut squash
1 cooking apple
25g/1oz/2 tbsp butter
1 onion, finely chopped

5–10ml/1–2 tsp curry powder
900ml/1½ pints/3¾ cups
    vegetable stock
5ml/1 tsp chopped fresh sage
150ml/¼ pint/⅔ cup
    apple juice
salt and ground black pepper
curry powder and finely shredded
    lime rind, to garnish
Curried Horseradish Cream
    (optional), to serve

1 Peel the squash, cut it in half and remove the seeds. Chop the flesh. Peel, core and chop the apple.

2 Heat the butter in a large, heavy-based saucepan. Add the onion and cook, stirring occasionally, for 5 minutes, until soft and translucent. Stir in the curry powder. Cook, stirring constantly, for 2 minutes.

3 Pour in the stock, then add the squash, apple and sage. Bring to the boil, lower the heat, cover and simmer for 20 minutes, until the squash and apple are tender.

4 Process the soup in a blender or food processor to a smooth purée. Return to the clean pan and add the apple juice. Season with salt and pepper to taste. Reheat gently, without allowing the soup to boil.

5 Serve the soup in heated bowls, topping each portion with a dusting of curry powder. Garnish with a few lime shreds. Add a spoonful of Curried Horseradish Cream, if you like.

> **Cook's Tip**
> Butternut squash looks rather like an oversize, elongated yellow pear. It is descriptively named, as the deep golden-yellow flesh has a buttery consistency and a nutty taste. However, other varieties of winter squash could also be used in this soup.

Curried Horseradish Cream

This is particularly good as a topping for the Butternut Squash Soup, but can be used with other vegetable soups as well. It is also excellent as a dipping sauce for crudités – use double or treble the quantity.

Serves 6 as a topping
60ml/4 tbsp double cream
10ml/2 tsp creamed horseradish
2.5ml/½ tsp curry powder

1 Whip the cream in a bowl until stiff, then stir in the creamed horseradish and curry powder.
2 Cover and chill in the fridge for up to 3 days.

Spiced Lentil Soup

A subtle blend of spices takes this warming soup to new heights. Serve it with warm crusty bread for a satisfying lunch.

Serves 6
2 onions, finely chopped
2 garlic cloves, crushed
4 tomatoes, roughly chopped

2.5ml/½ tsp ground turmeric
5ml/1 tsp ground cumin
6 cardamom pods
½ cinnamon stick
225g/8oz/1 cup red lentils
900ml/1½ pints/3¾ cups water
400g/14oz can coconut milk
15ml/1 tbsp fresh lime juice
salt and ground black pepper
cumin seeds, to garnish

1 Put the onions, garlic, tomatoes, turmeric, cumin, cardamoms, cinnamon and lentils into a saucepan. Pour in the water. Bring to the boil, lower the heat, cover and simmer gently for about 20 minutes, or until the lentils are soft.

2 Remove the cardamoms and cinnamon stick. Process the mixture in a blender or food processor to a smooth purée. Press the soup through a sieve, then return it to the clean pan.

3 Reserve a little of the coconut milk for the garnish and add the remainder to the pan, together with the lime juice. Stir well. Season to taste with salt and pepper. Reheat the soup gently without boiling. Ladle into heated bowls, swirl in the reserved coconut milk, garnish with the cumin seeds and serve.

> **Cook's Tips**
> • For maximum flavour, use sun-ripened vine tomatoes, rather than those ripened under glass. Alternatively, stir in a little tomato purée or use canned tomatoes.
> • When whole cardamom pods are used for flavouring – usually in soups and casseroles – they are removed before serving or processing to a purée. The small black seeds – usually used for flavouring desserts – may be eaten.
> • The cooking time for lentils may vary, depending on how long they have been stored.

Hot-&-sour Soup

This spicy, warming soup is the perfect introduction to a simple Chinese meal. Cloud ears are a type of Chinese fungi.

Serves 4

10g/ 1/4 oz dried cloud ears
8 fresh shiitake mushrooms
75g/3oz beancurd (tofu)
50g/2oz/ 1/2 cup sliced, drained, canned bamboo shoots
900ml/1 1/2 pints/3 3/4 cups vegetable stock
15ml/1 tbsp caster sugar
45ml/3 tbsp rice vinegar
15ml/1 tbsp light soy sauce
1.5ml/ 1/4 tsp chilli oil
1/2 tsp salt
large pinch of ground white pepper
15ml/1 tbsp cornflour
15ml/1 tbsp cold water
1 egg white
5ml/1 tsp sesame oil
2 spring onions, sliced into fine rings

1 Soak the cloud ears in hot water to cover for 30 minutes or until soft. Drain, trim off and discard the hard base from each and chop the cloud ears roughly.

2 Remove and discard the stalks from the shiitake mushrooms. Cut the caps into thin strips. Cut the beancurd (tofu) into 1cm/ 1/2 in cubes and shred the bamboo shoots finely.

3 Place the stock, shiitake mushrooms, beancurd, bamboo shoots and cloud ears in a large, heavy-based saucepan. Bring the stock to the boil, lower the heat and simmer for about 5 minutes.

4 Stir in the sugar, vinegar, soy sauce, chilli oil, salt and pepper. Mix the cornflour to a paste with the water. Add the mixture to the soup and stir constantly until it thickens slightly.

5 Lightly beat the egg white, then pour it slowly into the soup in a steady stream, stirring constantly. Cook, stirring constantly, until the egg white changes colour.

6 Add the sesame oil just before serving. Ladle into heated bowls and top each portion with spring onion rings.

North African Spiced Soup

Warm spices, such as cinnamon and ginger, give this thick vegetable and chick-pea soup an unforgettable flavour.

Serves 6

1 large onion, chopped
1.2 litres/2 pints/5 cups vegetable stock
5ml/1 tsp ground cinnamon
5ml/1 tsp ground turmeric
15ml/1 tbsp grated fresh root ginger
pinch of cayenne pepper
2 carrots, diced
2 celery sticks, diced
400g/14oz can chopped tomatoes
450g/1lb floury potatoes, diced
5 saffron strands
400g/14oz can chick-peas, drained
30ml/2 tbsp chopped fresh coriander
15ml/1 tbsp lemon juice
salt and ground black pepper
fried lemon wedges, to serve

1 Place the onion in a large pan with 300ml/ 1/2 pint/1 1/4 cups of the vegetable stock. Bring to the boil, lower the heat and simmer gently for about 10 minutes.

2 Meanwhile, spoon the cinnamon, turmeric, ginger and cayenne pepper into a bowl. Stir in 30ml/2 tbsp of the remaining stock to form a paste. Stir the spice paste into the onion mixture, together with the carrots and celery. Pour in the rest of the stock.

3 Bring the mixture to the boil, lower the heat, then cover and simmer gently for 5 minutes.

4 Stir in the tomatoes and potatoes. Cover and simmer gently for 20 minutes. Add the saffron, chick-peas, fresh coriander and lemon juice. Season to taste with salt and pepper. When piping hot, serve in heated bowls with fried lemon wedges.

> **Cook's Tip**
> *Although it is very expensive, do not stint on the saffron, as it adds a unique flavour to the spice combination.*

Jerusalem Artichoke Soup

Thanks to their mild, nutty flavour, Jerusalem artichokes make a remarkably good, creamy soup.

Serves 4
30ml/2 tbsp olive oil
1 large onion, chopped
1 garlic clove, chopped
1 celery stick, chopped
675g/1½ lb Jerusalem artichokes,
  peeled or scrubbed
  and chopped
1.2 litres/2 pints/5 cups
  vegetable stock
300ml/½ pint/1¼ cups milk
salt and ground black pepper
Gruyère Toasts, to serve (optional)

1 Heat the oil in a large saucepan and cook the onion, garlic and celery over a medium heat, stirring occasionally, for about 5 minutes, or until softened. Add the Jerusalem artichokes and cook for 5 minutes more.

2 Add the stock and season with salt and pepper to taste. Bring to the boil, lower the heat and simmer, stirring occasionally, for 20–25 minutes, until the artichokes are tender.

3 Transfer the soup to a food processor or blender and process until smooth. Return the soup to the pan, stir in the milk and heat through gently for 2 minutes. Ladle the soup into bowls and top with Gruyère Toasts, if using, and ground black pepper.

Gruyère Toasts

These are very good when floated on Jerusalem Artichoke Soup, but can also be served as snacks.

Makes 8
8 slices French bread
115g/4oz/1 cup grated
  Gruyère cheese

1 Spread out the slices of French bread in a grill pan and toast them lightly on one side under a hot grill.
2 Turn the slices of bread over and sprinkle the untoasted side of each with the grated Gruyère. Grill until the cheese melts and is golden.

Spinach & Rice Soup

Use young spinach leaves to prepare this light and fresh-tasting soup.

Serves 4
675g/1½ lb fresh young
  spinach, washed
45ml/3 tbsp extra virgin olive oil
1 small onion, finely chopped
2 garlic cloves, finely chopped
1 small fresh red chilli, seeded
  and finely chopped
200g/7oz/1 cup risotto rice
1.2 litres/2 pints/5 cups
  vegetable stock
salt and ground black pepper
60ml/4 tbsp grated Pecorino
  cheese, to serve

1 Place the spinach in a large pan with just the water that clings to its leaves after washing. Add a large pinch of salt. Heat gently until the spinach has just wilted, then remove from the heat and drain, reserving any liquid.

2 Either chop the spinach finely using a large knife or place it in a food processor and process to a fairly coarse purée.

3 Heat the oil in a large, heavy-based saucepan. Add the onion, garlic and chilli and cook over a low heat, stirring occasionally, for 4–5 minutes, until softened.

4 Add the rice and stir until all the grains are well coated, then pour in the stock and reserved spinach liquid. Bring to the boil over a medium heat, then lower the heat and simmer for about 10 minutes.

5 Add the spinach and season with salt and pepper to taste. Cook for 5–7 minutes more, until the rice is tender. Check the seasoning and serve in warmed soup plates with the grated Pecorino cheese.

Cook's Tip
Use arborio or carnaroli rice for the rice soup, or try one of the less familiar risotto rices, such as Vialone Nano.

Ribollita

Ribollita is an Italian soup, rather like minestrone, but with beans instead of pasta. It is traditionally served ladled over bread and a rich green vegetable.

Serves 6–8
45ml/3 tbsp olive oil
2 onions, chopped
2 carrots, sliced
4 garlic cloves, crushed
2 celery sticks, thinly sliced
1 fennel bulb, trimmed
  and chopped
2 large courgettes, thinly sliced

400g/14oz can
  chopped tomatoes
30ml/2 tbsp home-made or
  ready-made pesto
900ml/1½ pints/3¾ cups
  vegetable stock
400g/14oz can haricot or borlotti
  beans, drained
salt and ground black pepper

To finish
15ml/1 tbsp extra virgin olive oil,
  plus extra for drizzling
450g/1lb fresh young spinach
6–8 slices white bread
freshly ground black pepper

1 Heat the oil in a large saucepan. Add the onions, carrots, garlic, celery and fennel and fry gently for 10 minutes. Add the courgettes and fry for 2 minutes more.

2 Stir in the chopped tomatoes, pesto, stock and beans and bring to the boil. Lower the heat, cover and simmer gently for 25–30 minutes, until the vegetables are completely tender. Season with salt and pepper to taste.

3 To serve, heat the oil in a heavy-based frying pan and fry the spinach for 2 minutes, or until wilted. Put a slice of bread in each heated soup bowl, spoon the spinach on top, then ladle the soup over the spinach. Offer extra olive oil at the table, so that guests can drizzle it on to the soup. Freshly ground black pepper can be sprinkled on top.

Variation
Use other dark greens, such as chard or cabbage, instead of the spinach; shred and cook until tender.

Sweetcorn & Potato Chowder

This creamy yet chunky soup is rich with the sweet taste of corn. Serve it topped with grated Cheddar cheese.

Serves 4
30ml/2 tbsp sunflower oil
25g/1oz/2 tbsp butter
1 onion, chopped
1 garlic clove, crushed
1 medium baking potato, chopped

2 celery sticks, sliced
1 small green pepper, halved,
  seeded and sliced
600ml/1 pint/2½ cups vegetable
  stock or water
300ml/½ pint/1¼ cups milk
200g/7oz can flageolet beans
300g/11oz can sweetcorn kernels
good pinch of dried sage
salt and ground black pepper
grated Cheddar cheese, to serve
fresh sage leaves, to garnish

1 Heat the oil and butter in a large heavy-based pan. Add the onion, garlic, potato, celery and green pepper and cook over a low heat, stirring occasionally, for about 10 minutes, until the onion is softened and golden.

2 Pour in the stock or water, season with salt and pepper to taste and bring to the boil. Lower the heat, cover and simmer gently for about 15 minutes, until the vegetables are tender.

3 Add the milk, beans and sweetcorn – including the can liquids. Stir in the sage. Simmer, uncovered, for 5 minutes. Serve, sprinkled with the grated cheese, garnished with sage leaves.

Cook's Tip
Although the word "chowder" is most closely associated with a soup made from clams, this recipe contains the two traditional ingredients – vegetables and milk – so it is quite authentic.

Variation
If you are unable to locate canned flageolet beans, use frozen peas instead.

Borlotti Bean & Pasta Soup

A complete meal in a bowl, this is based on a classic Italian soup. Traditionally, the person who finds the bay leaf is honoured with a kiss from the cook.

Serves 4
75ml/5 tbsp olive oil
1 onion, chopped
1 celery stick, chopped
2 carrots, chopped
1 bay leaf
1.2 litres/2 pints/5 cups
  vegetable stock
400g/14oz can
  chopped tomatoes
175g/6oz/1½ cups dried
  pasta shapes
400g/14oz can borlotti
  beans, drained
250g/9oz fresh young spinach
salt and ground black pepper
50g/2oz/⅔ cup freshly grated
  Parmesan cheese, to serve

1 Heat the olive oil in a large, heavy-based saucepan and add the chopped onion, celery and carrots. Cook over a medium heat, stirring occasionally, for 5 minutes, or until the vegetables soften and the onion is translucent.

2 Add the bay leaf, stock and tomatoes and bring to the boil. Lower the heat and simmer for about 10 minutes, until the vegetables are just tender.

3 Bring the soup back to the boil, add the pasta and beans and simmer for 8 minutes, until the pasta is *al dente*. Stir the soup frequently to prevent the pasta from sticking to the bottom of the pan.

4 Season to taste with salt and pepper, add the spinach and cook for 2 minutes more. Serve in heated bowls, sprinkled with the grated Parmesan.

Variations
• Add a glass of white wine with the stock, if you wish.
• Substitute two shallots for the onion and ½ small fennel bulb for the celery.

Garlic, Chick-pea & Spinach Soup

Tahini, sesame seed paste, is the secret ingredient that gives this thick, creamy soup such a superb taste.

Serves 4
30ml/2 tbsp olive oil
4 garlic cloves, crushed
1 onion, roughly chopped
10ml/2 tsp ground cumin
10ml/2 tsp ground coriander
1.2 litres/2 pints/5 cups
  vegetable stock
350g/12oz potatoes,
  finely chopped
425g/15oz can chick-
  peas, drained
15ml/1 tbsp cornflour
150ml/¼ pint/⅔ cup
  double cream
30ml/2 tbsp light tahini (sesame
  seed paste)
200g/7oz fresh young
  spinach, shredded
salt and ground black pepper
cayenne pepper, to serve

1 Heat the olive oil in a large, heavy-based saucepan. Add the garlic and onion and cook over a medium heat, stirring occasionally, for 5 minutes, or until the onion has softened and is golden brown.

2 Stir in the cumin and coriander and cook for 1 minute more, then pour in the stock. Add the potatoes. Bring to the boil, lower the heat and simmer for 10 minutes.

3 Add the drained chick-peas and simmer for a further 5 minutes, or until the potatoes are just tender.

4 Mix the cornflour, cream and tahini in a bowl. Stir in plenty of seasoning. Stir the mixture into the soup and add the spinach. Bring to the boil, stirring constantly, then simmer for 2 minutes. Ladle the soup into heated bowls, sprinkle with a little cayenne pepper and serve immediately.

Variation
Ful medames would make a delicious alternative to chick-peas, but you would probably have to use dried beans. Soak them overnight and then simmer for 3–4 hours before using.

Pear & Parmesan Salad with Poppy Seed Dressing

This is a good starter when pears are at their seasonal best. Drizzle them with a poppy-seed dressing and top them with shavings of Parmesan cheese.

Serves 4

4 just-ripe dessert pears
50g/2oz piece of
   Parmesan cheese
watercress, to garnish
water biscuits or rye bread, to
   serve (optional)

For the dressing
30ml/2 tbsp cider vinegar
2.5ml/ ½ tsp soft light
   brown sugar
good pinch of dried thyme
30ml/2 tbsp extra virgin olive oil
15ml/1 tbsp sunflower oil
15ml/1 tbsp poppy seeds
salt and ground black pepper

1 Peel the pears if you wish, although they look more attractive with the skin on. Cut them in quarters and remove the cores.

2 Cut each pear quarter in half lengthways and arrange them on four small serving plates.

3 Make the dressing. Mix the vinegar, sugar and thyme in a jug. Gradually whisk in the olive oil, then the sunflower oil. Season with salt and pepper, then tip in the poppy seeds.

4 Trickle the dressing over the pears. Shave Parmesan over the top and garnish with watercress. Serve with water biscuits or thinly sliced rye bread, if you like.

Variation
Blue cheeses and pears also have a natural affinity. Stilton, dolcelatte, Gorgonzola or Danish blue (Danablu) can be used instead of the shavings of Parmesan. Allow about 200g/7oz and cut into wedges or cubes.

Dressed Salad of Fresh Ceps

Mushrooms make a marvellous salad, especially if you are able to obtain fresh ceps or bay boletus. Any wild or cultivated mushrooms can be used; remove the stems from shiitake mushrooms.

Serves 4

350g/12oz/4 cups fresh ceps or
   bay boletus, thinly sliced
175g/6oz ready-to-serve mixed
   salad leaves
50g/2oz/ ½ cup broken walnut
   pieces, toasted
50g/2oz piece of
   Parmesan cheese
salt and ground black pepper

For the dressing
2 egg yolks
2.5ml/ ½ tsp French mustard
75ml/5 tbsp groundnut oil
45ml/3 tbsp walnut oil
30ml/2 tbsp lemon juice
30ml/2 tbsp chopped
   fresh parsley
pinch of caster sugar

1 Make the dressing. Place the egg yolks in a screw-top jar with the mustard, groundnut oil, walnut oil, lemon juice, parsley and sugar. Close the jar tightly and shake well.

2 Place the mushrooms in a large salad bowl and pour over the dressing. Toss to coat, then set aside for 10–15 minutes to allow the flavours to mingle.

3 Add the salad leaves to the mushrooms and toss lightly. Season with plenty of salt and pepper.

4 Divide the salad among four large plates. Scatter each portion with toasted walnuts and shavings of Parmesan cheese.

Cook's Tip
The dressing for this salad uses raw egg yolks. Be sure to use only the freshest eggs from a reputable supplier. Expectant mothers, young children and the elderly are advised to avoid raw egg yolks. If this presents a problem, the dressing can be made without the egg yolks.

Grilled Goat's Cheese Salad

The fresh tangy flavour of goat's cheese contrasts beautifully with the mild salad leaves in this satisfying and attractive starter.

Serves 4
2 firm round whole goat's cheeses, about 65–115g/ 2½–4oz each
4 slices French bread
extra virgin olive oil, for drizzling
175g/6oz ready-to-serve mixed salad leaves
snipped fresh chives, to garnish

For the vinaigrette dressing
½ garlic clove
5ml/1 tsp Dijon mustard
5ml/1 tsp white wine vinegar
5ml/1 tsp dry white wine
45ml/3 tbsp extra virgin olive oil
salt and ground black pepper

1 To make the dressing, rub a large salad bowl with the cut side of the garlic clove. Combine the mustard, vinegar and wine in the bowl. Add salt and pepper to taste, then whisk in the oil, 15ml/1 tbsp at a time, to form a thick vinaigrette.

2 Using a sharp knife, cut the goat's cheeses in half across their width to make four "cakes".

3 Arrange the bread slices in a grill pan and toast them on one side under a hot grill. Turn them over and place a piece of cheese, cut side up, on each slice. Drizzle with olive oil and grill until the cheese is lightly browned.

4 Add the leaves to the salad bowl and toss to coat them with the dressing. Divide the salad among four plates, top each with a goat's cheese croûton and garnish with chives. Serve at once.

> **Cook's Tip**
> The best-known goat's cheeses are French, known generically as chèvre and also sold under specific names, such as Crottin de Chavignol. There are other excellent goat's milk cheeses, such as the English Cerney, Capricorn Goat and Vulscombe, and Caprile Banon and Chèvre de Provence from the United States.

Asparagus in Egg & Lemon Sauce

As a starter or light lunch, fresh asparagus is a special treat, especially when topped with a tangy, fresh-tasting sauce.

Serves 4
675g/1½ lb asparagus
15ml/1 tbsp cornflour
10ml/2 tsp granulated sugar
2 egg yolks
juice of 1½ lemons
salt

1 Trim the asparagus stalks, discarding the tough ends, then tie them in a bundle. Cook in a tall pan of boiling salted water over a medium heat for 7–10 minutes.

2 Drain well, reserving 200ml/7fl oz/scant 1 cup of the cooking liquid. Untie the asparagus stems and arrange them in a shallow serving dish.

3 Put the cornflour in a small pan. Stir in enough of the reserved cooking liquid to form a smooth paste, then stir in the remaining cooking liquid. Bring to the boil, stirring constantly, and cook over a low heat until the sauce thickens slightly. Stir in the sugar, then remove the pan from the heat. Set the sauce aside to cool slightly.

4 Beat the egg yolks with the lemon juice. Gradually stir the mixture into the cooled sauce. Cook over a very low heat, stirring constantly, until the sauce is fairly thick. Immediately remove the pan from the heat. Continue stirring for 1 minute.

5 Taste the sauce and add salt or sugar if needed. Let it cool slightly, then pour a little over the asparagus. Cover and chill for at least 2 hours before serving with the rest of the sauce.

> **Variation**
> This sauce goes very well with all sorts of young vegetables. Try it with baby leeks, cooked whole or chopped, or serve it with other baby vegetables, such as carrots and courgettes.

Baby Onions & Mushrooms à la Grecque

There are many variations of this classic dish. The mushrooms may be omitted, but they add immeasurably to the flavour.

Serves 4
2 carrots
350g/12oz baby onions
60ml/4 tbsp olive oil
120ml/4fl oz/ ½ cup dry
   white wine
5ml/1 tsp coriander seeds,
   lightly crushed

2 bay leaves
pinch of cayenne pepper
1 garlic clove, crushed
350g/12oz/4 cups
   button mushrooms
3 tomatoes, peeled, seeded
   and quartered
salt and ground black pepper
45ml/3 tbsp chopped fresh
   parsley, to garnish
crusty bread, to serve

1 Peel the carrots and cut them into small dice. Peel the baby onions and trim the tops and roots.

2 Heat 45ml/3 tbsp of the olive oil in a deep frying pan. Add the carrots and onions and cook, stirring occasionally, for about 20 minutes, until the vegetables have browned lightly.

3 Add the white wine, coriander seeds, bay leaves, cayenne, garlic, button mushrooms and tomatoes, with salt and pepper to taste. Cook, uncovered, for 20–30 minutes, until the vegetables are soft and the sauce has thickened.

4 Transfer to a serving dish and leave to cool. Cover and chill until needed. Before serving, pour over the remaining olive oil and sprinkle with the parsley. Serve with crusty bread.

Cook's Tip
Don't trim too much from either the top or root end of the onions: if you do, the centres will pop out during cooking.

Marinated Vegetable Antipasto

If you ever want to prove just how delectable vegetables can be, serve this sensational selection of Italian-style starters.

Serves 4
For the peppers
3 red peppers, halved and seeded
3 yellow peppers, halved
   and seeded
4 garlic cloves, sliced
a handful of fresh basil leaves,
   plus extra to garnish
extra virgin olive oil
salt

For the mushrooms
450g/1lb/6 cups open
   cap mushrooms
60ml/4 tbsp extra virgin olive oil

1 large garlic clove, crushed
15ml/1 tbsp chopped
   fresh rosemary
250ml/8fl oz/1 cup dry
   white wine
salt and ground black pepper
fresh rosemary sprigs, to garnish

For the olives
120ml/4fl oz/ ½ cup extra virgin
   olive oil
1 dried red chilli
grated rind of 1 lemon
225g/8oz/1 ¼ cups Italian
   black olives
30ml/2 tbsp chopped fresh flat
   leaf parsley
1 lemon wedge, to serve

1 Place the pepper halves, skin side up, on a grill rack and cook until the skins have charred. Transfer to a bowl and cover with crumpled kitchen paper. Leave to cool slightly.

2 When the pepper halves are cool enough to handle, peel off their skins, then cut the flesh into strips. Place the strips in a bowl and add the sliced garlic and basil leaves. Sprinkle over salt to taste, cover with olive oil and set aside to marinate for 3–4 hours, tossing occasionally. Chill in the fridge.

3 Slice the mushrooms thickly and place them in a large heatproof bowl. Heat the oil in a small pan and add the garlic and rosemary. Pour in the wine. Bring the mixture to the boil, then lower the heat and simmer for 3 minutes. Season with salt and pepper to taste.

4 Pour the mixture over the mushrooms. Mix thoroughly and set aside until cool, stirring occasionally. Cover and leave to marinate overnight in the fridge.

5 Prepare the olives. Place the oil in a small pan and crumble in the chilli. Add the lemon rind. Heat gently for about 3 minutes. Add the olives and heat for 1 minute more. Tip into a bowl and leave to cool. Set aside to marinate overnight.

6 Let the marinated mushrooms come to room temperature before serving. Garnish them with rosemary sprigs. Garnish the chilled peppers with basil leaves. Sprinkle the olives with parsley and serve with the lemon wedge.

Cook's Tip
The pepper antipasto can be stored in a screw-top jar in the fridge for up to 2 weeks.

Vegetable Terrine with Brandy

A feast for the eye and the palate – that's this luscious layer of brandy-flavoured custard and a colourful combination of vegetables.

Serves 4

oil, for greasing
1 red pepper, quartered
   and seeded
1 green pepper, quartered
   and seeded
75g/3oz/ ¾ cup fresh or
   frozen peas
6 fresh green asparagus stalks
2 carrots, cut into batons
150ml/ ¼ pint/ ⅔ cup milk
150ml/ ¼ pint/ ⅔ cup
   double cream
6 eggs, beaten
15ml/1 tbsp brandy
175g/6oz/ ¾ cup low-fat
   soft cheese
15ml/1 tbsp chopped
   fresh parsley
salt and ground black pepper
salad leaves, cucumber slices and
   halved tomatoes, to serve

1 Preheat the oven to 180°C/350°F/Gas 4. Grease and base-line a 900g/2lb loaf tin. Place the pepper quarters, skin side up, on a grill rack and cook until the skins have charred. Transfer to a bowl and cover with crumpled kitchen paper. Leave to cool.

2 Cook the peas, asparagus and carrots in separate pans of lightly salted boiling water until tender. Drain and dry on kitchen paper. Peel off the skins from the pepper quarters.

3 In a bowl, combine the milk, cream, eggs, brandy, soft cheese and parsley. Mix well and season with plenty of salt and pepper.

4 Arrange some of the vegetables in the base of the loaf tin, trimming to fit if necessary. Spoon some of the cheese mixture over the vegetables. Continue layering the vegetables and the cheese mixture, ending with a layer of peppers. Cover the tin with foil and stand it in a roasting tin. Pour in boiling water to come halfway up the sides of the loaf tin.

5 Bake for 45 minutes, or until the custard is just firm. Leave the terrine in the tin until cold, then remove it from the roasting tin. Invert it on to a plate. Lift off the lining paper and slice the terrine. Serve with the salad leaves, cucumber and tomatoes.

Aubergine & Spinach Terrines

These individual terrines make an elegant first course.

Serves 4

1 aubergine
30ml/2 tbsp extra virgin olive oil
2 courgettes, thinly sliced
leaves from 1 small fresh
   thyme sprig
4 firm tomatoes, peeled
   and seeded
4 fresh basil leaves, finely sliced
275g/10oz fresh baby
   spinach leaves
1 garlic clove, crushed
15g/ ½ oz/1 tbsp butter
pinch of freshly grated nutmeg
salt and ground black pepper
½ roasted red pepper, skinned
   and chopped, plus a little
   balsamic vinegar, to serve

1 Preheat the oven to 190°C/375°F/Gas 5. Seal four 6cm/2½ in diameter metal muffin rings at one end with clear film.

2 Slice the aubergine into four rounds of equal size. Heat half the oil in a frying pan and fry the aubergine slices on both sides until brown. Place them on a baking sheet and cook in the oven for 10 minutes. Transfer to a plate lined with kitchen paper.

3 Heat half the remaining oil in the same pan and fry the courgettes for 2 minutes, then drain on the kitchen paper. Season with salt and pepper and sprinkle with thyme leaves.

4 Place the tomatoes, basil and remaining oil in a heavy-based frying pan and cook for 5–8 minutes. Cook the spinach, garlic and butter in a saucepan, allowing all the water to evaporate. Drain well, add the nutmeg, then season with salt and pepper.

5 Line the base and 1cm/ ½ in of the sides of the muffin rings with the spinach leaves, leaving no gaps. Place courgette slices around the edges of each ring, overlapping them slightly. Divide the tomato mixture equally among the rings, pressing it down well. Place the aubergines on the top, trimming the edges to fit.

6 Seal the top with clear film and pierce the base to allow any liquid to escape. Chill overnight. Remove from the rings and serve with roasted pepper, drizzled with balsamic vinegar.

Red Pepper Polenta with Pipian

This recipe is inspired by
the fusion of Italian and
Mexican influences. A
polenta loaf, layered with
brightly coloured vegetables,
is served with a spicy salsa.

Serves 4
oil, for greasing
3 young courgettes, trimmed
1.2 litres/2 pints/5 cups
   vegetable stock
250g/9oz/2 cups fine polenta
   or cornmeal
200g/7oz can red peppers,
   drained and sliced
115g/4oz salad leaves

For the pipian
75g/3oz/generous 1 cup roasted
   sunflower seeds
1 slice white bread, crust removed
200ml/7fl oz/scant 1 cup
   vegetable stock
1 garlic clove, crushed
1/2 fresh red chilli, seeded
   and chopped
30ml/2 tbsp chopped
   fresh coriander
5ml/1 tsp granulated sugar
15ml/1 tbsp freshly squeezed
   lime juice
pinch of salt

1 Lightly oil a 23cm/9in loaf tin and line with a single sheet of
greaseproof paper. Cook the courgettes in a pan of lightly
salted simmering water for 2–3 minutes. Refresh under cold
running water and drain. When they are cool, cut into strips.

2 Heat the stock in a heavy-based saucepan until it is simmering.
Add the polenta in a steady stream, stirring constantly, and
continue to stir over the heat for 2–3 minutes, until thickened.

3 Partly fill the lined tin with the polenta mixture. Layer the
sliced courgettes and peppers over the polenta. Fill the tin with
the remaining polenta and leave to set for 10–15 minutes.

4 Meanwhile, make the pipian. Process the sunflower seeds in a
food processor to a thick paste. Add the remaining ingredients
and process again until well combined. Spoon into a bowl.

5 Turn the warm polenta loaf on to a board, remove the paper
and cut into thick slices with a large wet knife. Serve with the
salad leaves and the pipian salsa.

Sweet Potato Roulade

Sweet potato works
particularly well as the base
for this roulade. Slice thinly
for an impressive starter.

Serves 8
oil, for greasing
225g/8oz/1 cup low-fat
   soft cheese
75ml/5 tbsp natural yogurt
6–8 spring onions, thinly sliced

30ml/2 tbsp chopped Brazil
   nuts, roasted
450g/1lb sweet potatoes, peeled
   and cubed
12 allspice berries, crushed
4 eggs, separated
50g/2oz/ 1/2 cup finely grated
   Edam cheese
salt and ground black pepper
15ml/1 tbsp sesame seeds
ready-to-serve mixed salad leaves,
   to serve

1 Preheat the oven to 200°C/400°F/Gas 6. Grease and line a
33 x 25cm/13 x 10in Swiss roll tin with non-stick baking paper.
In a small bowl, mix together the soft cheese, yogurt, spring
onions and Brazil nuts. Set this filling aside.

2 Boil or steam the sweet potatoes until tender. Drain well.
Place in a food processor with the allspice and process until
smooth. Spoon into a bowl and stir in the egg yolks and grated
cheese. Season to taste with salt and pepper.

3 Whisk the egg whites until stiff, but not dry. Fold one-third of
the egg whites into the sweet potatoes to lighten the mixture
before gently folding in the rest.

4 Pour into the prepared tin, tipping it to get the mixture right
into the corners. Smooth gently with a palette knife and cook in
the oven for 10–15 minutes.

5 Meanwhile, lay a large sheet of greaseproof paper on a clean
dish towel and sprinkle with the sesame seeds.

6 When the roulade is cooked, tip it on to the paper, remove
the lining paper, trim the edges and roll it up. Leave to cool.
When cool, carefully unroll, spread with the filling and roll up
again. Cut into slices and serve with salad leaves.

Stuffed Vine Leaves

Whether you serve these as part of a meze or as a solo starter, they are certain to prove popular.

Makes about 40
40 fresh vine leaves
60ml/4 tbsp olive oil
lemon wedges and a crisp salad,
   to serve

For the stuffing
150g/5oz/ ¾ cup long grain
   rice, rinsed
2 bunches spring onions,
   finely chopped
40g/1 ½ oz/½ cup pine nuts
45ml/3 tbsp seedless raisins
30ml/2 tbsp chopped fresh
   mint leaves
60ml/4 tbsp chopped
   fresh parsley
4ml/ ¾ tsp ground black pepper
salt

1 Using a knife or a pair of scissors, snip out the thick, coarse stems from the vine leaves. Blanch the leaves in a large pan of boiling salted water until they just begin to change colour. Drain, refresh in cold water, then drain again.

2 To make the stuffing, mix all the ingredients together in a bowl and season to taste with salt. Open out the vine leaves, ribbed side uppermost. Place a heaped teaspoonful of the stuffing on each.

3 Fold over the two outer edges to secure the stuffing, then roll up each vine leaf from the stem end to form a neat roll.

4 Arrange the stuffed vine leaves neatly in a steamer and sprinkle over the olive oil. Steam over boiling water for 50–60 minutes, or until the rice is completely cooked. Serve cold, but not chilled, with lemon wedges and a salad.

Cook's Tip
If you can't obtain fresh vine leaves, use two packets of vine leaves preserved in brine. Rinse and drain them well, then pat dry with kitchen paper before filling.

Vermicelli with Lemon

Fresh and tangy, this makes an excellent first course for a dinner party. It has the additional advantage of being extremely quick and easy to prepare.

Serves 4
350g/12oz dried vermicelli
juice of 2 large lemons

50g/2oz/ ¼ cup butter
200ml/7fl oz/scant 1 cup
   double cream
15ml/1 tablespoon finely grated
   lemon rind
115g/4oz/1 ⅓ cups freshly grated
   Parmesan cheese
salt and ground black pepper

1 Cook the vermicelli in a large pan of lightly salted boiling water until *al dente*.

2 Meanwhile, pour the lemon juice into a medium saucepan. Add the butter and cream, then stir in the lemon rind. Season with salt and pepper to taste.

3 Bring to the boil, stirring frequently. Lower the heat and simmer, stirring occasionally, for about 5 minutes, until the cream has reduced slightly.

4 Drain the pasta and return it to the pan. Add the grated Parmesan to the sauce, then taste for seasoning and adjust if necessary. Pour the sauce over the pasta. Toss quickly over a medium heat until the pasta is evenly coated with the sauce, then divide among four warmed bowls and serve immediately.

Cook's Tips
• Lemons vary in the amount of juice they yield. On average, a large fresh lemon will yield 60–90ml/4–6 tbsp. The lemony flavour of this dish is quite pronounced – you can use less juice if you prefer.
• Try to find unwaxed lemons if you are going to grate the rind. (Waxed lemons have been treated with diphenyl to preserve the rind.) Otherwise, wash the lemons thoroughly first.

Chilled Stuffed Courgettes

Full of flavour but low in calories and fat, this makes a superb summer starter.

Serves 6
6 courgettes, topped and tailed
1 Spanish onion, very
   finely chopped
1 garlic clove, crushed
60–90ml/4–6 tbsp well-flavoured
   French dressing
1 green pepper, seeded and diced
3 tomatoes, peeled, seeded
   and diced
15ml/1 tbsp drained and chopped
   rinsed capers
5ml/1 tsp chopped fresh parsley
5ml/1 tsp snipped fresh basil
sea salt and ground black pepper
fresh parsley sprigs, to garnish

1 Bring a large shallow pan of lightly salted water to the boil. Add the courgettes and simmer for 2–3 minutes, until they are lightly cooked. Drain well.

2 Cut the courgettes in half lengthways. Carefully scoop out the flesh, leaving the courgette shells intact. Chop the flesh into small cubes. Place in a bowl and cover with half the chopped onion. Dot with the crushed garlic.

3 Drizzle 30ml/2 tbsp of the dressing over, cover and marinate for 2–3 hours. Wrap the courgette shells tightly in clear film, and chill them until they are required.

4 Stir the pepper, tomatoes and capers into the courgette mixture, with the remaining onion and the herbs. Season to taste with sea salt and pepper. Pour over enough of the remaining dressing to moisten the mixture, toss well and chill.

5 Spoon the filling into the courgette shells, arrange on a platter and serve garnished with parsley.

Cook's Tip
To make French dressing, whisk together 15ml/1 tbsp wine vinegar, 5ml/1 tsp Dijon mustard and 75ml/5 tbsp olive oil.

Stuffed Mushrooms

This is a classic mushroom dish, strongly flavoured with garlic. Use flat mushrooms or field mushrooms.

Serves 6
12 large or 18 medium
   flat mushrooms
butter, for greasing
45ml/3 tbsp olive oil
2 garlic cloves, very finely chopped
45ml/3 tbsp finely chopped
   fresh parsley
40–50g/1½–2oz/¾–1 cup fresh
   white breadcrumbs
salt and ground black pepper
flat leaf parsley sprig,
   to garnish

1 Preheat the oven to 180°C/350°F/Gas 4. Cut off the mushroom stalks and set them aside. Grease a shallow ovenproof dish with butter. Arrange the mushroom caps, gill side upwards, in the dish.

2 Heat 15ml/1 tbsp of the olive oil in a frying pan and fry the garlic briefly. Chop the mushroom stalks finely and mix them with the parsley and breadcrumbs. Add the garlic and 15ml/1 tbsp of the remaining oil and season with salt and pepper to taste. Mix thoroughly, then pile a little of the mixture on each mushroom cap.

3 Drizzle the remaining oil over the mushrooms, then cover them with buttered greaseproof paper. Bake for 15–20 minutes, removing the paper for the last 5 minutes to brown the tops.

4 Serve two or three mushrooms per portion, garnishing with flat leaf parsley.

Cook's Tips
• The cooking time for the mushroom caps depends on their size and thickness. If they are fairly thin, cook for slightly less time. They should be tender, but not too soft when cooked. Test them with the point of a sharp knife.
• If a stronger garlic flavour is preferred, do not cook the garlic before adding it to the breadcrumb mixture.

Hot Halloumi with Roasted Peppers

Salty and full of flavour, Halloumi cheese takes on a wonderful texture when grilled or fried. A tumble of roasted sweet peppers makes an especially fine accompaniment.

Serves 4

6 peppers of mixed colours, halved and seeded
olive oil
30ml/2 tbsp balsamic vinegar
small handful of raisins (optional)
300g/11oz Halloumi cheese, thickly sliced
salt and ground black pepper
flat leaf parsley, to garnish

1 Place the pepper halves, skin side up, on a grill rack and grill until the skins have blistered and charred. Transfer to a bowl and cover with crumpled kitchen paper. Leave to cool slightly, then peel off the skins. Slice the flesh into a bowl. Save any juices and mix these with the peppers.

2 Pour a little olive oil over the peppers. Add the vinegar and raisins, if using, and season with salt and pepper to taste. Toss lightly and leave to cool.

3 When ready to serve, divide the pepper salad among four plates. In a large heavy-based frying pan heat olive oil to a depth of about 5mm/ ¼ in. Fry the Halloumi slices over a medium-high heat for 2–3 minutes, or until golden brown on both sides, turning them halfway through cooking.

4 Drain the Halloumi thoroughly on kitchen paper and serve with the roasted peppers and a parsley garnish.

> **Cook's Tips**
> • For a crisp coating on the Halloumi, toss the slices in plain flour before frying them.
> • Halloumi can be grilled or griddled instead of fried. Preheat a grill or ridged griddling pan, add the cheese and cook until golden brown, turning once. It is good grilled on a barbecue, too.

Malfatti with Roasted Pepper Sauce

Deliciously light spinach dumplings are wonderful when served with a smoky pepper and tomato sauce.

Serves 5

500g/1¼ lb fresh leaf spinach
1 onion, finely chopped
1 garlic clove, crushed
15ml/1 tbsp extra virgin olive oil
350g/12oz/1½ cups ricotta cheese
3 eggs, beaten
50g/2oz/ ½ cup natural-coloured dried breadcrumbs

50g/2oz/ ½ cup plain flour
50g/2oz/ ⅔ cup freshly grated Parmesan cheese
freshly grated nutmeg
25g/1oz/2 tbsp butter, melted
salt and ground black pepper

For the sauce

2 red peppers, quartered and seeded
30ml/2 tbsp extra virgin olive oil
1 onion, chopped
400g/14oz can chopped tomatoes
150ml/ ¼ pint/ ⅔ cup water

1 Make the sauce. Grill the peppers, skin side up, until the skins have charred. Place in a bowl, cover with crumpled kitchen paper and leave to cool. Peel off the skins and chop the flesh.

2 Heat the oil in a saucepan and sauté the onion and peppers for 5 minutes. Add the tomatoes and water and season. Bring to the boil, lower the heat and simmer for 15 minutes. Process in a food processor or blender, then return to the clean pan.

3 Trim any thick stalks from the spinach, then blanch in a pan of boiling water for about 1 minute. Drain, refresh under cold water and drain again. Squeeze dry, then chop finely. Put the onion, garlic, oil, ricotta, eggs, breadcrumbs and spinach in a bowl. Mix well, then stir in the flour and 5ml/1 tsp salt. Add half the Parmesan, then season to taste with pepper and nutmeg. Roll the mixture into 15 small logs and chill lightly.

4 Bring a large saucepan of water to the boil. Cook the malfatti, in batches, for 5 minutes. Remove them with a fish slice and toss them with the melted butter. To serve, reheat the sauce and divide it among five plates. Arrange three malfatti on each and sprinkle over the remaining Parmesan. Serve at once.

Vegetable Tempura

These deep-fried fritters are based on Kaki-age, a popular Japanese dish.

vegetable oil, for deep-frying
salt and ground black pepper
sea salt flakes, lemon slices and
   Japanese soy sauce, to serve

Makes 8
2 medium courgettes
1/2 medium aubergine
1 large carrot
1/2 small Spanish onion

For the batter
1 egg
120ml/4fl oz/ 1/2 cup iced water
115g/4oz/1 cup plain flour

1 Using a potato peeler, pare strips of peel from the courgettes and aubergine to give a stripy effect. Cut the courgettes, aubergine and carrot into strips about 7.5–10cm/3–4in long and 3mm/1/8 in wide and put them in a colander.

2 Sprinkle the vegetable strips liberally with salt. Leave for about 30 minutes, then rinse thoroughly under cold running water. Drain well.

3 Thinly slice the onion from top to base, discarding the plump pieces in the middle. Separate the layers so that there are lots of fine long strips. Mix all the vegetables together and season to taste with salt and pepper.

4 Make the batter immediately before frying: mix the egg and iced water in a bowl, then sift in the flour. Mix very briefly with a fork or chopsticks – the batter should remain lumpy. Add the vegetables to the batter and mix to combine.

5 Half-fill a wok with oil and heat to 180°C/350°F or until a cube of day-old bread browns in 60 seconds. Scoop up one heaped tablespoon of the mixture at a time and carefully lower it into the oil to make a fritter. Deep-fry in batches for about 3 minutes until golden brown and crisp.

6 Drain the cooked fritters on kitchen paper, and serve at once, offering each diner sea salt flakes, lemon slices and a tiny bowl of Japanese soy sauce for dipping.

Spring Onion & Ricotta Fritters

These melt-in-the-mouth fritters make an unusual starter and are very tasty, especially if you serve them with a spicy avocado salsa.

30ml/2 tbsp chopped
   fresh coriander
sunflower oil, for frying
salt and ground black pepper

Serves 4–6
250g/9oz/generous 1 cup
   ricotta cheese
1 large egg, beaten
90ml/6 tbsp self-raising flour
90ml/6 tbsp milk
1 bunch spring onions,
   thinly sliced

To garnish
fresh coriander sprigs
lime wedges

To serve
Avocado & Tomato
   Dipping Sauce
200ml/7fl oz/scant 1 cup
   crème fraîche

1 Beat the ricotta in a bowl until smooth, then beat in the egg and flour, followed by the milk to make a smooth, thick batter. Beat in the spring onions and coriander. Season well with pepper and a little salt.

2 Heat a little oil in a non-stick frying pan over a medium heat. Add spoonfuls of the mixture, in batches, to make fritters about 7.5cm/3in across. Fry for 4–5 minutes each side, until set and browned. The mixture makes 12 fritters.

3 Drain the fritters on kitchen paper and serve immediately. Garnish with the coriander sprigs and lime wedges, and serve with the dipping sauce and crème fraîche.

> **Cook's Tip**
> It is important that the ricotta is well beaten before the other ingredients are added to make the batter. Once the flour has been added, beat lightly, just to ensure that it is thoroughly combined. Over-beating develops the gluten in the flour and the fritters will become stodgy.

Avocado & Tomato Dipping Sauce

This tastes superb with the Spring Onion & Ricotta Fritters, but can also be served with fried potato skins, crudités, pretzels or breadsticks.

grated rind and juice of 1 lime
1/2–1 fresh green or red chilli,
   seeded and finely chopped
225g/8oz tomatoes, peeled,
   seeded and diced
30–45ml/2–3 tbsp chopped
   mixed fresh mint and coriander
pinch of caster sugar
salt and ground black pepper

Serves 4–6
2 ripe, but not soft, avocados
1 small red onion, diced

1 Peel, stone and dice the avocados. Place in a bowl with the red onion, lime rind and juice. Add chilli to taste, the tomatoes, mint and coriander. Season, then stir in the sugar.

2 Cover closely and set aside for 30 minutes before using.

Indian Potato Pancakes

Although described as pancakes, these classic, crisp cakes are more like bhajis. They make an ideal starter for a curry supper.

Makes 10
2 potatoes, about 300g/11oz
   total weight
2.5ml/1½ tsp garam masala or
   curry powder
4 spring onions, finely chopped
1 large egg white, lightly beaten
30ml/2 tbsp vegetable oil
salt and ground black pepper
chutney and relishes, to serve

1 Peel the potatoes, then grate them into a large bowl. Taking a handful at a time, squeeze out the excess liquid, then pat the potatoes dry with kitchen paper and put them in a separate medium bowl.

2 Add the garam masala or curry powder, spring onions and egg white to the potatoes. Stir to combine, then season to taste with salt and pepper.

3 Heat the oil in a non-stick frying pan over a medium heat. Taking care not to overcrowd the pan, drop tablespoonfuls of the batter on to the surface and flatten each to a pancake with the back of the spoon.

4 Cook for a few minutes and then flip each pancake over. Cook for 3 minutes more.

5 Drain on kitchen paper and keep hot while cooking more pancakes in the same way. Serve hot, with chutney and relishes.

> **Cook's Tips**
> • Grate the potatoes at the last minute, as the flesh will turn brown if they are left standing.
> • Garam masala is a mixture of spices that usually includes dried chillies, cinnamon, curry leaves, coriander, cumin, mustard and fenugreek seeds, and black peppercorns.

Baked Eggs en Cocotte with Wild Mushrooms & Chives

These simple but utterly delicious baked eggs, served with toast, make a splendid start to a light meal.

Serves 6
65g/2½ oz/5 tbsp butter
2 shallots, finely chopped
1 small garlic clove,
   finely chopped
250g/9oz/3 cups wild
   mushrooms, finely chopped
15ml/1 tbsp lemon juice
5ml/1 tsp chopped fresh tarragon
30ml/2 tbsp crème fraîche
30ml/2 tbsp snipped fresh chives
6 eggs
salt and ground black pepper
whole chives, to garnish
buttered wholemeal toast, to serve

1 Melt 50g/2oz/4 tbsp of the butter in a frying pan and cook the shallots and garlic until softened but not browned.

2 Increase the heat and add the mushrooms, then cook briskly, stirring frequently, until the mushrooms lose their moisture and are just starting to brown slightly.

3 Stir in the lemon juice and tarragon and continue to cook, stirring occasionally, until the mushrooms have absorbed the liquid. Stir in half the crème fraîche and half the snipped chives and season to taste with salt and pepper.

4 Preheat the oven to 190°C/375°F/Gas 5. Distribute the mushroom mixture equally among six ramekins. Sprinkle the remaining snipped chives over the mushrooms.

5 Break an egg into each dish, add a dab of crème fraîche and season to taste with pepper. Dot with the remaining butter. Bake for 10–15 minutes, or until the whites of the eggs are set and the yolks cooked to your liking.

6 Serve immediately, garnished with the fresh chives and accompanied by lots of hot, buttered wholemeal toast.

Baked Eggs with Double Cream

This rich dish is very easy and quick to make.

Serves 4
15g/½oz/1 tbsp unsalted
   butter, softened, for greasing
120ml/4fl oz/½ cup
   double cream
30ml/2 tbsp snipped fresh chives
4 eggs
115g/4oz/1 cup finely grated
   Gruyère cheese
salt and ground black pepper

1 Preheat the oven to 180°C/350°F/Gas 4. Grease four individual gratin dishes. Mix the cream with the chives, and season to taste with salt and pepper.

2 Break an egg into each dish and top with the cream mixture. Sprinkle the cheese around the edge of each dish. Bake for 15–20 minutes. When cooked, brown the tops briefly under a hot grill, then serve.

Twice Baked Gruyère & Potato Soufflés

These were all the rage a few years ago and should not be forgotten. Easily prepared in advance, they are perfect for entertaining.

Serves 4
butter, for greasing
225g/8oz floury potatoes

2 eggs, separated
175g/6oz/1½ cups grated
   Gruyère cheese
50g/2oz/½ cup self-raising flour
50g/2oz fresh young spinach
   leaves, finely chopped
salt and ground black pepper
ready-to-serve salad leaves,
   to serve

1 Preheat the oven to 200°C/400°F/Gas 6. Grease four large ramekins. Cook the potatoes in lightly salted boiling water for 20 minutes, until very tender. Drain thoroughly and mash with the egg yolks.

2 Stir in half the Gruyère cheese and all the flour. Season to taste with salt and pepper, then fold in the spinach.

3 Whisk the egg whites until they form soft peaks. Stir a little of the egg white into the spinach mixture to loosen it slightly, then fold in the rest.

4 Place the ramekins on a baking sheet. Divide the mixture among them. Bake for 20 minutes. Remove from the oven and allow to cool.

5 Reheat the oven to 200°C/400°F/Gas 6. Carefully invert the soufflés on a baking sheet and scatter with the remaining Gruyère cheese. Bake for 5 minutes. Serve at once with salad leaves.

> **Variation**
> For a different flavouring, try replacing the Gruyère with a crumbled blue cheese, such as Stilton.

Cheese & Pesto Pasties

Dispense with a formal starter and serve these with drinks instead. They are also perfect for parties.

Serves 8
225g/8oz packet frozen
   chopped spinach
30ml/2 tbsp pine nuts

60ml/4 tbsp pesto sauce
115g/4oz/1 cup grated
   Gruyère cheese
50g/2oz/⅔ cup freshly grated
   Parmesan cheese
2 x 275g/10oz packets frozen filo
   pastry, thawed
30ml/2 tbsp olive oil
salt and ground black pepper

1 Preheat the oven to 190°C/375°F/Gas 5. Prepare the filling. Put the frozen spinach into a pan. Heat it gently, breaking it up as it thaws. Increase the heat to drive off any excess moisture. Transfer to a bowl and cool.

2 Spread out the pine nuts in a frying pan and stir over a very low heat until they are lightly toasted. Chop them and add them to the spinach, with the pesto. Stir in the Gruyère and Parmesan cheeses. Season to taste with salt and pepper.

3 Keeping the rest of the filo pastry covered, cut one sheet into 5cm/2in wide strips. Brush each strip with oil. Put a teaspoon of filling on one end of a strip of pastry. Fold the end over in a triangle, enclosing the filling.

4 Continue to fold the triangle over and over again until the end of the strip is reached. Repeat with the other strips, until all the filling has been used up.

5 Place the pasties on baking sheets, brush them with oil and bake for 20–25 minutes, or until golden brown. Cool slightly on a wire rack. Serve warm.

> **Cook's Tip**
> Keep the filo moist and pliable by keeping it covered with clear film or a damp dish towel. Remove one sheet at a time.

Brandied Roquefort Tarts

Light puff pastry rounds are topped with the irresistible combination of brandy and Roquefort cheese.

Makes 6
150g/5oz Roquefort cheese
30ml/2 tbsp brandy
30ml/2 tbsp olive oil
2 red onions (total weight about 225g/8oz), thinly sliced
225g/8oz puff pastry, thawed if frozen
flour, for dusting
beaten egg or milk, to glaze
6 walnut halves, chopped
30ml/2 tbsp snipped fresh chives
salt and ground black pepper
chive knots, to garnish
salad leaves, diced cucumber and thin tomato wedges, to serve

1 Crumble the Roquefort into a small bowl, pour the brandy over and leave to marinate for 1 hour. Meanwhile, heat the oil in a frying pan and fry the onions gently for 20 minutes, stirring occasionally. Set the pan aside.

2 Preheat the oven to 220°C/425°F/Gas 7. Grease a baking sheet. Roll out the pastry on a floured surface to a 5mm/¼in thickness and stamp out six rounds with a 10cm/4in fluted cutter. Put them on the baking sheet and prick with a fork.

3 Brush the edges of the pastry with a little beaten egg or milk. Add the walnuts and chives to the onion mixture and season with salt and pepper to taste. Divide the mixture among the pastry shapes, leaving the edges clear.

4 Spoon the brandied cheese mixture on top of the pastries and bake for 12–15 minutes, until golden. Serve warm, garnished with chive knots, on a bed of salad leaves, diced cucumber and thin tomato wedges.

> **Cook's Tip**
> To make the chive knots, simply tie chives together in groups of three, with a central knot. Blanch the chives briefly if they are not very pliable.

Quail's Egg & Vermouth Tartlets

The hard-boiled eggs have an attractive marbled surface.

Serves 4
10 quail's eggs
30ml/2 tbsp soy sauce
30ml/2 tbsp mustard seeds
15ml/1 tbsp green tea leaves
6 filo pastry sheets, thawed if frozen
50g/2oz/¼ cup butter, melted
1 small avocado
45ml/3 tbsp dry white vermouth
30ml/2 tbsp mayonnaise
10ml/2 tsp freshly squeezed lime juice
salt and ground black pepper
paprika, for dusting
lamb's lettuce, to serve

1 Put the quail's eggs into a saucepan. Pour over cold water to cover. Add the soy sauce, mustard seeds and tea leaves. Bring to the boil, then lower the heat and simmer for 3 minutes.

2 Remove the pan from the heat and lift out the eggs with a draining spoon. Gently tap them on a firm surface so that the shells crack all over. Put the eggs back into the liquid and leave in a cool place for 8 hours or overnight.

3 Preheat the oven to 190°C/375°F/Gas 5. Grease four 10cm/4in tartlet cases. Brush each sheet of filo pastry with a little melted butter and stack the six sheets on top of each other. Stamp out four rounds with a 15cm/6in cutter.

4 Line the tartlet cases with the pastry and frill the edge of each. Put a crumpled piece of foil in each filo case and bake for 12–15 minutes, until cooked and golden. Remove the foil and set the cases aside to cool.

5 Cut the avocado in half, remove the stone and scoop the flesh into a blender or food processor. Add the vermouth, mayonnaise and lime juice, and season to taste with salt and pepper. Process until smooth.

6 Shell and halve the eggs. Pipe or spoon the avocado mixture into the pastry cases and arrange the eggs on top. Dust them with a little paprika and serve at once, with the lamb's lettuce.

Spiced Carrot Dip

This is a delicious low-fat dip with a sweet and spicy flavour. Serve with wheat crackers or tortilla chips.

Serves 4
1 onion
4 carrots
grated rind and juice of 2 oranges
15ml/1 tbsp hot curry paste
150ml/ ¼ pint/ ⅔ cup low-fat natural yogurt
a handful of fresh basil leaves
15–30ml/1–2 tbsp fresh lemon juice, to taste
Tabasco sauce, to taste
salt and ground black pepper

1 Chop the onion finely. Peel and grate the carrots. Place three-quarters of the grated carrot in a small saucepan and add the onion, orange rind and juice and curry paste. Bring to the boil, lower the heat, cover and simmer for 10 minutes, until tender.

2 Allow to cool slightly, then process the mixture in a blender or food processor until smooth. Scrape into a bowl and leave to cool completely.

3 Stir in the yogurt, a little at a time. Tear the basil leaves into small pieces and stir them into the mixture.

4 Season with lemon juice, Tabasco, salt and pepper to taste. Mix well. Serve at room temperature within a few hours of making. Garnish with the remaining grated carrot.

Cook's Tip
The original Tabasco sauce, dating from the mid-nineteenth century, is made from red peppers, vinegar and salt. A green pepper version is also available.

Variation
Greek-style yogurt or soured cream can be used instead of natural yogurt to make a richer, creamy dip.

Fat-free Saffron Dip

Serve this mild dip with fresh vegetable crudités – it is particularly good with crunchy vegetables, such as cauliflower florets, baby corn cobs and celery.

Serves 4
15ml/1 tbsp boiling water
small pinch of saffron strands
200ml/7fl oz/scant 1 cup fat-free fromage frais
10 fresh chives
10 fresh basil leaves
salt and ground black pepper

1 Pour the boiling water into a small bowl and add the saffron strands. Leave to infuse for 3 minutes.

2 Beat the fromage frais until smooth, then stir in the infused saffron liquid.

3 Use a pair of scissors to snip the chives into the dip. Tear the basil leaves into small pieces and stir them in. Season with salt and pepper to taste and stir to combine. Serve immediately.

Variation
If preferred, you can omit the saffron and flavour the dip with a squeeze of lemon or lime juice instead.

Pesto Dip

This tastes great with roasted vegetables and also goes well with baked potato skins and chips.

Serves 4
250ml/8fl oz/1 cup soured cream or low-fat fromage frais
15ml/1 tbsp ready-made red or green pesto

1 Spoon the soured cream or fromage frais into a bowl. Stir in the pesto, swirling it on the surface of the dip.

2 Cover and chill until ready to serve.

Lemon Oil Dip with Charred Artichokes

A tangy lemon and garlic dip makes the perfect accompaniment to roasted globe artichokes. It would also go well with barbecued baby artichokes.

Serves 4

15ml/1 tbsp lemon juice or white wine vinegar
2 globe artichokes, trimmed
12 garlic cloves, unpeeled
90ml/6 tbsp olive oil
1 lemon
sea salt
flat leaf parsley sprigs, to garnish

1 Preheat the oven to 200°C/400°F/Gas 6. Add the lemon juice or vinegar to a bowl of cold water. Cut each artichoke lengthways into wedges. Pull out and discard the hairy choke from the centre of each wedge, then drop the wedges into the acidulated water to prevent discoloration.

2 Drain the artichoke wedges and place them in a roasting tin with the garlic. Add half the olive oil and toss well to coat. Sprinkle with sea salt and roast for 40 minutes, stirring once or twice, until the artichokes are tender and a little charred.

3 Meanwhile, make the dip. Using a small, sharp knife, thinly pare away two strips of rind from the lemon. Lay the strips on a board and carefully scrape away any remaining pith. Place the rind in a small pan with water to cover. Bring to the boil, then simmer for 5 minutes. Drain the rind, refresh it in cold water, then chop it roughly and set it aside.

4 Arrange the cooked artichokes on a serving plate and set them aside to cool for 5 minutes.

5 Press the garlic cloves to extract the flesh and put it in a bowl. Mash it to a purée, then add the lemon rind. Squeeze the juice from the lemon and whisk it into the garlic mixture. Finally, whisk in the remaining oil. Season with sea salt and serve with the warm artichokes. Garnish with flat leaf parsley.

Aïoli with Fried Potato

Today, aïoli is usually made in a food processor, rather than pounded with a pestle in a mortar, and is more like garlic mayonnaise.

Serves 4

vegetable oil, for deep-frying
4 potatoes, each cut into
   eight wedges
coarse sea salt

For the aïoli

1 large egg yolk, at room
   temperature
5ml/1 tsp white wine vinegar
75ml/5 tbsp olive oil
75ml/5 tbsp sunflower oil
4 garlic cloves, crushed
parsley sprig, to garnish

1 First, make the aïoli. Place the egg yolk and vinegar in a food processor. With the motor running, gradually add the olive oil, then the sunflower oil through the feeder tube, until the mixture has the consistency of a thick mayonnaise.

2 Scrape the mixture into a serving bowl and stir in the crushed garlic. Season with salt to taste, then cover closely and chill in the fridge until required.

3 Heat the vegetable oil in a saucepan or deep-fryer to a temperature of 180°C/350°F or until a cube of day-old bread turns golden in about 60 seconds. Add the potato wedges and fry for about 7 minutes, until pale golden.

4 Lift out the potato wedges with a draining spoon and drain them on kitchen paper. Increase the heat of the oil slightly, then return the potato wedges to the pan and fry them for a second time until crisp and golden brown. Remove with a slotted spoon and drain thoroughly on kitchen paper. Sprinkle with sea salt and serve hot with the aïoli, garnished with parsley.

Cook's Tip

For an aïoli with a milder flavour, use three parts sunflower oil to one part olive oil.

Mellow Garlic Dip

Two whole heads of garlic may seem like a lot but, once cooked, their flavour becomes sweet and mellow.

Serves 4
2 whole heads of garlic
15ml/1 tbsp olive oil

60ml/4 tbsp mayonnaise
75ml/5 tbsp Greek-style yogurt
5ml/1 tsp wholegrain mustard
salt and ground black pepper
crunchy breadsticks, to
  serve (optional)

1 Preheat the oven to 200°C/400°F/Gas 6. Separate the garlic cloves and place them in a small roasting tin. Pour the olive oil over them and turn them with a spoon to coat evenly. Roast for 20–30 minutes, until tender and softened. Set aside to cool for 5 minutes.

2 Trim off the root end from each garlic clove, then peel. Place the garlic cloves on a chopping board and sprinkle with salt. Mash with a fork until puréed. Scrape the purée into a small bowl and stir in the mayonnaise, yogurt and mustard.

3 Check and adjust the seasoning, then spoon the dip into a serving bowl. Cover closely and chill until ready to serve.

Easy Garlic and Coconut Dip

This tastes fabulous with crudités or breadsticks.

Serves 4
5 garlic cloves
150g/5oz/2 cups dry
  grated coconut

30ml/2 tbsp chilli powder
150ml/¼ pint/⅔ cup
  natural yogurt
salt
crudités, to serve

1 Pound the garlic with a pinch of salt. Gradually work in the coconut and chilli powder to make a paste.
2 Stir the paste into the yogurt and serve with crudités.

Butternut Squash & Parmesan Dip

Butternut squash makes an unusual but very tasty dip, which is best served warm.

Serves 4
1 butternut squash
15g/½ oz/1 tbsp butter

4 garlic cloves, unpeeled
30ml/2 tbsp freshly grated
  Parmesan cheese
45–75ml/3–5 tbsp double cream
salt and ground black pepper
Melba toast, cheese straws or
  crudités, to serve

1 Preheat the oven to 200°C/400°F/Gas 6. Cut the butternut squash in half lengthways, then scoop out and discard the seeds.

2 Use a small, sharp knife to score the flesh deeply in a criss-cross pattern; cut as close to the skin as possible, but take care not to cut through it. Arrange both halves in a small roasting tin and dot them with the butter. Sprinkle with salt and pepper and roast for 20 minutes. Tuck the garlic cloves around the squash in the roasting tin. Bake for 20 minutes more, until the squash is tender and softened.

3 Scoop the flesh out of the squash shells and place it in a blender or food processor. Slip the garlic cloves out of their skins and add the pulp to the squash. Process until smooth.

4 With the motor running, add half the grated Parmesan cheese, then add the double cream. Check the seasoning. Spoon the dip into a serving bowl, scatter the reserved cheese over the top and serve warm with Melba toast, cheese straws or crudités.

> **Cook's Tip**
> To make Melba toast, grill a slice of white bread on both sides until golden. Allow to cool slightly, then cut off and discard the crusts. Using a long, thin, very sharp knife, slice the bread in half horizontally to make two thinner slices. Toast the inner slices under the grill until golden. Allow to cool, then store in an airtight container until required.

Tzatziki

Cool, creamy and refreshing, tzatziki is wonderfully easy to make and even easier to eat. Serve this classic Greek dip with pitta bread, potato wedges or a selection of chargrilled vegetables.

Serves 4

1 mini cucumber, topped
   and tailed
4 spring onions
1 garlic clove
200ml/7fl oz/scant 1 cup
   Greek-style yogurt
45ml/3 tbsp chopped fresh mint
salt and ground black pepper
fresh mint sprig, to garnish
toasted mini pitta breads, to serve

1 Cut the cucumber into 5mm/ ¼ in dice. Trim the spring onions and garlic, then chop both very finely.

2 Beat the yogurt until smooth, if necessary, then gently stir in the cucumber, onions, garlic and mint.

3 Scrape the mixture into a serving bowl and season with salt and plenty of ground black pepper to taste. Cover and chill in the fridge until needed. Garnish with a small mint sprig and serve with toasted mini pitta breads.

Cook's Tip
Choose Greek-style yogurt for this dip – it has a higher fat content than most yogurts, which gives it a deliciously rich, creamy texture.

Variation
A similar, but smoother dip can be made in the food processor. Peel one mini cucumber and process with two garlic cloves and 75g/3oz/3 cups mixed fresh herbs to a purée. Stir the purée into 200ml/7fl oz/scant 1 cup soured cream and season to taste with salt and pepper.

Blue Cheese Dip

This dip can be mixed up in next-to-no-time and is delicious served with ripe pears cut into wedges. If you add a little more yogurt to give a softer consistency, it makes a good salad dressing.

Serves 4

150g/5oz blue cheese, such as
   Stilton or Danish blue
150g/5oz/ ⅔ cup low-fat
   soft cheese
about 75ml/5 tbsp Greek-
   style yogurt
salt and ground black pepper

1 Crumble the blue cheese into a bowl. Using a wooden spoon, beat the cheese to soften it.

2 Add the soft cheese and beat well to blend the cheeses.

3 Gradually beat in the Greek-style yogurt, adding enough to give you the consistency you prefer.

4 Season with lots of black pepper and a little salt. Cover and chill in the fridge until ready to serve.

Sun-dried Tomato Swirl

Try this with celery sticks or carrot batons. It is also delicious as a topping on baked potatoes.

Serves 4

30ml/2 tbsp sun-dried
   tomato paste

250ml/8fl oz/1 cup
   Greek-style yogurt
2 spring onions, finely chopped
2 sun-dried tomatoes in oil,
   drained and finely chopped
dash of Tabasco sauce (optional)
salt and ground black pepper

1 Mix the sun-dried tomato paste with a little of the yogurt until smooth, then gradually stir in the remaining yogurt.
2 Add the spring onions and chopped sun-dried tomatoes, season to taste with salt and pepper and mix well. If you like, spike the swirl with a dash of Tabasco.

Guacamole

One of the best-loved Mexican salsas, this blend of creamy avocado, tomatoes, garlic, chillies, coriander and lime now appears on tables the world over.

Serves 6–8

4 ripe avocados
juice of 1 lime
½ small onion
2 garlic cloves
small bunch of fresh
    coriander, chopped
3 fresh red chillies
4 medium tomatoes, peeled,
    seeded and roughly chopped
salt
tortilla chips, to serve

1 Cut the avocados in half and remove the stones. Scoop the flesh out of the shells and place it in a food processor or blender. Process until almost smooth, then scrape into a bowl and stir in the lime juice. For a chunkier dip, mash the avocado flesh roughly with a fork.

2 Chop the onion finely, then crush the garlic. Add both to the avocado and mix well. Stir in the coriander.

3 Remove the stalks from the chillies, slit the pods and scrape out the seeds with a small sharp knife. Chop the chillies finely and add them to the avocado mixture, together with the chopped tomatoes. Mix well.

4 Check the seasoning and add salt to taste. Cover closely with clear film or a tight-fitting lid and chill for 1 hour before serving as a dip with tortilla chips.

Cook's Tips
• If it is well covered, guacamole will keep in the fridge for 2–3 days, but it will tend to turn greyish.
• Submerging an avocado stone in the guacamole is said to inhibit discoloration.
• Traditionally, avocados are cut with a silver-bladed knife – again to prevent discoloration.

Aubergine & Pepper Spread

With its rich colour and robust texture, this mixture makes an excellent contrast to a creamy cheese dip. It goes especially well with black olives.

Serves 6–8

2 aubergines, total weight about
    675g/1½ lb, halved lengthways
2 green peppers, seeded
    and quartered
45ml/3 tbsp olive oil
2 firm ripe tomatoes, halved,
    seeded and finely chopped
45ml/3 tbsp chopped fresh
    parsley or coriander
2 garlic cloves, crushed
30ml/2 tbsp red wine vinegar
lemon juice, to taste
salt and ground black pepper
fresh parsley or coriander sprigs,
    to garnish
dark rye bread, lemon wedges
    and black olives, to serve

1 Place the aubergines and pepper quarters, skin side up, on a grill rack and grill until the skins have blistered and charred. Turn the vegetables over and cook for 3 minutes more. Transfer to a bowl, cover with crumpled kitchen paper and leave to cool for about 10 minutes.

2 Peel away the blackened skin. Place the aubergine and pepper flesh in a food processor and process to a purée.

3 With the motor running, pour in the olive oil in a continuous stream through the feeder tube and process until smooth and thoroughly combined.

4 Scrape the mixture into a serving bowl and stir in the chopped tomatoes, parsley or coriander, garlic, vinegar and lemon juice. Season to taste with salt and pepper, garnish with the parsley or coriander sprigs and serve with dark rye bread, wedges of lemon and black olives.

Cook's Tip
This dip is delicious served with any rustic bread, such as olive bread or ciabatta.

Baba Ganoush with Lebanese Flatbread

Baba Ganoush is a delectable aubergine dip from the Middle East.

Serves 6
2 small aubergines, halved
1 garlic clove, crushed
60ml/4 tbsp tahini
25g/1oz/ ¼ cup ground almonds
juice of ½ lemon
2.5ml/ ½ tsp ground cumin
30ml/2 tbsp fresh mint leaves

olive oil, for drizzling
salt and ground black pepper

For the Lebanese flatbread
4 pitta breads
45ml/3 tbsp toasted
  sesame seeds
45ml/3 tbsp chopped fresh
  thyme leaves
45ml/3 tbsp poppy seeds
150ml/ ¼ pint/ ⅔ cup olive oil

1 Make the flatbread. Split the pitta breads through the middle and carefully open them out. Mix the sesame seeds, thyme and poppy seeds in a mortar and crush them lightly with a pestle.

2 Stir in the olive oil. Spread the mixture lightly over the cut sides of the pitta bread. Grill until golden brown and crisp. When cool, break into rough pieces and set aside.

3 Place the aubergines, skin side up, on a grill rack and grill until the skins have blistered and charred. Transfer to a bowl, cover with crumpled kitchen paper and leave to cool for 10 minutes. Peel the aubergines, chop the flesh roughly and leave it to drain in a colander.

4 Squeeze out as much liquid from the aubergines as possible. Place the flesh in a blender or food processor. Add the garlic, tahini, ground almonds, lemon juice and cumin and process to a smooth paste. Roughly chop half the mint and stir into the dip. Season to taste with salt and pepper.

5 Spoon the dip into a serving bowl, scatter the remaining mint on top and drizzle lightly with olive oil. Serve the dip with the Lebanese flatbread.

Lemon & Coconut Dhal

A warm spicy dish, this is perfect with poppadums or can be served as a main-meal accompaniment.

Serves 8
30ml/2 tbsp sunflower oil
5cm/2in piece of fresh root
  ginger, chopped
1 onion, chopped
2 garlic cloves, crushed
2 small fresh red chillies, seeded
  and chopped

5ml/1 tsp cumin seeds
150g/5oz/ ⅔ cup red lentils
250ml/8fl oz/1 cup water
15ml/1 tbsp hot curry paste
200ml/7fl oz/scant 1 cup
  coconut cream
juice of 1 lemon
handful of fresh coriander leaves
25g/1oz/ ¼ cup flaked almonds
salt and ground black pepper
warm poppadums, to serve
a few thin slices of red chilli,
  to garnish

1 Heat the sunflower oil in a large, shallow saucepan. Add the ginger, onion, garlic, red chillies and cumin seeds. Cook over a medium heat, stirring occasionally, for about 5 minutes, until the onion is softened but not coloured.

2 Stir the lentils, water and curry paste into the pan and bring to the boil over a medium heat. Lower the heat, cover and cook gently for 15–20 minutes, stirring occasionally, until the lentils are just tender but not yet broken.

3 Stir in all but 30ml/2 tbsp of the coconut cream. Bring to the boil and cook, uncovered, for a further 15–20 minutes, until the mixture is thick and pulpy. Remove the pan from the heat, then stir in the lemon juice and the whole coriander leaves. Season with salt and pepper to taste.

4 Heat a large, heavy-based frying pan. Add the flaked almonds and dry-fry briefly over a medium heat, stirring frequently, until golden brown. Stir about three-quarters of the toasted almonds into the dhal.

5 Transfer the dhal to a serving bowl and swirl in the remaining coconut cream. Scatter the remaining toasted almonds and chilli slices on top. Serve warm, with poppadums.

Cannellini Bean Dip

This soft bean dip or pâté is good spread on wheaten crackers or toasted muffins. Serve it with wedges of tomato and salad leaves.

Serves 4
400g/14oz can cannellini beans, rinsed and drained
grated rind and juice of 1 lemon
30ml/2 tbsp olive oil
1 garlic clove, finely chopped
30ml/2 tbsp chopped fresh parsley
Tabasco sauce, to taste
cayenne pepper
salt and ground black pepper
chopped fresh parsley, to garnish

1 Put the beans in a shallow bowl and break them up roughly with a potato masher.

2 Stir in the lemon rind and juice and olive oil, then the chopped garlic and parsley. Add Tabasco sauce, salt and black pepper to taste.

3 Spoon the mixture into a small bowl, dust lightly with cayenne and sprinkle with parsley. Chill until ready to serve.

Vegetarian Tapenade

This famous black olive paste usually contains anchovies, but the vegetarian version is just as delicious.

Serves 4
350g/12oz/3 cups stoned black olives
5 pieces of sun-dried tomatoes in oil, drained
30ml/2 tbsp drained capers
1–2 garlic cloves, roughly chopped
5ml/1 tsp chopped fresh thyme
15ml/1 tbsp Dijon mustard
juice of ½ lemon
45ml/3 tbsp olive oil

1 Place all the ingredients in a food processor. Process to a smooth purée, then scrape into a serving dish. Cover and chill slightly before serving.

Chilli Bean Dip

This creamy bean dip is best served warm with grilled pitta bread.

Serves 4
30ml/2 tbsp vegetable oil
2 garlic cloves, crushed
1 onion, finely chopped
2 fresh green chillies, seeded and finely chopped
5–10ml/1–2 tsp hot chilli powder
400g/14oz can kidney beans
75g/3oz/¾ cup grated mature Cheddar cheese
1 fresh red chilli, seeded
salt and ground black pepper
triangles of grilled pitta bread, to serve

1 Heat the oil in a deep, heavy-based frying pan. Add the garlic, onion, green chillies and chilli powder and fry over a low heat, stirring frequently, for about 5 minutes, until the onions are softened and transparent, but not browned.

2 Drain the kidney beans, reserving the can juices. Set aside 30ml/2 tbsp of the beans and put the remainder in a food processor. Process to a purée.

3 Add the puréed beans to the onion mixture and moisten with 30–45ml/2–3 tbsp of the reserved can juices. Heat gently, stirring to mix well.

4 Stir in the reserved whole kidney beans and the grated Cheddar. Cook over a low heat, stirring constantly, for 2–3 minutes, until the cheese has melted. Season with salt and pepper to taste.

5 Cut the red chilli into thin strips. Spoon the dip into four individual serving bowls and scatter the chilli strips and extra cheese over the top. Serve warm, with the pitta triangles, garnished with green chillies.

> **Cook's Tip**
> For a dip with a coarser texture, do not purée the beans; instead, mash them with a potato masher.

Butterbean, Watercress & Herb Dip

A refreshing dip that is especially good served with crudités and breadsticks.

Serves 4–6
225g/8oz/1 cup plain
   cottage cheese
400g/14oz can butter beans,
   drained and rinsed
1 bunch spring onions, chopped
50g/2oz watercress, chopped
60ml/4 tbsp mayonnaise
45ml/3 tbsp chopped fresh
   mixed herbs
salt and ground black pepper
watercress sprigs, to garnish
crudités and breadsticks,
   to serve

1 Put the cottage cheese, butter beans, spring onions, watercress, mayonnaise and herbs in a blender or food processor and process to a rough purée.

2 Spoon the mixture into a dish, season to taste with salt and pepper and cover tightly with clear film. Chill in the fridge for several hours.

3 Transfer to a serving dish (or individual dishes) and garnish with watercress sprigs. Serve with crudités and breadsticks.

Curried Sweetcorn Dip

Serve this spicy dip with crudités, breadsticks or Melba toast.

Serves 6–8
30ml/2 tbsp mayonnaise
10–15ml/2–3 tsp curry paste
225g/8oz/1 cup cottage cheese
115g/4oz/1 cup grated
   Cheddar cheese
300ml/½ pint/1¼ cups
   soured cream
115g/4oz/⅔ cup canned
   sweetcorn, drained
salt and ground black pepper

1 Blend the mayonnaise, curry paste and cottage cheese together in a bowl. Stir in the grated Cheddar.
2 Stir in the soured cream and sweetcorn and season with salt and pepper to taste. Transfer to a serving bowl and serve.

Hummus with Crudités

Always a great family favourite, hummus can be made quickly at home with the help of a blender.

Serves 2–3
400g/14oz can chick-peas
30ml/2 tbsp tahini
30ml/2 tbsp lemon juice
1 garlic clove, crushed
salt and ground black pepper
olive oil and paprika, to garnish

To serve
whole baby carrots and radishes
strips of green and red pepper,
   chicory, celery and cucumber
bite-size chunks of bread, pitta or
   grissini sticks

1 Drain the chick-peas and put them in a blender or food processor. Add the tahini, lemon juice and garlic. Process to a smooth paste.

2 Season the hummus with plenty of salt and pepper. Spoon it into a bowl and swirl the top with the back of a spoon. Trickle over a little olive oil and sprinkle with paprika.

3 Arrange the baby carrots, radishes and the strips of salad vegetables around the rim of a large plate.

4 Add chunks of bread, pieces of pitta or grissini. Place the bowl of hummus in the centre. Serve at once.

Variation
Hummus is delicious served with hot celeriac fritters. Peel and slice one medium celeriac into strips about 1cm/½in wide and 5cm/2in long. Drop them into a bowl of water mixed with a little lemon juice. Lightly beat one egg in a shallow dish. In another shallow dish, combine 115g/4oz/1 cup ground almonds, 45ml/3 tbsp grated Parmesan cheese and 45ml/3 tbsp chopped fresh parsley. Heat vegetable oil for deep-frying to 180°C/350°F or until a cube of bread browns in about 60 seconds. Pat the celeriac dry and dip, first, in the egg and then in the almond mixture. Deep-fry, in batches, and serve.

Nutty Mushroom Pâté

Spread this delicious, medium-texture pâté on chunks of crusty French bread and eat with crisp leaves of lettuce and sweet cherry tomatoes.

Serves 4–6
15ml/1 tbsp sunflower oil
1 onion, chopped
1 garlic clove, crushed
30ml/2 tbsp water
15ml/1 tbsp dry sherry

225g/8oz/3 cups button
  mushrooms, chopped
75g/3oz/ ¾ cup cashew nuts or
  walnuts, chopped
150g/5oz/ ²⁄₃ cup low-fat
  soft cheese
15ml/1 tbsp soy sauce
few dashes of vegetarian
  Worcestershire sauce
salt and ground black pepper
fresh parsley, chopped, and a little
  paprika, to garnish

1 Heat the oil in a saucepan. Add the onion and garlic and fry over a medium heat, stirring occasionally, for 3 minutes. Stir in the water, sherry and mushrooms. Cook, stirring constantly, for about 5 minutes. Season to taste with salt and pepper. Remove the pan from the heat and allow to cool a little.

2 Put the mixture into a food processor and add the cashew nuts or walnuts, cheese, soy sauce and Worcestershire sauce. Process to a coarse purée – do not allow the mixture to become too smooth.

3 Check and adjust the seasoning, if necessary, then scrape the pâté into a serving dish. Swirl the top and chill lightly in the fridge. Serve the pâté sprinkled with parsley and paprika.

Cook's Tips
• *Conventional Worcestershire sauce is off-limits for vegetarians as it contains anchovies. Look out for the vegetarian version of this popular sauce. It is available in health-food stores.*
• *For extra flavour, add 15g/ ½ oz dried porcini mushrooms, soaked in hot water for 30 minutes. Substitute 30ml/2 tbsp of the strained soaking water for the plain water.*

Roast Garlic & Goat's Cheese Pâté

The flavour of mellow roasted garlic goes well with this classic goat's cheese, walnut and herb pâté.

pâté, Serves 2–4
4 large garlic bulbs
4 fresh rosemary sprigs
8 fresh thyme sprigs
60ml/4 tbsp extra virgin
  olive oil
salt and ground black pepper

For the pâté
175g/6oz soft goat's cheese
5ml/1 tsp finely chopped
  fresh thyme
15ml/1 tbsp chopped
  fresh parsley
50g/2oz/ ½ cup shelled
  walnuts, chopped
15ml/1 tbsp walnut oil (optional)

To serve
4–8 slices sourdough bread
shelled walnuts
sea salt

1 Preheat the oven to 180°C/350°F/Gas 4. Strip the papery skin from the garlic bulbs. Place them in an ovenproof dish large enough to hold them snugly.

2 Tuck in the rosemary and thyme, drizzle the oil over and season to taste with salt and pepper. Cover the dish closely with foil and bake for 50–60 minutes, basting once. Remove from the oven and leave to cool.

3 Make the pâté. Cream the cheese with the thyme, parsley and chopped walnuts. Beat in 15ml/1 tbsp of the cooking oil from the garlic. Season to taste with salt and pepper, then transfer the pâté to a serving bowl.

4 Spread out the slices of sourdough bread in a grill pan and brush them with the remaining cooking oil from the garlic. Grill until toasted.

5 If using the walnut oil, drizzle it over the goat's cheese pâté. Grind some black pepper over it. Place one or two bulbs of garlic on each plate and serve with the pâté and a couple of slices of toasted sourdough bread. Serve a few freshly shelled walnuts and a little sea salt with each portion.

Fontina Pan Bagna

When the weather is hot, a crusty flute or baguette filled with juicy tomatoes, crisp red onion, green pepper, thinly sliced Fontina cheese and sliced black olives makes a refreshing and substantial snack.

Serves 2–4
1 small red onion, thinly sliced
1 fresh flute or baguette
extra virgin olive oil
3 ripe plum tomatoes, thinly sliced
1 small green pepper, halved, seeded and thinly sliced
200g/7oz Fontina cheese, thinly sliced
about 12 stoned black olives, sliced
a handful of flat leaf parsley or basil leaves
salt and ground black pepper
fresh basil sprigs, to garnish

1 Soak the slices of red onion in plenty of cold water for at least 1 hour, then drain well in a colander, tip on to kitchen paper and pat dry.

2 Slice the flute or baguette in half lengthways and brush the cut sides well with olive oil. Lay the tomato slices down one side and season well with salt and black pepper.

3 Top with the green pepper slices, then add the onion slices. Arrange the cheese and olives on top. Scatter over the parsley or basil leaves and season with salt and pepper again.

4 Press the halves together, then wrap the filled loaf tightly in clear film to compress it. Chill for at least 1 hour. Unwrap and cut diagonally into thick slices. Garnish with basil sprigs and serve immediately.

> **Cook's Tips**
> • *This is a good choice for a picnic. Pack the loaf, uncut and still wrapped in clear film, and cut into slices just before serving. Do not forget to take a sharp knife with you.*
> • *Other springy-textured cheeses, such as Taleggio and Havarti, could be used instead of Fontina.*

Four Cheese Ciabatta Pizzas

Few dishes are as simple – or as satisfying – as this pizza made by topping a halved loaf of ciabatta.

Serves 2
1 loaf of ciabatta
1 garlic clove, halved
30–45ml/2–3 tbsp olive oil
about 90ml/6 tbsp passata
1 small red onion, thinly sliced
30ml/2 tbsp chopped stoned black olives
about 50g/2oz each of four cheeses, one mature (Parmesan or Cheddar), one blue-veined (Gorgonzola or Stilton), one mild (Fontina or Emmenthal) and a goat's cheese, sliced, grated or crumbled
pine nuts or cumin seeds, to sprinkle
salt and ground black pepper
fresh basil sprigs, to garnish

1 Preheat the oven to 200°C/400°F/Gas 6. Split the ciabatta loaf in half. Rub the cut sides with the cut sides of the garlic clove, then brush over the olive oil.

2 Spread the passata evenly over the ciabatta halves. Separate the onion slices into rings and arrange them on each cut loaf, with the chopped olives on top. Season generously with salt and pepper.

3 Divide the sliced, grated or crumbled cheeses equally among the ciabatta halves and then sprinkle the pine nuts or cumin seeds over the top.

4 Bake for 10–12 minutes, until the cheese topping is bubbling and golden brown. Cut the ciabatta pizzas into slices and serve immediately, garnished with basil sprigs.

> **Cook's Tip**
> *Passata is a very useful ingredient to keep in the store cupboard. Strained, puréed tomato pulp with an intense flavour, it comes in jars, cans and cartons and is widely available. Sugocasa can be used instead.*

Cannellini Bean & Rosemary Bruschetta

More brunch than breakfast, this dish is a sophisticated version of beans on toast.

Serves 4
150g/5oz/ ⅔ cup dried
   cannellini beans
5 tomatoes
45ml/3 tbsp olive oil, plus extra
   for drizzling
2 sun-dried tomatoes in oil,
   drained and finely chopped

1 garlic clove, crushed
30ml/2 tbsp chopped
   fresh rosemary
salt and ground black pepper
a handful of fresh basil leaves,
   to garnish

To serve
8 slices Italian-style bread, such as
   ciabatta
1 large garlic clove, halved

1 Place the beans in a large bowl and cover with water. Leave to soak overnight. Drain and rinse the beans, then place in a saucepan and cover with fresh water. Bring to the boil and boil rapidly for 10 minutes. Reduce the heat and simmer for 50–60 minutes, or until tender. Drain and set aside.

2 Meanwhile, place the tomatoes in a bowl, cover with boiling water and leave for 30 seconds. Remove with a draining spoon, then peel, seed and chop the flesh.

3 Heat the oil in a frying pan, add the fresh and sun-dried tomatoes, garlic and rosemary. Cook over a medium heat, stirring occasionally, for 2 minutes, until the tomatoes begin to break down and soften.

4 Add the tomato mixture to the cannellini beans, season to taste with salt and pepper and mix well. Keep warm.

5 When ready to serve, rub both sides of the bread slices with the cut sides of the garlic clove, then toast lightly. Spoon the cannellini bean and tomato mixture on top of the toast. Sprinkle with fresh basil leaves and drizzle with a little extra olive oil before serving.

Goat's Cheese & Gin Crostini

A gin marinade accentuates the flavour of goat's cheese, which melts beautifully over the spring onions on these tasty toasts.

Serves 4
8 slices chèvre
15ml/1 tbsp gin
30ml/2 tbsp walnut oil
30ml/2 tbsp olive oil
4 slices Italian or French bread

1 garlic clove, halved
2 spring onions, sliced
6 walnut halves, roughly broken
15ml/1 tbsp chopped
   fresh parsley
ground black pepper
cherry tomatoes and mixed salad
   leaves, to garnish
Orange and Tomato Salsa,
   to serve

1 Spread out the cheese slices in a single layer in a shallow bowl. Pour over the gin, walnut oil and olive oil, then cover and leave in a cool place to marinate for 1 hour.

2 Put the slices of bread on a grill rack. Toast them under a hot grill on one side, then turn them over and rub the untoasted surfaces with the cut pieces of garlic. Brush with a little of the marinade used for the goat's cheese, then sprinkle over the sliced spring onions. Top with the slices of marinated cheese.

3 Pour over any remaining marinade, season with pepper and cook the crostini under a hot grill until the cheese has melted and browned. Scatter over the walnuts and parsley. Garnish with the tomatoes and salad leaves and serve with the salsa.

> **Cook's Tip**
> Chèvre is French goat's milk cheese. It is often cylindrical in shape, which makes it perfect for this dish. Use a natural-rind cheese with a firm but not hard texture. Do not allow it to get wet in storage, as this will spoil it.

Orange & Tomato Salsa

Fruity, but not too sweet, this salsa is the perfect accompaniment for the crostini. It also tastes wonderful with Lancashire or Cheddar cheese and French bread as part of a simple ploughman's lunch.

Serves 4
2 oranges
5 tomatoes, peeled, seeded
   and chopped
15ml/1 tbsp shredded fresh basil
30ml/2 tbsp olive oil
pinch of soft light brown sugar
fresh basil sprig, to garnish

1 Cut a slice off the top and bottom of each orange. Place each orange in turn on a board and cut off the skin, taking care to remove all the bitter white pith. Working over a bowl to catch the juices, cut between the membranes to release the segments.

2 Add the segments to the bowl, with the tomatoes, shredded basil, olive oil and brown sugar. Mix well. Serve at room temperature, garnished with the basil.

Falafel

In North Africa, these spicy fritters are made using dried broad beans, but chick-peas are much easier to buy. They are lovely served as a snack with creamy yogurt or stuffed into warmed pitta bread pockets.

Serves 4
150g/5oz/ ⅔ cup dried
  chick-peas
1 large onion, roughly chopped
2 garlic cloves, roughly chopped

60ml/4 tbsp roughly
  chopped parsley
5ml/1 tsp cumin seeds, crushed
5ml/1 tsp coriander
  seeds, crushed
2.5ml/ ½ tsp baking powder
vegetable oil, for deep-frying
salt and ground black pepper

To serve
pitta bread
salad
natural yogurt

1 Put the chick-peas in a bowl with plenty of cold water. Leave to soak overnight.

2 Drain the chick-peas and put them in a large pan. Pour over enough water to cover them by at least 5cm/2in. Bring to the boil. Boil rapidly for 10 minutes, then lower the heat and simmer for 1–1½ hours, until soft.

3 Drain the chick-peas and place them in a food processor. Add the onion, garlic, parsley, cumin seeds, coriander seeds and baking powder. Season with salt and pepper to taste. Process until the mixture forms a fine paste.

4 As soon as the paste is cool enough to handle, shape it into walnut-size balls, flattening them slightly.

5 Pour oil to a depth of 5cm/2in into a deep frying pan. Heat until a little of the falafel mixture added to the hot oil sizzles on the surface.

6 Fry the falafel, in batches, until golden. Drain on kitchen paper and keep hot while frying the remainder. Serve warm in pitta bread, with salad and yogurt.

Courgettes, Carrots & Pecans in Pitta Bread

Easy to eat and very tasty, this makes a good, healthy after-school snack or a nourishing light lunch.

Serves 2
2 carrots
25g/1oz/ ¼ cup pecan nuts
4 spring onions, sliced

60ml/4 tbsp Greek-style yogurt
45ml/3 tbsp olive oil
5ml/1 tsp lemon juice
15ml/1 tbsp chopped fresh mint
2 courgettes
25g/1oz/ ¼ cup plain flour
2 pitta breads
salt and ground black pepper
shredded lettuce, to serve

1 Top and tail the carrots. Grate them coarsely into a bowl. Stir in the pecans and spring onions and toss well.

2 In a clean bowl, whisk the yogurt with 7.5ml/ 1½ tsp of the olive oil, the lemon juice and the fresh mint. Stir the dressing into the carrot mixture and mix thoroughly. Cover and chill in the fridge until required.

3 Top and tail the courgettes. Cut them diagonally into fairly thin slices. Season the flour with a little salt and pepper. Spread it out on a plate and coat the courgette slices. Shake off any excess flour.

4 Heat the remaining oil in a large frying pan. Add the coated courgette slices and cook for 3–4 minutes, turning once, until browned. Drain the courgettes on kitchen paper.

5 Make a slit in each pitta bread to form a pocket. Fill the pittas with the carrot mixture and the courgette slices. Serve immediately on a bed of shredded lettuce.

Cook's Tip
Warm the pitta breads, if you like. Do not fill them too soon or the carrot mixture will make the bread soggy.

Creamy Cannellini Beans with Asparagus

In this tasty toast topper, cannellini beans in a creamy sauce contrast with tender asparagus spears.

Serves 2
10ml/2 tsp butter
1 small onion, finely chopped
1 small carrot, grated
5ml/1 tsp fresh thyme leaves
400g/14oz can cannellini beans, drained
150ml/ ¼ pint/ ⅔ cup single cream
115g/4oz young asparagus spears, trimmed
2 slices Granary bread
salt and ground black pepper

1 Melt the butter in a pan. Add the onion and carrot and fry over a moderate heat, stirring occasionally, for 4 minutes, until soft. Add the thyme leaves.

2 Tip the cannellini beans into a sieve and rinse them under cold running water. Drain thoroughly, then add to the onion and carrot. Mix lightly.

3 Pour in the cream and heat slowly to just below boiling point, stirring occasionally. Remove the pan from the heat and season with salt and pepper to taste.

4 Place the asparagus spears in a saucepan. Pour over just enough boiling water to cover. Poach for 3–4 minutes, until the spears are just tender.

5 Meanwhile, toast the bread under a hot grill until both sides are golden. Place the toast on individual plates. Drain the asparagus and divide the spears between the slices of toast. Spoon the bean mixture over each portion and serve.

> **Variation**
> Try making this with other canned beans, such as borlotti, haricot or flageolets.

Parsley, Lemon & Garlic Mushrooms on Toast

Don't overwhelm the delicate flavour of wild mushrooms by adding too much garlic. Temper the taste with sherry, parsley and lemon juice.

Serves 4
25g/1oz/2 tbsp butter, plus extra for spreading
1 medium onion, chopped
1 garlic clove, crushed
350g/12oz/4 cups assorted wild mushrooms, sliced
45ml/3 tbsp dry sherry
75ml/5 tbsp chopped fresh flat leaf parsley
15ml/1 tbsp lemon juice
salt and ground black pepper
4 slices of brown or white bread

1 Melt the butter in a large non-stick frying pan. Add the onion and fry over a low heat, stirring occasionally, for 5 minutes without letting it colour.

2 Add the garlic and mushrooms, cover and cook over a medium heat for 3–5 minutes. Stir in the sherry, and cook, uncovered, until all the liquid has been absorbed.

3 Stir in the parsley and lemon juice, and then season to taste with salt and pepper.

4 Toast the bread, spread it with butter and place each piece on a serving plate. Spoon the mushroom mixture over the toast and serve immediately.

> **Cook's Tips**
> • Flat leaf parsley, also known as French parsley, has a good flavour and keeps well in the fridge. To keep it fresh, stand the bunch in a jar of water and cover with a plastic bag.
> • Use any mixture of wild mushrooms, such as field mushrooms, horse mushrooms and shaggy ink caps or, more economically, a mixture of wild and cultivated mushrooms.

Chive Scrambled Eggs in Brioches

Lift the lid on baked brioches and discover a glorious mixture of creamy scrambled egg and fried brown cap mushrooms.

Serves 4
115g/4oz/ 1/2 cup butter
75g/3oz/generous 1 cup brown cap mushrooms, finely sliced
4 individual brioches
8 eggs, lightly mixed
15ml/1 tbsp snipped fresh chives, plus extra to garnish
salt and ground black pepper

1 Preheat the oven to 180°C/350°F/Gas 4. Melt one-quarter of the butter in a frying pan. Fry the mushrooms for about 3 minutes, or until soft, then set aside and keep warm.

2 Slice the tops off the brioches, then scoop out the centres and save them for making breadcrumbs. Put the brioches and lids on a baking sheet and bake for 5 minutes, until hot and slightly crisp.

3 Meanwhile, beat the eggs lightly and season to taste. Heat the remaining butter in a heavy-based saucepan over a gentle heat.

4 Add the eggs. Using a wooden spoon, stir constantly until about three-quarters of the egg is semi-solid and creamy – this should take 2–3 minutes. Remove the pan from the heat and stir in the snipped chives.

5 Immediately spoon one-quarter of the fried mushrooms into the bottom of each brioche and top with the scrambled eggs, divided equally among them. Sprinkle with extra chives, balance the brioche lids on top and serve immediately.

> **Cook's Tip**
> Timing and temperature are crucial for perfect scrambled eggs. When cooked for too long over too high heat, eggs become dry and crumbly; undercooked eggs are sloppy and unappealing.

Mozzarella in Carozza with Fresh Tomato Salsa

These upmarket toasted sandwiches come from Italy. After being filled, they are dipped in beaten egg and fried like French toast.

Serves 4
200g/7oz mozzarella cheese, thinly sliced
8 thin slices of bread, crusts removed
pinch of dried oregano
30ml/2 tbsp freshly grated Parmesan cheese

3 eggs, beaten
olive oil, for frying
salt and ground black pepper
fresh herbs, to garnish

For the salsa
4 ripe plum tomatoes, peeled, seeded and finely chopped
15ml/1 tbsp chopped fresh parsley
5ml/1 tsp balsamic vinegar
15ml/1 tbsp extra virgin olive oil

1 Arrange the mozzarella on four slices of the bread. Season with salt and pepper and sprinkle with a little dried oregano and the Parmesan. Top with the other bread slices and press them firmly together.

2 Pour the beaten eggs into a large shallow dish and season with salt and pepper. Add the cheese sandwiches, two at a time, pressing them into the eggs with a fish slice until they are well coated. Repeat with the remaining sandwiches, then leave them to stand for 10 minutes.

3 Meanwhile, make the salsa. Put the chopped tomatoes in a bowl and add the parsley. Stir in the balsamic vinegar and the extra virgin olive oil. Season to taste with salt and pepper and set aside.

4 Pour olive oil to a depth of 5mm/ 1/4 in into a large frying pan. When it is hot, add the sandwiches carefully in batches and cook for about 2 minutes on each side, until golden and crisp. Drain well on kitchen paper. Cut in half. Serve on individual plates, garnished with fresh herbs and accompanied by the salsa.

Eggs Benedict with Quick Hollandaise

This classic American brunch dish originated in New York, and is ideal for serving on a special occasion, such as a birthday treat or New Year's day.

Serves 4
4 large eggs, plus 2 egg yolks
5ml/1 tsp dry mustard
15ml/1 tbsp white wine vinegar
   or lemon juice
175g/6oz/¾ cup butter, plus
   extra for spreading
4 muffins, split
30ml/2 tbsp rinsed capers
salt and ground black pepper
a little chopped fresh parsley,
   to garnish

1 Put the egg yolks in a blender or food processor. Add the mustard and a pinch of salt and pepper and process for a few seconds. Add the vinegar or lemon juice and process again.

2 Heat the butter until it is on the point of bubbling, then, with the motor running, slowly pour it through the lid or feeder tube. When the mixture is thick and creamy, switch off the blender or food processor and set the sauce aside.

3 Toast the split muffins under a hot grill. Cut four of the halves in two and butter them lightly. Place the four uncut halves on warmed plates and leave unbuttered.

4 Poach the eggs either in gently simmering water or in an egg poacher. Drain well and slip carefully on to the muffin halves. Spoon the hollandaise sauce over the muffins, then sprinkle with capers and parsley. Serve immediately with the buttered muffin quarters.

> **Variation**
> Instead of the toasted muffin, you could make more of a main meal by serving the poached eggs and sauce on a bed of lightly steamed or blanched spinach.

Mixed Pepper Pipérade

Every cook needs recipes like this one. Tasty, nourishing and made in moments, Pipérade is based on everyday ingredients.

Serves 4
30ml/2 tbsp olive oil
1 onion, chopped
1 red pepper
1 green pepper
4 tomatoes, peeled and chopped
1 garlic clove, crushed
4 large eggs, beaten with 15ml/
   1 tbsp water
4 large, thick slices of
   wholemeal bread
butter, for spreading (optional)
ground black pepper
fresh herbs, to garnish

1 Heat the oil in a large frying pan. Add the onion and sauté over a low heat, stirring occasionally, for 5 minutes, until it has softened but not browned.

2 Cut the peppers in half, remove the seeds and slice them thinly. Stir the pepper slices into the onion and cook gently for about 5 minutes.

3 Stir in the tomatoes and garlic, season generously with black pepper, and cook for 5 minutes more.

4 Pour the egg mixture over the vegetables and cook for 2–3 minutes, stirring occasionally, until the pipérade has thickened to the consistency of lightly scrambled eggs.

5 While the egg mixture is cooking, toast the bread. Butter it, if you like, and serve the toast and pipérade on individual plates, garnished with fresh herbs.

> **Cook's Tip**
> Choose eggs that have been date-stamped to ensure that they are fresh. Do not stir the pipérade too much or the eggs may become unpleasantly rubbery.

Cheese Scrolls

Fascinating filo pastries with a feta and yogurt filling, Cheese Scrolls make very good snacks.

Makes 14–16
450g/1lb/2 cups feta cheese, well drained and finely crumbled

90ml/6 tbsp Greek-style yogurt
2 eggs, beaten
14–16 sheets, 40 x 30cm/ 16 x 12in ready-made filo pastry, thawed if frozen
225g/8oz/1 cup butter, melted
sea salt and chopped spring onions, for the topping

1 Preheat the oven to 200°C/400°F/Gas 6. In a large bowl mix together the feta, yogurt and eggs, beating well until the mixture is smooth.

2 Fit a piping bag with a 1cm/ ½in plain round nozzle. Spoon half the cheese mixture into the bag.

3 Keeping the rest of the filo covered, lay one sheet on the work surface. Fold it in half to make a 30 x 20cm/12 x 8in rectangle, then brush with a little of the melted butter. Pipe a thick line of cheese mixture along one long edge, leaving a 5mm/ ¼in clear border.

4 Roll up the pastry to form a sausage shape, tucking in each end to prevent the filling from escaping. Brush with more melted butter. Form the "sausage" into a tight "S" or scroll-shape. Make more scrolls in the same way, refilling the piping bag as necessary.

5 Arrange the scrolls on a buttered baking sheet and sprinkle with a little sea salt and chopped spring onion. Bake for about 20 minutes, or until crisp and golden brown. Cool on a wire rack, before serving.

> **Cook's Tip**
> If you find it easier, you can shape the filled filo into crescents instead of scrolls.

Cheese Aigrettes

These choux buns, flavoured with mature Gruyère cheese and dusted with grated Parmesan, can be prepared ahead and deep-fried to serve.

Makes about 30
100g/3¾oz/scant 1 cup strong plain flour
2.5ml/ ½ tsp paprika
2.5ml/ ½ tsp salt

75g/3oz/6 tbsp cold butter, diced
200ml/7fl oz/scant 1 cup water
3 eggs, beaten
75g/3oz/ ¾ cup coarsely grated mature Gruyère cheese
vegetable oil, for deep-frying
50g/2oz piece of Parmesan cheese
ground black pepper
fresh flat leaf parsley sprigs, to garnish

1 Sift the flour, paprika and salt on to a sheet of greaseproof paper. Add a generous grinding of black pepper.

2 Put the butter and water into a medium saucepan and heat gently. As soon as the butter has melted and the liquid starts to boil, tip in all the seasoned flour at once and beat vigorously with a wooden spoon until the dough comes away from the sides of the pan.

3 Remove the pan from the heat and set the paste aside to cool for about 5 minutes. Gradually beat in enough of the beaten eggs to give a stiff dropping consistency. Add the grated Gruyère and mix well.

4 Heat the oil for deep-frying to 180°C/350°F or until a cube of day-old bread turns golden brown in 60 seconds. Take a teaspoonful of the choux paste and use a second spoon to slide it into the hot oil. Make more aigrettes in the same way, but don't overcrowd the pan. Fry for 3–4 minutes, until golden brown. Remove with a draining spoon and drain the aigrettes thoroughly on kitchen paper. Keep warm while cooking successive batches.

5 To serve, pile the aigrettes on a warmed serving dish, grate Parmesan over the top and garnish with fresh parsley sprigs.

Artichoke Rice Cakes with Melting Manchego

Cold cooked rice is very easy to mould. Shape it into balls, fill the centres with diced cheese and deep-fry to make a delectable snack.

Makes about 12 cakes
1 globe artichoke
50g/2oz/ 1/4 cup butter
1 small onion, finely chopped
1 garlic clove, finely chopped

115g/4oz/ 2/3 cup risotto rice
450ml/ 3/4 pint/scant 2 cups hot vegetable stock
50g/2oz/ 2/3 cup freshly grated Parmesan cheese
150g/5oz Manchego cheese, very finely diced
45–60ml/3–4 tbsp fine cornmeal
olive oil, for frying
salt and ground black pepper
flat leaf parsley, to garnish

1 Remove the stalk, leaves and choke to leave just the heart of the artichoke. Chop the heart finely. Melt the butter in a saucepan and gently fry the artichoke heart, onion and garlic for 5 minutes, until softened. Stir in the rice and cook for about 1 minute.

2 Add the stock a little at a time, stirring constantly and waiting until each addition has been absorbed before adding more.

3 After about 20 minutes the rice will be tender, but still firm at the centre of the grain, and all the liquid will have been absorbed. Season well, then stir in the Parmesan. Transfer to a bowl. Leave to cool, then cover and chill for at least 2 hours.

4 Spoon about 15ml/1 tbsp of the rice mixture into the palm of one hand, flatten slightly, and place a few pieces of diced Manchego in the centre. Shape the rice around the cheese to make a small ball. Flatten slightly then roll in the cornmeal, shaking off any excess. Repeat with the remaining mixture to make about 12 cakes.

5 Fry in hot olive oil for 4–5 minutes, until the rice cakes are crisp and golden brown. Drain on kitchen paper and serve hot, garnished with flat leaf parsley.

Wild Mushroom Pancakes with Chive Butter

Scotch pancakes are easy to make and taste wonderful with wild mushrooms. The unusual hedgehog fungus has been used here, but any wild or cultivated mushrooms could be used instead.

Makes 12 pancakes
350g/12oz/about 5 cups hedgehog fungus or other wild mushrooms

50g/2oz/ 1/4 cup butter
175g/6oz/1 1/2 cups self-raising flour
2 eggs
200ml/7fl oz/scant 1 cup milk
salt and ground white pepper

For the chive butter
15g/ 1/2 oz/scant 1 cup fresh finely snipped chives
115g/4oz/ 1/2 cup butter, softened
5ml/1 tsp lemon juice

1 First make the chive butter by mixing all the ingredients together. Turn out on to a 25cm/10in square of greaseproof paper and form into a sausage. Roll up, twist both ends of the paper and chill for about 1 hour, until the chive butter is firm.

2 Slice one-quarter of the mushrooms and set them aside. Chop the remaining mushrooms finely. Melt half the butter in a frying pan and fry the chopped mushrooms until they are soft, and all the moisture has evaporated. Spread them on a tray and leave to cool. Cook the sliced mushrooms in a knob of butter.

3 Sift the flour into a bowl and season with salt and pepper. Beat the eggs with the milk in a jug. Add to the flour, stirring to make a thick batter. Add the chopped mushrooms.

4 Heat the remaining butter in the clean frying pan. Arrange small heaps of sliced mushrooms on the bottom of the pan, using five mushroom slices each time, then pour a little batter over each heap to make 5cm/2in Scotch pancakes.

5 When bubbles appear on the surface, turn the pancakes over and cook for a further 10–15 seconds. Serve warm with slices of the chive butter.

Potato Pancakes

Crisp on the outside, with tender centres, these potato pancakes are delicious with soured cream and a refreshing salad or salsa.

Serves 6–8
6 large waxy potatoes, peeled
2 eggs, beaten
1–2 garlic cloves, crushed
115g/4oz/1 cup plain flour
5ml/1 tsp chopped
    fresh marjoram
50g/2oz/ 1/4 cup butter
60ml/4 tbsp vegetable oil
salt and ground black pepper

To serve
soured cream
chopped fresh parsley
tomato salad

1 Coarsely grate the potatoes on to a clean dish towel, then gather up the sides and squeeze tightly to remove as much moisture as possible.

2 Tip the potatoes into a bowl and add the beaten eggs, garlic, flour and marjoram. Season to taste with salt and pepper and mix well.

3 Heat half the butter and half the oil in a large frying pan, then add large spoonfuls of the potato mixture to form rounds. Using the back of a dampened spoon, carefully flatten the rounds into pancakes.

4 Fry the pancakes until crisp and golden brown, then turn them over carefully and cook on the other side. Drain on kitchen paper and keep hot while cooking the rest of the pancakes, adding the remaining butter and oil to the frying pan as necessary.

5 Serve the pancakes topped with soured cream, sprinkled with parsley, and accompanied by a fresh, juicy tomato salad.

Cook's Tip
Choose firm-fleshed potatoes, such as Charlotte or Kipfler.

Eggs in Baked Potatoes

Nestled in creamy baked potatoes, cheese-topped eggs make a substantial, nourishing and inexpensive snack for all the family.

Serves 4
4 large baking potatoes
40g/1 1/2 oz/3 tbsp butter
30ml/2 tbsp hot single cream
    or milk
30ml/2 tbsp snipped fresh chives
4 eggs
about 50g/2oz/ 1/2 cup finely
    grated mature Cheddar cheese
salt and ground black pepper
celery sticks and chives, to garnish

1 Preheat the oven to 200°C/400°F/Gas 6. Prick the potatoes with a fork and bake for 1–1 1/4 hours, until soft.

2 Working quickly, cut a slice about a quarter to a third of the way down from the top of each potato, then scoop the flesh into a bowl with a teaspoon, taking care not to pierce the potato skins. Reserve the skins.

3 Add the butter and cream or milk to the potato flesh, together with the chives. Season to taste with salt and pepper. Mash the ingredients together.

4 Divide the potato mixture among the potato skins, and make a hollow in each with the back of a spoon.

5 Break an egg into each hollow, season to taste with salt and pepper, then return to the oven for about 10 minutes, until the eggs are just set.

6 Sprinkle the cheese over the eggs, then place under a hot grill until golden. Serve, garnished with celery sticks and chives.

Cook's Tip
Bake the potatoes in the microwave, if you prefer. For crisp skins, pop them into a preheated 200°C/400°F/Gas 6 oven for about 10 minutes after microwave cooking.

Idaho Potato Slices

This dish is made from layered potatoes, cheese and herbs. Cooking the ingredients together gives them a very rich flavour.

Serves 4
3 large potatoes
butter, for greasing
1 small onion, thinly sliced
 into rings
200g/7oz/1¾ cups grated
 red Leicester or mature
 Cheddar cheese
fresh thyme sprigs
150ml/¼ pint/⅔ cup
 single cream
salt and ground black pepper
salad leaves, to serve

1 Preheat the oven to 200°C/400°F/Gas 6. Peel the potatoes and cook them in a large pan of lightly salted boiling water for 10 minutes, until they are just starting to soften. Remove from the water and pat dry.

2 Slice the potatoes thinly, using the straight edge of a grater or a mandoline. Grease the base and sides of an 18cm/7in cake tin with butter and lay some of the potatoes on the base to cover it completely. Season to taste with salt and pepper.

3 Scatter some of the onion rings over the potatoes and top with a little of the grated cheese. Scatter over some thyme leaves. Continue to layer the ingredients, finishing with a layer of cheese. Season to taste with salt and pepper. Press the potato layers right down. (The mixture may seem quite high at this point but it will cook down.)

4 Pour the cream over and bake for 35–45 minutes. Remove from the oven and cool. Invert on to a plate and cut into wedges. Serve with a few salad leaves.

> **Variation**
> If you want to make this snack more substantial, top the wedges with grilled red peppers.

Potato Skins with Cajun Dip

Divinely crisp and naughty, these potato skins taste great with this piquant dip.

Serves 2
2 large baking potatoes
vegetable oil, for deep-frying

For the dip
120ml/4fl oz/ ½ cup
 natural yogurt
1 garlic clove, crushed
5ml/1 tsp tomato purée
2.5ml/ ½ tsp green chilli purée
 or ½ small fresh green
 chilli, chopped
1.5ml/ ¼ tsp celery salt
pinch of cayenne
 pepper (optional)
salt and ground black pepper

1 Preheat the oven to 180°C/350°F/Gas 4. Prick the potatoes and bake for 1–1¼ hours, until tender. Cut them in half and scoop out the flesh, leaving a thin layer on the skins. Keep the flesh for another meal.

2 Meanwhile, make the dip. Put the yogurt, garlic, tomato purée, chilli purée or fresh chilli and celery salt in a bowl and mix thoroughly. Season to taste with cayenne, if using, salt and pepper. Cover with clear film and chill in the fridge.

3 Pour vegetable oil to a depth of about 1cm/½in into a large saucepan or deep-fat fryer. Heat to 180°C/350°F or until a cube of day-old bread turns golden brown in about 60 seconds. Cut each potato-skin half in half again, then fry them until crisp and golden on both sides.

4 Drain the fried potato skins on kitchen paper, sprinkle with salt and black pepper and serve with a bowl of dip or with a dollop of dip in each skin.

> **Cook's Tip**
> If you prefer, you can microwave the potatoes to save time. On the maximum setting, this will take about 10 minutes.

Thai Tempeh Cakes with Sweet Dipping Sauce

Made from soya beans, tempeh is similar to beancurd (tofu), but has a nuttier taste. Here, it is combined with spices and formed into small patties.

Makes 8 cakes

1 lemon grass stalk, outer leaves removed, roughly chopped
2 garlic cloves, chopped
2 spring onions, finely chopped
2 shallots, roughly chopped
2 fresh chillies, seeded and roughly chopped
2.5cm/1in piece of fresh root ginger, finely chopped
60ml/4 tbsp chopped fresh coriander, plus extra to garnish

250g/9oz tempeh, thawed if frozen, sliced
15ml/1 tbsp freshly squeezed lime juice
5ml/1 tsp caster sugar
45ml/3 tbsp plain flour
1 large egg, lightly beaten
vegetable oil, for frying
salt and ground black pepper

For the dipping sauce
45ml/3 tbsp mirin
45ml/3 tbsp white wine vinegar
2 spring onions, finely sliced
15ml/1 tbsp granulated sugar
2 fresh red chillies, chopped
30ml/2 tbsp chopped fresh coriander

1 To make the dipping sauce, mix the mirin, vinegar, spring onions, sugar, chillies, coriander and a large pinch of salt in a small bowl and set aside.

2 Place the lemon grass, garlic, spring onions, shallots, chillies, ginger and coriander in a food processor or blender and process to a coarse paste.

3 Add the tempeh, lime juice and sugar, then process until thoroughly combined. Add the flour and egg and season with plenty of salt and pepper. Process again until the mixture forms a coarse, sticky paste.

4 Using a tablespoon, scoop up a generous quantity of the tempeh mixture. Dampen your hands, then shape the mixture to a round, slightly flattened cake. Make seven more tempeh cakes in the same way.

5 Heat enough oil to cover the base of a large frying pan. Fry the tempeh cakes, in batches, for 5–6 minutes, turning once, until golden. Drain on kitchen paper and keep warm while cooking the remainder. Serve warm with the dipping sauce, garnished with the reserved coriander.

Cook's Tip
Use red or green chillies, choosing a variety with the degree of fieriness you require. In general, dark green chillies tend to be hotter than pale green ones, which, in turn, are hotter than red chillies. (As the chillies ripen, they become red and relatively sweeter.) Also, the small, pointed chillies tend to be fiercer than the larger, rounder ones. However, there are always exceptions and even different pods from the same plant can vary in their level of spiciness. Err on the side of caution, if in doubt.

Courgette Fritters with Chilli Jam

Rather like a thick chutney, chilli jam is hot, sweet and sticky. It adds a piquancy to these light courgette fritters but is also delicious with pies or a chunk of cheese.

Makes 12 fritters
450g/1lb courgettes
50g/2oz/ 2/3 cup freshly grated Parmesan cheese
2 eggs, beaten
60ml/4 tbsp unbleached plain flour

vegetable oil, for frying
salt and ground black pepper

For the chilli jam
75ml/5 tbsp olive oil
4 large onions, diced
4 garlic cloves, chopped
1–2 fresh Thai chillies, seeded and sliced
25g/1oz/2 tbsp soft dark brown sugar
a few thin slices of fresh red chilli, to garnish

1 First make the chilli jam. Heat the oil in a frying pan, add the onions and garlic, then lower the heat and cook the mixture, stirring frequently, for 20 minutes, until the onions are very soft.

2 Leave the onion mixture to cool, then put it into a food processor or blender. Add the Thai red chillies and brown sugar and process until smooth, then return the mixture to the saucepan. Cook over a low heat, stirring frequently, for about 10 minutes, or until the liquid evaporates and the mixture has the consistency of jam. Cool slightly.

3 To make the fritters, grate the courgettes roughly on to a clean dish towel, then gather up the sides and squeeze tightly to remove any excess moisture. Tip the courgettes into a bowl and stir in the grated Parmesan, eggs and flour and season to taste with salt and pepper.

4 Heat enough vegetable oil to cover the bottom of a large frying pan. Add 30ml/2 tbsp of the mixture for each fritter and cook three fritters at a time. Cook for 2–3 minutes on each side until golden, then keep warm while you cook the remaining fritters. Drain on kitchen paper and serve hot with a spoonful of the chilli jam, garnished with a slice of chilli.

Mexican Tortilla Parcels

Seeded green chillies add just a flicker of fire to the spicy filling in these parcels.

Serves 4
60ml/4 tbsp sunflower oil
1 large onion, thinly sliced
1 garlic clove, crushed
10ml/2 tsp cumin seeds
2 fresh green chillies, seeded and chopped
675g/1½ lb tomatoes, peeled and chopped
30ml/2 tbsp tomato purée
1 vegetable stock cube
200g/7oz can sweetcorn kernels, drained
15ml/1 tbsp chopped fresh coriander
115g/4oz/1 cup grated Cheddar cheese
12 wheat flour tortillas
fresh coriander leaves, shredded lettuce and soured cream, to serve
1 fresh red chilli, sliced, to garnish

1 Heat half the oil in a frying pan and fry the onion with the garlic and cumin seeds for 5 minutes, until the onion softens. Add the chillies and tomatoes, then stir in the tomato purée.

2 Crumble the stock cube over, stir well and cook gently for 5 minutes, until the chilli is soft but the tomatoes have not broken down completely. Stir in the sweetcorn and fresh coriander and heat gently to warm through. Keep hot.

3 Sprinkle grated cheese in the middle of each tortilla. Spoon some tomato mixture over the cheese. Fold over one edge of the tortilla, then the sides and finally the remaining edge to enclose the filling completely.

4 Heat the remaining oil in a frying pan and fry the filled tortillas for 1–2 minutes on each side, until crisp. Garnish with chillies and serve with coriander, lettuce and soured cream.

> **Cook's Tip**
> Mexican wheat flour tortillas are available in most supermarkets. Keep them in the cupboard as instant wraps for a variety of vegetable and cheese mixtures.

Spiced Sweet Potato Turnovers

A subtle hint of sweetness underscores the spicy flavour of these pasties.

Serves 4
15ml/1 tbsp olive oil
1 small egg
150ml/¼ pint/⅔ cup natural yogurt
115g/4oz/½ cup butter, melted
1.5ml/¼ tsp bicarbonate of soda
275g/10oz/2½ cups plain flour
10ml/2 tsp paprika
beaten egg, to glaze
salt and ground black pepper
fresh mint sprigs, to garnish

For the filling
1 sweet potato, about 225g/8oz
30ml/2 tbsp vegetable oil
2 shallots, finely chopped
10ml/2 tsp coriander seeds, crushed
5ml/1 tsp ground cumin
5ml/1 tsp garam masala
115g/4oz/1 cup frozen petit pois, thawed
15ml/1 tbsp chopped fresh mint

1 To make the filling, cook the sweet potato in boiling salted water for 15–20 minutes, until tender. Drain and leave to cool, then peel the potato and cut into 1cm/½in cubes.

2 Heat the vegetable oil in a frying pan and cook the shallots until softened. Add the potato and fry until it browns at the edges. Sprinkle over the spices and fry, stirring, for a few seconds. Remove the pan from the heat and add the peas and mint and season with salt and pepper to taste. Leave to cool.

3 Preheat the oven to 200°C/400°F/Gas 6. Grease a baking sheet. To make the pastry, whisk together the olive oil and egg, stir in the yogurt, then add the melted butter. Sift the bicarbonate of soda, flour, paprika and 5ml/1 tsp salt into a bowl, then stir into the yogurt mixture to form a soft dough.

4 Turn out the dough, and knead gently. Roll it out, then stamp out 10cm/4in rounds. Spoon 10ml/2 tsp of the filling on to one side of each round, fold over and seal the edges. Re-roll the trimmings and stamp out more rounds until the filling is used.

5 Arrange the turnovers on the baking sheet and brush with beaten egg. Bake for 20 minutes, until crisp. Garnish and serve.

Samosas

These are far too good to be served only as cocktail party nibbles. Enjoy them for lunches or snacks, too.

Makes about 20
1 packet 25cm/10in square
   spring roll wrappers, thawed
   if frozen
30ml/2 tbsp plain flour, mixed to
   a paste with water
vegetable oil, for deep-frying
fresh coriander leaves, to garnish

For the filling
25g/1oz/2 tbsp ghee
1 small onion, finely chopped

1cm/½ in piece of fresh root
   ginger, chopped
1 garlic clove, crushed
2.5ml/½ tsp chilli powder
1 large potato, about 225g/8oz,
   cooked until just tender, then
   finely diced
50g/2oz/½ cup cauliflower
   florets, lightly cooked, chopped
50g/2oz/½ cup frozen
   peas, thawed
5–10ml/1–2 tsp garam masala
15ml/1 tbsp chopped fresh
   coriander (leaves and stems)
squeeze of lemon juice
salt

1 To make the filling, heat the ghee in a large wok or frying pan and fry the onion, ginger and garlic for 5 minutes, until the onion has softened but not browned. Stir in the chilli powder and cook for 1 minute, then add the potato, cauliflower and peas. Mix well. Sprinkle with garam masala and set aside to cool. Stir in the chopped coriander, lemon juice and salt.

2 Cut the spring roll wrappers into three strips. Brush the edges with a little of the flour paste. Place a small spoonful of filling about 2cm/¾in from the edge of one strip. Fold one corner over it to make a triangle and continue this folding until the entire strip has been used and a triangular pastry has been formed. Seal any open edges with more flour and water paste.

3 Heat the oil for deep-frying to 180°C/350°F or until a cube of day-old bread turns golden brown in 60 seconds. Fry the samosas, a few at a time, until golden and crisp.

4 Drain well on kitchen paper. Serve hot, garnished with coriander leaves.

Spinach Empanadillas

These little Spanish pastry turnovers are filled with ingredients that have a strong Moorish influence – pine nuts and raisins.

Makes 20
25g/1oz/3 tbsp raisins
25ml/1½ tbsp olive oil
450g/1lb fresh young
   spinach, chopped

2 garlic cloves, finely chopped
25g/1oz/⅓ cup pine
   nuts, chopped
350g/12oz puff pastry, thawed
   if frozen
butter, for greasing
1 egg, beaten, to glaze
salt and ground black pepper

1 Put the raisins in bowl and pour over sufficient warm water to cover. Set aside to soak for 10 minutes. Drain thoroughly, then chop roughly.

2 Heat the oil in a large sauté pan or wok. Add the spinach, stir, then cover and cook over a low heat for about 2 minutes.

3 Take the lid off the pan, turn up the heat and let any liquid evaporate. Add the garlic and season with plenty of salt and pepper. Cook, stirring constantly, for 1 minute more. Remove the pan from the heat, stir in the raisins and pine nuts and set aside to cool.

4 Preheat the oven to 180°C/350°F/Gas 4. Roll out the pastry thinly. Using a 7.5cm/3in pastry cutter, cut out 20 rounds, re-rolling the dough if necessary.

5 Place about 10ml/2 tsp of the filling in the middle of a round, then brush the edges with a little water. Bring up the sides of the pastry and seal well to make a turnover. Press the edges together with the back of a fork. Make more turnovers in the same way.

6 Place the turnovers on a lightly greased baking sheet, brush with the beaten egg and bake for about 15 minutes, until golden. Serve warm.

Herb Omelette

It takes only moments to make a simple, herb-flavoured omelette. Serve it with a salad and a chunk of crusty bread and it becomes a nutritious light meal.

Serves 1

2 eggs
15ml/1 tbsp chopped fresh herbs, such as parsley or chives
5ml/1 tsp butter
salt and ground black pepper
fresh parsley, to garnish

1 Lightly beat the eggs in a bowl, add the fresh herbs and season to taste with salt and pepper.

2 Melt the butter in a heavy-based omelette pan or non-stick frying pan and swirl it around to coat the base evenly.

3 Keeping the heat fairly high, pour in the egg mixture. Let it start to set for 1–2 minutes, then lower the heat. Using a spoon or spatula, lift the edges of the omelette and push them gently towards the centre, so that the raw egg runs in to fill the gap, then starts to set as well.

4 Cook for about 2 minutes, without stirring, until the omelette is lightly set. Quickly fold it over and slide on to a plate. Serve at once, garnished with parsley.

Cook's Tips

• It is important to serve omelettes as soon as they are cooked, so this is one occasion when it would be unrealistic to expect everyone to be served simultaneously. Seat your guests and serve each omelette as soon as it is cooked.
• Omelettes have an undeserved reputation for being difficult to make. There are two secrets to success. A good-quality, heavy-based omelette or frying pan ensures an even distribution of heat throughout the base. It is essential to ensure that the butter has melted completely and to swirl it around so the entire base of the pan is evenly coated before adding the beaten egg mixture.

Classic Cheese Omelette

Perhaps the ultimate fast food – a couple of eggs, some well-flavoured cheese, a knob of butter and a good pan and you soon have a satisfying meal.

Serves 1

2 large eggs
15ml/1 tbsp chopped fresh herbs, such as chives, parsley or dill
5ml/1 tsp butter
50g/2oz/ 1/2 cup grated full-flavoured cheese, such as Gruyère, Gouda or Cheddar
salt and ground black pepper
fresh flat leaf parsley, to garnish
tomato wedges, to serve

1 Lightly beat the eggs in a bowl and quickly mix in the herbs. Season to taste with salt and pepper.

2 Melt the butter in a 20cm/8in heavy-based omelette pan or non-stick frying pan, swirling it around to coat the base evenly.

3 Keeping the heat fairly high, pour in the egg mixture. Let it set for 1–2 minutes, then lower the heat. Using a spoon or spatula, lift the edges of the omelette and push them gently towards the centre, so that the raw egg runs in to fill the gap, then starts to set as well.

4 When the egg at the sides is firm, but the centre remains soft, scatter over the cheese. Leave undisturbed to cook for about 30 seconds.

5 Fold the edge of the omelette nearest the handle over, then roll the omelette over on to a warmed plate. Serve at once with a garnish of fresh flat leaf parsley and tomato wedges.

Variation

You can add other ingredients to the cheese. Crunchy, garlicky croûtons are good, as are sautéed sliced mushrooms or chopped tomatoes.

Soufflé Omelette with Mushrooms

A soufflé omelette makes an ideal meal for one, especially with this delicious filling. Use a combination of different mushrooms, such as oyster and chestnut, if you like.

Serves 1
2 eggs, separated
15ml/1 tbsp water
15g/ ½ oz/1 tbsp butter
fresh flat leaf parsley or coriander leaves, to garnish

For the mushroom sauce
15g/ ½ oz/1 tbsp butter
75g/3oz/generous 1 cup button mushrooms, thinly sliced
15ml/1 tbsp plain flour
90–120ml/3–4fl oz/ ⅓–½ cup milk
5ml/1 tsp chopped fresh parsley (optional)
salt and ground black pepper

1 Start by making the mushroom sauce. Melt the butter in a pan over a low heat. Add the sliced mushrooms and fry gently, stirring occasionally, for 4–5 minutes, until tender.

2 Stir in the flour and cook, stirring constantly, for 1 minute, then gradually add the milk, stirring all the time until the sauce boils and thickens. Add the parsley, if using, and season to taste with salt and pepper. Keep the sauce hot while you are making the omelette.

3 Beat the egg yolks with the water and season with a little salt and pepper. Whisk the egg whites until stiff, then gently fold them into the egg yolks, using a metal spoon. Preheat the grill.

4 Melt the butter in a large, heavy-based frying pan which can safely be used under the grill. (Cover a wooden handle with foil to protect it.) Pour in the egg mixture. Cook over a gentle heat for 2–4 minutes, then place the frying pan under the grill and cook for 3–4 minutes more, until the top of the omelette is golden brown.

5 Slide the omelette on to a warmed serving plate, pour the mushroom sauce over the top and fold the omelette in half. Garnish with parsley or coriander leaves and serve.

Coriander Omelette Parcels with Oriental Vegetables

Stir-fried vegetables in black bean sauce make a remarkably good omelette filling, which is quick and easy to prepare.

Serves 4
130g/4½ oz broccoli, cut into small florets
30ml/2 tbsp groundnut oil
1cm/ ½ in piece of fresh root ginger, finely grated
1 large garlic clove, crushed
2 fresh red chillies, seeded and finely sliced
4 spring onions, sliced diagonally
175g/6oz/3 cups shredded pak choi
50g/2oz/2 cups fresh coriander leaves, plus extra to garnish
115g/4oz/1 cup beansprouts
45ml/3 tbsp black bean sauce
4 eggs
salt and ground black pepper

1 Bring a large pan of lightly salted water to the boil, add the broccoli and blanch for 2 minutes. Drain, refresh under cold running water, then drain again.

2 Heat half the oil in a wok and stir-fry the ginger, garlic and half the chillies for 1 minute. Add the spring onions, broccoli and pak choi, and stir-fry for 2 minutes more.

3 Chop three-quarters of the coriander leaves and add to the wok with the beansprouts. Stir-fry for 1 minute, then add the black bean sauce and toss over the heat for 1 minute more. Remove the pan from the heat and keep the vegetables hot.

4 Lightly beat the eggs and season well. Heat a little of the remaining oil in a small frying pan and add one-quarter of the beaten egg. Swirl the egg to cover the base of the pan, then scatter over one-quarter of the whole coriander leaves. Cook the omelette until set, then turn it out on to a plate. Make three more omelettes, adding more oil as required.

5 Divide the stir-fry among the omelettes and roll them up. Cut each one in half crossways and arrange the pieces on a plate. Garnish with coriander leaves and the remaining chillies.

Potato & Onion Tortilla

One of the signature dishes of Spain, this delicious thick potato and onion omelette is eaten at all times of the day, hot or cold.

Serves 4
300ml/ ½ pint/1 ¼ cups olive oil
6 large potatoes, sliced
2 Spanish onions, sliced
6 large eggs
salt and ground black pepper
cherry tomatoes, halved, to serve

1 Heat the oil in a large non-stick frying pan. Stir in the potato and onion slices and a little salt. Cover and cook gently for 20 minutes, until soft.

2 Beat the eggs. Transfer the onion and potato slices to the eggs with a draining spoon. Season to taste. Pour off some of the oil from the frying pan, leaving about 60ml/4 tbsp.

3 When the oil is very hot, pour in the egg mixture. Cook for 2–3 minutes. Cover the pan with a plate, then, holding them together, invert the tortilla on to the plate. Slide it back into the pan and cook for 5 minutes more. Serve with the tomatoes.

Pasta Frittata

This is a great way to use up cold leftover pasta.

Serves 4
225g/8oz cold cooked pasta, with any sauce

50g/2oz/⅔ cup freshly grated Parmesan cheese
5 eggs, lightly beaten
65g/2½oz/5 tbsp butter
salt and ground black pepper

1 Stir the pasta and Parmesan into the eggs. Season to taste.
2 Heat half the butter in a large pan. Pour in the egg mixture and cook for 4–5 minutes, gently shaking the pan.
3 Place a plate over the pan, then, holding them together, invert the frittata on to the plate. Melt the remaining butter in the pan, slide the frittata back in and cook for 3–4 minutes more.

Sweet Pepper & Courgette Frittata

Eggs, cheese and vegetables form the basis of this excellent supper dish. Served cold, in wedges, it makes tasty picnic fare too.

Serves 4
45ml/3 tbsp olive oil
1 red onion, thinly sliced
1 large red pepper, seeded and thinly sliced

1 large yellow pepper, seeded and thinly sliced
2 garlic cloves, crushed
1 medium courgette, thinly sliced
6 eggs
150g/5oz/1 ¼ cups grated Italian cheese, such as Fontina, Provolone or Taleggio
salt and ground black pepper
dressed mixed salad leaves, to serve

1 Heat 30ml/2 tbsp of the olive oil in a large heavy-based frying pan that can safely be used under the grill. (Cover a wooden handle with foil to protect it.) Add the onion and red and yellow pepper slices and fry over a low heat, stirring occasionally, for about 10 minutes, until softened.

2 Add the remaining oil to the pan. When it is hot, add the garlic and the courgette slices. Fry over a low heat, stirring constantly, for 5 minutes.

3 Beat the eggs with salt and pepper to taste. Stir in the grated cheese. Pour the mixture over the vegetables, stirring lightly to mix. Cook over a low heat until the mixture is just set.

4 Meanwhile, preheat the grill. When it is hot, slide the pan underneath and brown the top of the frittata lightly. Let the frittata stand in the pan for about 5 minutes before cutting into wedges. Serve hot or cold, with the salad.

Cook's Tips
• When adding the egg mixture to the vegetables, make sure that it covers the base of the pan evenly.
• Make sure that you use the freshest possible free-range eggs for maximum flavour.

Irish Colcannon

Curly kale is a vegetable that is often neglected, but if you mix it with mashed potatoes, eggs and cheese you will find that you have a dish fit for a feast.

Serves 4
1kg/2¼ lb potatoes, quartered
225g/8oz curly kale or crisp
　green cabbage, shredded
2 spring onions, chopped
butter, to taste
grated nutmeg
4 large eggs
75g/3oz/ ¾ cup grated mature
　Cheddar cheese
salt and ground black pepper

1 Cook the potatoes in a pan of lightly salted boiling water for about 30 minutes, until tender, then drain and mash well. Preheat the oven to 190°C/375°F/Gas 5.

2 Steam the kale or cabbage over boiling water until crisp-tender. Drain well. Add the greens to the potato with the onions, butter and nutmeg. Mix well and season to taste with salt and pepper.

3 Spoon the mixture into a shallow ovenproof dish and make four hollows in the mixture. Crack an egg into each hollow and season well with salt and pepper.

4 Bake for about 12 minutes or until the eggs are just set, then sprinkle with the cheese and serve.

Patrick's Posh Potato

This is one of many tasty variations on traditional Irish Colcannon.

Serves 6
675g/1½lb potatoes, quartered
115g/4oz/ ½ cup butter, plus
　extra for mashing
115g/4oz onion, finely chopped

115g/4oz celery sticks,
　finely chopped
225g/8oz green cabbage,
　finely shredded
6 juniper berries, lightly crushed
60ml/4 tbsp water
6 eggs
pinch of cayenne pepper
salt and ground black pepper

1 Cook the potatoes in a pan of lightly salted boiling water for about 30 minutes, until tender. Drain and mash well with butter to taste. Preheat the oven to 190°C/375°F/Gas 5.
2 Melt 115g/4oz/ ½ cup butter in a frying pan. Add the onion and celery and fry over a low heat, stirring occasionally, for about 5 minutes, until softened but not coloured.
3 Meanwhile, put the cabbage, juniper berries and water in a saucepan and cook over a low heat for 5 minutes, until tender. Drain well then add to the mashed potatoes.
4 Combine the potato mixture with the onion and celery and season to taste with salt and pepper. Spoon into an ovenproof dish and make six hollows in the mixture. Break an egg into each hollow and season with cayenne, salt and black pepper.
5 Bake for about 12 minutes, or until the eggs are just set. Serve immediately.

Vegetable Stir-fry with Eggs

A perfect family supper dish, this is very easy to prepare. Serve with plenty of fresh crusty bread.

Serves 4
30ml/2 tbsp olive oil
1 onion, roughly chopped
2 garlic cloves, crushed
225g/8oz courgettes, cut in
　long strips
1 red pepper, seeded and
　thinly sliced

1 yellow pepper, seeded and
　thinly sliced
10ml/2 tsp paprika
400g/14oz can
　chopped tomatoes
15ml/1 tbsp sun-dried tomato
　paste or tomato purée
4 eggs
115g/4oz/1 cup grated
　Cheddar cheese
salt and ground black pepper
crusty bread, to serve

1 Heat the oil in a deep, heavy-based frying pan which can safely be used under the grill. (Cover a wooden handle with foil to protect it.) Add the onion and garlic and cook over a low heat, stirring occasionally, for about 4 minutes, or until just beginning to soften.

2 Add the courgettes and red and yellow peppers to the onion. Cook over a medium heat, stirring occasionally, for 3–4 minutes, until beginning to soften.

3 Stir in the paprika, tomatoes and sun-dried tomato paste or tomato purée. Season with salt and pepper to taste. Bring to the boil, lower the heat and simmer gently for 15 minutes, until the vegetables are just tender.

4 Reduce the heat to a low setting. Make four wells in the tomato mixture, break an egg into each and season to taste with salt and pepper. Cook until the egg whites begin to set. Preheat the grill.

5 Sprinkle the cheese over the stir-fry, then slide the pan under the hot grill. Cook for about 5 minutes, until the cheese is melted golden and the eggs are lightly set. Serve at once with plenty of crusty bread.

Spring Vegetable Stir-fry

A dazzling and colourful medley of fresh and sweet young vegetables.

Serves 4

15ml/1 tbsp peanut oil
1 garlic clove, sliced
2.5cm/1in piece of fresh root
  ginger, finely chopped
115g/4oz baby carrots
115g/4oz small patty pan squash
115g/4oz baby sweetcorn
115g/4oz French beans, topped
  and tailed

115g/4oz sugar snap peas,
  topped and tailed
115g/4oz young asparagus, cut
  into 7.5cm/3in pieces
8 spring onions, trimmed and cut
  into 5cm/2in pieces
115g/4oz cherry tomatoes

For the dressing

juice of 2 limes
15ml/1 tbsp clear honey
15ml/1 tbsp soy sauce
5ml/1 tsp sesame oil

1 Heat the peanut oil in a wok and stir-fry the garlic and ginger over a high heat for 30 seconds.

2 Reduce the heat slightly and add the baby carrots, patty pan squash, sweetcorn and French beans and stir-fry for 3–4 minutes more.

3 Add the sugar snap peas, asparagus, spring onions and cherry tomatoes. Toss for a further 1–2 minutes.

4 Mix the dressing ingredients in a jug and pour them over the stir-fried vegetables. Stir well, cover and cook for 2–3 minutes more, until the vegetables are crisp-tender. Serve at once.

Variation
You can use any seasonal vegetables, provided they are tender enough to cook quickly. Cauliflower or broccoli florets, mange-touts, pepper strips and sliced courgettes would all be suitable. Make sure they are cut into similar sized pieces so that they cook simultaneously. Add thinly sliced red onion and celery when frying the garlic, if you like.

Lentil Stir-fry

Mushrooms, artichokes, sugar snap peas and lentils make a satisfying stir-fry for a mid-week supper.

Serves 2–3

115g/4oz sugar snap peas
25g/1oz/2 tbsp butter
1 small onion, chopped
115g/4oz/1½ cups cup or brown
  cap mushrooms, sliced

400g/14oz can artichoke hearts,
  drained and halved
400g/14oz can cooked green
  lentils, drained
60ml/4 tbsp single cream
25g/1oz/¼ cup flaked
  almonds, toasted
salt and ground black pepper
French bread, to serve

1 Bring a pan of lightly salted water to the boil and cook the sugar snap peas for 4 minutes, or until just tender. Drain, refresh under cold running water, then drain again. Pat the peas dry with kitchen paper and set them aside.

2 Melt the butter in a large, heavy-based frying pan. Add the chopped onion and cook over a medium heat, stirring occasionally for 2–3 minutes.

3 Stir in the sliced mushrooms, then cook, stirring occasionally, for 2–3 minutes, until just tender. Add the artichoke hearts, sugar snap peas and lentils to the pan. Stir-fry over a medium heat for 2 minutes.

4 Stir in the cream and almonds and cook for 1 minute. Season to taste. Serve immediately, with chunks of French bread.

Cook's Tip
Canned lentils are convenient, but it doesn't take long to cook dried lentils. Unlike most pulses, they don't need soaking. To add flavour, simmer them in vegetable stock or water to which you have added a little yeast extract. Do not add salt, as this tends to make the lentils tough. They will take 20–30 minutes, depending on type and the degree of freshness.

Quorn with Ginger, Chilli & Leeks

If you've never eaten Quorn, this would be a good recipe to try. Serve it over noodles or rice.

Serves 4
45ml/3 tbsp soy sauce
30ml/2 tbsp dry sherry
 or vermouth
225g/8oz/2 cups Quorn cubes
10ml/2 tsp clear honey
150ml/ ¼ pint/ ⅔ cup
 vegetable stock
10ml/2 tsp cornflour
45ml/3 tbsp sunflower oil
3 leeks, thinly sliced
1 fresh red chilli, seeded
 and sliced
2.5cm/1in piece of fresh root
 ginger, shredded
salt and ground black pepper

1 Mix the soy sauce and sherry or vermouth in a bowl. Add the Quorn cubes, toss until well coated and leave to marinate for about 30 minutes.

2 Using a draining spoon, lift out the Quorn cubes from the marinade and set them aside. Stir the honey, stock and cornflour into the remaining marinade to make a paste.

3 Heat the oil in a wok. When it is hot, stir-fry the Quorn cubes until they are crisp on the outside. Remove the Quorn and set aside.

4 Reheat the oil and stir-fry the leeks, chilli and ginger for about 2 minutes, until they are just soft. Season lightly.

5 Add the Quorn cubes to the vegetables in the wok and mix well. Stir the marinade mixture, pour it into the wok and stir until it forms a thick, glossy coating for the Quorn and vegetables. Serve at once.

> **Cook's Tip**
> *Quorn is a versatile mycoprotein food, which easily absorbs different flavours and retains a good firm texture. It is available from most supermarkets.*

Spiced Beancurd Stir-fry

Like Quorn, firm beancurd (tofu) is a boon to the vegetarian cook, as it readily absorbs the flavours of the other ingredients. In this recipe it is coated with warm spices before being stir-fried with a medley of mixed vegetables.

Serves 4
10ml/2 tsp ground cumin
15ml/1 tbsp paprika
5ml/1 tsp ground ginger
good pinch of cayenne pepper
15ml/1 tbsp caster sugar
275g/10oz beancurd (tofu), cubed
30ml/2 tbsp vegetable oil
2 garlic cloves, crushed
1 bunch spring onions, sliced
1 red pepper, seeded and sliced
1 yellow pepper, seeded
 and sliced
225g/8oz/generous 3 cups brown
 cap mushrooms, halved or
 quartered, if necessary
1 large courgette, sliced
115g/4oz/1 cup fine green
 beans, halved
50g/2oz/ ⅔ cup pine nuts
15ml/1 tbsp freshly squeezed
 lime juice
15ml/1 tbsp clear honey
salt and ground black pepper

1 Mix the cumin, paprika, ginger, cayenne and sugar in a bowl and add plenty of salt and pepper. Coat the beancurd (tofu) cubes in the spice mixture.

2 Heat 15ml/1 tbsp of the oil in a wok or large, heavy-based frying pan and cook the beancurd cubes over a high heat for 3–4 minutes, turning occasionally and taking care not to break them up too much. Remove the beancurd cubes with a draining spoon. Wipe out the pan with kitchen paper and return it to the heat.

3 Heat the remaining oil in the wok and stir-fry the garlic and spring onions for 3 minutes. Add the red and yellow peppers, mushrooms, courgette and beans and toss over a medium heat for about 6 minutes, or until beginning to soften and turn golden. Season well with salt and pepper.

4 Return the beancurd cubes to the wok with the pine nuts, lime juice and honey. Heat through, lightly stirring occasionally, then serve immediately.

Stir-fried Chick-peas

Most of the ingredients in this nourishing supper dish come straight from the store cupboard, so it is a useful standby for unexpected guests.

Serves 2–4
30ml/2 tbsp sunflower seeds
400g/14oz can chick-
  peas, drained and rinsed
5ml/1 tsp chilli powder
5ml/1 tsp paprika
30ml/2 tbsp vegetable oil
1 garlic clove, crushed
200g/7oz can chopped tomatoes
225g/8oz fresh spinach, coarse
  stalks removed
10ml/2 tsp chilli oil
salt and ground black pepper

1 Heat the wok and then add the sunflower seeds. Dry-fry, stirring frequently, until the seeds are golden and toasted, then tip them into a bowl.

2 Toss the chick-peas in the chilli powder and paprika. Heat the oil in the wok and stir-fry the garlic for 30 seconds. Add the chick-peas and stir-fry for 1 minute.

3 Stir in the tomatoes and stir-fry for 4 minutes. Add the spinach, season well with salt and pepper and toss over the heat for 1 minute.

4 Spoon the stir-fry into a serving dish and drizzle with chilli oil. Scatter the sunflower seeds over and serve immediately.

Cook's Tips
• If you have time, use dried chick-peas, but be prepared to soak them overnight. They are notorious for the time they take to cook, so it is worth making a big batch and either freezing the surplus or using it to make hummus.
• Ready-chopped canned tomatoes are usually slightly less watery than canned whole tomatoes, but are more expensive.
• Paprika, while never so hot as chilli powder, is available in two forms – mild (or sweet) and hot.

Black Bean & Vegetable Stir-fry

The secret of a quick stir-fry is to have everything ready before you begin to cook. This colourful vegetable mixture is coated in a classic Chinese sauce.

Serves 4
8 spring onions
225g/8oz/3 cups
  button mushrooms
1 red pepper
1 green pepper
2 large carrots
60ml/4 tbsp sesame oil
2 garlic cloves, crushed
60ml/4 tbsp black bean sauce
90ml/6 tbsp warm water
225g/8oz/2 cups beansprouts
salt and ground black pepper

1 Thinly slice the spring onions and button mushrooms. Cut both the peppers in half, remove the seeds and slice the flesh into thin strips.

2 Cut the carrots in half widthways, then cut each half into thin strips lengthways. Stack the slices and cut through them to make very fine strips.

3 Heat the oil in a large wok until it is very hot. Add the spring onions and garlic and stir-fry for 30 seconds.

4 Add the mushrooms, peppers and carrots and stir-fry over a high heat for 5–6 minutes, until the vegetables are just beginning to soften.

5 Mix the black bean sauce with the water. Add to the wok and cook, stirring occasionally, for 3–4 minutes. Stir in the beansprouts and stir-fry for 1 minute more, until all the vegetables are coated in the sauce. Season to taste with salt and pepper. Serve at once.

Cook's Tip
For best results the oil in the wok must be very hot before adding the vegetables.

Spaghetti with Garlic & Oil

This classic Italian dish has only a few ingredients, which must be of the very best quality. Chilli is always included to give the dish some bite.

Serves 4
400g/14oz fresh or
   dried spaghetti
90ml/6 tbsp extra virgin olive oil
2–4 garlic cloves, chopped
1 dried red chilli
1 small handful of fresh flat leaf
   parsley, roughly chopped
salt

1 Bring a large pan of generously salted water to the boil and cook the spaghetti until it is *al dente*. Dried spaghetti will take 10–12 minutes; fresh spaghetti will be ready in 2–3 minutes.

2 While the pasta is cooking, heat the oil in a small frying pan over a very low heat. Add the crushed garlic and whole dried chilli and stir over a low heat until the garlic is just beginning to brown. Remove the chilli and save as a garnish.

3 Drain the pasta and tip it into a warmed serving bowl. Pour on the oil and garlic mixture, add the parsley and toss until the pasta glistens. Serve immediately, garnished with the chilli.

Cook's Tips
• Don't use salt in the oil and garlic mixture, because it will not dissolve sufficiently. This is why plenty of salt is recommended for cooking the pasta.
• For an authentic Italian flavour, use peperoncino, fiery, dried, red chillies from Abruzzi. They are so hot that they are known locally as diavoletto – little devils. They are available from some Italian delicatessens.

Variation If liked, serve the pasta with 60ml/4 tbsp freshly grated Parmesan or Pecorino cheese.

Eliche with Pesto

Bottled pesto is a useful standby, but nothing beats the flavour of the freshly made mixture.

Serves 4
50g/2oz/1½ cups fresh basil
   leaves, plus extra
   to garnish
2–4 garlic cloves
60ml/4 tbsp pine nuts
120ml/4fl oz/½ cup extra virgin
   olive oil
115g/4oz/1⅓ cups freshly grated
   Parmesan cheese, plus shaved
   Parmesan to serve
25g/1oz/⅓ cup freshly grated
   Pecorino cheese
400g/14oz/3½ cups dried eliche
   or other pasta shapes
salt and ground black pepper

1 Put the basil leaves, garlic and pine nuts in a food processor. Add 60ml/4 tbsp of the olive oil. Process until the ingredients are finely chopped, then stop the machine, remove the lid and scrape down the sides of the bowl.

2 Switch the machine on again and slowly add the remaining oil in a thin, steady stream through the feeder tube. You may need to stop the machine and scrape down the sides of the bowl once or twice to make sure everything is evenly mixed.

3 Scrape the mixture into a large bowl and beat in the cheeses with a wooden spoon. Taste and season if necessary.

4 Bring a large pan of lightly salted water to the boil and cook the pasta for about 12 minutes, until it is *al dente*. Drain it thoroughly, then add it to the bowl of pesto and toss well. Serve immediately, garnished with the fresh basil leaves. Hand shaved Parmesan separately.

Cook's Tip
The pesto can be made up to 2–3 days in advance. To store pesto, transfer it to a bowl and pour a thin film of olive oil over the surface. Cover the bowl tightly with clear film and keep it in the fridge.

Spaghetti with Fresh Tomato Sauce

This famous Neapolitan sauce is very simple, so nothing detracts from the rich, sweet flavour of the tomatoes themselves.

Serves 4
675g/1½ lb ripe Italian
  plum tomatoes
60ml/4 tbsp olive oil
1 onion, finely chopped
350g/12oz fresh or
  dried spaghetti
a small handful of fresh basil
  leaves, shredded
salt and ground black pepper
coarsely shaved Parmesan cheese,
  to serve

1 Cut a cross in the blossom end of each tomato and put them in a heatproof bowl. Pour over boiling water to cover and leave for about 30 seconds, or until the skins wrinkle and start to peel back from the crosses. Drain, peel off the skin and roughly chop the flesh.

2 Heat the oil in a large saucepan and cook the onion over a low heat, for 5 minutes, until softened and lightly coloured. Stir in the tomatoes and season with salt and pepper to taste. Cover the pan and cook over a low heat for 30–40 minutes, stirring occasionally.

3 Bring a large pan of lightly salted water to the boil and cook the spaghetti until it is *al dente*. Dried pasta will take about 12 minutes and fresh spaghetti about 3–4 minutes.

4 Remove the sauce from the heat and taste for seasoning. Drain the pasta, tip it into a warmed bowl, pour the sauce over and toss well. Sprinkle the fresh basil over the top and serve immediately, with shaved Parmesan handed separately.

Cook's Tip
In summer, when sun-ripened tomatoes are plentiful, make this sauce in bulk and freeze it for later use. Let it cool, then freeze in usable quantities in rigid containers. Thaw before reheating.

Penne Rigate with Green Vegetable Sauce

Strictly speaking, this isn't a sauced dish, but a medley of vegetables and pasta tossed in butter and oil.

Serves 4
25g/1oz/2 tbsp butter
45ml/3 tbsp extra virgin olive oil
1 small leek, thinly sliced
2 carrots, diced
2.5ml/½ tsp granulated sugar
1 courgette, diced
75g/3oz French beans, cut in
  short lengths
115g/4oz/1 cup frozen peas
450g/1lb/4 cups dried penne
  rigate or other pasta shapes
a handful of fresh flat leaf
  parsley, chopped, plus extra,
  deep-fried, to garnish
2 ripe Italian plum tomatoes,
  peeled and diced
salt and ground black pepper

1 Melt the butter in the oil in a pan. When the mixture sizzles, add the leek and carrots. Sprinkle the sugar over and fry, stirring frequently, for about 5 minutes.

2 Stir in the courgette, French beans and peas, and season with salt and pepper. Cover and cook over a low heat for about 10 minutes until the vegetables are tender, stirring occasionally.

3 Meanwhile, bring a large pan of lightly salted water to the boil and cook the pasta until it is *al dente*.

4 Drain the pasta and return it to the pan. Stir the parsley and tomatoes into the sauce and season. Pour the sauce over the pasta, toss to mix, then serve with the deep-fried parsley.

Variation
For a quick and easy bake, make the vegetable mixture without the tomatoes. Toss it with the pasta and spoon it into an ovenproof dish. Slice three tomatoes and arrange the slices over the vegetable mixture. Top with a thick layer of grated cheese, then grill until the cheese melts to form a delicious topping.

Pasta with Slow-cooked Cabbage, Parmesan & Pine Nuts

This is an unusual, but quite delicious, way of serving pasta. Use cavolo nero, Italy's delicious black cabbage, if you can locate it.

Serves 4
25g/1oz/2 tbsp butter
15ml/1 tbsp extra virgin olive oil
500g/1¼ lb Spanish onions, halved and thinly sliced
5–10ml/1–2 tsp balsamic vinegar
400g/14oz cavolo nero, spring greens or kale, shredded
450g/1lb/4 cups dried pasta, such as penne or fusilli
75g/3oz/1 cup freshly grated Parmesan cheese
50g/2oz/⅔ cup pine nuts, toasted
salt and ground black pepper

1 Heat the butter and olive oil in a large saucepan. Add the onions, stirring to coat them in the butter mixture. Cover and cook over a very low heat, stirring occasionally, for about 20 minutes, until the onions are very soft.

2 Remove the lid and continue to cook the onions until they have turned golden yellow. Add the balsamic vinegar and season well with salt and pepper, then cook for a further 1–2 minutes. Set aside.

3 Bring a large pan of lightly salted water to the boil and blanch the greens for about 3 minutes. Remove the greens from the pan using a slotted spoon and drain them thoroughly. Add them to the onions, stir thoroughly to mix and cook over the lowest possible heat.

4 Bring the water in the pan back to the boil, add the pasta and cook for about 12 minutes, until *al dente*. Drain and return it to the pan. Add the onion mixture and toss over a medium heat until warmed through.

5 Season well with salt and pepper and stir in half the grated Parmesan. Spoon on to warmed plates. Scatter the pine nuts and more Parmesan on top and serve immediately.

Rustic Buckwheat Pasta Bake

A spicy combination of nutty-flavoured buckwheat pasta, vegetables and Fontina cheese, this makes a wonderful family supper.

Serves 6
45ml/3 tbsp olive oil, plus extra for greasing
2 potatoes, peeled and cubed
225g/8oz/2 cups dried buckwheat pasta shapes
275g/10oz/2½ cups shredded Savoy cabbage
1 onion, chopped
2 leeks, sliced
2 garlic cloves, chopped
175g/6oz/2½ cups brown cap mushrooms, sliced
5ml/1 tsp caraway seeds
5ml/1 tsp cumin seeds
150ml/¼ pint/⅔ cup vegetable stock
150g/5oz Fontina cheese, diced
25g/1oz/¼ cup walnuts, roughly chopped
salt and ground black pepper

1 Preheat the oven to 200°C/400°F/Gas 6. Grease a deep ovenproof dish with oil. Cook the cubed potatoes in a pan of lightly salted water for 8–10 minutes, until tender, then drain and set aside.

2 Meanwhile, bring a large pan of lightly salted water to the boil. Add the pasta and cook until it is just tender. Add the cabbage in the last minute of cooking time. Drain, then rinse under cold running water.

3 Heat the olive oil in a large heavy-based saucepan and fry the onion and leeks over a medium heat, stirring occasionally, for 5 minutes, until softened.

4 Add the garlic and mushrooms and cook, stirring occasionally, for 3 minutes more, until tender. Stir in the caraway seeds and cumin seeds and cook, stirring constantly, for 1 minute.

5 Stir in the cooked potatoes, pasta and cabbage. Season well with salt and pepper. Spoon the mixture into the prepared dish. Pour the stock over the mixture, then sprinkle with the cheese and walnuts. Bake for 15 minutes, or until the cheese is melted and bubbling.

Five-spice Vegetable Noodles

Vary this stir-fry by substituting mushrooms, bamboo shoots, beansprouts, mangetouts or water chestnuts for some or all of the vegetables.

Serves 2–3
225g/8oz dried egg noodles
30ml/2 tbsp sesame oil
2 carrots
1 celery stick
1 small fennel bulb
2 courgettes, halved lengthways and sliced
1 fresh red chilli
2.5cm/1in piece of fresh root ginger, grated
1 garlic clove, crushed
7.5ml/1½ tsp Chinese five-spice powder
2.5ml/½ tsp ground cinnamon
4 spring onions, sliced
60ml/4 tbsp warm water

1 Bring a large pan of salted water to the boil. Add the noodles and cook for 2–3 minutes, until they are just tender. Drain the noodles, return them to the pan and toss them with a little of the oil. Set aside.

2 Cut the carrots and celery into matchstick strips. Cut the fennel bulb in half and cut out the hard core. Cut into slices, then cut the slices into matchstick strips.

3 Heat the remaining oil in a wok until very hot. Add the carrots, celery, fennel and courgettes and stir-fry over a medium heat for 7–8 minutes.

4 Cut half the chilli into rings, discarding any seeds, and set aside. Chop the rest of the chilli and add it to the wok.

5 Add the ginger and garlic and stir-fry for 2 minutes, then add the Chinese five-spice powder and cinnamon. Stir-fry for 1 minute, then toss in the spring onions and stir-fry for a further minute.

6 Pour in the warm water and cook for 1 minute. Stir in the noodles and toss over the heat until they have warmed through. Transfer to a warmed serving dish and serve sprinkled with the reserved sliced red chilli.

Fried Noodles with Beansprouts & Asparagus

Soft fried noodles contrast beautifully with crisp beansprouts and asparagus.

Serves 2
115g/4oz dried egg noodles
45ml/3 tbsp vegetable oil
1 small onion, chopped
2.5cm/1in piece of fresh root ginger, grated
2 garlic cloves, crushed
175g/6oz young asparagus spears, trimmed
115g/4oz/1 cup beansprouts
4 spring onions, sliced
45ml/3 tbsp soy sauce
salt and ground black pepper

1 Bring a pan of lightly salted water to the boil. Add the noodles and cook for 2–3 minutes, until just tender. Drain and toss with 15ml/1 tbsp of the oil.

2 Heat the remaining oil in a wok until very hot. Add the onion, ginger and garlic and stir-fry for 2–3 minutes. Add the asparagus and stir-fry for 2–3 minutes more.

3 Add the noodles and beansprouts and toss over a high heat for 2 minutes.

4 Stir in the spring onions and soy sauce. Season to taste with salt and pepper. Stir-fry for 1 minute, then serve.

Cook's Tip
When seasoning the stir-fry, add salt sparingly, as the soy sauce will impart quite a salty flavour.

Variation
If preferred, substitute the same quantity of mangetouts for the asparagus spears.

New Potato, Rosemary & Garlic Pizza

New potatoes, smoked mozzarella, rosemary and garlic make the flavour of this pizza unique.

Serves 2–3
350g/12oz new potatoes
45ml/3 tbsp olive oil
2 garlic cloves, crushed
1 pizza base, 25–30cm/10–12in
  in diameter
1 red onion, very thinly sliced
150g/5oz/1¼ cups grated
  smoked mozzarella cheese
10ml/2 tsp chopped
  fresh rosemary
salt and ground black pepper
30ml/2 tbsp freshly grated
  Parmesan cheese, to garnish

1 Preheat the oven to 220°C/425°F/Gas 7. Bring a large pan of lightly salted water to the boil and cook the potatoes for 5 minutes. Drain well. When cool, peel the potatoes and slice them thinly.

2 Heat 30ml/2 tbsp of the oil in a frying pan. Add the sliced potatoes and garlic and fry over a medium heat, stirring occasionally, for 5–8 minutes until tender.

3 Brush the pizza base with the remaining oil. Scatter over the onion, then arrange the potatoes on top.

4 Sprinkle over the mozzarella and rosemary. Grind over plenty of black pepper. Bake for 15–20 minutes until the crust is crisp and golden. Sprinkle over the grated Parmesan and serve.

Quattro Formaggi Pizzas

As the Italian title suggests, these tasty little pizzas are topped with four different types of cheese and have a very rich flavour.

Serves 4
1 quantity Basic Pizza Dough
flour, for dusting
15ml/1 tbsp olive oil
1 small red onion, very
  thinly sliced
50g/2oz dolcelatte cheese
50g/2oz mozzarella cheese
50g/2oz Gruyère cheese
30ml/2 tbsp freshly grated
  Parmesan cheese
15ml/1 tbsp chopped fresh thyme
ground black pepper

1 Preheat the oven to 220°C/425°F/Gas 7. Divide the dough into four pieces and roll out each one on a lightly floured surface into a 13cm/5in circle.

2 Place well apart on two greased baking sheets, then push up the dough edges to make a thin rim.

3 Heat the olive oil in a small frying pan. Add the red onion slices and fry over a low heat, stirring occasionally for 4–5 minutes, until softened. Divide them among the pizza bases, then brush over any oil remaining in the pan.

4 Cut the dolcelatte and mozzarella into cubes and scatter over the pizza bases. Grate the Gruyère cheese into a bowl. Add the Parmesan and thyme and mix thoroughly. Sprinkle the mixture over the bases.

5 Grind over plenty of black pepper. Bake for 15–20 minutes, until the crust on each pizza is crisp and golden and the cheese is bubbling. Serve immediately.

> **Cook's Tips**
> • It's easy to overestimate how many new potatoes you need to cook for a family meal. Next time you find yourself with leftovers, use them to make this tasty pizza.
> • Smoked mozzarella, also known as mozzarella affumicata, is available from supermarkets and delicatessens.

> **Variations**
> There's no need to stick slavishly to the suggested cheeses. Any variety that melts readily can be used, but a mixture of soft and hard cheeses gives the best result.

Polenta Pan-pizza

This yeast-free pizza is cooked in a frying pan rather than in the oven.

Serves 2
30ml/2 tbsp olive oil
1 large red onion, sliced
3 garlic cloves, crushed
115g/4oz/1 1/2 cups brown cap
   mushrooms, sliced
5ml/1 tsp dried oregano
115g/4oz mozzarella
   cheese, sliced
tomato wedges and fresh basil
   leaves, to garnish

For the pizza base
50g/2oz/ 1/2 cup plain flour, sifted
2.5ml/ 1/2 tsp salt
115g/4oz/scant 1 cup
   fine polenta
5ml/1 tsp baking powder
1 egg, beaten
150ml/ 1/4 pint/ 2/3 cup milk
25g/1oz/ 1/3 cup freshly grated
   Parmesan cheese
2.5ml/ 1/2 tsp dried chilli flakes
15ml/1 tbsp olive oil
baby plum tomatoes, halved and
   basil, to serve

1 Heat half the oil in a heavy-based frying pan, and fry the onion for 10 minutes, stirring occasionally. Remove the onion from the pan and set aside. Heat the remaining oil in the pan and fry the garlic for 1 minute. Add the mushrooms and oregano and cook for 5 minutes.

2 To make the pizza base, mix the flour, salt, polenta and baking powder in a bowl. Make a well in the centre and add the egg. Gradually add the milk, mixing well to make into a thick, smooth batter. Stir in the Parmesan and chilli flakes.

3 Heat the oil in a 25cm/10in heavy-based frying pan that can safely be used under the grill. (Cover a wooden handle with foil to protect it.) Spoon in the batter in an even layer. Cook for 3 minutes, or until set. Remove the pan from the heat and run a knife around the edge of the pizza base. Place a plate over the pan and, holding them together, invert the pizza on to the plate. Slide it back into the pan. Cook for 2 minutes until golden.

4 Preheat the grill to high. Spoon the onion over the base, then top with the mushroom mixture and the mozzarella, then grill for about 6 minutes. Serve in wedges with tomatoes and basil.

Potato Gnocchi

These tasty Italian dumplings are made with mashed potato and flour.

Serves 4–6
1kg/2 1/4 lb waxy potatoes
250–300g/9–11oz/2 1/4–2 3/4 cups
   plain flour, plus more
   if necessary

1 egg
pinch of freshly grated nutmeg
25g/1oz/2 tbsp butter
salt
fresh basil leaves shaved
   Parmesan cheese and freshly
   ground black pepper,
   to garnish

1 Bring a large saucepan of lightly salted water to the boil. Add the potatoes and cook for 25–30 minutes, until tender, but not falling apart. Drain and peel while the potatoes are still hot.

2 Spread a layer of flour on a work surface. Pass the hot potatoes through a food mill, dropping them directly on to the flour. Sprinkle with about half the remaining flour and mix in very lightly. Break the egg into the mixture. Finally, add the nutmeg to the dough and knead lightly, adding more flour if needed in order to make a dough that is light to the touch and no longer moist.

3 Divide the dough into four pieces. On a lightly floured surface, form each into a roll about 2cm/3/4in in diameter. Cut the rolls crossways into pieces about 2cm/3/4in long.

4 Press and roll the gnocchi lightly along the tines of a fork towards the points, making ridges on one side, and a depression from your thumb on the other.

5 Bring a large pan of salted water to a fast boil, then drop in about half the prepared gnocchi. As soon as they rise to the surface, after 3–4 minutes, lift them out with a draining spoon, drain well, and place in a warmed serving bowl. Dot with butter. Cover to keep warm while cooking the remainder.

6 As soon as all the gnocchi are cooked, toss them with the butter, garnish with basil, Parmesan and black pepper and serve.

Saffron Risotto

This classic risotto makes a delicious first course or light supper dish.

Serves 4

about 1.2 litres/2 pints/5 cups
  vegetable stock
good pinch of saffron strands
75g/3oz/6 tbsp butter
1 onion, finely chopped
275g/10oz/1½ cups risotto rice
75g/3oz/1 cup freshly grated
  Parmesan cheese
salt and ground black pepper
freshly ground black pepper,
  to garnish

1 Bring the stock to the boil in a large pan, then lower the heat so that it barely simmers. Ladle a little stock into a small bowl. Add the saffron strands and leave to infuse.

2 Melt 50g/2oz/4 tbsp of the butter in a large saucepan and cook the onion over a low heat for 3 minutes, stirring frequently, until softened.

3 Add the rice. Stir until coated, then add a few ladlefuls of the stock, with the saffron liquid and salt and pepper to taste. Stir over a low heat until the stock has been absorbed.

4 Add the remaining stock in the same way, allowing the rice to absorb all the liquid before adding more, and stirring constantly. After 20–25 minutes, the rice should be *al dente* and the risotto golden yellow, moist and creamy.

5 Gently stir in about two-thirds of the grated Parmesan and the remaining butter. Cover the pan and leave the risotto to stand for 2–3 minutes. Spoon it into a warmed serving bowl and serve immediately, with the remaining grated Parmesan sprinkled on top and some freshly ground black pepper.

> **Cook's Tip**
> Risotto rice, such as arborio, has rounder grains than long grain rice and is able to absorb large quantities of liquid, giving the dish its characteristic creamy texture.

Risotto with Summer Vegetables

This is one of the prettiest risottos, especially if you can get yellow courgettes.

Serves 4

150g/5oz/1¼ cups shelled
  fresh peas
115g/4oz/1 cup French beans,
  cut into short lengths
30ml/2 tbsp olive oil
75g/3oz/6 tbsp butter
2 small yellow courgettes, cut into
  matchstick strips
1 onion, finely chopped
275g/10oz/1½ cups risotto rice
120ml/4fl oz/½ cup Italian dry
  white vermouth
about 1 litre/1¾ pints/4 cups
  simmering vegetable stock
75g/3oz/1 cup freshly grated
  Parmesan cheese
a small handful of fresh basil
  leaves, finely shredded, plus a
  few whole leaves, to garnish
salt and ground black pepper

1 Bring a large pan of lightly salted water to the boil and blanch the peas and beans for 2–3 minutes, until just tender. Drain, refresh under cold running water, drain again and set aside.

2 Heat the oil and 25g/1oz/2 tbsp of the butter in a medium saucepan. Add the courgettes and cook over a low heat for 2–3 minutes. Remove with a draining spoon and set aside.

3 Add the onion to the pan and cook, stirring occasionally, for about 3 minutes, until softened.

4 Stir in the rice until coated, then add the vermouth. When most of it has been absorbed, add a few ladlefuls of the stock and season with salt and pepper to taste. Stir over a low heat until the stock has been absorbed.

5 Continue adding the stock, a little at a time, and stirring constantly for about 20 minutes, until all the stock has been added and the risotto is moist and creamy.

6 Gently stir in the vegetables, the remaining butter and about half the grated Parmesan. Heat through, then stir in the shredded basil. Serve at once, garnished with a few whole basil leaves. Offer the remaining grated Parmesan separately.

Leek, Mushroom & Lemon Risotto

Leeks and lemon go together beautifully in this light risotto, while mushrooms add texture and extra flavour.

Serves 4

30ml/2 tbsp olive oil
3 garlic cloves, crushed
225g/8oz trimmed leeks, sliced
225g/8oz/2–3 cups brown cap
    mushrooms, sliced
75g/3oz/6 tbsp butter
1 large onion, roughly chopped
350g/12oz/1¾ cups risotto rice
1.2 litres/2 pints/5 cups
    simmering vegetable stock
grated rind of 1 lemon
45ml/3 tbsp lemon juice
50g/2oz/⅔ cup freshly grated
    Parmesan cheese
60ml/4 tbsp mixed chopped fresh
    chives and flat leaf parsley
salt and ground black pepper

1 Heat the olive oil in a large pan and cook the garlic for 1 minute. Add the leeks and mushrooms and season to taste with salt and pepper. Cook over a low heat, stirring occasionally, for about 10 minutes, or until the leeks have softened and browned. Spoon the mixture into a bowl and set aside.

2 Melt 25g/1oz/2 tbsp of the butter in the pan and cook the onion, stirring occasionally, for 5 minutes, until it has softened and is golden. Stir in the rice until coated, then add a ladleful of hot stock. Cook gently, stirring frequently, until all the liquid has been absorbed.

3 Continue to add the remaining stock, a little at a time, and stirring constantly. After about 25–30 minutes, the rice will have absorbed all the stock and the risotto will be moist and creamy.

4 Add the leeks and mushrooms, with the remaining butter. Stir in the lemon rind and juice, then the grated Parmesan and the herbs. Adjust the seasoning, spoon into a bowl and serve.

Cook's Tip
Always wash leeks very thoroughly, as soil and grit may be trapped within the leaves.

Nutty Rice with Mushrooms

This delicious and substantial supper dish can be eaten either hot, or cold with salads.

Serves 4–6

350g/12oz/1¾ cups long
    grain rice
45ml/3 tbsp sunflower oil
1 small onion, roughly chopped
225g/8oz/3 cups field
    mushrooms, sliced
50g/2oz/½ cup hazelnuts,
    roughly chopped
50g/2oz/½ cup pecan nuts,
    roughly chopped
50g/2oz/½ cup almonds,
    roughly chopped
60ml/4 tbsp chopped
    fresh parsley
salt and ground black pepper
fresh flat leaf parsley sprigs,
    to garnish

1 Bring a large pan of water to the boil. Add the rice and cook for about 10 minutes, or until just tender. Drain, refresh under cold water and drain again. Leave to dry.

2 Heat half the oil in a wok. Add the rice and stir-fry over a medium heat for 2–3 minutes. Remove and set aside.

3 Add the remaining oil to the wok. Add the onion and stir-fry for 2 minutes, until softened, then mix in the sliced mushrooms and stir-fry for 2 minutes more.

4 Add all the nuts and stir-fry for 1 minute. Return the rice to the wok and toss over the heat for 3 minutes. Season with salt and pepper to taste. Stir in the chopped parsley and serve with a garnish of flat leaf parsley sprigs.

Cook's Tips
• *When cooking in a wok, always preheat it. When it is hot, add the oil and swirl it around to coat the sides. Then allow the oil to heat up before adding any ingredients.*
• *It is possible to stir-fry in a frying pan, if you don't have a wok. However, the heat will be less evenly distributed and it is harder to toss the ingredients without making a mess.*

Vedgeree with French Beans & Mushrooms

Crunchy French beans and mushrooms are the star ingredients in this vegetarian version of an old favourite.

Serves 2

115g/4oz/¾ cup basmati rice
3 eggs
175g/6oz/1½ cups French
  beans, trimmed
50g/2oz/¼ cup butter
1 onion, finely chopped
225g/8oz/3 cups brown cap
  mushrooms, quartered
30ml/2 tbsp single cream
15ml/1 tbsp chopped
  fresh parsley
salt and ground black pepper

1 Rinse the rice several times in cold water. Drain thoroughly. Bring a large saucepan of lightly salted water to the boil, add the rice and cook for 10–12 minutes, until tender. Drain thoroughly and set aside.

2 Half fill a second pan with water, add the eggs and bring to the boil over a medium heat. Lower the heat and simmer gently for 8 minutes. Drain the eggs, cool them under cold water, then remove the shells.

3 Bring another pan of water to the boil and cook the French beans for 5 minutes. Drain, refresh under cold running water, then drain again.

4 Melt the butter in a large, heavy-based frying pan. Add the onion and mushrooms and fry over a moderate heat, stirring occasionally, for 2–3 minutes.

5 Stir in the beans and rice and cook for 2 minutes. Cut the hard-boiled eggs into wedges and add them to the pan.

6 Stir in the cream and parsley, taking care not to break up the eggs. Season to taste with salt and pepper. Reheat the vedgeree, but do not allow it to boil. Transfer to a warmed serving dish and serve at once.

Golden Vegetable Paella

Hearty enough for the hungriest guests, this takes very little time to prepare and cook.

Serves 4

pinch of saffron strands
750ml/1¼ pints/3 cups hot
  vegetable stock
90ml/6 tbsp olive oil
2 large onions, sliced
3 garlic cloves, chopped
275g/10oz/1½ cups long
  grain rice
50g/2oz/⅓ cup wild rice
175g/6oz pumpkin, chopped
1 large carrot, cut into
  matchstick strips
1 yellow pepper, seeded
  and sliced
4 tomatoes, peeled and chopped
115g/4oz/1½ cups oyster
  mushrooms, quartered
salt and ground black pepper
strips of red, yellow and green
  pepper, to garnish

1 Place the saffron in a small bowl with 60ml/4 tbsp of the hot stock. Leave to stand for 5 minutes.

2 Meanwhile, heat the oil in a paella pan or large, heavy-based frying pan. Add the onions and garlic and fry over a low heat, stirring occasionally, for 3 minutes, until just beginning to soften.

3 Add the long grain rice and wild rice to the pan and toss for 2–3 minutes, until coated in oil. Add the stock to the pan, together with the pumpkin and the saffron strands and liquid. Stir the mixture as it comes to the boil, then reduce the heat to the lowest setting.

4 Cover and cook very gently for 15 minutes, without lifting the lid. Add the carrot strips, yellow pepper and chopped tomatoes and season to taste with salt and pepper. Replace the lid and cook very gently for a further 5 minutes, or until the rice is almost tender.

5 Add the oyster mushrooms, check the seasoning and cook, uncovered, for just enough time to soften the mushrooms without letting the paella stick to the pan. Garnish with the peppers and serve.

Middle-Eastern Rice with Lentils

Part of the appeal of this spicy main meal dish lies in its sheer simplicity as well as the speed with which it can be cooked.

Serves 4
30ml/2 tbsp sunflower oil
1 large onion, sliced
4–5 cardamom pods
2.5ml/ ½ tsp coriander
   seeds, crushed
2.5ml/ ½ tsp cumin
   seeds, crushed

small piece of fresh root ginger,
   finely chopped
1 cinnamon stick
1 garlic clove, crushed
115g/4oz/ ¾ cup brown rice
about 900ml/1 ½ pints/3¾ cups
   vegetable stock
2.5ml/ ½ tsp ground turmeric
115g/4oz/ ½ cup split red lentils
25g/1oz/ ¼ cup flaked
   almonds, toasted
50g/2oz/ ⅓ cup raisins
natural yogurt, to serve

1 Heat the sunflower oil in a large saucepan. Add the onion and fry over a medium heat, stirring occasionally, for 5 minutes, until softened.

2 Crush the cardamom pods, extract the seeds and add them to the pan, together with the coriander seeds, cumin seeds, ginger, cinnamon stick and garlic. Stir over a moderate heat for 2–3 minutes.

3 Add the rice, stirring to coat the grains in the spice mixture, then pour in the stock. Stir in the turmeric. Bring to the boil and then lower the heat, cover the pan with a tight-fitting lid and simmer for 15 minutes.

4 Add the lentils to the pan, replace the lid and cook for 20 minutes more, or until the rice and lentils are tender and all the stock has been absorbed. If the mixture seems to be drying out, stir in a little more stock.

5 When all the stock has been absorbed, tip the rice mixture into a heated serving dish. Remove and discard the cinnamon stick. Scatter the toasted almonds and raisins over the top. Serve with the yogurt.

Quick Basmati & Nut Pilaff

Light and fragrant basmati rice cooks perfectly using this simple pilaff method.

Serves 4–6
225g/8oz/generous 1 cup
   basmati rice
15–30ml/1–2 tbsp sunflower oil
1 onion, chopped
1 garlic clove, crushed
1 large carrot, coarsely grated

5ml/1 tsp cumin seeds
10ml/2 tsp ground coriander
10ml/2 tsp black mustard seeds
4 cardamom pods
450ml/ ¾ pint/scant 2 cups
   vegetable stock
1 bay leaf
75g/3oz/ ¾ cup unsalted nuts
salt and ground black pepper
chopped fresh parsley or
   coriander, to garnish

1 Rinse the rice in several changes of cold water. If there is sufficient time, leave it to soak for 30 minutes in the water used for the final rinse.

2 Heat the oil in a large shallow pan and fry the onion, garlic and carrot for 2–3 minutes. Stir in the rice and spices and cook for 1–2 minutes, so that the grains are coated in oil.

3 Pour in the stock, add the bay leaf and season to taste with salt and pepper. Bring to the boil, then lower the heat, cover and simmer very gently for about 10 minutes.

4 Remove from the heat without lifting the lid – this helps the rice to firm up and cook further. Leave for about 5 minutes, then check the rice. If it is cooked, there will be small steam holes in the centre. Discard the bay leaf and cardamom pods.

5 Stir in the nuts and check the seasoning. Spoon the mixture into a serving dish and scatter the chopped parsley or coriander over the surface. Serve at once.

Cook's Tip
Use whatever nuts are your favourites, such as almonds, cashews or pistachios – even unsalted peanuts are good.

Vegetable Couscous with Saffron & Harissa

A North African favourite, this spicy dish makes an excellent midweek supper.

Serves 4
45ml/3 tbsp olive oil
1 onion, chopped
2 garlic cloves, crushed
5ml/1 tsp ground cumin
5ml/1 tsp paprika
400g/14oz can chopped tomatoes
300ml/½ pint/1¼ cups vegetable stock
1 cinnamon stick
generous pinch of saffron strands
4 baby aubergines, quartered
8 baby courgettes, trimmed and quartered lengthways
8 baby carrots
225g/8oz/1⅓ cups couscous
400g/14oz can chick-peas, drained and rinsed
175g/6oz/¾ cup prunes
45ml/3 tbsp chopped fresh parsley
45ml/3 tbsp chopped fresh coriander
10–15ml/2–3 tsp harissa
salt

1 Heat the olive oil in a large saucepan and cook the onion and garlic gently for 5 minutes, until soft. Add the cumin and paprika and cook, stirring, for 1 minute. Stir in the tomatoes, stock, cinnamon stick, saffron, aubergines, courgettes and carrots. Season with salt. Bring to the boil, lower the heat, cover and cook for 20 minutes.

2 Select a colander that will fit over the pan of vegetables. Line it with a double thickness of muslin. Soak the couscous according to the instructions on the packet.

3 Add the chick-peas and prunes to the vegetables and cook for 5 minutes. Fork the couscous to break up any lumps and spread it in the colander. Place it on top of the vegetables, cover, and cook for 5 minutes until the couscous is hot.

4 Tip the couscous into a warmed dish. Using a draining spoon, add the vegetables. Spoon over a little of the cooking liquid, add the parsley and coriander and toss gently to combine. Stir the harissa into the remaining sauce and serve separately.

Spiced Couscous with Halloumi

Courgette ribbons add colour and flavour to this delicious dish.

Serves 4
275g/10oz/1⅔ cups couscous
500ml/17fl oz/generous 2 cups boiling water
1 bay leaf
1 cinnamon stick
30ml/2 tbsp olive oil, plus extra for brushing
1 large red onion, chopped
2 garlic cloves, chopped
5ml/1 tsp mild chilli powder
5ml/1 tsp ground cumin
5ml/1 tsp ground coriander
5 cardamom pods, bruised
50g/2oz/⅓ cup whole blanched almonds, toasted
1 peach, stoned and diced
25g/1oz/2 tbsp butter
3 courgettes, sliced lengthways into ribbons
225g/8oz Halloumi cheese, sliced
salt and ground black pepper
chopped fresh flat leaf parsley, to garnish

1 Place the couscous in a bowl and pour over the boiling water. Add the bay leaf and cinnamon stick and season with salt. Leave the couscous for 10 minutes.

2 Meanwhile, heat the oil in a large, heavy-based pan and sauté the onion and garlic until the onion has softened, stirring occasionally. Stir in the chilli powder, cumin, coriander and cardamom pods and cook for a further 3 minutes.

3 Fork the couscous to break up any lumps, then add it to the pan, with the almonds, diced peach and butter. Heat through for 2 minutes.

4 Brush a griddle pan with olive oil and heat until very hot. Turn down the heat to medium, then place the courgettes on the griddle and cook for 5 minutes, until tender and slightly charred. Turn them over, add the Halloumi and continue cooking for 5 minutes more, turning the Halloumi halfway through.

5 Remove the cinnamon stick, bay leaf and cardamom pods from the couscous mixture, then pile it on a plate and season to taste with salt and pepper. Top with the Halloumi and courgettes. Sprinkle the parsley over the top and serve.

Goat's Cheese Kasha

Kasha is a Russian staple of cooked grains. Buckwheat is conventionally used, but has a strong flavour. Here it is moderated with couscous.

Serves 4

175g/6oz/1 cup couscous
45ml/3 tbsp buckwheat
15g/½ oz/¼ cup dried ceps
3 eggs, lightly beaten
60ml/4 tbsp chopped
   fresh parsley
10ml/2 tsp chopped fresh thyme
60ml/4 tbsp olive oil
45ml/3 tbsp walnut oil
175g/6oz crumbly white
   goat's cheese
50g/2oz/½ cup broken
   walnuts, toasted
salt and ground black pepper
fresh parsley sprigs,
   to garnish
rye bread and a mixed salad,
   to serve

1 Place the couscous, buckwheat and ceps in a bowl, cover with boiling water and leave to soak for 15 minutes. Drain off any excess liquid.

2 Place the mixture in a large non-stick frying pan and stir in the eggs. Season with plenty of salt and pepper. Cook over a medium heat, stirring with a wooden spoon until the mixture looks like grainy scrambled eggs. Do not let it get too dry.

3 Stir in the parsley, thyme, olive oil and walnut oil. Crumble in the goat's cheese and stir in the walnuts.

4 Transfer to a large serving dish, garnish with fresh parsley sprigs, and serve hot with rye bread and a mixed salad.

Cook's Tip
Cep is the French name for the Boletus edulis *mushroom. It is also known as the penny bun in England. As the dried mushrooms are widely used in Italian cuisine, packets may also be labelled porcini (little pigs), the Italian name. Dried bay boletus mushrooms* (Boletus badius) *are also available, but the flavour is inferior to that of ceps.*

Aubergine Pilaff

This hearty dish is made with bulgur wheat and aubergine, flavoured with fresh mint. It is a perfect choice for a mid-week supper as it can be prepared within 15 minutes.

Serves 2

2 medium aubergines
60–90ml/4–6 tbsp sunflower oil
1 small onion, finely chopped
175g/6oz/1 cup bulgur wheat
450ml/¾ pint/scant 2 cups
   vegetable stock
30ml/2 tbsp pine nuts, toasted
15ml/1 tbsp chopped fresh mint
salt and ground black pepper

For the garnish
lime wedges
lemon wedges
torn mint leaves

1 Trim the ends from the aubergines, then slice them lengthways. Cut each slice into neat sticks and then into 1cm/½ in dice.

2 Heat 60ml/4 tbsp of the oil in a large, heavy-based frying pan. Add the onion and fry over a medium heat for 1 minute. Add the diced aubergine. Increase the heat to high and cook, stirring frequently, for about 4 minutes, until just tender. Add the remaining oil if needed.

3 Stir in the bulgur wheat, mixing well, then pour in the vegetable stock. Bring to the boil, then lower the heat and simmer for 10 minutes or until all the liquid has evaporated. Season to taste with salt and pepper.

4 Stir in the pine nuts and mint, then spoon the pilaff on to individual plates. Garnish each portion with lime and lemon wedges. Sprinkle with torn mint leaves for extra colour and serve immediately.

Variation
Use courgettes instead of aubergine, or, for something completely different, substitute pumpkin or acorn squash.

Beetroot Casserole

Maybe beetroot isn't the obvious choice for a casserole, but this sweet and sour dish is delicious.

Serves 4
50g/2oz/ ¼ cup butter
1 onion, chopped
2 garlic cloves, crushed
675g/1½ lb raw beetroot, peeled and diced
2 large carrots, diced
115g/4oz/1½ cups button mushrooms
300ml/ ½ pint/1 ¼ cups vegetable stock
grated rind and juice of ½ lemon
2 bay leaves
15ml/1 tbsp chopped fresh mint
salt and ground black pepper

For the hot dressing
150ml/ ¼ pint/ ⅔ cup soured cream
2.5ml/ ½ tsp paprika, plus extra to garnish

1 Melt the butter in a non-aluminium pan. Add the onion and garlic and fry over a low heat for 5 minutes. Add the beetroot, carrots and mushrooms and fry for 5 minutes more. Pour in the stock, then add the lemon rind and bay leaves. Season with salt and pepper. Bring to the boil, lower the heat, cover and simmer for 1 hour, or until the vegetables are soft.

2 Turn off the heat and stir in the lemon juice and mint. Cover the pan and leave it to stand for 5 minutes.

3 Meanwhile, make the dressing. Gently heat the soured cream and paprika in a small pan, stirring all the time, until bubbling.

4 Transfer the beetroot mixture to a serving bowl, spoon over the dressing and sprinkle with a little more paprika. Serve.

Cook's Tips
• *Wear rubber or plastic gloves to avoid staining your hands when preparing beetroot.*
• *Cooking beetroot in an aluminium pan may cause discoloration of pan and food.*

Braised Barley & Vegetables

One of the oldest cultivated cereals, pot barley has a nutty colour and slightly chewy texture. It makes a warming and filling dish when combined with a selection of root vegetables.

Serves 4
30ml/2 tbsp sunflower oil
1 large onion, chopped
2 celery sticks, sliced
2 carrots, halved lengthways and sliced
225g/8oz/1 cup pearl or pot barley
1 large piece of swede, about 225g/8oz, cubed
1 large potato, about 225g/8oz, cubed
475ml/16fl oz/2 cups vegetable stock
salt and ground black pepper
celery leaves, to garnish

1 Heat the oil in a large pan. Add the onion and fry over a low heat, stirring occasionally, for 5 minutes, until softened. Add the sliced celery and carrots and cook for 3–4 minutes, or until the onion is starting to brown.

2 Add the barley, then stir in the swede and potato. Pour in the stock and season to taste with salt and pepper. Bring to the boil, then lower the heat and cover the pan.

3 Simmer, stirring occasionally, for 40 minutes, or until most of the stock has been absorbed and the barley is tender.

4 Spoon on to warmed serving plates, garnish with the celery leaves and serve.

Variations
• *This tastes good with feta cheese, especially if you use the cubes that are conveniently packed in oil. Toss them in to the mixture just before serving and drizzle over a little of the oil from the jar, if you like.*
• *You can substitute or add other vegetables, such as celeriac or parsnips. For a more summery version of the dish, use fennel, courgettes and broad beans.*

Vegetable Hot-pot with Cheese Triangles

A sort of savoury cobbler, this hot-pot is topped with a scone mixture. The combination is irresistible.

Serves 6
30ml/2 tbsp oil
2 garlic cloves, crushed
1 onion, roughly chopped
5ml/1 tsp mild chilli powder
450g/1lb potatoes, peeled and
roughly chopped
450g/1lb celeriac, peeled and
roughly chopped
350g/12oz carrots,
roughly chopped
350g/12oz trimmed leeks,
roughly chopped
225g/8oz/3 cups brown cap
mushrooms, halved

20ml/4 tsp plain flour
600ml/1 pint/2½ cups
vegetable stock
400g/14oz can
chopped tomatoes
15ml/1 tbsp tomato purée
30ml/2 tbsp chopped fresh thyme
400g/14oz can kidney beans,
drained and rinsed
salt and ground black pepper

For the topping
225g/8oz/2 cups self-raising flour
115g/4oz/½ cup butter
115g/4oz/1 cup grated
Cheddar cheese
30ml/2 tbsp snipped fresh chives
about 75ml/5 tbsp milk

1 Preheat the oven to 180°C/350°F/Gas 4. Heat the oil in a large flameproof casserole. Add the garlic and onion and fry over a low heat, stirring occasionally, for 5 minutes. Stir in the chilli powder and cook for 1 minute more.

2 Add the potatoes, celeriac, carrots, leeks and mushrooms. Cook for 3–4 minutes. Stir in the flour and cook, stirring constantly, for 1 minute more.

3 Stir in the stock, then the tomatoes, tomato purée and thyme and season well with salt and pepper. Bring to the boil, stirring. Cover and cook in the oven for 30 minutes.

4 Meanwhile, make the topping. Sift the flour into a bowl and rub in the butter with your fingertips, then stir in half the grated cheese, together with the chives and plenty of seasoning. Add just enough milk to bind the dry ingredients and mix quickly to form a soft dough.

5 Pat out the dough to a round, about 2.5cm/1in thick. Cut it into 12 triangles. Brush with a little milk.

6 Remove the casserole from the oven and stir in the beans. Overlap the triangles on top, and sprinkle with the remaining cheese. Return to the oven, uncovered, for 20–25 minutes, or until the scone topping is golden brown and cooked through. Serve at once.

Cook's Tip
Use any of your favourite vegetables, as long as the overall weight remains the same. Firm vegetables may need a little longer cooking.

Vegetarian Cassoulet

Every town in south-west France has its own version of this popular classic. Serve this hearty vegetable version with warm French bread.

Serves 4–6
400g/14oz/1¾ cups dried
haricot beans, soaked overnight
in water to cover
1 bay leaf
1.75 litres/3 pints/7½ cups
cold water
2 onions
3 cloves
5ml/1 tsp olive oil

2 garlic cloves, crushed
2 leeks, thickly sliced
12 baby carrots
115g/4oz/1½ cups
button mushrooms
400g/14oz can
chopped tomatoes
15ml/1 tbsp tomato purée
5ml/1 tsp paprika
15ml/1 tbsp chopped fresh thyme
30ml/2 tbsp chopped
fresh parsley
115g/4oz/2 cups fresh
white breadcrumbs
salt and ground black pepper

1 Drain the beans. Rinse them under cold running water, then put them in a large pan. Add the bay leaf, then pour in the water. Bring to the boil and cook rapidly for 10 minutes.

2 Peel one of the onions and spike it with cloves. Add it to the beans and lower the heat. Cover and simmer gently for 1 hour, until the beans are almost tender. Drain, reserving the stock but discarding the bay leaf and onion.

3 Preheat the oven to 160°C/325°F/Gas 3. Chop the remaining onion. Heat the oil in a large flameproof casserole. Add the chopped onion and garlic and fry over a low heat, stirring occasionally, for 5 minutes, or until softened. Add the leeks, carrots, mushrooms, chopped tomatoes, tomato purée, paprika and thyme to the casserole. Stir in 400ml/14fl oz/1¾ cups of the reserved stock.

4 Bring to the boil, cover and simmer gently for 10 minutes. Stir in the cooked beans and parsley. Season to taste, sprinkle with the fresh breadcrumbs and bake, uncovered, for 35 minutes, or until the topping is golden brown and crisp.

Baked Cheese Polenta with Tomato Sauce

Polenta, or cornmeal, is a staple food in Italy. It is cooked like porridge, and can be eaten soft. This version uses squares of set polenta, baked in a rich tomato sauce.

Serves 4

1 litre/1¾ pints/4 cups water
5ml/1 tsp salt
250g/9oz/2 cups quick-
    cook polenta
5ml/1 tsp paprika
2.5ml/½ tsp ground nutmeg
30ml/2 tbsp olive oil, plus extra
    for greasing
1 large onion, finely chopped
2 garlic cloves, crushed
2 x 400g/14oz cans
    chopped tomatoes
15ml/1 tbsp tomato purée
5ml/1 tsp granulated sugar
75g/3oz Gruyère cheese, grated
salt and ground black pepper

1 Preheat the oven to 200°C/400°F/Gas 6. Line a 28 x 18cm/ 11 x 7in baking tin with clear film. Pour the water into a large heavy-based pan and add the salt.

2 Bring the water to the boil. Pour in the polenta in a steady stream and cook, stirring constantly, for 5 minutes. Beat in the paprika and nutmeg, then pour the mixture into the prepared tin. Level the surface. Leave to cool.

3 Heat the oil in a pan. Add the onion and garlic and fry over a low heat, stirring occasionally, for 5 minutes, until soft. Stir in the tomatoes, tomato purée and sugar and season with salt and pepper to taste. Simmer for 20 minutes.

4 Turn out the polenta on to a chopping board and cut it into 5cm/2in squares. Place half the polenta squares in a greased ovenproof dish. Spoon over half the tomato sauce and sprinkle with half the grated cheese. Repeat the layers of polenta, sauce and cheese.

5 Bake the polenta for about 25 minutes, until the top is golden and bubbling. Serve immediately.

Polenta with Mushroom Sauce

This is a fine example of just how absolutely delicious soft polenta can be. Topped with a robust mushroom and tomato sauce, it tastes quite sublime.

Serves 4

1.2 litres/2 pints/5 cups
    vegetable stock
350g/12oz/3 cups fine
    polenta or cornmeal
50g/2oz/⅔ cup freshly grated
    Parmesan cheese
salt and ground black pepper

For the sauce
15g/½ oz/¼ cup dried
    porcini mushrooms
150ml/¼ pint/⅔ cup hot water
15ml/1 tbsp olive oil
50g/2oz/¼ cup butter
1 onion, finely chopped
1 carrot, finely chopped
1 celery stick, finely chopped
2 garlic cloves, crushed
450g/1lb/6 cups mixed chestnut
    and large flat mushrooms,
    roughly chopped
120ml/4fl oz/½ cup red wine
400g/14oz can
    chopped tomatoes
5ml/1 tsp tomato purée
15ml/1 tbsp chopped fresh thyme

1 Make the sauce. Soak the dried mushrooms in the hot water for 20 minutes. Drain, reserving the liquid, and chop roughly.

2 Heat the oil and butter in a saucepan and fry the onion, carrot, celery and garlic for 5 minutes, until beginning to soften. Raise the heat and add the both mushrooms. Cook for another 10 minutes. Pour in the wine and cook rapidly for 2–3 minutes, then add the tomatoes and strained, reserved soaking liquid. Stir in the tomato purée and thyme and season with salt and pepper. Lower the heat and simmer for 20 minutes.

3 Meanwhile, heat the stock in a large heavy-based saucepan. Add a pinch of salt. As soon as it simmers, tip in the polenta in a fine stream, whisking until the mixture is smooth. Cook for 30 minutes, stirring constantly, until the polenta comes away from the pan. Stir in half the Parmesan and some pepper.

4 Divide among four heated bowls and top each with sauce. Sprinkle with the remaining Parmesan.

Onions Stuffed with Goat's Cheese & Sun-dried Tomatoes

Roasted onions and creamy goat's cheese truly are a winning combination.

Serves 4

4 large onions
oil, for greasing
150g/5oz goat's cheese, crumbled
50g/2oz/1 cup fresh breadcrumbs
8 sun-dried tomatoes in olive oil, drained and chopped
1–2 garlic cloves, finely chopped
2.5ml/ 1/2 tsp chopped fresh thyme
30ml/2 tbsp chopped fresh parsley, plus extra to garnish
1 small egg, beaten
45ml/3 tbsp pine nuts, toasted
30ml/2 tbsp olive oil (from the tomatoes)
salt and ground black pepper

1 Bring a large pan of lightly salted water to the boil. Add the whole onions in their skins and boil for 10 minutes. Drain and cool, then cut each onion in half horizontally and peel.

2 Using a teaspoon to scoop out the flesh, remove the centre of each onion, leaving a thick shell. Reserve the flesh and place the shells in an oiled ovenproof dish. Preheat the oven to 190°C/375°F/Gas 5.

3 Chop the scooped-out onion flesh and place it in a bowl. Add the goat's cheese, breadcrumbs, sun-dried tomatoes, garlic, thyme, parsley and egg. Mix well, then season to taste with salt and pepper. Add the toasted pine nuts.

4 Divide the stuffing among the onions and cover with foil. Bake for about 25 minutes. Uncover, drizzle with the oil and cook for 30–40 minutes more, until bubbling and well cooked. Baste occasionally during cooking. Serve, garnished with parsley.

Variation
• Omit the goat's cheese and add 115g/4oz finely chopped mushrooms and 1 grated carrot.

Baked Peppers with Egg & Lentils

A breadcrumb or rice filling is commonly used for peppers. Lentils make a delicious change and the eggs add extra protein.

Serves 4

75g/3oz/scant 1/2 cup Puy lentils
2.5ml/ 1/2 tsp ground turmeric
2.5ml/ 1/2 tsp ground coriander
2.5ml/ 1/2 tsp paprika
450ml/ 3/4 pint/scant 2 cups vegetable stock
2 large peppers, halved lengthways and seeded
a little vegetable oil
15ml/1 tbsp chopped fresh mint
4 eggs
salt and ground black pepper
fresh coriander sprigs, to garnish

1 Put the lentils in a pan with the spices and stock. Bring to the boil, stirring occasionally, then lower the heat and simmer for 30–40 minutes. If necessary, add some water during cooking.

2 Preheat the oven to 190°C/375°F/Gas 4. Brush the peppers lightly with oil and place them close together, cut sides upwards, in a roasting tin. Stir the mint into the lentils, then fill the peppers with the mixture.

3 Beat one egg in a small jug and carefully pour it over the lentil mixture in one of the peppers. Uising a small spoon, gently stir it into the lentils and season with salt and pepper to taste. Repeat with the remaining eggs and peppers. Bake for 10 minutes, garnish with coriander and serve.

Variations
• Add a little extra flavour to the lentil mixture by mixing in chopped onion and tomatoes sautéed in olive oil before filling the peppers.
• Use beef tomatoes instead of peppers. Cut a lid off the tomatoes and scoop out the flesh with a teaspoon. Fill with the lentils and egg and bake.
• For an extra touch of spice, add one or two finely chopped fresh green chillies to the lentils.

Baked Stuffed Squash

A creamy, sweet and nutty filling makes the perfect topping for tender squash.

Serves 4
2 butternut or acorn squash, about 500g/1¼ lb each
15ml/1 tbsp olive oil
175g/6oz/1 cup drained canned sweetcorn kernels
115g/4oz/½ cup unsweetened chestnut purée
75ml/5 tbsp low-fat yogurt
50g/2oz fresh goat's cheese
salt and ground black pepper
snipped chives, to garnish
mixed salad leaves, to serve

1 Preheat the oven to 180°C/350°F/Gas 4. Cut the squash in half lengthwise, scoop out the seeds and place the halves, skin side down, on a baking sheet.

2 Brush the squash flesh lightly with the olive oil, then bake for about 30 minutes.

3 Meanwhile, mix the sweetcorn, chestnut purée and yogurt in a bowl. Season to taste with salt and pepper.

4 Remove the squash from the oven and divide the chestnut mixture between them, spooning it into the hollows.

5 Top each half with one-quarter of the goat's cheese and return to the oven for 10–15 minutes. Garnish with snipped chives and serve immediately with salad leaves.

> **Variations**
> • Use mozzarella or other mild, soft cheeses in place of the goat's cheese. The cheese can be omitted entirely for a lower-fat alternative.
> • Add 15–30ml/1–2 tbsp finely chopped nuts, such as almonds or pistachios to the filling.
> • This filling also goes well with courgettes. Cut four to six large courgettes in half lengthways and bake for about 20 minutes.

Stuffed Mushrooms with Pine Nut Tarator

Portabello mushrooms have a rich flavour and a meaty texture. They go well with this fragrant and tasty herb and lemon stuffing.

Serves 4–6
45ml/3 tbsp olive oil, plus extra for brushing
1 onion, finely chopped
2 garlic cloves, crushed
30ml/2 tbsp chopped fresh thyme or 5ml/1 tsp dried thyme
8 portabello mushrooms, stalks removed and finely chopped
400g/14oz can aduki beans, drained and rinsed
50g/2oz/1 cup fresh wholemeal breadcrumbs
juice of 1 lemon
185g/6½ oz goat's cheese, crumbled
salt and ground black pepper

For the pine nut tarator
50g/2oz/⅔ cup pine nuts, toasted
50g/2oz/1 cup cubed white bread
2 garlic cloves, chopped
200ml/7fl oz/scant 1 cup milk
45ml/3 tbsp olive oil

1 Preheat the oven to 200°C/400°F/Gas 6. Heat the oil in a large, heavy-based frying pan. Add the onion and garlic and fry over a low heat, stirring occasionally, for 5 minutes until softened. Add the thyme and the mushroom stalks and cook for 3 minutes more, stirring occasionally, until tender.

2 Stir the aduki beans into the mixture with the breadcrumbs and lemon juice, season well with salt and pepper, then cook for 2 minutes, until heated through.

3 Remove the pan from the heat and, using a fork or potato masher, mash the mixture until about two-thirds of the beans are broken up, leaving the remaining beans whole.

4 Brush an ovenproof dish and the tops and sides of the mushroom caps with oil. Place them, gills uppermost, in the dish and top each one with a spoonful of the bean mixture. Cover with foil and bake for 20 minutes.

5 Remove the foil. Top each mushroom with goat's cheese and bake for 15 minutes more, or until the cheese has melted and the mushrooms are tender.

6 Meanwhile, make the pine nut tarator. Put the pine nuts, bread and garlic in a food processor and process briefly. Add the milk and olive oil and process until creamy. Serve the tarator with the mushrooms.

> **Cook's Tip**
> Use dried beans if you prefer. Soak 200g/7oz/1 cup beans overnight in cold water, then drain and rinse well. Place in a pan with water to cover and boil rapidly for 10 minutes. Reduce the heat, cook for 30 minutes, until tender, then drain. Alternatively, cover the dried beans with boiling water and leave to soak for about 3 hours before draining and cooking.

Aubergine Parmigiana

A classic Italian dish, in which blissfully tender sliced aubergines are layered with melting creamy mozzarella, fresh Parmesan and a good home-made tomato sauce.

Serves 4–6
3 medium aubergines, thinly sliced
olive oil, for brushing
300g/11oz mozzarella
   cheese, sliced
115g/4oz/1⅓ cups freshly grated
   Parmesan cheese
30–45ml/2–3 tbsp natural-
   coloured dried breadcrumbs
salt and ground black pepper
fresh basil sprigs, to garnish

For the sauce
30ml/2 tbsp olive oil
1 onion, finely chopped
2 garlic cloves, crushed
400g/14oz can
   chopped tomatoes
5ml/1 tsp granulated sugar
about 6 fresh basil leaves

1 Layer the aubergine slices in a colander, sprinkling each layer with a little salt. Drain over a sink for about 20 minutes, then rinse thoroughly under cold running water and pat dry with kitchen paper.

2 Preheat the oven to 200°C/400°F/Gas 6. Lay the aubergine slices on non-stick baking sheets, brush the tops with olive oil and bake for 10–15 minutes until softened.

3 Meanwhile, make the sauce. Heat the oil in a pan. Add the onion and garlic and fry over a low heat, stirring occasionally, for 5 minutes. Add the canned tomatoes and sugar and season with salt and pepper to taste. Bring to the boil, then lower the heat and simmer for about 10 minutes, until reduced and thickened. Tear the basil leaves into small pieces and stir them into the sauce.

4 Layer the aubergines in a greased shallow ovenproof dish with the sliced mozzarella, the tomato sauce and the grated Parmesan, ending with a layer of Parmesan mixed with the breadcrumbs. Bake for 20–25 minutes, until golden brown and bubbling. Allow to stand for 5 minutes before cutting. Serve garnished with basil.

Savoy Cabbage Stuffed with Mushroom Barley

The veined texture of Savoy cabbage provides good cover for a hearty stuffing of barley and wild mushrooms.

Serves 4
50g/2oz/¼ cup butter
2 medium onions, chopped
1 celery stick, sliced
225g/8oz/3 cups assorted wild
   and cultivated mushrooms
175g/6oz/¾ cup pearl barley
1 fresh thyme sprig
750ml/1¼ pints/3 cups water
30ml/2 tbsp cashew nut butter
½ vegetable stock cube
1 Savoy cabbage
salt and ground black pepper

1 Melt the butter in a large pan and fry the onions and celery over a low heat, stirring occasionally, for 5 minutes, until soft. Add the mushrooms and cook until they release their juices, then add the barley, thyme, water and the nut butter. Bring to the boil, lower the heat, cover and simmer for 30 minutes. Crumble in the piece of stock cube, cover again and simmer for 20 minutes more. Season to taste with salt and pepper.

2 Separate the cabbage leaves and cut away the thick stem. Blanch the leaves in a pan of lightly salted boiling water for 3–4 minutes. Drain, refresh under cold running water and then drain well again.

3 Lay a 45cm/18in square of muslin over a steaming basket. Reconstruct the cabbage by lining the muslin with large cabbage leaves. Spread a layer of mushroom barley over the leaves.

4 Cover with a second layer of leaves and filling. Continue until the centre is full. Draw together opposite corners of the muslin and tie firmly.

5 Set the steaming basket in a saucepan containing 2.5cm/1in of simmering water. Cover and steam for 30 minutes.

6 To serve, place on a warmed serving plate, untie the muslin and carefully pull it away from underneath the cabbage.

Potato Rösti & Beancurd Stacks

Although this dish has several components, it is not difficult to make. Serve it with mixed salad leaves.

Serves 4
425g/15oz firm beancurd (tofu),
   cut into 1cm/ ¹/₂ in cubes
4 large potatoes, total weight
   about 900g/2lb, peeled
sunflower oil, for frying
30ml/2 tbsp sesame
   seeds, toasted
salt and ground black pepper

For the marinade
30ml/2 tbsp tamari or dark
   soy sauce
15ml/1 tbsp clear honey
2 garlic cloves, crushed
4cm/1 ¹/₂ in piece of fresh root
   ginger, grated
5ml/1 tsp toasted sesame oil

For the sauce
15ml/1 tbsp olive oil
8 tomatoes, halved, seeded
   and chopped

1 Mix all the marinade ingredients in a shallow dish. Add the beancurd, spoon the marinade over and marinate for 1 hour.

2 Cook the potatoes in a large pan of boiling water for 10–15 minutes, until almost tender. Leave to cool, then grate coarsely. Season well. Preheat the oven to 200°C/400°F/Gas 6.

3 Lift out the beancurd from the marinade. Spread it out on a baking sheet and bake for 20 minutes, turning occasionally, until the cubes are golden and crisp.

4 Form the potato mixture into four cakes. Heat a frying pan with just enough oil to cover the base. Place the cakes in the pan and flatten them to rounds about 1cm/ ½ in thick. Cook for 6 minutes, until golden and crisp underneath. Carefully turn them over and cook the undersides for 6 minutes, until golden.

5 Meanwhile, make the sauce. Heat the oil in a pan, add the reserved marinade and the tomatoes and simmer, stirring occasionally, for 10 minutes. Press through a sieve, then reheat.

6 To serve, place a rösti on each plate. Pile the beancurd on top, spoon over the sauce and sprinkle with the sesame seeds.

Tomato Bread & Butter Pudding

This is a great family dish and is ideal when you don't have time to cook on the day, because it can be prepared in advance.

Serves 4
50g/2oz/ ¹/₄ cup butter, softened
15ml/1 tbsp red pesto sauce
1 garlic and herb focaccia

150g/5oz mozzarella cheese,
   thinly sliced
2 large ripe tomatoes, sliced
300ml/ ¹/₂ pint/1 ¹/₄ cups milk
3 large eggs
5ml/1 tsp fresh chopped oregano,
   plus extra leaves to garnish
50g/2oz/ ¹/₂ cup grated
   Pecorino cheese
salt and ground black pepper

1 Preheat the oven to 180°C/350°F/Gas 4. Mix the butter and pesto sauce in a small bowl. Slice the herb bread and spread one side of each slice with the pesto mixture.

2 In an oval ovenproof dish, layer the slices of herb bread with the mozzarella and tomatoes, overlapping each new layer with the next.

3 Beat the milk, eggs and oregano in a jug, season well with salt and pepper and pour over the bread. Leave to stand for at least 5 minutes.

4 Sprinkle over the grated cheese and bake the pudding for 40 minutes or until golden brown and just set. Sprinkle with whole oregano leaves, and serve immediately.

> **Cook's Tip**
> The longer this stands before baking, the better it will be. Try to leave it for at least half an hour before baking, if you have time.

> **Variation**
> Other cheeses that would go well with this pudding include Fontina, Beaufort, Bel Paese and Taleggio.

Vegetable Crumble

This dish is perennially popular with children, and even those who claim to dislike Brussels sprouts will tuck into it eagerly.

Serves 8
450g/1lb potatoes, peeled
    and halved
25g/1oz/2 tbsp butter
225g/8oz leeks, sliced
450g/1lb carrots, chopped
2 garlic cloves, crushed
225g/8oz/3 cups mushrooms,
    thinly sliced
450g/1lb Brussels sprouts, sliced
salt and ground black pepper

For the cheese crumble
50g/2oz/ ½ cup plain flour
50g/2oz/ ¼ cup butter
50g/2oz/1 cup fresh
    white breadcrumbs
50g/2oz/ ½ cup grated
    Cheddar cheese
30ml/2 tbsp chopped
    fresh parsley
5ml/1 tsp English
    mustard powder

1 Add the potatoes to a pan of lightly salted water. Bring them to the boil and cook for about 15 minutes, until just tender.

2 Meanwhile, melt the butter in a large pan. Add the leeks and carrots and cook over a low heat, stirring occasionally, for 2–3 minutes. Add the garlic and mushrooms and cook, stirring occasionally for 3 minutes more.

3 Add the Brussels sprouts to the pan. Season to taste with pepper. Transfer the vegetable mixture to a 2.5 litre/4 pint/ 10 cup ovenproof dish.

4 Preheat the oven to 200°C/400°F/Gas 6. Drain the potatoes and cut them into 1cm/½in-thick slices. Arrange them in an even layer on top of the other vegetables.

5 To make the crumble, sift the flour into a bowl and rub in the butter with your fingertips. Alternatively, process in a food processor until combined. Add the breadcrumbs and mix in the grated Cheddar, parsley and mustard powder. Spoon the crumble mixture evenly over the vegetables and bake for 20–30 minutes. Serve hot.

Gorgonzola, Cauliflower & Walnut Gratin

A bubbly blue cheese sauce sprinkled with chopped nuts makes a marvellous topping for cauliflower.

Serves 4
1 large cauliflower, broken
    into florets
25g/1oz/2 tbsp butter
1 medium onion, finely chopped
45ml/3 tbsp plain flour
450ml/ ¾ pint/scant 2 cups milk
150g/5oz Gorgonzola, cut
    into pieces
2.5ml/ ½ tsp celery salt
pinch of cayenne pepper
75g/3oz/ ¾ cup chopped walnuts
salt
fresh parsley, to garnish

1 Bring a large saucepan of lightly salted water to the boil and cook the cauliflower for 6 minutes. Drain and place in a flameproof gratin dish.

2 Heat the butter in a heavy-based pan. Add the onion and fry over a low heat, stirring occasionally, for 4–5 minutes, until softened but not coloured.

3 Stir in the flour and cook, stirring constantly, for 1 minute, then gradually add the milk, stirring until the sauce boils and thickens. Stir in the cheese, celery salt and cayenne.

4 Preheat the grill to moderately hot. Spoon the sauce over the cauliflower, scatter with the chopped walnuts and grill until golden. Garnish with the parsley and serve.

Variations
• For a delicious alternative, replace the cauliflower with 1.1kg/2½ lb fresh broccoli or use a combination.
• For a milder flavour, use dolcelatte or Buxton blue cheese instead of Gorgonzola.
• For an even richer sauce, substitute 250ml/8fl oz/1 cup single cream for the same quantity of milk.

Pan Haggerty

A wonderfully old-fashioned dish, this has endured because it is easy to make and always tastes delicious.

Serves 2
30ml/2 tbsp olive oil
25g/1oz/2 tbsp butter

450g/1lb potatoes, thinly sliced
1 large onion, halved and sliced
2 garlic cloves, crushed
115g/4oz/1 cup grated mature
    Cheddar cheese
45ml/3 tbsp snipped fresh chives,
    plus extra to garnish
salt and ground black pepper

1 Heat the oil and butter in a large heavy-based frying pan which can safely be used under the grill. (Cover a wooden handle with foil to protect it.) Remove the pan from the heat and cover the base with a layer of potatoes, followed by layers of onion, garlic, cheese, chives and seasoning.

2 Continue layering, ending with cheese. Cover with foil and cook over a gentle heat for about 30 minutes, or until the potatoes and onion are tender. Remove the foil.

3 Preheat the grill and slide the frying pan under it. Cook until the topping has browned. Garnish with chives and serve.

Bubble & Squeak

Another classic British dish, this is very easy to make. It is a traditional way of using up leftover vegetables, but is also worth cooking with fresh ingredients.

Serves 4
500g/1¼ lb/6 cups
    mashed potato
225g/8oz/2 cups cooked cabbage
60ml/4 tbsp sunflower oil
salt and ground black pepper

1 Mix together the potato and cabbage and season to taste.
2 Heat the oil in a frying pan. Add the potato mixture and press down to make a cake. Fry over a low heat until golden underneath. Invert on to a plate and return to the pan. Cook for about 10 minutes, until golden.

Root Vegetable Gratin with Indian Spices

Subtly spiced with curry powder, turmeric, coriander and mild chilli powder, this rich gratin is substantial enough to serve on its own for lunch or supper.

Serves 4
2 large potatoes, total weight
    about 450g/1lb
2 sweet potatoes, total weight
    about 275g/10oz
175g/6oz celeriac

15g/½ oz/1 tbsp butter
5ml/1 tsp curry powder
5ml/1 tsp ground turmeric
2.5ml/½ tsp ground coriander
5ml/1 tsp mild chilli powder
3 shallots, chopped
150ml/¼ pint/⅔ cup
    single cream
150ml/¼ pint/⅔ cup semi-
    skimmed milk
salt and ground black pepper
chopped fresh flat leaf parsley,
    to garnish

1 Using a sharp knife or the slicing attachment of a food processor, slice the potatoes, sweet potatoes and celeriac thinly. Immediately place the vegetables in a bowl of cold water to prevent them from discolouring.

2 Preheat the oven to 180°C/350°F/Gas 4. Heat half the butter in a heavy-based pan, and add the curry powder, turmeric and coriander and half the chilli powder. Cook for 2 minutes, then leave to cool slightly.

3 Drain the vegetables, then pat them dry with kitchen paper. Place them in a bowl, add the spice mixture and the shallots and mix well.

4 Arrange the vegetables in a gratin dish, seasoning each layer. Mix the cream and milk in a jug. Pour the mixture over the vegetables, then sprinkle the remaining chilli powder on top.

5 Cover with greaseproof paper and bake for 45 minutes. Remove the greaseproof paper, dot with the remaining butter and bake for 50 minutes more, until the top is golden. Serve garnished with chopped fresh parsley.

Cheese & Onion Quiche

Perfect for picnics, parties and family suppers, this classic quiche celebrates a timeless combination.

Serves 6–8
200g/7oz/1¾ cups plain flour
2.5ml/½ tsp salt
90g/3½ oz/scant ½ cup butter
about 60ml/4 tbsp iced water

For the filling
25g/1oz/2 tbsp butter
1 large onion, thinly sliced
3 eggs
300ml/½ pint/1¼ cups
   single cream
1.5ml/¼ tsp freshly
   grated nutmeg
90g/3½ oz/scant 1 cup grated
   hard cheese, such as mature
   Cheddar, Gruyère or Manchego
salt and ground black pepper

1 To make the pastry, sift the flour and salt into a bowl. Rub in the butter with your fingertips, then add enough iced water to make a firm dough. Knead lightly, wrap in clear film and chill in the fridge for 20 minutes.

2 Roll out the dough and line a 23cm/9in loose-based flan tin. Prick the pastry base a few times. Line the flan case with foil and baking beans and chill again for about 15 minutes.

3 Preheat the oven to 200°C/400°F/Gas 6. Place a baking sheet in the oven. Stand the flan tin on the baking sheet and bake blind for 15 minutes. Remove the beans and foil and return the pastry case to the oven for 5 minutes more. Reduce the oven temperature to 180°C/350°F/Gas 4.

4 To make the filling, melt the butter in a heavy-based frying pan. Add the onion and fry over a low heat, stirring occasionally, for 5 minutes, until softened. In a jug, beat together the eggs and cream. Add the nutmeg and season with salt and pepper.

5 Spoon the onion mixture into the cooked pastry case and scatter over the grated cheese. Pour in the egg and cream mixture. Bake the quiche for 35–40 minutes, or until the filling has just set. Cool, then gently ease the quiche out of the tin and place it on a plate for serving.

Mushroom Tart

A mixture of fresh wild mushrooms is best for this simple tart, but if the only mushrooms you can find are cultivated, it is still well worth making.

Serves 4
350g/12oz shortcrust pastry,
   thawed if frozen
50g/2oz/¼ cup butter
3 medium onions, halved
   and sliced

350g/12oz/4 cups mushrooms,
   such as field mushrooms, ceps
   and oyster mushrooms, sliced
leaves from 1 fresh thyme
   sprig, chopped
pinch of freshly grated nutmeg
45ml/3 tbsp milk
60ml/4 tbsp single cream
1 egg, plus 2 egg yolks
salt and ground black pepper

1 Roll out the pastry on a lightly floured surface and line a 23cm/9in loose-based flan tin. Place the flan case in the fridge to rest for about 1 hour.

2 Preheat the oven to 190°C/375°F/Gas 5. Prick the pastry base a few times with a fork, then line the flan case with foil and fill it with baking beans. Bake blind for 25 minutes. Lift out the paper and baking beans and leave the case to cool without removing it from the tin.

3 Melt the butter in a heavy-based frying pan, add the sliced onions, cover and cook over a very low heat, stirring occasionally, for about 20 minutes, until very soft and beginning to caramelize. Add the sliced mushrooms and thyme leaves, and continue cooking, stirring occasionally, for a further 10 minutes. Season to taste with salt, freshly ground black pepper and nutmeg.

4 Mix the milk and cream in a jug and beat in the egg and egg yolks. Spoon the mushroom mixture into the flan case and level the surface. Pour over the milk and egg mixture. Bake for 15–20 minutes, until the centre is just firm to the touch. Cool slightly, then gently ease the tart out of the tin and place it on a plate for serving.

Cheese & Leek Sausages with Spicy Tomato Sauce

These are based on Glamorgan sausages, which are traditionally made using white or wholemeal breadcrumbs alone. However, adding a little mashed potato lightens the sausages and makes them much easier to handle.

Serves 4
25g/1oz/2 tbsp butter
175g/6oz leeks, finely chopped
90ml/6 tbsp cold mashed potato
115g/4oz/2 cups fresh
 white breadcrumbs
150g/5oz/1¼ cups grated
 Caerphilly cheese
30ml/2 tbsp chopped
 fresh parsley
5ml/1 tsp chopped fresh sage

2 large eggs, beaten
cayenne pepper
65g/2½ oz/1 cup dry
 white breadcrumbs
oil, for shallow frying
salt and ground black pepper

For the sauce
30ml/2 tbsp olive oil
2 garlic cloves, thinly sliced
1 fresh red chilli, seeded and
 finely chopped
1 small onion, finely chopped
500g/1¼ lb tomatoes, peeled,
 seeded and chopped
2–3 fresh thyme sprigs
10ml/2 tsp balsamic vinegar
pinch of light muscovado sugar
15–30ml/1–2 tbsp chopped
 fresh marjoram

1 Melt the butter in a frying pan. Add the leeks and fry over a low heat, stirring occasionally, for 4–5 minutes, until softened but not browned.

2 Mix the leeks with the mashed potato, fresh breadcrumbs, grated cheese, parsley and sage. Add about two-thirds of the beaten eggs to bind the mixture. Season well with salt and pepper and add a good pinch of cayenne.

3 Shape the mixture into 12 sausages. Put the remaining egg in a shallow dish and the dry breadcrumbs in another shallow dish. Dip the sausages first in egg, then in the dry breadcrumbs, shaking off any excess. Place the coated sausages on a plate, cover and chill in the fridge.

4 To make the sauce, heat the olive oil over a low heat. Add the garlic, chilli and onion and fry, stirring occasionally, for 3–4 minutes. Add the tomatoes, thyme and vinegar. Season to taste with salt, pepper and sugar.

5 Cook the sauce for 40–50 minutes, until much reduced. Remove the thyme and process the sauce in a blender to a purée. Return to the clean pan and add the marjoram. Reheat gently, then adjust the seasoning, adding more sugar, if necessary.

6 Fry the sausages in shallow oil until golden brown on all sides. Drain on kitchen paper and serve with the sauce.

Variation
These sausages are also delicious served with aïoli, guacamole or chilli jam.

Mixed Vegetables with Artichokes

Baking a vegetable medley in the oven is a wonderfully easy way of producing a quick, simple, wholesome mid-week meal.

Serves 4
30ml/2 tbsp olive oil
675g/1½ lb frozen broad beans
4 turnips, peeled and sliced

4 leeks, sliced
1 red pepper, seeded and sliced
200g/7oz fresh spinach leaves
2 x 400g/14oz cans artichoke
 hearts, drained
60ml/4 tbsp pumpkin seeds
soy sauce
salt and ground black pepper

1 Preheat the oven to 180°C/350°F/Gas 4. Pour the olive oil into a casserole and set aside.

2 Cook the broad beans in a saucepan of lightly salted boiling water for about 10 minutes.

3 Drain the broad beans and place them in the casserole. Add the turnips, leeks, red pepper slices, spinach and canned artichoke hearts.

4 Cover the casserole and place it in the oven. Bake for 30–40 minutes, or until the turnips are soft.

5 Stir in the pumpkin seeds and a little soy sauce to taste. Season with ground black pepper and serve.

Cook's Tip
Serve this with pasta, rice, new potatoes or bread.

Variation
For a delicious change, top the cooked vegetables with a mixture of wholemeal breadcrumbs and grated Cheddar cheese. Grill until the cheese melts and the topping is golden.

Vegetable Stew with Roasted Tomato & Garlic Sauce

This lightly-spiced, richly flavoured stew makes a perfect match for couscous.

Serves 6
45ml/3 tbsp olive oil
250g/9oz shallots
1 large onion, chopped
2 garlic cloves, chopped
5ml/1 tsp cumin seeds
5ml/1 tsp ground coriander seeds
5ml/1 tsp paprika
10cm/4in piece cinnamon stick
2 fresh bay leaves
about 450ml/³/₄ pint/scant
    2 cups vegetable stock
good pinch of saffron strands
450g/1lb carrots, thickly sliced
2 green peppers, seeded and
    thickly sliced
115g/4oz/¹/₂ cup ready-to-eat
    dried apricots, halved if large
5–7.5ml/1–1¹/₂ tsp ground
    toasted cumin seeds
450g/1lb squash, peeled, seeded
    and cut into chunks
salt and ground black pepper
45ml/3 tbsp fresh coriander
    leaves, to garnish

For the sauce
1kg/2¹/₄ lb tomatoes, halved
about 5ml/1 tsp granulated sugar
45ml/3 tbsp olive oil
1–2 fresh red chillies, seeded
    and chopped
2–3 garlic cloves, chopped
5ml/1 tsp fresh thyme leaves

1 Preheat the oven to 180°C/350°F/Gas 4. First make the sauce. Place the tomatoes, cut sides uppermost, in an ovenproof dish. Season with salt and pepper to taste, sprinkle the sugar over the top, then drizzle with the olive oil. Roast for 30 minutes.

2 Scatter the chillies, garlic and thyme over the tomatoes. Stir, then roast for a further 30–45 minutes, until the tomatoes have collapsed, but are still a little juicy. Cool, then process in a food processor or blender to make a thick sauce. Sieve to remove the seeds.

3 Heat 30ml/2 tbsp of the oil in a large, deep, frying pan. Add the shallots and cook over a low heat, stirring frequently, until browned all over. Remove them from the pan and set aside.

4 Add the chopped onion to the pan and cook over a low heat, stirring occasionally, for 5–7 minutes, until softened. Stir in the garlic and cumin seeds and cook for 3–4 minutes more.

5 Add the ground coriander seeds, paprika, cinnamon stick and bay leaves. Cook, stirring constantly, for 2 minutes, then mix in the stock, saffron, carrots and peppers. Season well with salt and pepper, cover and simmer gently for 10 minutes.

6 Stir in the apricots, 5ml/1 tsp of the ground toasted cumin, the browned shallots and the squash. Stir in the tomato sauce. Cover and cook for a further 5 minutes.

7 Uncover the pan and continue to cook, stirring occasionally, for 10–15 minutes, until the vegetables are all fully cooked. Adjust the seasoning, adding more cumin and a pinch of sugar to taste. Remove and discard the cinnamon stick and bay leaves. Serve, scattered with the fresh coriander leaves.

Roasted Vegetables with Salsa Verde

Fresh herbs are at the heart of the Italian salsa verde (green sauce). It tastes wonderful with the vegetable mixture. Serve it with rice or a mixture of rice and vermicelli.

Serves 4
3 courgettes, sliced lengthways
1 large fennel bulb, cut
    into wedges
450g/1lb butternut squash, cut
    into 2cm/³/₄in chunks
12 shallots
2 red peppers, seeded and
    thickly sliced
4 plum tomatoes, halved
    and seeded
45ml/3 tbsp olive oil
2 garlic cloves, crushed
5ml/1 tsp balsamic vinegar
salt and ground black pepper

For the salsa verde
45ml/3 tbsp chopped fresh mint
90ml/6 tbsp chopped fresh flat
    leaf parsley
15ml/1 tbsp Dijon mustard
juice of ¹/₂ lemon
30ml/2 tbsp olive oil

1 Preheat the oven to 220°C/425°F/Gas 7. Make the salsa verde. Place all the ingredients, except the olive oil, in a food processor or blender. Blend to a coarse paste, then add the oil, a little at a time, until the mixture forms a smooth purée. Season to taste with salt and pepper.

2 In a large bowl, toss the courgettes, fennel, squash, shallots, peppers and tomatoes in the olive oil, garlic and balsamic vinegar. Leave for 10 minutes to allow the flavours to mingle.

3 Place all the vegetables – apart from the squash and tomatoes – in a roasting tin. Brush with half the oil and vinegar mixture and season with plenty of salt and pepper.

4 Roast for 25 minutes. Remove the roasting tin from the oven, turn the vegetables over and brush with the rest of the oil and vinegar mixture. Add the squash and tomatoes and cook for 20–25 minutes more, until all the vegetables are tender and lightly charred around the edges. Spoon the roasted vegetables on to a serving platter and serve with the salsa verde.

Bean Feast with Mexican Salsa

Canned beans really come into their own when you need to make a nutritious meal in double-quick time.

Serves 4

400g/14oz can red kidney beans
400g/14oz can flageolet beans
400g/14oz can borlotti beans
15ml/1 tbsp olive oil
1 small onion, finely chopped
3 garlic cloves, finely chopped
1 fresh red chilli, seeded and
   finely chopped
1 red pepper, seeded and
   coarsely chopped
2 bay leaves
10ml/2 tsp chopped
   fresh oregano
10ml/2 tsp ground cumin

5ml/1 tsp ground coriander
2.5ml/½ tsp ground cloves
15ml/1 tbsp soft dark
   brown sugar
300ml/½ pint/1¼ cups
   vegetable stock
salt and ground black pepper
fresh coriander sprigs, to garnish

For the salsa

1 ripe but firm avocado
45ml/3 tbsp freshly squeezed
   lime juice
1 small red onion, chopped
1 small fresh hot green chilli,
   finely sliced
3 ripe plum tomatoes, peeled,
   seeded and chopped
45ml/3 tbsp chopped
   fresh coriander

1 Drain all the beans in a colander and rinse thoroughly. Heat the oil in a heavy-based saucepan. Add the onion and fry over a low heat, stirring occasionally, for 3 minutes, until soft and transparent. Add the garlic, chilli, red pepper, bay leaves, oregano, cumin, coriander and cloves.

2 Stir well and cook for a further 3 minutes, then add the sugar, beans and stock and cook for 8 minutes. Season with salt and pepper, and leave over a low heat while you make the salsa.

3 Cut the avocado in half, remove the stone, then peel it and dice the flesh. Toss it with the lime juice, then add all the remaining salsa ingredients and season with plenty of black pepper. Mix well.

4 Spoon the beans into four serving bowls. Garnish with sprigs of fresh coriander and serve with the salsa.

Tuscan Baked Beans

Cannellini beans are delicious with garlic and sage in this tasty bake, which can be served hot or at room temperature.

Serves 6–8

600g/1lb 6oz/3½ cups dried
   cannellini beans
60ml/4 tbsp olive oil
2 garlic cloves, crushed
3 fresh sage leaves
1 leek, thinly sliced
400g/14oz can
   chopped tomatoes
salt and ground black pepper

1 Carefully pick over the beans, place them in a large bowl and cover with water. Soak for at least 6 hours, or overnight.

2 Preheat the oven to 180°C/350°F/Gas 4. Heat the oil in a small saucepan. Add the garlic cloves and sage leaves and sauté over a low heat, stirring occasionally, for 3–4 minutes. Remove the pan from the heat.

3 Drain the cannellini beans and put them in a saucepan with cold water to cover. Bring to the boil and boil vigorously for 10 minutes. Drain again.

4 Tip the beans into a casserole and add the leek and tomatoes. Stir in the garlic and sage, with the oil in which they were cooked. Add enough cold water to cover the beans by 2.5cm/1in. Mix well. Cover the casserole and bake for 1¾ hours.

5 Remove the casserole from the oven, stir the bean mixture, and season to taste with salt and pepper. Return the casserole to the oven, uncovered, and cook for 15 minutes more, until the beans are tender. Remove from the oven and allow to stand for 7–8 minutes before serving.

Cook's Tip
Cannellini beans are also known as Italian haricot beans.

Chick-pea Stew

This hearty chick-pea and vegetable stew makes a filling meal.

Serves 4
30ml/2 tbsp olive oil
1 small onion, chopped
225g/8oz carrots, halved and
    thinly sliced
2.5ml/ ½ tsp ground cumin
5ml/1 tsp ground coriander
30ml/2 tbsp plain flour

225g/8oz courgettes, halved
    lengthways and sliced
200g/7oz can sweetcorn
    kernels, drained
400g/14oz can chick-peas,
    drained and rinsed
30ml/2 tbsp tomato purée
200ml/7fl oz/scant 1 cup hot
    vegetable stock
salt and ground black pepper
garlic-flavoured mashed potato,
    to serve

1 Heat the oil in a frying pan. Add the onion and carrots. Toss to coat the vegetables in the oil, then cook over a medium heat, stirring occasionally, for 4 minutes.

2 Stir in the ground cumin, coriander and flour. Cook, stirring constantly, for 1 minute.

3 Add the courgette slices to the pan with the sweetcorn, chick-peas, tomato purée and vegetable stock. Stir well. Cook for 10 minutes, stirring frequently.

4 Taste the stew and season with salt and pepper. Serve at once, with garlic-flavoured mashed potato (see Cook's Tip), if you like.

Cook's Tip
For speedy garlic-flavoured mashed potatoes, simply mash 675g/1½lb potatoes with garlic butter and stir in chopped fresh parsley and a little crème fraîche. Alternatively, add 10–12 peeled garlic cloves to the potatoes during cooking and then mash with the potatoes, adding butter, herbs and crème fraîche to taste. This may seem an alarming quantity of garlic, but the flavour is actually quite subtle.

Shepherdess Pie

A no-meat version of the timeless classic, this dish does not contain any dairy products, so it is also suitable for vegans.

Serves 6–8
1kg/2¼ lb potatoes
45ml/3 tbsp extra virgin olive oil
45ml/3 tbsp sunflower oil
1 large onion, chopped
1 green pepper, chopped
2 carrots, coarsely grated

2 garlic cloves
115g/4oz/1¼ cups mushrooms,
    roughly chopped
2 x 400g/14oz cans aduki
    beans, drained
600ml/1 pint/2½ cups
    vegetable stock
5ml/1 tsp yeast extract
2 bay leaves
5ml/1 tsp dried mixed herbs
dried breadcrumbs or chopped
    nuts, for the topping
salt and ground black pepper

1 Bring a large pan of water to the boil. Add the unpeeled potatoes and cook for about 30 minutes, until tender. Drain, reserving a little of the cooking water.

2 As soon as the potatoes are cool enough to handle, remove the skins. Put the skinned potatoes in a bowl and mash them with the olive oil, adding enough of the reserved cooking water to make a smooth purée. Season well with salt and pepper.

3 Heat the sunflower oil in a large, heavy-based frying pan. Add the chopped onion, green pepper, carrots and garlic and fry over a low heat, stirring occasionally, for about 5 minutes, until softened.

4 Stir in the mushrooms and beans. Cook for 2 minutes more, then stir in the stock, yeast extract, bay leaves and mixed herbs. Simmer for 15 minutes.

5 Preheat the grill. Remove and discard the bay leaves from the vegetable and bean mixture, then tip it into a gratin dish. Spoon on the mashed potatoes in dollops and sprinkle the breadcrumbs or chopped nuts over the top. Grill for 5 minutes, until the topping is golden brown. Serve immediately straight from the dish.

Veggie Burgers

Unlike some commercially-produced veggie burgers, which are decidedly dreary, these are full of flavour.

Serves 4

115g/4oz/1¼ cups mushrooms, finely chopped
1 small onion, chopped
1 small courgette, chopped
1 carrot, chopped
25g/1oz/¼ cup unsalted peanuts or cashews
115g/4oz/2 cups fresh breadcrumbs
30ml/2 tbsp chopped fresh parsley
5ml/1 tsp yeast extract
fine oatmeal or flour, for shaping
a little vegetable oil, for frying
salt and ground black pepper
salad, to serve

1 Cook the mushrooms in a non-stick pan without oil, stirring them constantly, for 8–10 minutes to drive off all the moisture.

2 Process the onion, courgette, carrot and nuts in a food processor until the mixture starts to bind together. Scrape it into a bowl.

3 Stir in the mushrooms, breadcrumbs, parsley and yeast extract to taste. Season to taste. Coat your hands and a board with the oatmeal or flour, then shape the mixture into four burgers. Chill in the fridge for 30 minutes.

4 Heat a little oil in a non-stick frying pan and cook the burgers for 8–10 minutes, turning once, until they are cooked and golden brown. Serve hot with a crisp salad.

> **Cook's Tip**
> These burgers can be cooked on a barbecue, but do not place them directly on the grill, as they are quite delicate and likely to break up. Use a wire rack or foil dish and brush with a little vegetable oil on both sides.

Marinated Beancurd Kebabs

Perfect partners for both the vegetarian burgers featured here, these kebabs are very easy to make.

Serves 4

30ml/2 tbsp soy sauce
5ml/1 tsp groundnut oil
5ml/1 tsp sesame oil
1 garlic clove, crushed
15ml/1 tbsp grated fresh root ginger
15ml/1 tbsp clear honey
225g/8oz firm beancurd (tofu), cut into 1cm/½ in cubes
2 small courgettes, thickly sliced
8 baby onions
8 mushrooms

1 Mix together the soy sauce, groundnut oil, sesame oil, garlic, ginger and honey in a shallow dish. Add the beancurd (tofu) cubes and marinate for 1–2 hours.
2 Drain the beancurd cubes, reserving the marinade, and thread onto four long metal skewers, alternating with the vegetables. Brush with the reserved marinade and grill or barbecue until golden, turning occasionally.

Red Bean & Mushroom Burgers

Whether you cook these tasty burgers under the grill or on the barbecue, they are certain to prove popular with everyone.

Serves 4

15ml/1 tbsp olive oil, plus extra for brushing
1 small onion, finely chopped
1 garlic clove, crushed
5ml/1 tsp ground cumin
5ml/1 tsp ground coriander
2.5ml/½ tsp ground turmeric
115g/4oz/1½ cups finely chopped mushrooms
400g/14oz can red kidney beans, drained and rinsed
30ml/2 tbsp chopped fresh coriander
wholemeal flour, for forming the burgers
salt and ground black pepper

To serve

warm pitta bread
Greek-style yogurt
salad leaves and tomatoes

1 Heat the olive oil in a deep, heavy-based frying pan. Add the onion and garlic and fry over a medium heat, stirring occasionally, for about 4 minutes, until softened. Add the cumin, ground coriander and turmeric and cook for 1 minute more, stirring constantly.

2 Add the mushrooms and cook, stirring, until softened and dry. Remove the pan from the heat.

3 Tip the beans into a bowl and then mash them with a fork. Stir them into the mushroom mixture, then add the fresh coriander, mixing thoroughly. Season well with salt and pepper.

4 Using floured hands, form the mixture into four flat burger shapes. If the mixture is too sticky to handle, mix in a little flour. Preheat the grill.

5 Brush the burgers with oil and grill them for 8–10 minutes, turning once, until golden brown. Alternatively, cook on the barbecue, using a wire rack to turn them easily.

6 Serve immediately with warm pitta bread, Greek-style yogurt, crisp green salad leaves and tomatoes.

Pasta with Spicy Aubergine Sauce

There's no better way to satisfy hearty appetites than with a big bowl of pasta in a rich and robust sauce.

Serves 4–6
30ml/2 tbsp olive oil
1 small fresh red chilli
2 garlic cloves
2 handfuls fresh flat leaf parsley, roughly chopped
450g/1lb aubergines, roughly chopped
1 handful of fresh basil leaves
200ml/7fl oz/scant 1 cup water
1 vegetable stock cube
8 ripe Italian plum tomatoes, peeled and finely chopped
60ml/4 tbsp red wine
5ml/1 tsp granulated sugar
1 sachet saffron powder
2.5ml/ 1/2 tsp ground paprika
350g/12oz/3 cups dried pasta shapes
salt and ground black pepper
fresh chopped herbs, to garnish

1 Heat the oil in a large pan and add the chilli, garlic cloves and half the chopped parsley. Smash the garlic cloves with a wooden spoon to release their juices, then cover the pan and cook over a low heat, stirring occasionally, for about 10 minutes.

2 Remove and discard the chilli. Add the aubergines to the pan with the rest of the parsley and all the basil. Pour in half the water. Crumble in the stock cube and stir until it has dissolved, then cover and cook, stirring frequently, for about 10 minutes.

3 Add the tomatoes, wine, sugar, saffron and paprika, season with salt and pepper, then pour in the remaining water. Stir well, replace the lid and cook, stirring occasionally, for 30–40 minutes.

4 When the sauce is almost ready, bring a pan of lightly salted water to the boil. Cook the pasta for about 12 minutes, until it is *al dente*. Drain, tip into a bowl and toss with the aubergine sauce. Garnish with fresh herbs, and serve.

> **Variation**
> This sauce can be layered with sheets of pasta and béchamel or cheese sauce to make a delicious vegetarian lasagne.

Pasta with Sugocasa & Chilli

This is a quick version of a popular Italian dish, *pasta arrabbiata*. The name literally translates as "furious pasta", a reference to the heat generated by the chilli.

Serves 4
475ml/16fl oz/2 cups bottled sugocasa (see Cook's Tip)
2 garlic cloves, crushed
150ml/ 1/4 pint/ 2/3 cup dry white wine
15ml/1 tbsp sun-dried tomato paste
1 fresh red chilli
300g/11oz dried penne or other pasta shapes
60ml/4 tbsp finely chopped fresh flat leaf parsley
salt and ground black pepper
freshly grated Pecorino cheese, to serve

1 Put the sugocasa, garlic, wine, sun-dried tomato paste and chilli in a saucepan and bring to the boil. Lower the heat, cover and simmer for about 15 minutes, until thick.

2 Meanwhile, bring a large pan of lightly salted water to the boil. Add the pasta shapes and cook for 10–12 minutes, until they are *al dente*.

3 Using tongs, remove the chilli from the sauce. Taste for seasoning. If you prefer a hotter taste, chop some or all of the chilli and return it to the sauce.

4 Drain the pasta and tip it into a large bowl. Stir half the parsley into the sauce, then pour the sauce over the pasta and toss to mix. Serve at once, sprinkled with grated Pecorino and the remaining parsley.

> **Cook's Tip**
> Sugocasa is sold in bottles and is sometimes labelled "crushed Italian tomatoes". It is finer than canned chopped tomatoes and coarser than passata, and so is ideal for pasta sauces, soups and stews.

Mushroom & Chilli Carbonara

Classic spaghetti carbonara hits the hot spot when chillies and mushrooms enter the equation.

Serves 4

15g/ ½ oz dried
   porcini mushrooms
300ml/ ½ pint/1¼ cups
   hot water
225g/8oz spaghetti
25g/1oz/2 tbsp butter
15ml/1 tbsp olive oil
1 garlic clove, crushed
225g/8oz/3 cups button or
   chestnut mushrooms, sliced
5ml/1 tsp dried chilli flakes
2 eggs
300ml/ ½ pint/1¼ cups
   single cream
salt and ground black pepper
freshly shaved Parmesan cheese
   and chopped parsley, to serve

1 Put the dried mushrooms in a bowl, cover with the hot water and soak for 20–30 minutes. Drain, reserving the soaking liquid.

2 Bring a large pan of lightly salted water to the boil and cook the spaghetti for 10–12 minutes, until it is *al dente*. Drain, rinse under cold water and drain again.

3 Melt the butter in the oil in a separate pan. Add the garlic and cook gently for 30 seconds, then add the mushrooms, including the soaked dried mushrooms. Stir in the dried chilli flakes and cook for about 2 minutes. Strain the liquid used for soaking the mushrooms and add it to the pan. Bring to the boil and cook over a high heat until the sauce has reduced slightly.

4 Beat the eggs with the cream and plenty of salt and pepper. Add the cooked spaghetti to the mushroom mixture and toss in the eggs and cream. Reheat, without boiling, and serve hot, sprinkled with the Parmesan and chopped parsley.

> **Variation**
> *If chilli flakes are too hot and spicy for your taste, try the delicious alternative of peeled and chopped tomatoes with torn, fresh basil leaves.*

Spinach, Tomato & Chilli Pizza

The fiery flavour of hot chillies is soothed slightly by the spinach in the colourful topping on this pizza.

Serves 2–3

6 sun-dried tomatoes in oil,
   drained, plus 45ml/3 tbsp oil
   from the jar
1 onion, chopped
2 garlic cloves, chopped
1–2 fresh red chillies, seeded and
   finely chopped
400g/14oz can
   chopped tomatoes
15ml/1 tbsp tomato purée
175g/6oz fresh spinach
1 pizza base, 25–30cm/10–12in
   in diameter
75g/3oz/¾ cup grated smoked
   Bavarian cheese
175g/6oz/1½ cups grated
   mature Cheddar cheese
salt and ground black pepper

1 Pour 30ml/2 tbsp of the oil from the jar of sun-dried tomatoes into a large, heavy-based pan. Heat gently, then add the onion, garlic and chillies and fry over a low heat, stirring occasionally, for about 5 minutes, until softened.

2 Roughly chop the sun-dried tomatoes. Add them to the pan, together with the chopped tomatoes and tomato purée. Season with plenty of salt and pepper. Simmer uncovered, over a low heat, stirring occasionally, for 15 minutes.

3 Remove the stalks from the spinach and wash the leaves in plenty of cold water. Drain well and pat dry with kitchen paper. Chop the spinach roughly.

4 Stir the spinach into the sauce. Cook, stirring constantly, for 5–10 minutes more, until the spinach has just wilted and no excess moisture remains. Remove the pan from the heat and set aside to cool.

5 Preheat the oven to 220°C/425°F/Gas 7. Brush the pizza base with the remaining tomato oil, then spoon the spinach mixture evenly over the surface, leaving a 1 cm/½in border all around. Sprinkle over the grated cheeses and bake the pizza for 15–20 minutes, until crisp and golden. Serve immediately.

Indian Mee Goreng

This is a truly international dish combining Indian, Chinese and Western ingredients. It is a delicious treat for lunch or supper.

Serves 4–6
450g/1lb fresh yellow egg noodles
60–90ml/4–6 tbsp vegetable oil
150g/5oz firm beancurd
    (tofu), cubed
2 eggs
30ml/2 tbsp water
1 onion, sliced
1 garlic clove, crushed
15ml/1 tbsp light soy sauce
30–45ml/2–3 tbsp
    tomato ketchup
15ml/1 tbsp chilli sauce
1 large cooked potato, diced
4 spring onions, shredded
1–2 fresh green chillies, seeded
    and finely sliced
salt and ground black pepper

1 Bring a large pan of water to the boil, add the fresh egg noodles and cook for just 2 minutes. Drain the noodles and immediately rinse them under cold water. Drain well again and then set aside.

2 Heat 30ml/2 tbsp of the oil in a large frying pan. Fry the beancurd (tofu) until brown, then lift it out with a draining spoon and set it aside.

3 Beat the eggs with the water and a little seasoning. Make an omelette by adding it to the oil in the frying pan and cooking it, without stirring, until it sets. Flip over, cook the other side, then slide it out of the pan, roll up and slice thinly.

4 Heat the remaining oil in a wok and fry the onion and garlic for 2–3 minutes. Add the drained noodles, soy sauce, ketchup and chilli sauce. Toss well over medium heat for 2 minutes, then add the diced potato.

5 Reserve a few spring onions for garnishing, then stir the rest into the noodles. Add the chillies and the beancurd and toss lightly until heated through.

6 Stir in the omelette. Pile on a hot platter, garnish with the remaining spring onions and serve immediately.

Crispy Noodles with Mixed Vegetables

Deep-frying noodles gives them a lovely, crunchy texture. They taste great in this colourful stir-fry.

Serves 3–4
115g/4oz dried vermicelli rice
    noodles or cellophane noodles
groundnut oil, for deep-frying
115g/4oz yard-long beans or
    green beans, cut into
    short lengths
2.5cm/1in piece of fresh root
    ginger, cut into shreds
1 fresh red chilli, sliced
115g/4oz/1½ cups fresh shiitake
    or button mushrooms,
    thickly sliced
2 large carrots, cut into thin strips
2 courgettes, cut into thin strips
a few Chinese cabbage leaves,
    coarsely shredded
75g/3oz/¾ cup beansprouts
4 spring onions, shredded
30ml/2 tbsp light soy sauce
30ml/2 tbsp Chinese rice wine
5ml/1 tsp granulated sugar
30ml/2 tbsp roughly torn fresh
    coriander leaves

1 Break the noodles into 7.5cm/3in lengths. Half-fill a wok with oil and heat it to 180°C/350°F. Deep-fry the raw noodles, in batches, for 1–2 minutes until puffed and crispy. Drain on kitchen paper. Carefully pour off all but 30ml/2 tbsp of the oil.

2 Reheat the oil in the wok. When hot, add the beans and stir-fry for 2–3 minutes. Add the ginger, chilli, mushrooms, carrots and courgettes and stir-fry for 1–2 minutes.

3 Add the Chinese cabbage, beansprouts and spring onions. Toss over the heat for 1 minute, then add the soy sauce, rice wine and sugar. Cook, stirring, for about 30 seconds.

4 Add the noodles and coriander and toss to mix, without crushing the noodles. Serve at once, piled on a plate.

Cook's Tip
If a milder flavour is preferred, remove the seeds from the chilli.

Chillies Rellenos

Slice open one of these delicious deep-fried chillies or peppers and you'll be rewarded with a melted cheese filling.

Serves 4

8 large fresh green chillies or
    small green peppers
15–30ml/1–2 tbsp vegetable oil,
    plus extra for frying
450g/1lb/4 cups grated
    Cheddar cheese
4 eggs, separated

40g/1½ oz/⅔ cup flour
fresh coriander sprigs, to garnish

For the sauce
15ml/1 tbsp vegetable oil
1 small onion, finely chopped
1.5ml/¼ tsp salt
5–10ml/1–2 tsp dried chilli flakes
2.5ml/½ tsp ground cumin
250ml/8fl oz/1 cup
    vegetable stock
2 x 400g/14oz cans
    chopped tomatoes

1 First, make the sauce. Heat the oil in a heavy-based frying pan. Add the onion and fry over a low heat, stirring occasionally, for 5 minutes, until just soft. Stir in the salt, chilli flakes, cumin, stock and tomatoes. Cover and simmer gently for 5 minutes, stirring occasionally.

2 Remove the pan from the heat and cool slightly. Tip the mixture into a food processor or blender and process until smooth. Strain into a clean pan. Bring to the boil, then lower the heat to a bare simmer.

3 Preheat the grill. Brush the chillies or peppers lightly all over with vegetable oil. Spread them out in a single layer on a baking sheet. Grill as close to the heat as possible until charred all over. Place them in a bowl, cover with kitchen paper and set aside for 5–10 minutes.

4 When the chillies or peppers are cool enough to handle, rub off the skins. Carefully slit the chillies or peppers and scoop out the seeds.

5 Form the cheese into eight cylinders and place them inside the chillies or peppers. Secure the slits with wooden cocktail sticks. Set aside.

6 Beat the egg whites until just stiff. Add the egg yolks, one at a time, beating on low speed just to incorporate them. Beat in 15ml/1 tbsp of the flour.

7 Pour vegetable oil into a large frying pan to a depth of 2.5cm/1in and heat. Coat the chillies or peppers lightly in flour. Dip them into the egg batter, then place in the hot oil. Fry for about 2 minutes, until brown on one side. Turn carefully and brown the other side. Drain, garnish with coriander sprigs and serve immediately with the sauce.

Variation
If using peppers instead of fresh chillies, mix the grated cheese with about 10ml/2 tsp hot chilli powder for a more authentic, Tex-Mex taste.

Jalapeño & Onion Quiche

Not too fiery, but with a distinctive Tex-Mex flavour, this is good served hot or at room temperature.

Serves 6
15g/½ oz/1 tbsp butter
2 onions, sliced
4 spring onions, chopped
2.5ml/½ tsp ground cumin
15–30ml/1–2 tbsp chopped
    canned jalapeño chillies
4 eggs

300ml/½ pint/1¼ cups milk
2.5ml/½ tsp salt
75g/3oz/¾ cup grated
    Cheddar cheese
fresh parsley sprig, to garnish

For the pastry
175g/6oz/1½ cups plain flour
1.5ml/¼ tsp salt
1.5ml/¼ tsp cayenne pepper
75g/3oz/6 tbsp cold butter
75g/3oz/6 tbsp cold margarine
30–60ml/2–4 tbsp iced water

1 First, make the pastry. Sift the flour, salt and cayenne into a bowl. Rub in the butter and margarine until the mixture resembles breadcrumbs, then add enough iced water to bind the mixture. Wrap in clear film and chill for at least 30 minutes.

2 Preheat the oven to 190°C/375°F/Gas 5. Roll out the pastry and line a 23cm/9in loose-based quiche tin. Prick the base of the pastry case, then line with non-stick baking paper and fill with baking beans.

3 Bake for 15 minutes, then remove from the oven and carefully lift out the paper and baking beans. Return the pastry case to the oven and bake for 5–8 minutes more until golden. Leave the oven on.

4 Melt the butter in a pan and cook the sliced onions until softened. Add the spring onions and cook for 1 minute more. Stir in the cumin and jalapeños and set aside.

5 In a jug, whisk the eggs with the milk and salt.

6 Spoon the onion mixture into the pastry case. Sprinkle with the cheese, then pour in the egg mixture. Bake for about 40 minutes, until the filling is golden and set. Garnish with parsley.

Chilli Cheese Tortilla with Salsa

Good warm or cold, this is like a quiche without the pastry base. Cheese and chillies are more than a match for each other.

Serves 4
45ml/3 tbsp olive oil
1 small onion, thinly sliced
2–3 fresh green jalapeño chillies, sliced
200g/7oz cold cooked potato, thinly sliced
130g/4¼ oz/generous 1 cup grated Cheddar cheese
6 eggs, beaten
salt and ground black pepper
fresh herbs, to garnish

For the salsa
500g/1¼ lb tomatoes, peeled, seeded and finely chopped
1 fresh mild green chilli, seeded and finely chopped
2 garlic cloves, crushed
45ml/3 tbsp chopped fresh coriander
juice of 1 lime
2.5ml/½ tsp salt

1 First, make the salsa. Put the tomatoes in a bowl and add the chilli, garlic, coriander, lime juice and salt. Mix well and set aside.

2 Heat half the oil in a large omelette pan and gently fry the onion and jalapeños, stirring occasionally, for 5 minutes, until softened. Add the potato and cook for 5 minutes more, until lightly browned, taking care to keep the slices whole.

3 Using a draining spoon, transfer the vegetables to a warm plate. Wipe the pan with kitchen paper, then pour in the remaining oil. Heat well, return the vegetable mixture to the pan and season to taste. Scatter the cheese over the top.

4 Pour in the eggs, making sure that they seep under the vegetables. Cook over a gentle heat until set. Serve in wedges, garnished with fresh herbs, with the salsa on the side.

> **Cook's Tip**
> If you use a frying pan with a flameproof handle, you can brown the top of the tortilla under a hot grill.

Rice & Beans with Avocado Salsa

Mexican-style rice and beans make a tasty supper dish.

Serves 4
4 tomatoes, halved and seeded
2 garlic cloves, chopped
1 onion, sliced
45ml/3 tbsp olive oil
225g/8oz/generous 1 cup long grain brown rice, rinsed
600ml/1 pint/2½ cups vegetable stock
75g/3oz/½ cup canned kidney beans, rinsed and drained
2 carrots, diced
75g/3oz green beans
salt and ground black pepper
4 wheat tortillas and soured cream, to serve
15ml/1 tbsp chopped fresh coriander, to garnish

For the salsa
1 avocado
juice of 1 lime
1 small red onion, diced
1 small fresh red chilli, seeded and chopped

1 Preheat the grill. Spread out the tomatoes, garlic and onion in a grill pan. Pour over 15ml/1 tbsp of the olive oil and toss to coat. Grill for 10 minutes, turning once. Set aside to cool.

2 Heat the remaining oil in a saucepan, add the rice and cook for 2 minutes, stirring constantly, until light golden.

3 Process the cooked tomato mixture in a food processor or blender, then scrape into the rice and cook for 2 minutes more, stirring frequently. Pour in the stock, cover and cook gently for 20 minutes, stirring occasionally.

4 Reserve 30ml/2 tbsp of the kidney beans for the salsa. Add the rest to the rice mixture with the carrots and green beans. Cook for 10 minutes, until the vegetables are tender. Season well. Remove the pan from the heat and leave to stand, covered, for 15 minutes.

5 Make the salsa. Halve and stone the avocado. Peel and dice the flesh, then toss it in the lime juice. Add the onion, chilli and reserved kidney beans, then season with salt. To serve, spoon the hot rice and beans on to warm tortillas and sprinkle with the coriander. Hand round the salsa and soured cream.

Vegetable Fajitas

A colourful medley of mushrooms and peppers in a spicy sauce, wrapped in tortillas and served with creamy guacamole.

Serves 2
1 onion, sliced
1 red pepper, seeded and sliced
1 green pepper, seeded and sliced
1 yellow pepper, seeded and sliced
1 garlic clove, crushed
225g/8oz/3 cups mushrooms, sliced
90ml/6 tbsp vegetable oil
30ml/2 tbsp medium chilli powder
6 warm wheat flour tortillas
salt and ground black pepper
fresh coriander sprigs and lime wedges, to garnish

For the guacamole
1 ripe avocado
1 shallot, roughly chopped
1 fresh green chilli, seeded and roughly chopped
juice of 1 lime

1 Combine the onion and red, green and yellow peppers in a large bowl. Add the garlic and mushrooms and mix lightly. Mix the oil and chilli powder in a cup, pour over the vegetable mixture and stir well. Set aside.

2 To make the guacamole, cut the avocado in half lengthways and remove the stone. Scoop the flesh into a food processor or blender and add the chopped shallot, green chilli and lime juice. Process for about 1 minute, until smooth. Scrape the guacamole into a small bowl, cover closely with clear film and chill in the fridge until required.

3 Heat a large, heavy-based frying pan or wok until very hot. Add the marinated vegetables and stir-fry over a high heat for 5–6 minutes, until the mushrooms and peppers are just tender. Season well with salt and pepper.

4 Spoon a little of the filling on to each warm tortilla and roll up. Place three fajitas on each of two individual serving plates, garnishing them with the fresh coriander and lime wedges. Offer the guacamole separately.

Black Bean Burritos

Some of the world's most delectable vegetarian dishes come from Mexico. Burritos make a delicious supper.

Serves 4
225g/8oz/1 cup dried black beans, soaked overnight
1 bay leaf
30ml/2 tbsp coarse salt
oil, for greasing
1 small red onion, finely chopped
225g/8oz/2 cups grated Cheddar cheese
15–45ml/1–3 tbsp chopped pickled jalapeño chillies
15ml/1 tbsp chopped fresh coriander
900ml/1½ pints/3¾ cups ready-made tomato salsa
8 wheat flour tortillas
diced avocado and salad, to serve

1 Drain the beans and put them in a large pan. Add fresh cold water to cover and the bay leaf. Bring to the boil, then lower the heat, and simmer, covered, for 30 minutes. Add the salt and continue to simmer for about 30 minutes, until tender. Drain and tip into a bowl. Discard the bay leaf and leave to cool.

2 Preheat the oven to 180°C/350°F/Gas 4. Grease a rectangular ovenproof dish. Add the onion, half the cheese, the jalapeños and coriander to the beans, with 250ml/8fl oz/1 cup of the salsa. Stir and taste for seasoning.

3 Place one tortilla on a board. Spread a spoonful of the filling down the middle, then roll up. Place the burrito in the prepared dish, seam side down. Repeat with the remaining tortillas.

4 Sprinkle the remaining cheese over the burritos, in a line down the middle. Bake for about 15 minutes, until the cheese melts. Serve the burritos immediately, with diced avocado, salad and the remaining salsa.

Variation
• Use passata if you don't have any ready-made salsa. Add some chopped onion and diced peppers to the portion used as a serving sauce.

Spiced Coconut Mushrooms

These delicious mushrooms can be served with almost any vegetarian meal, and are also good as a toast topping.

Serves 3–4
30ml/2 tbsp groundnut oil
2 garlic cloves, finely chopped
2 fresh red chillies, seeded and
  sliced into rings
3 shallots, finely chopped
225g/8oz/1½ cups brown cap
  mushrooms, thickly sliced
150ml/¼ pint/⅔ cup
  coconut milk
30ml/2 tbsp chopped
  fresh coriander
salt and ground black pepper

1 Heat the oil in a wok, add the garlic and chillies, then stir-fry for a few seconds. Add the shallots and stir-fry for 2–3 minutes, until softened. Add the mushrooms and cook for 3 minutes.

2 Pour in the coconut milk and bring to the boil. Boil rapidly until the liquid is reduced by half and coats the mushrooms. Season to taste with salt and pepper. Sprinkle over the chopped coriander and toss gently to mix. Serve at once.

Pickled Mushrooms

Add a little olive oil to the liquid when serving these spicy mushrooms.

Makes I jar
250ml/8fl oz/1 cup white
  wine vinegar
150ml/¼ pint/⅔ cup water
5ml/1 tsp salt
I fresh red chilli
10ml/2 tsp coriander seeds
10ml/2 tsp black peppercorns
225g/8oz/3 cups firm
  button mushrooms

1 Pour the vinegar and water into a stainless steel pan. Bring to simmering point, add the remaining ingredients and cook for 10 minutes.
2 Pour into a hot sterilized jar. Seal, label and leave to cool. Store in the fridge for at least 10 days before opening.

Sprouting Beans & Pak Choi

Health-food shops are a good source of the more unusual sprouting beans, or you can sprout your own.

Serves 4
45ml/3 tbsp groundnut oil
3 spring onions, sliced
2 garlic cloves, cut in slivers
2.5cm/1in piece of fresh root
  ginger, cut in slivers
I carrot, cut in thin sticks
150g/5oz/1¼ cups
  sprouting beans
200g/7oz pak choi,
  shredded
50g/2oz/½ cup unsalted cashew
  nuts or halved almonds

For the sauce
45ml/3 tbsp light soy sauce
30ml/2 tbsp dry sherry
15ml/1 tbsp sesame oil
15ml/1 tbsp chilli sauce
150ml/¼ pint/⅔ cup cold water
5ml/1 tsp cornflour
5ml/1 tsp clear honey
ground black pepper

1 Heat the oil in a large wok and stir-fry the onions, garlic, ginger and carrot for 2 minutes. Add the sprouting beans and stir-fry for 2 minutes more, stirring and tossing them together.

2 Add the pak choi and cashew nuts or almonds. Toss over the heat for 2–3 minutes, until the cabbage leaves are just wilting.

3 Quickly mix all the sauce ingredients in a jug and pour them into the wok, stirring constantly until the sauce is hot and coats the vegetables. Season and serve immediately.

Cook's Tip
To sprout your own beans, soak dried mung beans, soya beans, lentils, aduki beans or chick-peas overnight in cold water. Drain then put them in a large glass jar, filling it no more than one-sixth full. Pour in cold water and cover with muslin, kept in place by an elastic band. Pour away the water, so that the beans are just damp, and put the jar in a cool, dark place. Rinse daily. You should have edible sprouts in 5–6 days.

Spiced Vegetables with Coconut

This spicy and substantial dish could be served as a starter for four people, or as a vegetarian main course for two.

Serves 2–4
30ml/2 tbsp grapeseed oil
2.5cm/1in piece of fresh root
  ginger, grated
1 garlic clove, crushed
1 fresh red chilli, seeded
  and chopped
2 large carrots, diagonally sliced
6 celery stalks, diagonally sliced
1 fennel bulb, roughly chopped
3 spring onions, sliced
400ml/14fl oz can or carton
  coconut milk
15ml/1 tbsp chopped
  fresh coriander
salt and ground black pepper
fresh coriander sprigs, to garnish

1 Swirl the grapeseed oil into a preheated wok and heat. Lower the heat and add the grated ginger and garlic. Stir-fry over a medium heat for 1–2 minutes, until the garlic is pale golden in colour.

2 Add the chilli, carrots, celery, fennel and spring onions. Stir-fry for 2 minutes.

3 Stir in the coconut milk with a large spoon and bring to the boil. Cook, stirring constantly, until the coconut milk reduces slightly and the vegetables are crisp-tender.

4 Toss in the chopped coriander, season to taste with salt and pepper and serve immediately, garnished with the sprigs of fresh coriander.

> **Cook's Tips**
> • Serve this with rice or offer chunks of farmhouse-style bread for mopping up the sauce.
> • Slicing the vegetables diagonally ensures the maximum surface area so that they cook quickly and evenly. When stir-frying, try to make the ingredients about the same size.

Spicy Potatoes & Cauliflower

Serve this easy dish with a cucumber and yogurt raita.

Serves 2
about 225g/8oz potatoes
75ml/5 tbsp groundnut oil
5ml/1 tsp ground cumin
5ml/1 tsp ground coriander
1.5ml/¼ tsp ground turmeric
1.5ml/¼ tsp cayenne pepper
1 fresh green chilli, seeded and
  finely chopped
1 medium cauliflower, broken into
  small florets
60ml/4 tbsp water
5ml/1 tsp cumin seeds
2 garlic cloves, cut into shreds
15–30ml/1–2 tbsp chopped
  fresh coriander
salt

1 Bring a pan of lightly salted water to the boil and cook the potatoes in their skins for 20 minutes, until just tender. Drain and leave to cool, then peel and cut into 2.5cm/1in cubes.

2 Heat 45ml/3 tbsp of the oil in a wok. Add the ground spices and chilli. Let them sizzle for a few seconds, then add the cauliflower and water. Stir-fry for 6–8 minutes over a medium heat. Add the potatoes, tossing them until coated. Stir-fry for 2–3 minutes. Season with salt and remove from the heat.

3 Heat the remaining oil in a frying pan. Add the cumin seeds and garlic and cook until golden. Pour the mixture over the vegetables. Sprinkle with the chopped coriander and serve.

Cucumber & Yogurt Raita

Refreshing and cooling, this tastes wonderful with any spicy vegetable dish.

Serves 2–4
1 cucumber, finely diced
250ml/8fl oz/1 cup natural yogurt
20ml/4 tsp chopped fresh mint
salt and ground black pepper

1 Place the cucumber in a colander and sprinkle with salt. Leave for 2 hours, then rinse well, drain and pat dry.
2 Mix the yogurt and mint, stir in the cucumber and season.

Middle-Eastern Vegetable Stew

Serve this spicy dish of mixed vegetables as a side dish for six or as a main course for four. Children may prefer less chilli.

Serves 4–6
45ml/3 tbsp vegetable stock
1 green pepper, seeded and sliced
2 medium courgettes, sliced
2 medium carrots, sliced
2 celery stocks, sliced
2 medium potatoes, diced
400g/14oz can
   chopped tomatoes
5ml/1 tsp hot chilli powder
30ml/2 tbsp chopped fresh mint
15ml/1 tbsp ground cumin
400g/14oz can chick-peas,
   drained and rinsed
salt and ground black pepper
fresh mint sprigs, to garnish

1 Pour the vegetable stock into a large flameproof casserole and bring to the boil, then add the sliced pepper, courgettes, carrots and celery. Stir over a high heat for 2–3 minutes, until the vegetables are just beginning to soften.

2 Add the diced potatoes, tomatoes, chilli powder, chopped mint and cumin. Stir in the chick-peas and bring the mixture back to the boil.

3 Lower the heat, cover the casserole and simmer for about 30 minutes, or until all the vegetables are tender. Season to taste with salt and pepper and serve immediately, garnished with mint sprigs.

Cook's Tip
Cooking the vegetables in a small amount of stock rather than oil works extremely well, and makes this dish ideal for anyone on a low-fat diet.

Variation
You can use kidney beans or haricot beans instead of chick-peas, if you prefer.

Deep-fried Courgettes with Chilli Sauce

Crunchy coated courgettes are great served with a fiery tomato sauce.

Serves 2
15ml/1 tbsp olive oil
1 onion, finely chopped
1 fresh red chilli, seeded and
   finely diced
10ml/2 tsp hot chilli powder
400g/14oz can
   chopped tomatoes
1 vegetable stock cube
60ml/4 tbsp hot water
150ml/¼ pint/⅔ cup milk
50g/2oz/½ cup plain flour
450g/1lb courgettes, sliced
oil, for deep-frying
salt and ground black pepper
fresh thyme sprigs, to garnish

To serve
lettuce leaves
watercress sprigs
slices of seeded bread

1 Heat the oil in a pan. Add the onion and fry over a low heat, stirring occasionally, for 2–3 minutes. Add the chilli, then stir in the chilli powder and cook for 30 seconds.

2 Tip in the canned tomatoes. Crumble in the stock cube and stir in the water. Cover and cook for 10 minutes, then leave the sauce over a very low heat until needed. Check for seasoning.

3 Pour the milk into a shallow dish and spread out the flour in another dish. Dip the courgette slices in the milk, then into the flour, until well-coated.

4 Heat the oil for deep-frying to 180°C/350°F or until a cube of bread, added to the oil, browns in 45–60 seconds. Add the courgettes, in batches, and deep-fry for 3–4 minutes, until crisp. Drain on kitchen paper.

5 Place two or three lettuce leaves on each serving plate. Add a few sprigs of watercress and fan out the bread slices to one side. Lightly mix the deep-fried courgettes into the sauce, then spoon some on to each plate. Garnish with the thyme sprigs and serve at once.

Turkish-style New Potato Casserole

A one-pot bake that's both easy to make and tastes delicious – who could ask for more?

Serves 4

60ml/4 tbsp olive oil
1 large onion, chopped
2 small–medium aubergines, cut into small cubes
4 courgettes, cut into small chunks
1 green pepper, seeded and chopped
1 red or yellow pepper, seeded and chopped
115g/4oz/1 cup fresh or frozen peas

115g/4oz French beans
450g/1lb new potatoes, cubed
2.5ml/ ½ tsp cinnamon
2.5ml/ ½ tsp ground cumin
5ml/1 tsp paprika
4–5 tomatoes, halved, seeded and chopped
400g/14oz can chopped tomatoes
30ml/2 tbsp chopped fresh parsley
3–4 garlic cloves, crushed
350ml/12fl oz/1 ½ cups vegetable stock
salt and ground black pepper
black olives and fresh parsley, to garnish

1 Preheat the oven to 190°C/375°F/Gas 5. Heat 45ml/3 tbsp of the oil in a heavy-based pan. Add the onion and fry over a medium heat, stirring occasionally, for 5–7 minutes, until golden.

2 Add the aubergines, sauté for about 3 minutes, then add the courgettes, peppers, peas, beans and potatoes. Stir in the cinnamon, cumin and paprika and season to taste with salt and pepper. Continue to cook for 3 minutes, stirring all the time. Transfer to a shallow ovenproof dish.

3 Mix the fresh and canned tomatoes in a bowl. Stir in the parsley, garlic and the remaining olive oil.

4 Pour the stock over the aubergine mixture, and spoon the prepared tomato mixture over the top.

5 Cover with foil and bake for 30–45 minutes, until the vegetables are tender. Serve immediately, garnished with black olives and parsley.

Spicy Potato Strudel

Take a tasty mixture of vegetables in a spicy, creamy sauce and wrap in crisp filo pastry for a stylish and satisfying main course.

Serves 4

65g/2½ oz/5 tbsp butter
1 onion, chopped
2 carrots, coarsely grated
1 courgette, chopped
350g/12oz firm potatoes, finely chopped

10ml/2 tsp mild curry paste
2.5ml/ ½ tsp dried thyme
150ml/ ¼ pint/ ⅔ cup of water
1 egg, beaten
30ml/2 tbsp single cream
50g/2oz/ ½ cup grated Cheddar cheese
8 sheets filo pastry, thawed if frozen
sesame seeds, for sprinkling
salt and ground black pepper
lamb's lettuce, to garnish

1 Melt 25g/1oz/2 tbsp of the butter in a large frying pan and cook the onion, carrots, courgette and potatoes for 5 minutes, tossing them frequently so they cook evenly. Stir in the curry paste and continue to cook the vegetables, stirring frequently, for 1–2 minutes more.

2 Add the thyme and water and season with salt and pepper to taste. Bring to the boil, then lower the heat and simmer for 10 minutes, until tender, stirring occasionally.

3 Remove the pan from the heat and tip the mixture into a large bowl. When cool, mix in the egg, cream and cheese. Chill until ready to fill the filo pastry.

4 Preheat the oven to 190°C/375°F/Gas 5. Melt the remaining butter. Lay out four sheets of filo pastry, slightly overlapping them to form a fairly large rectangle. Brush with some melted butter and fit the other sheets on top. Brush again.

5 Spoon the filling along one long side, then roll up the pastry. Form it into a circle and set on a baking sheet. Brush again with the last of the butter and sprinkle over the sesame seeds. Bake for about 25 minutes, until golden and crisp. Leave to stand for 5 minutes before cutting. Garnish with lamb's lettuce.

Aubergine & Sweet Potato Stew

Inspired by Thai cooking, this has a tasty coconut sauce scented with fragrant lemon grass and ginger.

Serves 6
60ml/4 tbsp groundnut oil
450g/1lb baby aubergines, halved
225g/8oz shallots
5ml/1 tsp fennel seeds, lightly crushed
4–5 garlic cloves, thinly sliced
25ml/5 tsp finely chopped fresh root ginger
475ml/16fl oz/2 cups vegetable stock
2 lemon grass stalks, outer layers discarded, finely chopped
15g/ ½ oz/ ½ cup fresh coriander, stalks and leaves chopped separately
3 kaffir lime leaves, lightly bruised
2–3 small red chillies
45–60ml/3–4 tbsp Thai green curry paste
675g/1 ½ lb sweet potatoes, peeled and cut into chunks
400ml/14fl oz/1⅔ cups coconut milk
2.5–5ml/ ½–1 tsp light muscovado sugar
250g/9oz/1⅔ cups mushrooms, thickly sliced
juice of 1 lime
salt and ground black pepper
fresh basil leaves, to serve

1 Heat half the oil in a wide pan and cook the aubergines, stirring occasionally, until lightly browned on all sides. Remove with a draining spoon and set aside. Slice four of the shallots and set them aside. Fry the remaining whole shallots in the oil remaining in the pan, until lightly browned. Set aside.

2 Add the remaining oil to the pan and cook the sliced shallots, fennel seeds, garlic and ginger until soft. Add the stock, lemon grass, chopped coriander stalks and any roots, lime leaves and whole chillies. Cover and simmer over a low heat for 5 minutes.

3 Stir in 30ml/2 tbsp of the curry paste and the sweet potatoes. Simmer for 10 minutes, then return the aubergines and shallots to the pan and cook for 5 minutes more. Stir in the coconut milk and sugar. Stir in the mushrooms and simmer for 5 minutes, or until all the vegetables are cooked.

4 Season and add more curry paste and lime juice to taste. Stir in the coriander leaves, scatter basil leaves over and serve.

Thai Vegetable Curry

Making your own spice paste gives this curry an authentic flavour.

Serves 4
10ml/2 tsp vegetable oil
400ml/14fl oz/1⅔ cups coconut milk
300ml/ ½ pint/1¼ cups vegetable stock
225g/8oz new potatoes, halved if large
130g/4½ oz baby corn cobs
5ml/1 tsp golden caster sugar
175g/6oz broccoli florets
1 red pepper, seeded and sliced lengthways
115g/4oz spinach, tough stalks removed and shredded
salt and ground black pepper
cooked jasmine rice, to serve

30ml/2 tbsp chopped fresh coriander, to garnish

For the spice paste
1 fresh red chilli, seeded and chopped
3 fresh green chillies, seeded and chopped
1 lemon grass stalk, outer layers discarded and finely chopped
2 shallots, chopped
finely grated rind of 1 lime
2 garlic cloves, chopped
5ml/1 tsp ground coriander
2.5ml/ ½ tsp ground cumin
1cm/ ½in fresh galangal or root ginger, finely chopped
30ml/2 tbsp chopped fresh coriander

1 First, make the spice paste. Place all the ingredients in a food processor or blender and process to a coarse paste.

2 Heat the oil in a large, heavy-based pan and fry the spice paste for 1–2 minutes, stirring constantly. Add the coconut milk and stock, and bring to the boil.

3 Lower the heat, add the potatoes and simmer gently for 15 minutes. Add the baby corn cobs, season to taste with salt and black pepper and cook for 2 minutes. Stir in the sugar, broccoli and red pepper and cook for 2 minutes more, until the vegetables are tender.

4 Stir in the shredded spinach and half the fresh coriander. Cook for 2 minutes. Serve over jasmine rice, garnished with the remaining chopped coriander.

Peppers Filled with Spiced Vegetables

Indian spices season the potato and aubergine stuffing in these colourful baked peppers.

Serves 6

1 aubergine
30ml/2 tbsp groundnut oil, plus
   extra for brushing
6 large even-shaped red or
   yellow peppers
500g/1¼ lb waxy potatoes
1 small onion, chopped
4–5 garlic cloves, chopped
5cm/2in piece of fresh root
   ginger, chopped
1–2 fresh green chillies, seeded
   and chopped
105ml/7 tbsp water
10ml/2 tsp cumin seeds
5ml/1 tsp kalonji seeds
2.5ml/½ tsp ground turmeric
5ml/1 tsp ground coriander
5ml/1 tsp ground toasted
   cumin seeds
pinch of cayenne pepper
about 30ml/2 tbsp lemon juice
salt and ground black pepper
chopped fresh coriander,
   to garnish

1 Preheat the oven to 230°C/450°F/Gas 8. Cut the aubergine in half lengthways and score the skin. Brush a roasting tin lightly with oil. Put the aubergine halves, cut side down, in the tin and bake for 20 minutes. Leave to cool.

2 Cut the tops off the peppers and carefully scoop out and discard the seeds. Cut a thin slice off the base of the peppers, if necessary, so they stand upright. Bring a large saucepan of lightly salted water to the boil. Cook the peppers for 5–6 minutes. Lift out with a draining spoon and drain upside down in a colander.

3 Bring the water back to the boil and cook the potatoes until just tender. Drain, cool and peel, then cut into 1cm/½in dice. Peel the aubergine and cut the flesh into similar dice.

4 Put the chopped onion, garlic, ginger and green chillies in a food processor or blender with 60ml/4 tbsp of the water and process to a purée.

5 Heat half the oil in a large, deep, frying pan and stir-fry the aubergine until browned. Remove from the pan and set aside. Add the remaining oil to the pan and cook the potatoes until lightly browned. Remove from the pan and set aside.

6 Dry-fry the cumin and kalonji seeds in a non-stick pan. When the seeds darken, add the turmeric, coriander and ground cumin. Cook for 15 seconds. Stir in the onion and garlic purée and fry, scraping the pan with a spatula, until it begins to brown.

7 Add the potatoes and aubergines to the pan, and season with salt, pepper and cayenne. Add the remaining water and half the lemon juice and cook, stirring, until the liquid evaporates. Preheat the oven to 190°C/375°F/Gas 5.

8 Place the peppers on a baking sheet and fill with the potato mixture. Brush lightly with oil and bake for 30–35 minutes, until the peppers are cooked. Allow to cool a little, then sprinkle with more lemon juice, garnish with the coriander and serve.

Mixed Vegetable Curry

A good all-round vegetable curry that goes well with most Indian dishes.

Serves 4

30ml/2 tbsp oil
2.5ml/½ tsp black
   mustard seeds
2.5ml/½ tsp cumin seeds
1 onion, thinly sliced
2 curry leaves
1 fresh green chilli, seeded and
   finely chopped
2.5cm/1in piece of fresh root
   ginger, grated
30ml/2 tbsp curry paste
1 small cauliflower, broken
   into florets
1 large carrot, thickly sliced
115g/4oz French beans, cut into
   short lengths
1.5ml/¼ tsp ground turmeric
1.5ml/¼ tsp hot chilli powder
2.5ml/½ tsp salt
2 tomatoes, finely chopped
50g/2oz/½ cup frozen
   peas, thawed
150ml/¼ pint/⅔ cup hot
   vegetable stock
fresh curry leaves, to garnish

1 Heat the oil in a large saucepan and fry the mustard seeds and cumin seeds for 2 minutes, until they begin to splutter. Add the onion and the curry leaves and fry for 5 minutes more.

2 Stir in the chilli and ginger and fry for 2 minutes. Add the curry paste, mix well and fry for 3–4 minutes.

3 Add the cauliflower, carrot and French beans and cook for 4–5 minutes. Stir in the turmeric, chilli powder, salt and tomatoes and cook for 2–3 minutes.

4 Add the thawed peas and cook for 2–3 minutes more. Pour in the stock. Cover and simmer gently over a low heat for 10–13 minutes, until all the vegetables are tender. Serve, garnished with the curry leaves.

Cook's Tip

Keep root ginger in the freezer and it will be very easy to grate. There's no need to peel it first, and it will thaw on contact with any hot mixture.

Vegetable Kashmiri

A spicy yogurt sauce coats the vegetables in this aromatic curry.

Serves 4

10ml/2 tsp cumin seeds
8 black peppercorns
seeds from 2 green
 cardamom pods
5cm/2in piece of cinnamon stick
2.5ml/ 1/2 tsp grated nutmeg
45ml/3 tbsp oil
2.5cm/1in piece of fresh root
 ginger, grated

1 fresh green chilli, chopped
5ml/1 tsp chilli powder
2.5ml/ 1/2 tsp salt
2 large potatoes, cut into chunks
225g/8oz cauliflower, broken
 into florets
225g/8oz okra, thickly sliced
150ml/ 1/4 pint/ 2/3 cup
 natural yogurt
150ml/ 1/4 pint/ 2/3 cup
 vegetable stock
toasted flaked almonds and fresh
 coriander sprigs, to garnish

1 Grind the cumin seeds, peppercorns, cardamom seeds, cinnamon stick and nutmeg to a fine powder, using a spice grinder or a pestle and mortar.

2 Heat the oil in a large saucepan and stir-fry the ginger and fresh chilli for 2 minutes. Add the chilli powder, salt and ground spice mixture and fry for about 2–3 minutes, stirring all the time to prevent the spices from sticking.

3 Stir in the potatoes until coated, cover, and cook over a low heat for 10 minutes, stirring from time to time. Add the cauliflower and okra and cook for 5 minutes.

4 Add the yogurt and stock. Bring to the boil, then lower the heat. Cover and simmer for 20 minutes, or until all the vegetables are tender. Spoon on to a platter, garnish with toasted almonds and coriander sprigs, and serve.

> **Cook's Tip**
> *An electric coffee grinder will make short work of preparing whole spices. Don't use it for anything else, though.*

Masala Okra

Okra or "ladies fingers" are a popular vegetable in India, where they are known as bhindi. In this recipe they are stir-fried with spices.

Serves 4

450g/1lb okra
2.5ml/ 1/2 tsp ground turmeric
5ml/1 tsp mild chilli powder
15ml/1 tbsp ground cumin
15ml/1 tbsp ground coriander
1.5ml/ 1/4 tsp salt

1.5ml/ 1/4 tsp granulated sugar
15ml/1 tbsp lemon juice
15ml/1 tbsp desiccated coconut
30ml/2 tbsp chopped
 fresh coriander
45ml/3 tbsp vegetable oil
2.5ml/ 1/2 tsp cumin seeds
2.5ml/ 1/2 tsp black
 mustard seeds
chopped fresh tomatoes,
 to garnish
poppadums, to serve

1 Wash, dry and trim the okra. In a bowl, mix together the turmeric, chilli powder, cumin, ground coriander, salt, sugar, lemon juice, desiccated coconut and fresh coriander.

2 Heat the oil in a large, heavy-based frying pan. Add the cumin seeds and mustard seeds and fry over a low heat, stirring occasionally, for about 2 minutes, or until they begin to splutter and give off their aroma.

3 Stir in the spice and coconut mixture and fry for 2 minutes more. Add the okra, cover, and cook over a low heat for about 10 minutes, or until tender.

4 Spoon into a serving bowl, garnish with chopped fresh tomatoes and serve with poppadums.

> **Cook's Tips**
> • *When buying okra, choose firm, brightly coloured pods that are less than 10cm/4in long. They should snap cleanly. Avoid any that are bendy or browning at the edges or tips.*
> • *Prepare okra by washing, drying and carefully cutting off the stalk without breaking the seed pod.*

Curried Mushrooms

This is a delicious way of
cooking mushrooms. The
mixture would make a tasty
filling for samosas.

Serves 4
30ml/2 tbsp vegetable oil
2.5ml/ ½ tsp cumin seeds
1.5ml/ ¼ tsp black peppercorns
4 green cardamom pods
1.5ml/ ¼ tsp ground turmeric
1 onion, finely chopped
5ml/1 tsp ground cumin

5ml/1 tsp ground coriander
2.5ml/ ½ tsp garam masala
1 fresh green chilli, finely chopped
2 garlic cloves, crushed
2.5cm/1in piece of fresh root
  ginger, grated
400g/14oz can
  chopped tomatoes
1.5ml/ ¼ tsp salt
450g/1lb/6 cups button
  mushrooms, halved
chopped fresh coriander,
  to garnish

1 Heat the oil in a large saucepan. Add the cumin seeds,
peppercorns, cardamom pods and turmeric and fry over a low
heat, stirring occasionally, for 2–3 minutes.

2 Add the onion and fry for about 5 minutes, stirring
occasionally, until golden. Stir in the cumin, ground coriander
and garam masala and fry for 2 minutes more.

3 Add the chilli, garlic and ginger and fry for 2–3 minutes,
stirring all the time to prevent the spices from sticking to the
pan. Stir in the tomatoes and salt. Bring to the boil, then simmer
for 5 minutes.

4 Add the mushrooms. Cover and simmer over a low heat for
10 minutes. Spoon into a serving dish and remove and discard
the cardamom pods. Garnish with chopped fresh coriander and
serve immediately.

Variation
This recipe would work well with any small, firm mushrooms,
such as chestnut mushrooms or their pink or white equivalents,
called champignons de Paris.

Broad Bean & Cauliflower Curry

A tasty mid-week curry, this
is especially good with
basmati rice, baby
poppadums and cucumber
and yogurt raita.

Serves 4
2 garlic cloves, chopped
2.5cm/1in piece of fresh
  root ginger
1 fresh green chilli, seeded
  and chopped
15ml/1 tbsp vegetable oil
30ml/2 tbsp ghee or butter
1 onion, sliced

1 large potato, chopped
15ml/1 tbsp mild or hot
  curry powder
1 medium cauliflower, cut into
  small florets
600ml/1 pint/2½ cups
  vegetable stock
25g/1oz/2 tbsp creamed coconut
275g/10oz can broad beans
juice of ½ lemon (optional)
salt and ground black pepper
chopped fresh coriander or
  parsley, to garnish
cooked white basmati rice,
  to serve

1 Put the garlic, ginger, chilli and oil in a food processor and
process until the mixture forms a smooth paste.

2 Heat the ghee or butter in a large, heavy-based pan. Add the
onion and potato and fry over a low heat, stirring occasionally,
for about 5 minutes, until the onion is soft and pale golden. Stir
in the spice paste and curry powder. Cook, stirring constantly,
for 1 minute more.

3 Stir in the cauliflower florets, then pour in the stock. Bring to
the boil over a medium heat and mix in the creamed coconut,
stirring until it melts.

4 Season well with salt and pepper, then lower the heat, cover
and simmer for 10 minutes.

5 Add the broad beans, with the can juices, stir gently to mix
and cook, uncovered, for 10 minutes more.

6 Check the seasoning and add a good squeeze of lemon juice
if liked. Spoon into a serving bowl, garnish with coriander or
parsley, and serve immediately with basmati rice.

Aloo Gobi

Cauliflower and potatoes are coated in classic Indian spices in this dish.

Serves 4

450g/1lb potatoes, cut into
   2.5cm/1in chunks
30ml/2 tbsp vegetable oil
5ml/1 tsp cumin seeds
1 fresh green chilli, finely chopped
450g/1lb cauliflower, broken
   into florets
5ml/1 tsp ground coriander
5ml/1 tsp ground cumin
1.5ml/¼ tsp chilli powder
2.5ml/½ tsp ground turmeric
2.5ml/½ tsp salt
chopped fresh coriander,
   to garnish
tomato and onion salad and lime
   pickle, to serve

1 Bring a large pan of lightly salted water to the boil and cook the potatoes for 10 minutes. Drain well and set aside.

2 Heat the oil in a heavy-based, deep frying pan. Add the cumin seeds and fry over a low heat, stirring occasionally, for 2 minutes, until they begin to splutter. Add the chilli and fry for 1 minute more.

3 Toss in the cauliflower florets. Stir well to coat them all over with the spice mixture. Continue to stir-fry, over a low to medium heat for 5 minutes more.

4 Add the potatoes, ground coriander, cumin, chilli powder, turmeric and salt. Cook for 7–10 minutes, or until the vegetables are tender.

5 Spoon into a warmed serving dish, garnish with chopped fresh coriander and serve immediately with the tomato and onion salad and lime pickle.

Variation
Try using sweet potatoes instead of ordinary potatoes for a curry with a sweeter flavour.

Aubergine Curry

A simple and delicious way of cooking aubergines which makes sure their full flavour is retained.

Serves 4

2 large aubergines, about
   450g/1lb each
45ml/3 tbsp vegetable oil
2.5ml/½ tsp black
   mustard seeds
1 bunch spring onions,
   finely chopped
115g/4oz/1½ cups button
   mushrooms, halved
2 garlic cloves, crushed
1 fresh red chilli, finely chopped
2.5ml/½ tsp mild chilli powder
5ml/1 tsp ground cumin
5ml/1 tsp ground coriander
1.5ml/¼ tsp ground turmeric
5ml/1 tsp salt
400g/14oz can
   chopped tomatoes
15ml/1 tbsp chopped
   fresh coriander
fresh coriander sprig, to garnish

1 Preheat the oven to 200°C/400°F/Gas 6. Brush both of the aubergines with 15ml/1 tbsp of the oil. Prick them with a fork and place in a roasting tin. Bake for 30–35 minutes, until soft.

2 Meanwhile, heat the remaining oil in a large pan and fry the mustard seeds for 2 minutes, until they begin to splutter. Add the spring onions, mushrooms, garlic and fresh chilli and fry for about 5 minutes. Stir in the ground spices and salt and fry for 3–4 minutes. Add the tomatoes and simmer for 5 minutes.

3 Cut each of the aubergines in half lengthways and scoop out the soft flesh into a bowl. Mash the flesh roughly.

4 Add the mashed aubergines and fresh coriander to the saucepan. Bring to the boil, then simmer for 5 minutes, or until the sauce thickens. Serve, garnished with a fresh coriander sprig.

Cook's Tip
If you want to omit the oil, wrap the aubergines in foil and bake in the oven for 1 hour.

Aloo Saag

Potatoes, spinach and spices are the main ingredients in this authentic curried vegetable dish.

Serves 4

450g/1lb fresh young
  spinach leaves
30ml/2 tbsp vegetable oil
5ml/1 tsp black mustard seeds
1 onion, thinly sliced
2 garlic cloves, crushed
2.5cm/1in piece of fresh root
  ginger, finely chopped
675g/1½lb potatoes, cut into
  2.5cm/1in chunks
5ml/1 tsp mild chilli powder
5ml/1 tsp salt
120ml/4fl oz/½ cup water

1 Bring a large pan of lightly salted water to the boil and blanch the spinach leaves for 3–4 minutes. Drain thoroughly and set aside. When the spinach is cool enough to handle, use your hands to squeeze out any remaining liquid.

2 Heat the oil in a large saucepan. Add the mustard seeds and fry over a low heat, stirring occasionally, for 2 minutes, or until they begin to splutter.

3 Add the onion, garlic and ginger. Fry for 5 minutes, stirring constantly, then add the potatoes, chilli powder, salt and water. Stir well and cook for 8 minutes.

4 Stir in the spinach. Cover and simmer for 10–15 minutes, or until the potatoes are tender. Spoon on to a warmed serving dish and serve immediately.

> **Cook's Tips**
> • *Use a waxy variety of potato for this dish, such as Ausonia, Spunta, Maris Bard or Morag, so the pieces do not break up during cooking.*
> • *To make certain that the spinach is completely dry after it has been blanched and drained, you can put it in a clean dish towel, roll up tightly and then squeeze gently to remove the excess liquid.*

Cumin-spiced Marrow & Spinach

Tender chunks of marrow with spinach in a creamy, cumin-flavoured sauce.

Serves 2

½ marrow, about 450g/1lb
30ml/2 tbsp vegetable oil
10ml/2 tsp cumin seeds
1 small fresh red chilli, seeded
  and finely chopped
30ml/2 tbsp water
50g/2oz fresh young spinach
  leaves, torn into pieces
90ml/6 tbsp single cream
salt and ground black pepper
boiled rice or naan bread,
  to serve

1 Peel the marrow and cut it in half. Scoop out and discard the seeds. Cut the flesh into cubes.

2 Heat the oil in a large, heavy-based frying pan. Add the cumin seeds and the chopped chilli. Cook over a low heat, stirring occasionally, for 1 minute.

3 Add the marrow and water to the pan. Cover with foil or a lid and simmer gently, stirring occasionally, for 8 minutes, until the marrow is just tender. Remove the foil cover or lid and cook for about 2 minutes more, or until most of the water has evaporated.

4 Add the spinach to the marrow, with just the water that clings to the leaves after washing and draining. Replace the cover and cook gently for 1 minute.

5 Stir in the cream and cook over a high heat for 2 minutes. Season to taste and serve with rice or naan bread.

> **Cook's Tip**
> *Be careful when handling chillies, as the juice can burn sensitive skin. Wear rubber gloves to protect your hands or wash your hands very thoroughly after preparation.*

Courgette Curry

Next time you have a glut of courgettes in the garden, treat yourself to this colourful curry.

Serves 4

45ml/3 tbsp vegetable oil
2.5ml/ ½ tsp cumin seeds
2.5ml/ ½ tsp mustard seeds
I onion, thinly sliced
2 garlic cloves, crushed
1.5ml/ ¼ tsp ground turmeric
1.5ml/ ¼ tsp mild chilli powder
5ml/I tsp ground coriander
5ml/I tsp ground cumin
2.5ml/ ½ tsp salt
675g/I ½ lb courgettes, cut in
 I cm/ ½in slices
15ml/I tbsp tomato purée
400g/14oz can
 chopped tomatoes
150ml/ ¼ pint/ ⅔ cup water
15ml/I tbsp chopped
 fresh coriander
5ml/I tsp garam masala

1 Heat the oil in a large, heavy-based pan. Add the cumin seeds and mustard seeds and fry over a low heat, stirring occasionally, for 2 minutes, until they begin to splutter.

2 Add the onion and garlic and fry, stirring occasionally, for about 5 minutes, until softened.

3 Stir in the turmeric, chilli powder, ground coriander, ground cumin and salt. Cook, stirring constantly, for 2–3 minutes.

4 Add the sliced courgettes, all at once, and cook for 5 minutes. Meanwhile, mix together the tomato purée, chopped tomatoes and water in a bowl.

5 Add the tomato mixture to the pan, stir well and simmer for 10 minutes, until the sauce thickens. Stir in the fresh coriander and garam masala, then cook for 5 minutes more, until the courgettes are tender. Serve immediately.

> **Variation**
> This curry is also delicious made with other summer squash, such as patty pans.

Sweetcorn & Pea Curry

Chunks of corn on the cob not only look interesting in this unusual curry, they taste pretty good too!

Serves 4

6 pieces of frozen corn on the cob
45ml/3 tbsp vegetable oil
2.5ml/ ½ tsp cumin seeds
I onion, finely chopped
2 garlic cloves, crushed
I fresh green chilli, finely chopped
15ml/I tbsp curry paste
5ml/I tsp ground coriander
5ml/I tsp ground cumin
1.5ml/ ¼ tsp ground turmeric
2.5ml/ ½ tsp salt
2.5ml/ ½ tsp granulated sugar
400g/14oz can
 chopped tomatoes
15ml/I tbsp tomato purée
150ml/ ¼ pint/ ⅔ cup water
115g/4oz/I cup frozen
 peas, thawed
30ml/2 tbsp chopped
 fresh coriander

1 Cut each piece of corn in half crossways to make 12 equal pieces in total. Bring a large saucepan of water to the boil and cook the corn cob pieces for 10–12 minutes. Drain well.

2 Heat the oil in a large pan. Add the cumin seeds and fry over a low heat, stirring occasionally, for about 2 minutes, or until they begin to splutter. Add the onion, garlic and chilli and fry for 5–6 minutes, until the onions are golden.

3 Stir in the curry paste and fry for 2 minutes. Stir in the remaining spices, salt and sugar and fry for 2–3 minutes.

4 Add the chopped tomatoes, tomato purée and water and simmer for 5 minutes, or until the sauce thickens. Add the peas and cook for 5 minutes more.

5 Add the pieces of corn and the fresh coriander. Cook for 6–8 minutes, or until the corn and peas are tender.

> **Cook's Tip**
> Use fresh corn on the cob when it is in season. Do not salt the water or the corn will become tough.

Vegetable Korma

The blending of spices is an ancient art in India. Here the aim is to produce a subtle, aromatic curry rather than an assault on the senses.

Serves 4
50g/2oz/ ¼ cup butter
2 onions, sliced
2 garlic cloves, crushed
2.5cm/1in piece of fresh root
    ginger, grated
5ml/1 tsp ground cumin
15ml/1 tbsp ground coriander
6 cardamom pods
5cm/2in piece of cinnamon stick
5ml/1 tsp ground turmeric
1 fresh red chilli, seeded and
    finely chopped
1 potato, cut into 2.5cm/
    1in cubes
1 small aubergine, chopped
115g/4oz/1½ cups mushrooms,
    thickly sliced
175ml/6fl oz/¾ cup water
115g/4oz French beans, cut into
    short lengths
60ml/4 tbsp natural yogurt
150ml/ ¼ pint/ ⅔ cup
    double cream
5ml/1 tsp garam masala
salt and ground black pepper
fresh coriander sprigs, to garnish
poppadums, to serve

1 Melt the butter in a heavy-based pan and cook the onions for 5 minutes, until soft. Add the garlic and ginger and cook for 2 minutes, then stir in the cumin, ground coriander, cardamoms, cinnamon stick, turmeric and chilli. Stir-fry for 30 seconds.

2 Add the potato, aubergine, mushrooms and water. Cover the pan, bring to the boil, then lower the heat and simmer for 15 minutes. Add the beans and cook, uncovered, for 5 minutes.

3 With a draining spoon, remove the vegetables to a warmed serving dish and keep hot. Boil the cooking liquid until it reduces a little. Season with salt and pepper, then stir in the yogurt, cream and garam masala. Pour the sauce over the vegetables and garnish with coriander. Serve with poppadums.

Variation
Any combination of vegetables can be used for this korma, including carrots, cauliflower, broccoli, peas and chick-peas.

Beancurd & Green Bean Red Curry

This Thai curry is simple and quick to make.

Serves 4–6
600ml/1 pint/2½ cups
    coconut milk
15ml/1 tbsp red curry paste
45ml/3 tbsp vegetarian "oyster"
    sauce (mushroom-based)
10ml/2 tsp sugar
225g/8oz/1½ cups
    button mushrooms
115g/4oz green beans, trimmed
175g/6oz firm beancurd (tofu),
    cut into 2cm/ ¾in cubes
4 kaffir lime leaves, torn
2 fresh red chillies, sliced
fresh coriander leaves, to garnish

1 Pour about one-third of the coconut milk into a pan. Cook until it starts to separate and an oily sheen appears.

2 Stir in the curry paste, "oyster" sauce and sugar, then add the mushrooms. Stir and cook for 1 minute. Stir in the rest of the coconut milk and bring to the boil. Add the green beans and cubes of beancurd (tofu) and simmer gently for 4–5 minutes more. Stir in the kaffir lime leaves and sliced chillies. Serve immediately, garnished with the coriander leaves.

Beancurd with Chillies

This is quick, easy and deliciously spicy.

Serves 4
450g/1lb beancurd (tofu), diced
15ml/1tbsp dark soy sauce
4 fresh red Thai chillies
3 garlic cloves
30ml/2 tbsp vegetable oil
30ml/2 tbsp light soy sauce
30ml/2 tbsp vegetarian "oyster"
    sauce (mushroom-based)
15ml/1 tbsp granulated sugar
fresh Thai basil leaves, to garnish

1 Mix the beancurd (tofu) and dark soy sauce in a bowl and set aside to marinate for 10 minutes.
2 Meanwhile, pound the chillies and garlic together to a paste. Heat the oil in a wok and stir-fry the spice paste and beancurd for 1 minute. Stir in the remaining ingredients and stir-fry for a further 2 minutes. Serve, garnished with the basil leaves.

Stir-fried Beancurd & Beansprouts

Beancurd (tofu) is a boon to the busy vegetarian cook, providing plenty of protein in this simple stir-fry.

Serves 4
225g/8oz firm beancurd (tofu)
groundnut oil, for deep-frying
175g/6oz medium egg noodles
15ml/1 tbsp sesame oil
5ml/1 tsp cornflour
10ml/2 tsp dark soy sauce
30ml/1 tbsp Chinese rice wine
5ml/1 tsp granulated sugar
6–8 spring onions, cut diagonally into 2.5cm/1in lengths
3 garlic cloves, sliced
1 fresh green chilli, seeded and sliced
115g/4oz pak choi leaves, coarsely shredded
50g/2oz/1 cup beansprouts
50g/2oz/½ cup cashew nuts, toasted

1 Drain the beancurd (tofu) and pat it dry with kitchen paper. Cut it into 2.5cm/1in cubes. Half-fill a wok with groundnut oil and heat to 180°C/350°F or until a cube of day-old bread browns in 30–60 seconds. Deep-fry the beancurd cubes, in batches, for 1–2 minutes, until golden and crisp. Remove the cubes with a draining spoon and drain them on kitchen paper. Carefully pour all but 30ml/2 tbsp of the oil from the wok.

2 Bring a large pan of water to the boil, add the noodles and remove the pan from the heat. Cover and leave to stand for about 4 minutes, until the noodles are just tender. Drain, rinse under cold water and drain again. Toss in 10ml/2 tsp of the sesame oil and set aside.

3 In a bowl, blend together the cornflour, soy sauce, rice wine, sugar and the remaining sesame oil.

4 Reheat the 30ml/2 tbsp of groundnut oil in the wok. Add the spring onions, garlic, chilli, pak choi and beansprouts and stir-fry for 1–2 minutes.

5 Add the beancurd cubes, together with the noodles and sauce. Cook, stirring, for about 1 minute, until thoroughly mixed and heated through. Transfer to a warmed serving dish, sprinkle over the cashew nuts and serve at once.

Peanut Noodles

Add any of your favourite vegetables to this quick and easy recipe and increase the number of chillies, if you can take the heat!

Serves 4
200g/7oz medium egg noodles
30ml/2 tbsp olive oil
2 garlic cloves, crushed
1 large onion, roughly chopped
1 red pepper, seeded and roughly chopped
1 yellow pepper, seeded and roughly chopped
350g/12oz courgettes, roughly chopped
150g/5oz/1¼ cups roasted unsalted peanuts, roughly chopped
snipped fresh chives, to garnish

For the dressing
60ml/4 tbsp good-quality olive oil
grated rind and juice of 1 lemon
1 fresh red chilli, seeded and finely chopped
45ml/3 tbsp snipped fresh chives
15–30ml/1–2 tbsp balsamic vinegar
salt and ground black pepper

1 Bring a large pan of water to the boil, add the noodles and remove the pan from the heat. Cover and leave to stand for about 4 minutes, until the noodles are tender. Drain, rinse under cold water and drain again.

2 Heat the olive oil in a wok. Add the garlic and onion and stir-fry for 3–4 minutes, until the onion is beginning to soften. Add the red and yellow peppers and the courgettes and stir-fry for 3–4 minutes, until crisp-tender. Add the peanuts and cook for 1 minute more.

3 Make the dressing. In a jug, whisk together the olive oil, grated lemon rind and 45ml/3 tbsp of the lemon juice. Add the chilli and chives and whisk in balsamic vinegar to taste. Season well with salt and pepper.

4 Add the noodles to the vegetables and toss over the heat to heat through. Add the dressing and stir to coat. Transfer to a warmed serving dish and serve immediately, garnished with snipped chives.

Parsnip & Aubergine Biryani

It always seems such a humble vegetable, yet the parsnip has a superb flavour and brings a touch of sweetness to spicy dishes such as this one.

Serves 4–6
1 small aubergine, sliced
275g/10oz/1 1/4 cups basmati rice
3 onions
2 garlic cloves, roughly chopped
2.5cm/1in piece of fresh root
   ginger, peeled
45ml/3 tbsp water
about 60ml/4 tbsp vegetable oil

175g/6oz/1 1/2 cups unsalted
   cashew nuts
40g/1 1/2oz/ 1/4 cup sultanas
1 red pepper, seeded and sliced
3 parsnips, chopped
5ml/1 tsp ground cumin
5ml/1 tsp ground coriander
2.5ml/ 1/2 tsp mild chilli powder
120ml/4fl oz/ 1/2 cup
   natural yogurt
300ml/ 1/2 pint/1 1/4 cups
   vegetable stock
25g/1oz/2 tbsp butter
salt
fresh coriander sprigs and wedges
   of hard-boiled egg, to garnish

1 Layer the aubergine slices in a colander, sprinkling each layer with salt. Leave to drain in the sink for 30 minutes. Rinse, pat dry with kitchen paper and cut into bite-size pieces.

2 Soak the rice in a bowl of cold water while you cook the vegetables. Roughly chop one onion and put it in a food processor or blender with the garlic and ginger. Add the water and process to a paste.

3 Thinly slice the remaining onions. Heat 45ml/3 tbsp of the oil in a large flameproof casserole. Add the onion slices and fry over a low heat, stirring occasionally, for about 10 minutes, until deep golden brown. Remove and drain. Add one-quarter of the cashews to the pan and stir-fry for 2 minutes. Add the sultanas and fry until they swell. Remove and drain.

4 Add the aubergine and red pepper to the casserole and stir-fry for 4–5 minutes. Drain on kitchen paper. Add the parsnips to the casserole and fry for 4–5 minutes. Stir in the remaining cashews and fry for 1 minute. Transfer to a plate with the aubergine and pepper.

5 Add the remaining 15ml/1 tbsp of oil to the casserole. Add the onion paste. Cook, stirring constantly, for 4–5 minutes. Stir in the cumin, ground coriander and chilli powder. Cook, stirring, for 1 minute, then lower the heat and add the yogurt.

6 Stir in the stock, parsnips, aubergine and peppers. Bring to the boil, then lower the heat, cover and simmer for 30–40 minutes, until the parsnips are tender.

7 Preheat the oven to 150°C/300°F/Gas 2. Drain the rice and cook it in salted boiling water for 6 minutes. Drain, then pile in a mound on top of the spiced vegetables. Make a hole from the top to the base using the handle of a wooden spoon.

8 Scatter the reserved fried onions, cashew nuts and sultanas over the rice and dot with the butter. Cover with a foil lid. Bake for 35–40 minutes, then spoon on to a warmed serving dish and garnish with the coriander sprigs and egg.

Kitchiri

This is the Indian original that inspired the classic breakfast dish, kedgeree. Made with basmati rice and small tasty lentils, this will make an ample supper or brunch dish.

Serves 4
115g/4oz/ 2/3 cup Indian masoor
   dhal or continental green lentils
50g/2oz/ 1/4 cup ghee or butter
30ml/2 tbsp sunflower oil
1 onion, chopped
1 garlic clove, crushed

225g/8oz/generous 1 cup easy-
   cook basmati rice
10ml/2 tsp ground coriander
10ml/2 tsp cumin seeds
2 cloves
3 cardamom pods
2 bay leaves
1 cinnamon stick
1 litre/1 3/4 pints/4 cups
   vegetable stock
30ml/2 tbsp tomato purée
45ml/3 tbsp chopped fresh
   coriander or parsley
salt and ground black pepper

1 Put the dhal or lentils in a bowl. Pour over boiling water to cover and leave to soak for 30 minutes. Meanwhile, bring a pan of water to the boil. Drain the soaked dhal or lentils and add to the pan. Cook for 10 minutes. Drain once more and set aside.

2 Heat the ghee or butter and oil in a large saucepan and fry the onion and garlic for about 5 minutes.

3 Add the rice, stir well to coat the grains, then stir in the spices. Cook gently for 1–2 minutes, then add the lentils, stock, tomato purée and seasoning.

4 Bring to the boil, lower the heat, cover and simmer for 20 minutes, until the stock has been absorbed. Stir in the coriander or parsley and check the seasoning. Remove and discard the cinnamon stick and bay leaf and serve.

> **Cook's Tip**
> In summer, it is worth growing coriander in a pot, as it has an inimitable flavour and adds authenticity to many ethnic dishes.

Oriental Fried Rice

This is a great way to use leftover cooked rice. It not only looks colourful, but also tastes delicious.

Serves 4–6
60ml/4 tbsp oil
115g/4oz shallots, halved and
    thinly sliced
3 garlic cloves, crushed
1 fresh red chilli, seeded and
    finely chopped
6 spring onions, finely chopped
1 red pepper, seeded and
    finely chopped
225g/8oz white cabbage,
    finely shredded

175g/6oz cucumber,
    finely chopped
50g/2oz/ ½ cup frozen
    peas, thawed
3 eggs, beaten
5ml/1 tsp tomato purée
30ml/2 tbsp freshly squeezed
    lime juice
1.5ml/ ¼ tsp Tabasco sauce
675g/1½lb/6 cups very cold
    cooked white rice
115g/4oz/1 cup cashew nuts,
    roughly chopped
about 30ml/2 tbsp chopped
    fresh coriander, plus extra to
    garnish
salt and ground black pepper

1 Heat the oil in a wok. Add the shallots and cook, stirring frequently, until very crisp and golden. Remove with a draining spoon and drain well on kitchen paper.

2 Add the garlic and chilli and cook for 1 minute. Add the spring onions and red pepper and cook for 3–4 minutes, or until beginning to soften. Add the cabbage, cucumber and peas and cook for 2 minutes more.

3 Make a gap and add the beaten eggs. Scramble the eggs, stirring occasionally, then stir them into the vegetables.

4 Stir in the tomato purée, lime juice and Tabasco. Add the rice, cashews and coriander, with plenty of seasoning. Toss over a high heat for 3–4 minutes, until the rice is piping hot. Serve garnished with the crisp shallots and coriander.

Egyptian Rice with Lentils

Two important staple foods come together in this simple but tasty Middle-Eastern dish, which owes its warm flavour to the inclusion of ground cumin and cinnamon.

Serves 6
350g/12oz/1½ cups large brown
    lentils, soaked overnight
    in water
2 large onions
45ml/3 tbsp olive oil
15ml/1 tbsp ground cumin
2.5ml/ ½ tsp ground cinnamon
225g/8oz/generous 1 cup long
    grain rice
salt and ground black pepper
flat leaf parsley, to garnish

1 Drain the lentils and put them in a large pan. Add enough water to cover them by 5cm/2in. Bring to the boil, lower the heat, cover and simmer for 40 minutes–1½ hours, or until tender. Drain thoroughly.

2 Finely chop one onion, and slice the other. Heat 15ml/1 tbsp of the oil in a pan. Add the chopped onion and fry over a low heat, stirring occasionally, for 5 minutes, until soft. Add the lentils, cumin and cinnamon. Stir well and season to taste with salt and pepper.

3 Measure the volume of rice and add it, with the same volume of water, to the lentil mixture. Cover and simmer for about 20 minutes, until both the rice and lentils are tender.

4 Heat the remaining oil in a frying pan and cook the sliced onion for about 15 minutes, until very dark brown. Tip the rice mixture into a serving bowl, sprinkle with the sliced onion and serve hot or cold, garnished with flat leaf parsley.

Cook's Tip
Use two 400g/14oz cans of cooked lentils, if you prefer. Simply add them to the fried chopped onion in Step 2.

Lentil Dhal with Roasted Garlic

This spicy lentil dhal makes a comforting, starchy meal when served with boiled rice or Indian breads and a vegetable dish.

Serves 4–6
1 head of garlic
30ml/2 tbsp extra virgin olive oil, plus extra for brushing
40g/1½ oz/3 tbsp ghee or butter
1 onion, chopped
2 fresh green chillies, seeded and chopped
15ml/1 tbsp chopped fresh root ginger
225g/8oz/1 cup yellow or red split lentils

900ml/1½ pints/3¾ cups water
5ml/1 tsp ground cumin
5ml/1 tsp ground coriander
2 tomatoes, peeled and diced
a little lemon juice
salt and ground black pepper
30–45ml/2–3 tbsp fresh coriander sprigs, to garnish

For the spice mix
30ml/2 tbsp groundnut oil
4–5 shallots, sliced
2 garlic cloves, thinly sliced
15g/½oz/1 tbsp ghee or butter
5ml/1 tsp cumin seeds
5ml/1 tsp mustard seeds
3–4 small dried red chillies
8–10 fresh curry leaves

1 Preheat the oven to 180°C/350°F/Gas 4. Place the garlic in an oiled roasting tin and roast it whole for 30 minutes.

2 Meanwhile, melt the ghee or butter in a large pan. Add the onion, fresh chillies and ginger and cook over a low heat, stirring occasionally, for 10 minutes, until golden.

3 Stir in the lentils and water. Bring to the boil, then lower the heat and partially cover the pan. Simmer, stirring occasionally, for about 35 minutes, until the mixture looks like a very thick soup.

4 When the garlic is soft and tender, remove it from the oven and let it cool slightly. Cut off the top third and, holding the garlic over a bowl, dig out the flesh from each clove so that it drops into the bowl. Mash it to a paste with the oil.

5 Stir the roasted garlic purée, cumin and ground coriander into the lentil mixture and season with salt and pepper to taste. Cook for 10 minutes, uncovered, stirring frequently. Stir in the diced tomatoes, then adjust the seasoning, adding a little lemon juice to taste.

6 For the spice mix, heat the oil in a small, heavy-based pan and fry the shallots until crisp and browned. Add the garlic and cook until it colours slightly. Remove the mixture from the pan and set it aside.

7 Melt the ghee or butter in the same pan and fry the cumin and mustard seeds until the mustard seeds pop. Stir in the dried chillies, curry leaves and the shallot mixture, then swirl the hot mixture into the cooked dhal. Garnish with the coriander sprigs and serve immediately.

Cook's Tip
Do not be alarmed by the quantity of garlic; when roasted, it acquires a mild and mellow flavour.

Tomato & Lentil Dhal with Toasted Almonds

Richly flavoured with spices, coconut milk and tomatoes, this lentil dish is good enough to serve as part of a celebration supper.

Serves 4
30ml/2 tbsp vegetable oil
1 large onion, finely chopped
3 garlic cloves, chopped
1 carrot, diced
10ml/2 tsp cumin seeds
10ml/2 tsp yellow mustard seeds
2.5cm/1in piece of fresh root ginger, grated

10ml/2 tsp ground turmeric
5ml/1 tsp mild chilli powder
5ml/1 tsp garam masala
225g/8oz/1 cup red split lentils
400ml/14fl oz/1⅔ cups water
400ml/14fl oz/1⅔ cups coconut milk
5 tomatoes, peeled, seeded and chopped
juice of 2 limes
60ml/4 tbsp chopped fresh coriander
salt and ground black pepper
25g/1oz/¼ cup flaked almonds, toasted, to serve

1 Heat the oil in a large, heavy-based pan. Sauté the onion over a low heat, stirring occasionally, for 5 minutes, until softened. Add the garlic, carrot, cumin and mustard seeds and ginger. Cook for 5 minutes, stirring constantly, until the seeds begin to pop and the carrot softens slightly.

2 Stir in the ground turmeric, chilli powder and garam masala, and cook for 1 minute, or until the flavours begin to mingle, stirring to prevent the spices from burning.

3 Add the lentils, water, coconut milk and tomatoes, and season well with salt and pepper. Bring to the boil, then lower the heat, cover and simmer, for about 15 minutes, stirring occasionally to prevent the lentils from sticking.

4 Stir in the lime juice and 45ml/3 tbsp of the fresh coriander and check the seasoning. Cook for 10–15 minutes more, until the lentils are tender. Spoon into a warmed serving dish and sprinkle with the remaining coriander and the toasted flaked almonds. Serve at once.

Egg & Lentil Curry

Hard-boiled eggs combine well with all pulses.

Serves 4
75g/3oz/scant ½ cup
    green lentils
750ml/1¼ pints/3 cups
    vegetable stock
6 eggs
30ml/2 tbsp vegetable oil
3 cloves
1.5ml/¼ tsp black peppercorns
1 onion, finely chopped

2 fresh green chillies,
    finely chopped
2 garlic cloves, crushed
2.5cm/1in piece of fresh root
    ginger, chopped
30ml/2 tbsp curry paste
400g/14oz can
    chopped tomatoes
2.5ml/½ tsp granulated sugar
175ml/6fl oz/¾ cup water
2.5ml/½ tsp garam masala
roughly chopped parsley,
    to garnish

1 Put the lentils in a large, heavy-based pan and add the stock. Bring to the boil, cover, lower the heat and simmer for about 30 minutes, or until the lentils are soft. Drain and set aside.

2 Cook the eggs in boiling water for 10 minutes. Cool slightly, then shell and cut in half lengthways.

3 Heat the oil in a large frying pan and fry the cloves and peppercorns for 2 minutes. Add the onion, chillies, garlic and ginger and cook for 5–6 minutes, stirring frequently.

4 Stir in the curry paste and fry for 2 minutes, stirring constantly. Add the tomatoes, sugar and water and simmer, stirring occasionally, for 5 minutes, until the sauce thickens.

5 Add the boiled eggs, lentils and garam masala. Cover and simmer for 10 minutes more, then serve, garnished with parsley.

Cook's Tip
As soon as the eggs are hard-boiled, lift them out of the water and plunge them into cold water. This prevents a dark ring from forming around the yolks.

Lentils with Fried Spices

If you've got a saucepan and a frying pan, you can cook this classic Indian dish. It is ideal for hungry students.

Serves 4–6
115g/4oz/½ cup split red lentils
50g/2oz/¼ cup yellow split peas
350ml/12fl oz/1½ cups water
4 fresh green chillies
5ml/1 tsp ground turmeric
1 large onion, sliced

400g/14oz can
    chopped tomatoes
60ml/4 tbsp vegetable oil
1.5ml/¼ tsp mustard seeds
1.5ml/¼ tsp cumin seeds
1 garlic clove, crushed
6 curry leaves
2 dried red chillies
1.5ml/¼ tsp asafoetida
salt
deep-fried onions, to garnish

1 Combine the lentils and split peas in a heavy pan and add the water, chillies, turmeric and onion slices. Bring to the boil. Lower the heat, cover and simmer for about 30 minutes, or until the lentils are soft and the water has evaporated.

2 Mash the lentils with the back of a spoon. When nearly smooth, add the tomatoes and season with salt to taste. Mix well. If necessary, thin the mixture with hot water.

3 Heat the oil in a frying pan and add the mustard and cumin seeds, garlic and curry leaves. Crumble in the dried chillies and stir in the asafoetida. Fry over a low heat, stirring constantly, until the garlic browns.

4 Pour the oil and spices over the lentils and cover the pan. After 5 minutes, mix well, garnish with the deep-fried onions and serve immediately.

Cook's Tip
If you buy lentils loose, pick them over carefully and remove any small stones. Wash them thoroughly under cold running water. It is not necessary to soak the lentils, but if you soak the brown ones, it will speed up the cooking process.

Spinach Dhal

Yellow split peas cook down to a creamy consistency, which combines well with the spinach in this delicious, lightly spiced dish.

Serves 4

175g/6oz/ ¾ cup chana dhal or
  yellow split peas
175ml/6fl oz/ ¾ cup water
15ml/1 tbsp vegetable oil
1.5ml/ ¼ tsp black
  mustard seeds
1 onion, thinly sliced
2 garlic cloves, crushed
2.5cm/1in piece of fresh root
  ginger, grated
1 fresh red chilli, finely chopped
275g/10oz frozen spinach,
  thawed and drained
1.5ml/ ¼ tsp mild chilli powder
2.5ml/ ½ tsp ground coriander
2.5ml/ ½ tsp garam masala
salt

1 Wash the chana dhal or split peas in several changes of cold water. Put into a bowl and pour over plenty of water to cover. Leave to soak for 30 minutes.

2 Drain the pulses and put them in a large pan with the measured water. Bring to the boil, lower the heat, cover and simmer for 20–25 minutes, until soft.

3 Meanwhile, heat the oil in a large, heavy-based frying pan and fry the mustard seeds over a low heat for 2 minutes, until they begin to splutter.

4 Add the onion, garlic, ginger and chilli to the pan and fry, stirring occasionally, for 5–6 minutes, or until the onion has softened but not coloured.

5 Add the spinach and cook for about 10 minutes, or until the spinach is dry and the liquid has been absorbed. Stir in the chilli powder, ground coriander and garam masala and season to taste with salt. Cook for 2–3 minutes.

6 Drain the chana dhal or split peas, add them to the spinach mixture and cook for about 5 minutes. Transfer to a warmed serving dish and serve at once.

Madras Sambal

There are many variations of this everyday Indian dish, which can be served solo but is often presented as part of a meal.

Serves 4

225g/8oz/1 cup toovar dhal or
  red split lentils
600ml/1 pint/2½ cups water
2.5ml/ ½ tsp ground turmeric
2 large potatoes, cut into
  2.5cm/1in chunks
30ml/2 tbsp vegetable oil
2.5ml/ ½ tsp black
  mustard seeds
1.5ml/ ¼ tsp fenugreek seeds
4 curry leaves
1 onion, thinly sliced
115g/4oz French beans, cut into
  short lengths
2.5ml/ ½ tsp mild chilli powder
15ml/1 tbsp lemon juice
60ml/4 tbsp desiccated coconut
salt
toasted coconut, to garnish
chutney, to serve

1 Wash the toovar dhal or lentils in several changes of water. Place in a heavy-based saucepan with the measured water and the turmeric. Bring to the boil, then lower the heat and simmer, covered, for 20–30 minutes, until the lentils are soft.

2 Meanwhile, bring a large pan of lightly salted water to the boil. Add the potatoes and boil for 10 minutes. Drain well.

3 Heat the oil in a large, deep frying pan and fry the seeds and curry leaves for 2–3 minutes, until the seeds begin to splutter. Add the onion and the French beans and fry for 7–8 minutes. Stir in the potatoes and cook for 2 minutes more.

4 Drain any free liquid from the lentils, then stir them into the vegetables with the chilli powder, lemon juice and salt. Simmer for 2 minutes. Stir in the coconut and simmer for 5 minutes. Garnish with toasted coconut and serve with chutney.

> **Cook's Tip**
> Toovar dhal are split yellow pigeon peas. Look for these pulses in Indian groceries.

Hot & Sour Chick-peas

If you visit India, you will find bowls of this tasty snack food on sale from stalls on the street.

Serves 4
45ml/3 tbsp vegetable oil
2 onions, very finely chopped
2 tomatoes, peeled and
    finely chopped
15ml/1 tbsp ground coriander
15ml/1 tbsp ground cumin
5ml/1 tsp ground fenugreek
5ml/1 tsp ground cinnamon
2 x 400g/14oz cans
    chick-peas, drained
350ml/12fl oz/1½ cups
    vegetable stock
1–2 fresh hot green chillies,
    seeded and thinly sliced
2.5cm/1in piece of fresh root
    ginger, grated
60ml/4 tbsp lemon juice
salt
15ml/1 tbsp chopped
    fresh coriander, to garnish

1 Heat the oil in a large flameproof casserole. Reserve about 30ml/2 tbsp of the chopped onions and fry the remainder, stirring frequently, for 4–5 minutes, until tinged with brown.

2 Add the tomatoes and continue cooking over a moderately low heat for 5–6 minutes, until soft. Stir frequently, mashing the tomatoes to a pulp.

3 Stir in the ground spices. Cook for 30 seconds, then add the chick-peas and vegetable stock. Season with salt, cover and simmer very gently for 15–20 minutes, stirring occasionally and adding water if the mixture becomes too dry.

4 Meanwhile, mix the reserved onion with the chilli, ginger and lemon juice. Just before serving, stir this mixture into the chick-peas, with more salt, if needed, and garnish with fresh coriander.

> **Cook's Tip**
> In India, dried chick-peas would be used. If you want to follow suit, soak 350g/12oz/2 cups dried chick-peas overnight in water, then drain them and boil them in fresh water for 1–1¼ hours, until tender.

Masala Chana

Tamarind gives this dish a deliciously tangy flavour.

Serves 4
50g/2oz pressed tamarind
120ml/4fl oz/½ cup
    boiling water
30ml/2 tbsp vegetable oil
2.5ml/½ tsp cumin seeds
1 onion, finely chopped
2 garlic cloves, crushed
2.5cm/1in piece of fresh root
    ginger, grated
1 fresh green chilli, finely chopped
5ml/1 tsp ground cumin
5ml/1 tsp ground coriander
1.5ml/¼ tsp ground turmeric
2.5ml/½ tsp salt
2 tomatoes, peeled and
    finely chopped
2 x 400g/14oz cans
    chick-peas, drained
2.5ml/½ tsp garam masala
chopped fresh chillies and
    chopped onion, to garnish

1 Break up the tamarind and soak in the boiling water for about 15 minutes. Rub the mixture through a sieve into a bowl, discarding what remains in the sieve.

2 Heat the oil in a large, heavy-based pan and fry the cumin seeds for 2 minutes, until they splutter. Add the onion, garlic, ginger and chilli and fry over a low heat, stirring occasionally, for 5 minutes, until the onion has softened.

3 Stir in the ground cumin, ground coriander, turmeric and salt and fry for 3–4 minutes. Add the tomatoes and tamarind pulp. Mix thoroughly, bring to the boil, then lower the heat and simmer for 5 minutes.

4 Add the chick-peas and stir in the garam masala. Cover and simmer for about 15 minutes. Spoon into a serving dish, garnish with the chopped chillies and onion, and serve.

> **Cook's Tip**
> Peeled, seeded tamarind pods compressed into bricks are sold in Indian grocers. Break off as much as you need and soak it as described in the recipe.

Spicy Chick-peas with Fresh Ginger

Here's another excellent chick-pea recipe, this time with ginger, spring onions and fresh mint.

Serves 4–6
30ml/2 tbsp vegetable oil
1 small onion, chopped
4cm/1 ½in piece of fresh root
  ginger, finely chopped
2 garlic cloves, finely chopped
1.5ml/ ¼ tsp ground turmeric
450g/1lb tomatoes, peeled,
  seeded and chopped
2 x 400g/14oz cans
  chick-peas, drained

30ml/2 tbsp chopped
  fresh coriander
10ml/2 tsp garam masala
salt and ground black pepper
fresh coriander sprigs, to garnish

For the raita
150ml/ ¼ pint/ ⅔ cup
  natural yogurt
2 spring onions, finely chopped
5ml/1 tsp roasted cumin seeds
30ml/2 tbsp chopped fresh mint
pinch of cayenne pepper

1 Heat the oil in a large pan. Add the onion and fry over a low heat, stirring occasionally, for 2–3 minutes. Add the ginger, garlic and turmeric. Fry for a few seconds more.

2 Stir in the tomatoes and chick-peas and season with salt and pepper to taste. Bring to the boil, then simmer for 10–15 minutes, until the mixture has reduced to a thick sauce.

3 Meanwhile, make the raita. Mix the yogurt, spring onions, roasted cumin seeds, mint and cayenne pepper in a small serving bowl. Set aside.

4 Just before the end of cooking, stir the chopped coriander and garam masala into the chick-pea mixture. Serve at once, garnished with coriander sprigs and accompanied by the raita.

> **Variation**
> Try this with drained canned beans, if you like. Butter beans make an interesting alternative to chick-peas.

Curried Spinach & Chick-peas

Serve this with natural yogurt and naan bread, for a complete, satisfying and very tasty meal.

Serves 6
30ml/2 tbsp vegetable oil
2 garlic cloves, crushed
1 onion, roughly chopped
30ml/2 tbsp medium curry paste
15ml/1 tbsp black mustard seeds

450g/1lb potatoes, diced
475ml/16fl oz/2 cups water
450g/1lb frozen leaf
  spinach, thawed
400g/14oz can
  chick-peas, drained
225g/8oz Halloumi cheese, cubed
15ml/1 tbsp freshly squeezed
  lime juice
salt and ground black pepper
fresh coriander sprigs, to garnish

1 Heat the oil in a large, heavy-based pan. Add the garlic and onion and fry over a medium heat, stirring occasionally, for about 5 minutes. Stir in the curry paste and mustard seeds and cook the mixture for 1 minute.

2 Add the diced potatoes and pour in the measured water. Bring to the boil and cook gently, stirring occasionally, for 20–25 minutes, until the potatoes are almost tender and most of the liquid has evaporated.

3 Meanwhile, place the thawed spinach in a sieve and press out as much liquid as possible. Chop it roughly, then stir it into the potato mixture, with the chick-peas. Cook for 5 minutes, or until the potatoes are tender, stirring frequently.

4 Stir in the cheese cubes and lime juice, season to taste with salt and pepper and serve immediately, garnished with sprigs of fresh coriander.

> **Cook's Tip**
> In India, paneer, rather than Halloumi, would be used. This cheese is made at home by curdling boiled milk with vinegar or lemon juice, straining the curds and then pressing them with a weight for a short while.

Parsnips & Chick-peas in an Aromatic Paste

The sweet flavour of parsnips goes very well with the spices in this special-occasion stew.

Serves 4

200g/7oz/scant 1 cup dried
　chick-peas, soaked overnight
7 garlic cloves, finely chopped
1 small onion, chopped
5cm/2in piece of fresh root
　ginger, chopped
2 fresh green chillies, seeded and
　finely chopped
550ml/18fl oz/2½ cups water
30ml/2 tbsp groundnut oil
5ml/1 tsp cumin seeds
10ml/2 tsp ground
　coriander seeds
5ml/1 tsp ground turmeric
2.5–5ml/½–1 tsp mild
　chilli powder
50g/2oz/½ cup cashew nuts,
　toasted and ground
2 tomatoes, peeled and chopped
900g/2lb parsnips, cut
　into chunks
5ml/1 tsp ground roasted
　cumin seeds
juice of 1 lime
salt and ground black pepper
fresh coriander leaves and toasted
　cashew nuts, to serve

1 Drain the chick-peas and put them in a heavy-based pan. Cover with cold water and bring to the boil. Boil vigorously for 10 minutes, then lower the heat to a steady boil and cook for 1–1½ hours, or until tender.

2 Set 10ml/2 tsp of the garlic aside. Place the remaining garlic in a food processor or blender with the onion, ginger and half the fresh chillies. Add 75ml/5 tbsp of the water and process to a smooth paste.

3 Heat the oil in a large, deep frying pan and cook the cumin seeds for 30 seconds. Stir in the coriander seeds, turmeric, chilli powder and the ground cashews.

4 Add the ginger and chilli paste and cook, stirring frequently, until the water begins to evaporate. Add the tomatoes and stir-fry until the mixture begins to turn red-brown in colour.

5 Drain the chick-peas and stir them into tomato mixture with the parsnips. Pour in the remaining water. Add 5ml/1 tsp salt and plenty of black pepper. Bring to the boil, stir well, then simmer, uncovered, for 15–20 minutes, until the parsnips are completely tender.

6 Reduce the liquid, if necessary, by boiling fiercely until the sauce is thick. Add the ground roasted cumin with lime juice to taste. Stir in the reserved garlic and chilli, and cook for a final 1–2 minutes. Scatter the coriander leaves and toasted cashew nuts over and serve immediately.

Cook's Tip
Dried chick-peas are used here, but they do demand some forethought as they require soaking. For an impromptu meal, use two cans of chick-peas, adding them when the parsnips have been cooking for about 5 minutes.

Aubergine & Chick-pea Ragoût

The perfect dish for a winter supper party, this combines two hearty main ingredients with a blend of warming spices.

Serves 4

3 large aubergines, cubed
200g/7oz/scant 1 cup dried
　chick-peas, soaked overnight
45ml/3 tbsp olive oil
3 garlic cloves, chopped
2 large onions, chopped
2.5ml/½ tsp ground cumin
2.5ml/½ tsp ground cinnamon
2.5ml/½ tsp ground coriander
3 x 400g/14oz cans
　chopped tomatoes
salt and ground black pepper
cooked rice, to serve

For the garnish
30ml/2 tbsp olive oil
1 onion, sliced
1 garlic clove, sliced
fresh coriander sprigs

1 Put the aubergine cubes in a colander, sprinkling each layer with salt. Stand in the sink for 30 minutes, then rinse very well. Drain thoroughly and pat dry with kitchen paper.

2 Drain the chick-peas and put them in a pan with enough water to cover. Bring to the boil. Boil vigorously for 10 minutes, then lower the heat and simmer for 1–1¼ hours, or until tender. Drain.

3 Heat the oil in a large, heavy-based pan. Add the garlic and onions and fry over a low heat, stirring occasionally, for 5 minutes, until softened.

4 Add the cumin, cinnamon and ground coriander and cook, stirring constantly, for a few seconds. Stir in the aubergine until coated with the spice mixture. Cook for 5 minutes.

5 Add the tomatoes and chick-peas and season to taste with salt and pepper. Cover and simmer for 20 minutes.

6 Make the garnish. Heat the oil in a frying pan. When it is very hot, add the sliced onion and garlic and fry, stirring frequently until golden and crisp. Serve the ragoût with rice, topped with the onion and garlic and garnished with coriander.

Curried Kidney Beans

This is a very popular Punjabi-style dish. It also tastes good when made with butter beans.

Serves 4

30ml/2 tbsp vegetable oil
2.5ml/ ½ tsp cumin seeds
1 onion, thinly sliced
1 fresh green chilli, finely chopped
2 garlic cloves, crushed
2.5cm/1in piece of fresh root
   ginger, grated

30ml/2 tbsp curry paste
5ml/1 tsp ground cumin
5ml/1 tsp ground coriander
2.5ml/ ½ tsp mild chilli powder
400g/14oz can
   chopped tomatoes
2 x 400g/14oz cans red kidney
   beans, drained and rinsed
30ml/2 tbsp chopped
   fresh coriander
salt and ground black pepper

1 Heat the oil in a large, heavy-based frying pan. Add the cumin seeds and fry for 2 minutes, until they begin to splutter.

2 Add the onion, chilli, garlic and ginger and fry over a low heat, stirring occasionally, for 5 minutes, until the onion has softened.

3 Stir in the curry paste, cumin, ground coriander, chilli powder and salt to taste and cook for 5 minutes.

4 Add the tomatoes and simmer for 5 minutes. Add the beans and fresh coriander, reserving a little for the garnish. Cover and cook for 15 minutes, stirring in a little water if necessary.

5 Taste the mixture and add salt and pepper, if needed. Garnish with the remaining chopped coriander and serve.

> **Cook's Tip**
> If you prefer to use dried red kidney beans, soak 225g/8oz/ 1 ¼ cups overnight in cold water, then drain and put in a pan with plenty of cold water. Bring to the boil and boil vigorously for 10 minutes, then lower the heat slightly and cook for 1–1 ¼ hours, until soft.

Mixed Bean Curry

When your stock of dried beans is running low, mix the remains of several packets to make this marvellous curry. Start early, as the beans will need to soak overnight.

Serves 4

50g/2oz/ ⅓ cup dried red
   kidney beans
50g/2oz/ ⅓ cup dried
   black-eyed beans
50g/2oz/ ⅓ cup dried
   haricot beans
50g/2oz/ ⅓ cup dried
   flageolet beans

30ml/2 tbsp vegetable oil
5ml/1 tsp cumin seeds
5ml/1 tsp black mustard seeds
1 onion, finely chopped
2 garlic cloves, crushed
2.5cm/1in piece of fresh root
   ginger, grated
2 fresh green chillies,
   finely chopped
30ml/2 tbsp curry paste
2.5ml/ ½ tsp salt
400g/14oz can
   chopped tomatoes
30ml/2 tbsp tomato purée
250ml/8fl oz/1 cup water
30ml/2 tbsp chopped fresh
   coriander, plus extra to garnish

1 Mix the beans in a large bowl. Add sufficient cold water to cover and soak overnight.

2 Drain the beans and put them into a large, heavy-based pan with at least double the volume of cold water. Bring to the boil and boil vigorously for 10 minutes. Lower the heat, cover and simmer for 1–1 ½ hours, or until all the beans are soft.

3 Heat the oil in a large pan and fry the cumin and mustard seeds for 2 minutes until they splutter. Add the onion, garlic, ginger and chillies and fry over a low heat, stirring occasionally, for 5 minutes, until the onion has softened.

4 Stir in the curry paste. Fry for 2–3 minutes more, stirring all the time, then add the salt. Add the tomatoes, tomato purée and the measured water, mix well and simmer for 5 minutes.

5 Add the drained beans and the fresh coriander. Cover and simmer for 30 minutes, until the sauce thickens. Garnish with the extra coriander and serve immediately.

Dry Mung Dhal with Courgettes

Most dhal dishes are quite runny, but this one has a bit of texture – mainly thanks to the courgettes.

Serves 4–6
175g/6oz/³⁄₄ cup mung dhal
2.5ml/ ¹⁄₂ tsp ground turmeric
300ml/ ¹⁄₂ pint/1¹⁄₄ cups water
30ml/2 tbsp vegetable oil
1 large onion, thinly sliced
2 garlic cloves, crushed
2 fresh green chillies, chopped
2.5ml/ ¹⁄₂ tsp mustard seeds
2.5ml/ ¹⁄₂ tsp cumin seeds
1.5ml/ ¹⁄₄ tsp asafoetida
a few fresh coriander and mint
    leaves, chopped
6–8 curry leaves
2.5ml/ ¹⁄₂ tsp granulated sugar
200g/7oz can tomatoes, drained
    and chopped
225g/8oz courgettes, diced
salt
60ml/4 tbsp lemon juice

1 Soak the mung dhal in water to cover for about 4 hours. Drain thoroughly, then put into a heavy-based pan.

2 Add the turmeric and measured water. Bring to the boil, then lower the heat. Cover and simmer for 15 minutes, until the dhal is cooked but not mushy. Drain, reserving the cooking liquid.

3 Heat the oil in a frying pan and add all the remaining ingredients, except the lemon juice. Cover and cook, stirring occasionally, until the courgettes are almost tender.

4 Fold in the mung dhal and lemon juice. If the dish is too dry, add a little of the reserved cooking liquid. Reheat and serve.

Cook's Tips
• *Mung dhal, also known as green gram, is one of those pulses most likely to be found at an Indian grocery or ethnic food shop. It consists of split mung beans, which have been hulled.*
• *Asafoetida is made from the resinous sap of a rather foul-smelling fennel plant. When dried and powdered, it gives an onion flavour to Indian and Middle Eastern dishes and is also considered to have digestive properties.*

Mung Beans with Potatoes

One of the quicker-cooking pulses, mung beans are very easy to use.

Serves 4
175g/6oz/ ³⁄₄ cup mung beans
750ml/1¹⁄₄ pints/3 cups water
2 potatoes, cut into 2cm/
    ³⁄₄ in chunks
30ml/2 tbsp vegetable oil
2.5ml/ ¹⁄₂ tsp cumin seeds
1 fresh green chilli, finely chopped
1 garlic clove, crushed
2.5cm/1in piece of fresh root
    ginger, finely chopped
1.5ml/ ¹⁄₄ tsp ground turmeric
2.5ml/ ¹⁄₂ tsp mild chilli powder
5ml/1 tsp salt
5ml/1 tsp granulated sugar
4 curry leaves, plus extra
    to garnish
5 tomatoes, peeled and
    finely chopped
15ml/1 tbsp tomato purée

1 Put the beans in a saucepan and add the water. Bring to the boil, then lower the heat and simmer for 30 minutes, until soft. Drain and set aside.

2 Meanwhile, par-boil the potatoes in a separate pan of boiling water for 10 minutes. Drain and set aside.

3 Heat the oil in a large, heavy-based pan and fry the cumin seeds until they splutter. Add the chilli, garlic and ginger and fry over a low heat, stirring frequently, for 3–4 minutes.

4 Stir in the turmeric, chilli powder, salt and sugar. Cook for 2 minutes, stirring constantly to prevent the mixture from sticking to the pan.

5 Add the curry leaves, tomatoes and tomato purée and simmer for 5 minutes, until the sauce thickens. Stir in the mung beans and potatoes and reheat. Spoon on to a serving platter or dish, garnish with the extra curry leaves and serve.

Cook's Tip
Unlike many other pulses, mung beans do not require soaking before they are cooked.

Chilli Beans with Basmati Rice

Red kidney beans, tomatoes and chilli make a great combination. Serve with pasta or pitta bread instead of rice, if you prefer.

Serves 4
350g/12oz/1¾ cups basmati rice
30ml/2 tbsp olive oil
1 large onion, chopped
1 garlic clove, crushed
15ml/1 tbsp hot chilli powder
15ml/1 tbsp plain flour
15ml/1 tbsp tomato purée
400g/14oz can
　chopped tomatoes
400g/14oz can red kidney beans,
　drained and rinsed
150ml/¼ pint/⅔ cup hot
　vegetable stock
salt and ground black pepper
chopped fresh parsley, to garnish

1 Rinse the rice several times in cold water. If there is sufficient time, leave it to soak for about 30 minutes in the water used for the final rinse.

2 Bring a large pan of water to the boil. Drain the rice, then cook it in the water for 10–12 minutes, until tender.

3 Meanwhile, heat the oil in a heavy-based frying pan. Add the onion and garlic and cook over a low heat, stirring occasionally, for 2 minutes. Stir in the chilli powder and flour. Cook, stirring frequently, for 2 minutes.

4 Stir in the tomato purée, tomatoes, beans and hot vegetable stock. Cover and cook for 12 minutes, stirring occasionally.

5 Taste the mixture and stir in salt and pepper, if needed. Drain the rice and serve at once, with the chilli beans, sprinkled with a little chopped fresh parsley.

Cook's Tip
Basmati is generally considered to be the long grain rice with the finest flavour and texture. However, if you prefer to use another type, including brown rice, there is, of course, no reason why you shouldn't.

Red Bean Chilli

White wine and soy sauce may not be standard ingredients in chilli, but they give this spicy bean dish a depth of flavour unmatched by more mundane mixtures.

Serves 4
30ml/2 tbsp vegetable oil
1 onion, chopped
400g/14oz can
　chopped tomatoes
2 garlic cloves, crushed
300ml/½ pint/1¼ cups
　white wine
about 300ml/½ pint/1¼ cups
　vegetable stock
115g/4oz/½ cup red split lentils
2 fresh thyme sprigs or 5ml/1 tsp
　dried thyme
10ml/2 tsp ground cumin
45ml/3 tbsp dark soy sauce
½ fresh hot chilli, seeded and
　finely chopped
5ml/1 tsp mixed spice
225g/8oz can red kidney beans,
　drained and rinsed
10ml/2 tsp granulated sugar
salt
boiled rice and sweetcorn, to serve

1 Heat the oil in a large, heavy-based pan. Add the onion and fry over a low heat, stirring occasionally for about 5 minutes, until slightly softened.

2 Add the tomatoes and garlic, cook for 10 minutes, then stir in the wine and stock. Bring to the boil.

3 Add the lentils, thyme, cumin, soy sauce, chilli and mixed spice. Cover, then simmer for 40 minutes, or until the lentils are cooked, stirring occasionally and adding more water if the lentils begin to dry out.

4 Stir in the kidney beans and sugar and continue cooking for 10 minutes, adding a little extra stock or water if the mixture is becoming too dry. Season to taste with salt and serve hot with boiled rice and sweetcorn.

Cook's Tip
If you have a taste for very hot, spicy food, do not seed the chilli before chopping it.

Mixed Vegetable Stir-fry

Serve this stir-fry with rice
or noodles.

Serves 4
15ml/1 tbsp vegetable oil
5ml/1 tsp toasted sesame oil
1 garlic clove, chopped
2.5cm/1in piece of fresh root
   ginger, finely chopped

225g/8oz baby carrots
350g/12oz broccoli florets
175g/6oz asparagus tips
2 spring onions, cut diagonally
175g/6oz spring greens, shredded
30ml/2 tbsp light soy sauce
15ml/1 tbsp apple juice
15ml/1 tbsp sesame
   seeds, toasted

1 Heat the oils in a wok and sauté the garlic over a low heat
for 2 minutes. Raise the heat, add the ginger, carrots, broccoli
and asparagus and stir-fry for 4 minutes. Add the cut spring
onions and spring greens and stir-fry for 2 minutes more.

2 Drizzle over the soy sauce and apple juice and toss over the
heat for 1–2 minutes, until the vegetables are crisp-tender.
Sprinkle the sesame seeds on top and serve.

Mixed Cabbage Stir-fry

Use three or four different
types of cabbage, including
pak choi.

Serves 4
15ml/1 tbsp vegetable oil
1 garlic clove, chopped
2.5cm/1in piece of fresh root
   ginger, finely chopped

450g/1lb mixed cabbage leaves,
   finely shredded
10ml/2 tsp light soy sauce
5ml/1 tsp clear honey
15ml/1 tbsp sesame
   seeds, toasted

1 Heat the oil in a wok and sauté the garlic over a low heat for
2 minutes. Raise the heat and add the ginger and shredded
cabbage. Stir-fry for 4 minutes.
2 Drizzle over the soy sauce and honey and toss over the heat
for 1–2 minutes. Sprinkle with the sesame seeds and serve.

Braised Aubergine & Courgettes

Fresh red chillies add a
flicker of fire to a dish that
is simple, spicy and quite
sensational. If you don't like
your food quite so hot, use
mild chillies or even sweet
red peppers.

Serves 4
1 aubergine, about 350g/12oz
2 small courgettes
15ml/1 tbsp vegetable oil

2 garlic cloves, finely chopped
2 fresh red chillies, seeded and
   finely chopped
1 small onion, diced
15ml/1 tbsp black bean sauce
15ml/1 tbsp dark soy sauce
45ml/3 tbsp water
salt

1 Trim the aubergine and slice it in half lengthways, then cut it
across into 1cm/½in slices. Layer the slices in a colander,
sprinkling each layer with salt. Leave the colander in the sink for
about 20 minutes, so the liquid that is drawn from the
aubergine drains away.

2 Meanwhile, roll cut each courgette by slicing off one end
diagonally, then rolling the courgette through 180° and taking
off another diagonal slice to form a triangular wedge. Make
more wedges of courgette in the same way.

3 Rinse the aubergine slices well under cold running water,
drain and dry thoroughly on kitchen paper.

4 Heat the oil in a preheated wok. Add the finely chopped
garlic, chopped chillies and diced onion and stir-fry over a
medium heat for 2–3 minutes. Stir in the black bean sauce,
coating the onions well.

5 Lower the heat and add the aubergine slices. Stir-fry for
2 minutes, sprinkling over a little water, if necessary, to prevent
them from burning.

6 Stir in the courgettes, soy sauce and measured water. Cook,
stirring occasionally, for 5 minutes. Serve hot.

Braised Beancurd with Mushrooms

The mushrooms flavour the beancurd (tofu) to make this the perfect low-fat vegetarian main course.

Serves 4
350g/12oz firm beancurd (tofu)
2.5ml/ 1/2 tsp sesame oil
10ml/2 tsp light soy sauce
15ml/1 tbsp vegetable oil
2 garlic cloves, finely chopped
2.5ml/ 1/2 tsp grated fresh
   root ginger
115g/4oz/1 1/2 cups shiitake
   mushrooms, stalks removed

175g/6oz/2 cups
   oyster mushrooms
115g/4oz/1 1/2 cups drained,
   canned straw mushrooms
115g/4oz/1 1/2 cups button
   mushrooms, cut in half
15ml/1 tbsp Chinese rice wine or
   medium-dry sherry
15ml/1 tbsp dark soy sauce
90ml/6 tbsp vegetable stock
5ml/1 tsp cornflour
15ml/1 tbsp water
salt and ground white pepper
2 spring onions, shredded,
   to garnish

1 Put the beancurd (tofu) in a dish and sprinkle with the sesame oil, light soy sauce and a large pinch of pepper. Leave to marinate for 10 minutes, then drain and cut into 2.5 × 1cm/1 × 1/2in pieces, using a sharp knife.

2 Heat the vegetable oil in a wok. Add the garlic and ginger and stir-fry over a low heat for a few seconds. Raise the heat, add all the mushrooms and stir-fry for 2 minutes.

3 Stir in the Chinese rice wine or sherry, soy sauce and stock and season with salt and pepper to taste. Toss over the heat for about 4 minutes.

4 Mix the cornflour to a paste with the water. Stir the mixture into the wok and cook, stirring constantly, until thickened.

5 Carefully add the pieces of beancurd, toss gently to coat thoroughly and simmer for 2 minutes.

6 Transfer the stir-fry to a large, warmed serving dish and scatter the shredded spring onions over the top to garnish. Serve immediately.

Red-cooked Beancurd with Chinese Mushrooms

Red-cooked is a term used for Chinese dishes cooked with dark soy sauce.

Serves 2–4
6 dried Chinese mushrooms
225g/8oz firm beancurd (tofu)
45ml/3 tbsp dark soy sauce
30ml/2 tbsp Chinese rice wine or
   medium-dry sherry
10ml/2 tsp soft dark brown sugar
1 garlic clove, crushed

15ml/1 tbsp grated fresh
   root ginger
2.5ml/ 1/2 tsp Chinese five-
   spice powder
pinch of ground roasted
   Szechuan peppercorns
5ml/1 tsp cornflour
30ml/2 tbsp groundnut oil
5–6 spring onions, sliced into
   short lengths
small fresh basil leaves, to garnish
cooked rice noodles, to serve

1 Soak the dried Chinese mushrooms in warm water for 20–30 minutes, until soft.

2 Meanwhile, cut the beancurd (tofu) into 2.5cm/1in cubes. Place in a shallow dish. Combine the soy sauce, rice wine or sherry, sugar, garlic, ginger, five-spice powder and Szechuan pepper. Pour this over the beancurd, toss lightly and marinate for 10 minutes. Drain, reserve the marinade and stir in the cornflour.

3 Drain the mushrooms, reserving 90ml/6 tbsp of the soaking liquid. Strain this into the cornflour mixture, mix well and set aside. Squeeze out any excess liquid from the mushrooms, remove the tough stalks and slice the caps.

4 Heat the oil in a wok and fry the beancurd for 2–3 minutes, until golden. Remove it with a draining spoon and set aside.

5 Add the mushrooms and the white parts of the spring onions to the wok and stir-fry for 2 minutes. Pour in the cornflour mixture and stir for 1 minute, until the mixture thickens. Return the beancurd to the wok with the green parts of the spring onions. Simmer for 1–2 minutes. Serve at once with a scattering of basil leaves and rice noodles.

Harvest Vegetable & Lentil Casserole

In autumn, thoughts turn to hearty, satisfying food. This sustaining, yet low-fat dish is the ideal choice.

Serves 6
15ml/1 tbsp sunflower oil
2 leeks, sliced
1 garlic clove, crushed
4 celery sticks, chopped
2 carrots, sliced
2 parsnips, diced
1 sweet potato, diced
225g/8oz swede, diced

175g/6oz/ 3/4 cup whole brown or
  green lentils
450g/1lb tomatoes, peeled,
  seeded and chopped
15ml/1 tbsp chopped fresh thyme
15ml/1 tbsp chopped
  fresh marjoram
900ml/1 1/2 pints/3 3/4 cups
  vegetable stock
15ml/1 tbsp cornflour
45ml/3 tbsp water
salt and ground black pepper
fresh thyme sprigs, to garnish

1 Preheat the oven to 180°C/350°F/Gas 4. Heat the oil in a large flameproof casserole. Add the leeks, garlic and celery and cook over a low heat, stirring occasionally, for 3 minutes, until the onion is beginning to soften.

2 Add the carrots, parsnips, sweet potato, swede, lentils, tomatoes, herbs and stock. Stir well and season with salt and pepper to taste. Bring to the boil, stirring occasionally.

3 Cover the casserole, put it in the oven and bake for about 50 minutes, until the vegetables and lentils are tender, stirring the vegetable mixture once or twice.

4 Remove the casserole from the oven. Blend the cornflour with the water in a small bowl. Stir the mixture into the casserole and heat it gently on top of the stove, stirring continuously, until the mixture boils and thickens. Lower the heat and simmer gently for 2 minutes, stirring.

5 Spoon on to warmed serving plates or into bowls, garnish with the thyme sprigs and serve.

Mushroom & Fennel Hot-pot

Marvellous flavours permeate this unusual main course or accompaniment, which makes the most of dried and fresh mushrooms.

Serves 4
25g/1oz/2 cups dried
  shiitake mushrooms
30ml/2 tbsp olive oil
12 shallots, peeled and left whole

1 small head of fennel,
  roughly chopped
225g/8oz/3 cups button
  mushrooms, halved
300ml/ 1/2 pint/1 1/4 cups dry cider
2 large pieces sun-dried tomatoes
  in oil, drained and sliced
30ml/2 tbsp sun-dried
  tomato paste
1 bay leaf
chopped fresh parsley, to garnish

1 Place the dried mushrooms in a bowl. Pour over boiling water to cover and set aside for 20 minutes. Drain, reserving the liquid. Discard the stalks and chop the caps into pieces.

2 Heat the oil in a flameproof casserole. Add the shallots and fennel and sauté over a low heat, stirring occasionally, for 10 minutes, or until the mixture has softened and the shallots are lightly browned.

3 Add the button mushrooms and fry for 2–3 minutes, then stir in the shiitake mushrooms and fry for 1 minute more.

4 Pour in the cider and stir in the sun-dried tomatoes and sun-dried tomato paste. Add the bay leaf. Bring to the boil, then lower the heat, cover the casserole and simmer gently for about 30 minutes.

5 If the mixture seems dry, stir in the reserved liquid from the soaked mushrooms. Reheat briefly, then remove the bay leaf and serve, sprinkled with plenty of chopped parsley.

Cook's Tip
Dried mushrooms swell up a great deal after soaking, so a little goes a long way in terms of both flavour and quantity.

Balti Stir-fried Vegetables with Cashews

This versatile stir-fry recipe will accommodate most other combinations of vegetables – you do not have to use the selection suggested here.

Serves 4

2 medium carrots
1 medium red pepper, seeded
1 medium green pepper, seeded
2 courgettes
115g/4oz green beans, halved
1 medium bunch of spring onions
15ml/1 tbsp virgin olive oil
4–6 curry leaves
2.5ml/ ½ tsp white cumin seeds
4 dried red chillies
10–12 cashew nuts
5ml/1 tsp salt
30ml/2 tbsp lemon juice
fresh mint leaves, to garnish

1 Prepare the vegetables: cut the carrots, peppers and courgettes into matchsticks, halve the beans and chop the spring onions. Set aside.

2 Heat the oil in a wok and stir-fry the curry leaves, cumin seeds and dried chillies for 1 minute.

3 Add the vegetables and nuts and toss them over the heat for 3–4 minutes. Add the salt and lemon juice. Continue to stir and toss over the heat for 2 minutes more, or until the vegetables are crisp-tender.

4 Transfer to a warmed serving dish. Remove the dried chillies, if you like. Serve immediately, garnished with mint leaves.

> **Cook's Tips**
> • When making any of the stir-fries in this section, it is a good idea to use a non-stick wok to minimize the amount of oil needed. However, it cannot be heated to the same high temperature as a conventional wok.
> • You can reduce the fat content still further by using a light oil cooking spray instead of the olive oil.

Carrot & Cauliflower Stir-fry

There's plenty of crunch in this tasty, quick-cooking supper dish, which is high in fibre, but very low in fat.

Serves 4

15ml/1 tbsp olive oil
1 bay leaf
2 cloves
1 small cinnamon stick
2 cardamom pods
3 black peppercorns
5ml/1 tsp salt
2 large carrots, cut into thin batons
1 small cauliflower, broken into florets
50g/2oz/ ½ cup frozen peas
10ml/2 tsp lemon juice
15ml/1 tbsp chopped fresh coriander
fresh coriander leaves, to garnish

1 Heat the oil in a wok and add the bay leaf, cloves, cinnamon stick, cardamoms and peppercorns. Stir-fry over a medium heat for 30–35 seconds, then add the salt.

2 Add the carrot and cauliflower and stir-fry for 3–5 minutes. Add the peas, lemon juice and chopped coriander and cook for 2–3 minutes more. Serve, garnished with the coriander leaves.

Broccoli Stir-fry

Ginger and orange make this quick stir-fry deliciously tangy and flavoursome.

Serves 4

675g/1½lb broccoli, broken into florets
2 slices fresh root ginger
juice of 1 orange
10ml/2 tsp cornflour
2.5ml/½ tsp sugar
60ml/4 tbsp water
15ml/1 tbsp olive oil
1 garlic clove, thinly sliced
matchstick strips of orange rind, soaked in cold water

1 Slice the broccoli stems and cut the ginger into matchsticks. Mix the orange juice with the cornflour, sugar and water.
2 Heat the oil in a wok. Stir-fry the stems for 2 minutes. Add the ginger, garlic and florets and stir-fry for 3 minutes. Stir in the orange mixture until thickened. Toss in the rind and serve.

Balti Mushrooms in a Creamy Garlic Sauce

Low-fat and virtually fat-free fromage frais are real finds for anyone who is trying to limit the amount of fat he or she consumes. It gives this stir-fry a deceptively creamy taste.

Serves 4

15ml/1 tbsp olive oil
1 bay leaf
3 garlic cloves, roughly chopped
2 fresh green chillies, seeded
   and chopped
350g/12oz/4½ cups button
   mushrooms, halved
30–45ml/2–3 tbsp
   vegetable stock
225g/8oz/1 cup low-fat
   fromage frais
15ml/1 tbsp chopped fresh mint
15ml/1 tbsp chopped
   fresh coriander
5ml/1 tsp salt
fresh mint and coriander leaves,
   to garnish

1 Heat the oil in a wok, add the bay leaf, garlic and chillies and cook for about 1 minute.

2 Add the mushrooms and moisten them with the stock. Cook over a high heat, stirring constantly, for 3–5 minutes, until the stock has been absorbed.

3 Remove the wok from the heat and stir in the fromage frais, mint, coriander and salt. Return the wok to the heat and cook, stirring constantly, for 2 minutes, until heated through. Transfer to a warmed serving dish. Garnish with the mint and coriander leaves and serve immediately.

> **Cook's Tip**
> All kinds of mushrooms will absorb an astonishing amount of fat, as anyone who has fried them in butter or oil will appreciate. Try using a well-flavoured, home-made vegetable stock instead; the mushrooms will cook beautifully and will remain lovely and juicy.

Sweetcorn & Cauliflower Balti

This quick and tasty vegetable dish is easily made with frozen sweetcorn.

Serves 4

15ml/1 tbsp corn oil
4 curry leaves
1.5ml/¼ tsp onion seeds
2 medium onions, diced
1 fresh red chilli, seeded
   and diced
175g/6oz/1 cup frozen
   sweetcorn kernels
½ small cauliflower, cut into
   small florets
6 fresh mint leaves

1 Heat the oil in a wok. Add the curry leaves and the onion seeds and stir-fry for about 30 seconds.

2 Add the onions and stir-fry for 5–8 minutes, until golden brown. Stir in the chilli, sweetcorn and cauliflower and stir-fry for 5–8 minutes.

3 Finally, add the mint leaves and serve at once.

Glazed Mangetouts & Peppers

A delectable sauce coats the crisp-tender vegetables in this simple stir-fry.

Serves 2–4

5ml/1 tsp cornflour
10ml/2 tsp dry sherry
15ml/1 tbsp soy sauce
90ml/6 tbsp vegetable stock
15ml/1 tbsp sweet chilli sauce
15ml/1 tbsp sunflower oil
2 red peppers, seeded and sliced
115g/4oz/1 cup mangetouts

1 Mix the cornflour to a paste with the sherry. Stir in the soy sauce, stock and chilli sauce.
2 Heat the oil in a wok and stir-fry the pepper slices and mangetouts for 2–3 minutes, until crisp-tender.
3 Stir in the cornflour mixture and toss over the heat for 1–2 minutes, until the vegetables are glistening and the sauce is hot. Serve at once.

Balti Potatoes with Aubergines

Using baby vegetables adds to the attractiveness and the flavour of this dish.

Serves 4

10–12 baby potatoes, unpeeled
15ml/1 tbsp corn oil
2 medium onions, sliced
4–6 curry leaves
2.5ml/½ tsp onion seeds
5ml/1 tsp crushed
  coriander seeds
2.5ml/1 tsp cumin seeds
1 medium red pepper, seeded
  and sliced
5ml/1 tsp grated fresh root ginger
5ml/1 tsp crushed garlic
5ml/1 tsp crushed dried
  red chillies
15ml/1 tbsp chopped
  fresh fenugreek
6 small aubergines, cut
  in quarters
5ml/1 tsp chopped
  fresh coriander
15ml/1 tbsp natural
  low-fat yogurt
fresh coriander leaves, to garnish

1 Bring a pan of water to the boil, add the potatoes and cook them for about 20 minutes, until just soft. Drain and set aside.

2 Heat the oil in a wok and fry the onions, curry leaves, onion seeds, crushed coriander seeds and cumin seeds until the onions are a pale golden brown.

3 Add the pepper strips, ginger, garlic, crushed chillies and fenugreek, followed by the aubergines and potatoes. Stir everything together and cover with a lid. Lower the heat and cook for 5–7 minutes.

4 Remove the lid and add the fresh coriander. Stir in the yogurt. Serve garnished with the coriander leaves.

> **Cook's Tip**
> To prevent curdling it is always best to whisk the yogurt before adding it to a hot dish. If using a larger quantity of yogurt than is required for this recipe, stabilize it with 5ml/1 tsp cornflour before adding it to a hot dish.

Balti French Beans with Sweetcorn

Frozen French beans are useful for this, as they cook quickly. This dish makes a colourful accompaniment.

Serves 4

15ml/1 tbsp sunflower oil
1.5ml/¼ tsp mustard seeds
1 medium red onion, diced
50g/2oz/⅓ cup frozen
  sweetcorn kernels
50g/2oz/⅓ cup drained canned
  red kidney beans, rinsed
175g/6oz frozen French beans
1 fresh red chilli, seeded
  and diced
1 garlic clove, chopped
2.5cm/1in piece of fresh root
  ginger, finely chopped
15ml/1 tbsp chopped
  fresh coriander
5ml/1 tsp salt
1 tomato, seeded and diced,
  to garnish

1 Heat the oil in a wok. Add the mustard seeds and onion and fry over a low heat, stirring occasionally, for about 2 minutes, until the seeds begin to pop and give off their aroma and the onion is beginning to soften.

2 Add the sweetcorn, kidney beans and French beans. Toss over the heat for about 3–5 minutes, until the frozen vegetables have thawed and the beans are crisp-tender.

3 Add the chilli, garlic, ginger, coriander and salt and toss over the heat for 2–3 minutes.

4 Remove the wok from the heat. Transfer the mixture to a warmed serving dish and garnish with the diced tomato.

> **Cook's Tip**
> Strictly speaking, Balti dishes are cooked in a karahi or Balti pan, which is similar to a wok and available in a range of sizes and materials. It is possible to stir-fry in an ordinary frying pan, as long as it is quite deep, but the heat is not distributed so evenly. In Pakistan, the food is often served directly from the karahi, placed on a special stand on the table.

Mushroom & Okra Curry

This simple but delicious curry is served with a fresh gingery mango relish.

Serves 4

4 garlic cloves, roughly chopped
2.5cm/1in piece of fresh root
  ginger, roughly chopped
1–2 fresh red chillies, seeded
  and chopped
175ml/6fl oz/ ¾ cup cold water
15ml/1 tbsp sunflower oil
5ml/1 tsp coriander seeds
5ml/1 tsp cumin seeds
5ml/1 tsp ground cumin
seeds from 2 green cardamom
  pods, ground
pinch of ground turmeric
400g/14oz can
  chopped tomatoes

450g/1lb/6 cups mushrooms,
  quartered if large
225g/8oz okra, trimmed and cut
  into 1cm/ ½in slices
30ml/2 tbsp chopped
  fresh coriander
cooked basmati rice, to serve

For the mango relish

1 large ripe mango, about
  500g/1¼lb
1 small garlic clove, crushed
1 onion, finely chopped
10ml/2 tsp grated fresh
  root ginger
1 fresh red chilli, seeded and
  finely chopped
pinch of granulated sugar
pinch of salt

1 First. make the relish. Peel the mango and cut the flesh from the stone. Mash it in a bowl or pulse it in a food processor. Stir in the rest of the relish ingredients. Set aside.

2 Put the garlic, ginger, chillies and 45ml/3 tbsp of the water into a blender and blend until smooth.

3 Heat the oil in a large pan. Add the coriander and cumin seeds and let them sizzle for a few seconds. Add the ground cumin, cardamom and turmeric and cook for 1 minute. Add the paste from the blender, the tomatoes, the remaining water, the mushrooms and okra. Stir and bring to the boil. Lower the heat, cover, and simmer for 5 minutes.

4 Uncover and cook for 10 minutes more, until the okra is tender. Stir in the coriander and serve with the relish and rice.

Bengali-style Vegetables

Many curries need to be cooked slowly if their full flavour is to be realized. This one is very quick and easy, thanks to spices that rapidly release their properties.

Serves 4

½ cauliflower, broken into florets
1 large potato, peeled and cut
  into 2.5cm/1in dice
115g/4oz French beans, trimmed
2 courgettes, halved lengthways
  and sliced
2 fresh green chillies, seeded
  and chopped

2.5cm/1in piece of fresh root
  ginger, finely chopped
120ml/4fl oz/ ½ cup
  natural yogurt
10ml/2 tsp ground coriander
2.5ml/ ½ tsp ground turmeric
25g/1oz/2 tbsp ghee or
  clarified butter
2.5ml/ ½ tsp garam masala
5ml/1 tsp cumin seeds
10ml/2 tsp granulated sugar
pinch of ground cloves
pinch of ground cinnamon
pinch of ground cardamom
salt and ground black pepper

1 Bring a large pan of lightly salted water to the boil. Add the cauliflower and potato and cook for 5 minutes. Add the beans and courgettes and cook for 2–3 minutes more.

2 Drain the vegetables and tip them into a bowl. Add the chillies, ginger, yogurt, ground coriander and turmeric. Season with plenty of salt and pepper and mix well.

3 Heat the ghee in a large frying pan. Add the vegetable mixture and cook over a high heat for 2 minutes, stirring.

4 Stir in the garam masala and whole cumin seeds and fry for 2 minutes. Stir in the sugar and the remaining spices. Cook for about 1 minute or until all the liquid has evaporated. Serve.

Cook's Tip
To clarify butter, melt 50g/2oz/ ¼ cup butter in a small pan. Remove from the heat and leave for 5 minutes. Pour off the clear yellow clarified butter, leaving the sediment in the pan.

Spinach with Mushrooms & Red Pepper

This is a wonderful way to cook three tasty and nutritious vegetables. Serve the stir-fry very hot, with freshly made chapatis.

Serves 4
450g/1lb fresh or frozen spinach
30ml/2 tbsp corn oil
2 onions, diced
6–8 curry leaves
1.5ml/ ¼ tsp onion seeds
5ml/1 tsp crushed garlic
5ml/1 tsp grated fresh root ginger
5ml/1 tsp mild chilli powder
5ml/1 tsp salt
7.5ml/1 ½ tsp ground coriander
1 large red pepper, seeded and sliced
115g/4oz/1 ½ cups mushrooms, roughly chopped
225g/8oz/1 cup low-fat fromage frais
30ml/2 tbsp fresh coriander leaves

1 Blanch fresh spinach briefly in boiling water and drain thoroughly. Thaw frozen spinach, then drain. Set aside.

2 Heat the oil in a wok. Add the onions, curry leaves and onion seeds and fry, stirring occasionally, for 1–2 minutes. Add the garlic, ginger, chilli powder, salt and ground coriander. Stir-fry for 2–3 minutes more.

3 Add half the red pepper slices and all the mushrooms and continue to stir-fry for 2–3 minutes.

4 Add the spinach and stir-fry for 4–6 minutes. Finally, stir in the fromage frais and half the fresh coriander, followed by the remaining red pepper slices. Fry over a medium heat, stirring constantly, for 2–3 minutes more before serving, garnished with the remaining coriander.

Variation
For a spicier dish, add one finely chopped fresh red chilli with the pepper slices in step 3.

Rice Noodles with Vegetable Chilli Sauce

A mixture of fresh and canned ingredients, this is a very versatile dish.

Serves 4
15ml/1 tbsp sunflower oil
1 onion, chopped
2 garlic cloves, crushed
1 fresh red chilli, seeded and finely chopped
1 red pepper, seeded and diced
2 carrots, finely chopped
175g/6oz/1 ½ cups baby sweetcorn, halved
225g/8oz can sliced bamboo shoots, drained and rinsed
400g/14oz can red kidney beans, drained and rinsed
300ml/ ½ pint/1 ¼ cups passata or sieved tomatoes
15ml/1 tbsp soy sauce
5ml/1 tsp ground coriander
250g/9oz rice noodles
30ml/2 tbsp chopped fresh coriander
salt and ground black pepper
fresh parsley sprigs, to garnish

1 Heat the oil in a large pan and fry the onion, garlic, chilli and red pepper, stirring occasionally, for 5 minutes. Stir in the carrots, sweetcorn, bamboo shoots, kidney beans, passata or sieved tomatoes, soy sauce and ground coriander. Bring to the boil, then lower the heat, cover and simmer gently, stirring occasionally, for 30 minutes, until the vegetables are tender. Season with salt and pepper to taste.

2 Meanwhile, bring a large pan of water to the boil, add the noodles and remove the pan from the heat. Cover and leave to stand for about 4 minutes, until the noodles are just tender. Drain thoroughly, rinse with boiling water and drain again.

3 Stir the coriander into the sauce. Spoon the noodles into bowls, top with the sauce, garnish with parsley and serve.

Cook's Tip
Rice noodles are specified here, but you can use any type of noodles or even spaghetti.

Penne with Artichokes

The sauce for this pasta dish is garlicky and richly flavoured. It would make the perfect first course for a dinner party during the globe artichoke season.

Serves 6
juice of ½ lemon
2 globe artichokes
15ml/1 tbsp olive oil
1 small fennel bulb, thinly sliced, with feathery tops reserved
1 onion, finely chopped
4 garlic cloves, finely chopped
a handful of fresh flat leaf parsley, roughly chopped
400g/14oz can chopped Italian plum tomatoes
150ml/¼ pint/⅔ cup dry white wine
350g/12oz/3 cups dried penne
10ml/2 tsp capers, chopped
salt and ground black pepper
freshly grated Parmesan cheese, to serve

1 Fill a bowl with cold water and add the lemon juice. Cut off the artichoke stalks, then pull off and discard the outer leaves. Cut off the tops of the pale inner leaves so that the base remains. Cut this in half lengthways, then prise out and discard the hairy choke. Cut the artichokes lengthways into 5mm/¼in slices, adding these to the bowl of acidulated water.

2 Bring a large pan of salted water to the boil, add the artichokes and boil them for 5 minutes. Drain and set aside.

3 Heat the oil in a large frying pan and cook the fennel, onion, garlic and parsley over a low heat for about 10 minutes, until the fennel has softened and is lightly coloured. Add the tomatoes and wine, with salt and pepper to taste. Bring to the boil, stirring, then simmer for 10–15 minutes. Stir in the artichokes, replace the lid and simmer for 10 minutes more.

4 Meanwhile, bring a pan of lightly salted water to the boil and cook the pasta for about 12 minutes, until it is al dente.

5 Drain the pasta and return it to the clean pan. Stir the capers into the sauce, pour it over the pasta and toss well. Serve immediately, garnished with the reserved fennel fronds. Offer grated Parmesan separately.

Conchiglie with Roasted Vegetables

Nothing could be simpler – or more delicious – than tossing freshly cooked pasta with roasted vegetables.

Serves 4
1 small aubergine
30ml/2 tbsp extra virgin olive oil, plus extra for brushing
1 red pepper, seeded and cut into 1cm/½in squares
1 yellow or orange pepper, seeded and cut into 1cm/½in squares
2 courgettes, roughly diced
15ml/1 tbsp chopped fresh flat leaf parsley
5ml/1 tsp dried oregano
250g/9oz baby Italian plum tomatoes, halved lengthways
2 garlic cloves, roughly chopped
350g/12oz/3 cups dried conchiglie
salt and ground black pepper
4–6 fresh herb flowers, to garnish

1 Preheat the oven to 230°C/450°F/Gas 8. Cut the aubergine in half and score the cut sides deeply. Brush a roasting tin lightly with oil and place the aubergines on it, cut sides down. Roast for 15 minutes. Remove the aubergine from the oven and lower the temperature to 190°C/375°F/Gas 5.

2 Cut the aubergine halves into chunks and return them to the roasting tin. Add the peppers and courgettes.

3 Pour the olive oil over the vegetables and sprinkle with the herbs and salt and pepper to taste. Stir well. Roast for about 30 minutes, stirring twice. Stir in the tomatoes and garlic, then roast for 20 minutes more, stirring once or twice.

4 Meanwhile, bring a large pan of lightly salted water to the boil and cook the pasta for about 12 minutes or until it is al dente.

5 Drain the pasta and tip it into a warmed bowl. Add the roasted vegetables and toss well. Garnish with herb flowers.

> **Cook's Tip**
> Roasting the aubergine first releases some of its liquid and also makes it less likely to absorb fat.

Rigatoni with Winter Tomato Sauce

In winter, when fresh tomatoes are not at their best, Italians use canned tomatoes to make this superb sauce, which is particularly good with chunky pasta shapes.

Serves 6–8
30ml/2 tbsp olive oil
1 garlic clove, thinly sliced
1 onion, finely chopped
1 carrot, finely chopped
1 celery stick, finely chopped
a few leaves each fresh
   basil, thyme and oregano
   or marjoram

2 x 400g/14oz cans chopped
   Italian plum tomatoes
15ml/1 tbsp sun-dried
   tomato paste
5ml/1 tsp granulated sugar
about 90ml/6 tbsp dry red or
   white wine (optional)
350g/12oz/3 cups dried rigatoni
salt and ground black pepper
chopped fresh mixed herbs,
   such as thyme and basil, to
   garnish (optional)
coarsely shaved Parmesan
   cheese, to serve

1 Heat the olive oil in a medium saucepan, add the garlic slices and stir over a very low heat for 1–2 minutes.

2 Add the onion, carrot, celery, basil, thyme and oregano or marjoram. Cook over a low heat, stirring frequently, for 5–7 minutes, until all the vegetables have softened and are lightly coloured.

3 Add the canned tomatoes, tomato paste and sugar, then stir in the wine, if using. Season with salt and pepper to taste. Bring to the boil, stirring constantly, then lower the heat and simmer for about 45 minutes, stirring occasionally.

4 Meanwhile, bring a large pan of lightly salted water to the boil and cook the pasta for 12 minutes or until *al dente*. Drain it and tip it into a warmed bowl.

5 Pour the sauce over the rigatoni and toss well. If you like, garnish with extra chopped herbs. Serve immediately, with shavings of Parmesan handed separately.

Wholemeal Pasta with Caraway Cabbage

Crunchy cabbage and Brussels sprouts are the perfect partners for pasta in this healthy dish.

Serves 6
30ml/2 tbsp olive oil
3 onions, roughly chopped
400ml/14fl oz/1²/₃ cups
   vegetable stock

350g/12oz round white cabbage,
   roughly chopped
350g/12oz Brussels sprouts,
   trimmed and halved
10ml/2 tsp caraway seeds
15ml/1 tbsp chopped fresh dill
200g/7oz/1³/₄ cups fresh or dried
   wholewheat pasta spirals
salt and ground black pepper
fresh dill sprigs, to garnish

1 Heat the oil in a large saucepan. Add the onions and fry over a low heat, stirring occasionally, for 10 minutes, until softened and golden in colour. If they start to stick to the pan, moisten them with a little of the stock.

2 Add the chopped cabbage and Brussels sprouts and cook for 2–3 minutes, then stir in the caraway seeds and chopped dill. Pour in the remaining stock and season with salt and pepper to taste. Cover and simmer for 5–10 minutes, until the cabbage and sprouts are crisp-tender.

3 Meanwhile, bring a pan of lightly salted water to the boil and cook the pasta for 12 minutes, or until *al dente*.

4 Drain the pasta, tip it into a warmed bowl and add the cabbage mixture. Toss lightly, adjust the seasoning, if necessary, and serve immediately, garnished with dill.

> **Cook's Tips**
> • If tiny baby Brussels sprouts are available, they can be used whole for this dish.
> • Not only do caraway seeds complement the flavour of cabbage, they also make it more digestible.

Tagliatelle with Pea Sauce, Asparagus & Broad Beans

A creamy pea sauce provides a wonderful contrast to the crunchy young vegetables.

Serves 4
15ml/1 tbsp olive oil
1 garlic clove, crushed
6 spring onions, sliced
225g/8oz/2 cups frozen
 peas, thawed
30ml/2 tbsp chopped fresh sage,
 plus extra leaves to garnish
finely grated rind of 2 lemons
450ml/3/4 pint/scant 2 cups
 vegetable stock
350g/12oz fresh young
 asparagus, trimmed and cut
 into 5cm/2in lengths
225g/8oz/2 cups frozen broad
 beans, thawed
450g/1lb/2 cups fresh or
 dried tagliatelle
60ml/4 tbsp low-fat
 yogurt, whisked

1 Heat the oil in a pan. Add the garlic and spring onions and fry over a low heat, stirring occasionally, for 2–3 minutes, until softened, but not coloured.

2 Add the peas, sage, lemon rind and stock. Stir in one-third of the asparagus stalks. Bring to the boil, lower the heat and simmer for 10 minutes, until tender. Process in a blender until smooth, then scrape into a saucepan.

3 Pop the broad beans out of their skins and set them aside. Bring a large pan of water to the boil, add the remaining asparagus and blanch for 2 minutes. Transfer the asparagus pieces to a colander with a draining spoon and set aside.

4 Bring the water in the pan back to the boil, add the tagliatelle and cook for about 10 minutes, until it is *al dente*.

5 Meanwhile, add the cooked asparagus and shelled beans to the sauce and reheat. Off the heat, stir the yogurt into the sauce. Drain the pasta and divide among four warmed plates. Top the pasta with the sauce. Garnish with a few extra sage leaves and serve immediately.

Mushroom Bolognese

A quick – and exceedingly tasty – vegetarian version of the classic Italian meat dish.

Serves 4
15ml/1 tbsp olive oil
1 onion, chopped
1 garlic clove, crushed
450g/1lb/6 cups
 mushrooms, quartered
15ml/1 tbsp tomato purée
400g/14oz can
 chopped tomatoes
15ml/1 tbsp chopped
 fresh oregano
450g/1lb fresh pasta
salt and ground black pepper
chopped fresh oregano, to garnish
Parmesan cheese, to
 serve (optional)

1 Heat the oil in a large pan. Add the chopped onion and garlic and fry over a low heat, stirring occasionally, for 2–3 minutes, until just beginning to soften.

2 Add the mushrooms to the pan and cook over a high heat, stirring occasionally, for 3–4 minutes.

3 Stir in the tomato purée, chopped tomatoes and oregano. Lower the heat, cover and cook for 5 minutes.

4 Meanwhile, bring a large pan of lightly salted water to the boil. Cook the pasta for 2–3 minutes until *al dente*.

5 Season the mushroom sauce to taste with salt and pepper. Drain the pasta, tip it into a bowl and add the mushroom mixture. Toss thoroughly to mix. Serve in individual bowls. Add a sprinkling of extra oregano and top with shavings of fresh Parmesan cheese, if you like.

> **Cook's Tips**
> • If you prefer to use dried pasta, make it the first thing that you cook. It will take 10–12 minutes, during which time you can make the mushroom sauce.
> • This dish is even more delicious if you use wild mushrooms, such as ceps, oysters and chanterelles.

Mixed Vegetable & Macaroni Bake

A tasty change from macaroni cheese, this dish is great for a family meal.

Serves 6

225g/8oz/2 cups
  wholewheat macaroni
450ml/¾ cup/scant 2 cups
  vegetable stock
225g/8oz leeks, sliced
225g/8oz broccoli florets
50g/2oz/4 tbsp half-fat spread
50g/2oz/ ½ cup plain
  wholemeal flour

600ml/1 pint/2½ cups
  skimmed milk
115g/4oz/1 cup grated reduced-
  fat mature Cheddar cheese
5ml/1 tsp prepared
  English mustard
350g/12oz can sweetcorn
  kernels, drained
25g/1oz/ ½ cup fresh
  wholemeal breadcrumbs
30ml/2 tbsp chopped
  fresh parsley
2 tomatoes, cut into eighths
salt and ground black pepper

1 Preheat the oven to 200°C/400°F/Gas 6. Bring a large pan of lightly salted water to the boil and cook the macaroni for 8–10 minutes, until *al dente*.

2 Meanwhile, heat the stock in a separate pan and cook the leeks for 8 minutes. Add the broccoli florets and cook for 2 minutes more. Drain, reserving 300ml/½ pint/1¼ cups of the vegetable stock.

3 Put the half-fat spread, flour and milk in a saucepan. Add the reserved stock. Heat gently, whisking constantly, until the sauce comes to the boil and has thickened. Simmer gently for 3 minutes, stirring constantly.

4 Remove the pan from the heat, stir in two-thirds of the cheese, then add the macaroni, leeks, broccoli, mustard and sweetcorn. Mix well and season with salt and pepper to taste. Transfer the mixture to an ovenproof dish.

5 Mix the remaining cheese, breadcrumbs and parsley and sprinkle the mixture over the surface. Arrange the tomatoes on top and then bake for 30–40 minutes, until the topping is golden brown and bubbling.

Spinach & Hazelnut Lasagne

Using low-fat fromage frais instead of a white sauce makes this a healthy version of a popular vegetarian dish, and spinach and hazelnuts provide variations, on the usual themes.

Serves 4

900g/2lb fresh spinach
300ml/ ½ pint/1¼ cups
  vegetable stock

1 medium onion, finely chopped
1 garlic clove, crushed
75g/3oz/ ¾ cup hazelnuts
30ml/2 tbsp chopped fresh basil
6 sheets no pre-cook lasagne
400g/14oz can
  chopped tomatoes
200g/7oz/scant 1 cup low-fat
  fromage frais
salt and ground black pepper
flaked hazelnuts and chopped
  fresh parsley, to garnish

1 Preheat the oven to 200°C/400°F/Gas 6. Wash the spinach and place it in a pan with just the water that is still clinging to the leaves. Cover and cook over a fairly high heat for about 2 minutes, until the spinach has wilted. Drain well and set aside until required.

2 Heat 30ml/2 tbsp of the stock in a large pan. Add the onion and garlic, bring to the boil, then simmer until softened. Stir in the spinach, hazelnuts and basil.

3 In a large ovenproof dish, make layers of the spinach, lasagne and tomatoes. Season each layer with salt and pepper to taste. Pour over the remaining stock. Spread the fromage frais evenly over the top.

4 Bake the lasagne for about 45 minutes, or until golden brown. Serve hot, garnished with lines of flaked hazelnuts and chopped fresh parsley.

Cook's Tip
The flavour of hazelnuts is improved if they are roasted. Place them on a baking sheet and bake in a moderate oven or under a hot grill until light golden.

Courgette, Sweetcorn & Plum Tomato Wholewheat Pizza

This tasty wholewheat pizza has a colourful topping. It is good hot or cold.

Serves 6

225g/8oz/2 cups plain
    wholemeal flour
pinch of salt
10ml/2 tsp baking powder
50g/2oz/4 tbsp margarine
150ml/¼ pint/⅔ cup
    skimmed milk
30ml/2 tbsp tomato purée
10ml/2 tsp dried herbes
    de Provence

10ml/2 tsp olive oil
1 onion, sliced
1 garlic clove, crushed
2 small courgettes, sliced
115g/4oz/1½ cups
    mushrooms, sliced
115g/4oz/⅔ cup frozen
    sweetcorn kernels
2 plum tomatoes, sliced
50g/2oz/½ cup grated reduced-
    fat Red Leicester cheese
50g/2oz/½ cup grated half-fat
    mozzarella cheese
salt and ground black pepper
fresh basil sprigs, to garnish

1 Preheat the oven to 220°C/425°F/Gas 7. Line a baking sheet with non-stick baking paper. Put the flour, salt and baking powder in a bowl and rub in the margarine until the mixture resembles breadcrumbs. Add enough milk to form a soft dough and knead lightly. Roll the dough out on a lightly floured surface, to a round about 25cm/10in in diameter.

2 Place the dough on the prepared baking sheet and pinch the edges to make a rim. Spread the tomato purée over the base and sprinkle the herbs on top.

3 Heat the oil in a frying pan and cook the onion, garlic, courgettes and mushrooms gently for 10 minutes, stirring occasionally. Spread the vegetable mixture over the pizza base, sprinkle over the sweetcorn and season to taste with salt and pepper. Arrange the tomato slices on top.

4 Mix the cheeses and sprinkle over the pizza. Bake for 25–30 minutes, until cooked and golden brown. Serve the pizza hot or cold in slices, garnished with basil sprigs.

Low-fat Calzone

Like pizza, calzone conjures up an image of sheer indulgence in terms of its fat content, but here's one you can eat with a completely clear conscience.

Makes 4

450g/1lb/4 cups plain flour
pinch of salt
1 sachet easy-blend dried yeast
about 350ml/12fl oz/1½ cups
    warm water

For the filling

5ml/1 tsp olive oil, plus extra
    for greasing
1 medium red onion, thinly sliced
3 medium courgettes, total weight
    about 350g/12oz, sliced
2 large tomatoes, diced
150g/5oz half-fat mozzarella
    cheese, diced
15ml/1 tbsp chopped fresh
    oregano, plus extra sprigs,
    to garnish
skimmed milk, to glaze
salt and ground black pepper

1 Sift the flour and salt into a bowl and stir in the yeast. Stir in just enough warm water to mix to a soft dough. Knead for about 5 minutes, until smooth.

2 Return to the clean bowl, cover with clear film and leave in a warm place for about 1 hour, or until doubled in bulk.

3 Meanwhile, make the filling. Heat the oil. Add the onion and courgettes and fry over a low heat, stirring occasionally, for 3–4 minutes, until softened but not coloured. Remove from the heat and add the tomatoes, cheese and oregano, then season with salt and pepper to taste.

4 Preheat the oven to 220°C/425°F/Gas 7. Knead the dough lightly and divide into four pieces. Roll out each piece on a floured surface to a 20cm/8in round. Place one-quarter of the filling on one half of each round.

5 Brush the edges of each round with milk and fold the dough over, pastie-style, to enclose the filling. Press the edges together firmly to seal. Brush each calzone with milk to glaze.

6 Bake on a lightly oiled baking sheet for 15–20 minutes. Serve.

Polenta with Baked Tomatoes & Olives

A staple of northern Italy, polenta is a nourishing, filling food, served here with a delicious fresh tomato and olive topping.

Serves 4–6
2 litres/3½ pints/9 cups water
500g/1¼ lb/4½ cups quick-
  cook polenta

10ml/2 tsp olive oil, plus extra
  for greasing
12 large ripe plum
  tomatoes, sliced
4 garlic cloves, thinly sliced
30ml/2 tbsp chopped fresh
  oregano or marjoram
115g/4oz/1 cup pitted
  black olives
salt and ground black pepper

1 Pour the water into a large saucepan and bring it to the boil. Add the polenta, whisking constantly, and continue to whisk while simmering for 5 minutes.

2 Remove the pan from the heat and pour the polenta into a 33 x 23cm/13 x 9in Swiss roll tin. Smooth the surface level and leave to cool.

3 Preheat the oven to 180°C/350°F/Gas 4. When the polenta is cool and set, stamp out 12 rounds with a 7.5cm/3in round pastry cutter. Lay them so that they overlap slightly in a lightly oiled ovenproof dish.

4 Layer the tomatoes, garlic, fresh herbs and olives on top of the polenta, seasoning the layers with salt and pepper to taste as you go. Drizzle with the olive oil, and bake, uncovered, for 30–35 minutes. Serve immediately.

> **Cook's Tip**
> Olive oil contains a high proportion of monounsaturated fats – the "good" fats – as well as vitamin A. It is a healthy choice, as it helps to lower levels of blood cholesterol and forms a useful part of a low-fat diet.

Potato Gnocchi with Hazelnut Sauce

These delicate potato dumplings are dressed with a light creamy-tasting hazelnut sauce.

Serves 4
675g/1½lb large potatoes
115g/4oz/1 cup plain flour, plus
  extra for dusting

For the hazelnut sauce
115g/4oz/1 cup
  hazelnuts, roasted
1 garlic clove, roughly chopped
2.5ml/½ tsp grated lemon rind
2.5ml/½ tsp lemon juice
30ml/2 tbsp sunflower oil
150g/5oz/scant ¾ cup low-fat
  fromage blanc
salt and ground black pepper

1 Make the sauce. Put just over half of the hazelnuts in a food processor or blender with the garlic, grated lemon rind and juice. Process until coarsely chopped. With the motor running, gradually add the oil until the mixture is smooth. Spoon into a heatproof bowl and mix in the fromage blanc. Season to taste.

2 Put the potatoes in a pan of cold water. Bring to the boil and cook for 20–25 minutes. Drain well. When cool enough to handle, peel them and pass through a food mill into a bowl.

3 Add the flour, a little at a time, until the mixture is smooth and slightly sticky. Add salt to taste. Roll out the mixture on a floured board to a long sausage 1cm/ ½in in diameter. Cut into 2cm/ ¾in lengths. Roll one piece at a time on a floured fork to make the characteristic ridges. Flip on to a floured plate or tray.

4 Bring a large pan of water to the boil and drop in about 20 gnocchi at a time. They will rise to the surface. Cook for 10–15 seconds, then lift them out with a draining spoon. Drop into a dish and keep hot. Continue with the rest of the gnocchi.

5 To heat the sauce, place the bowl over a pan of simmering water and heat gently, being careful not to let it curdle. Pour the sauce over the gnocchi. Roughly chop the remaining hazelnuts, scatter them over the top and serve.

Spring Vegetable Omelette

This resembles a Spanish omelette in that it is not flipped, but finished off under the grill. Packed with tender vegetables, it makes a very tasty light lunch.

Serves 4
50g/2oz/ ½ cup fresh
　asparagus tips
50g/2oz spring greens, shredded
15ml/1 tbsp sunflower oil
1 onion, sliced
175g/6oz cooked new potatoes,
　halved or diced
2 tomatoes, chopped
6 eggs
15–30ml/1–2 tbsp chopped fresh
　mixed herbs
salt and ground black pepper
salad, to serve

1 Steam the asparagus tips and spring greens over a saucepan of boiling water for 5–10 minutes, until tender. Drain the vegetables and keep them warm.

2 Heat the oil in a large frying pan, that can safely be used under the grill. (Cover a wooden handle with foil to protect it.) Add the onion and cook over a low heat, stirring occasionally, for 5–10 minutes, until softened.

3 Add the new potatoes and cook, stirring constantly for 3 minutes. Stir in the tomatoes, asparagus and spring greens. Beat the eggs lightly with the herbs and season to taste with salt and pepper.

4 Preheat the grill. Pour the egg mixture over the vegetables, then cook over a gentle heat until the base of the omelette is golden brown. Slide the pan under the grill and cook the omelette for 2–3 minutes, until the top is golden brown. Serve immediately, cut into wedges, with salad.

Cook's Tip
Remember to use a low-fat dressing for the salad, such as cider vinegar and low-fat fromage frais.

Mushroom & Sunflower Seed Flan

Mushrooms, baby corn and spinach make a delectable filling for a flan.

Serves 6
175g/6oz/1½ cups
　wholemeal flour
75g/3oz/6 tbsp low-fat spread
15ml/1 tbsp olive oil
175g/6oz baby corn, each cut into
　2–3 pieces
30ml/2 tbsp sunflower seeds
225g/8oz/3 cups mushrooms
75g/3oz fresh spinach
　leaves, chopped
juice of 1 lemon
salt and ground black pepper
tomato salad, to serve

1 Preheat the oven to 180°C/350°F/Gas 4. Sift the flour into a bowl, then tip in the bran from the sieve. Rub in the low-fat spread until the mixture resembles breadcrumbs. Add enough water to make a firm dough.

2 Roll out the dough on a lightly floured surface and line a 23cm/9in flan dish. Prick the base, line the flan case with foil and add a layer of baking beans. Bake blind for 15 minutes, then remove the foil and beans. Return the pastry case to the oven and bake for 10 minutes more, or until the pastry is crisp and golden brown.

3 Meanwhile, heat the oil in a heavy-based pan. Add the corn with the sunflower seeds and fry, stirring occasionally, for 5–8 minutes until lightly browned all over.

4 Add the mushrooms, lower the heat slightly and cook the mixture for 2–3 minutes. Stir in the chopped spinach, cover the pan and cook for 2–3 minutes.

5 Sharpen the filling with a little lemon juice. Stir in salt and pepper to taste. Spoon into the flan case. Serve warm or cold, with a tomato salad.

Cook's Tip
If the mushrooms are large, cut them in half or quarters.

Carrot Mousse with Mushroom Sauce

This impressive yet easy-to-make mousse makes healthy eating a pleasure.

Serves 4
about 350g/12oz carrots, roughly chopped
1 small red pepper, seeded and roughly chopped
45ml/3 tbsp vegetable stock
2 eggs, plus 1 egg white
115g/4oz/½ cup Quark or low-fat soft cheese
15ml/1 tbsp chopped fresh tarragon
salt and ground black pepper
fresh tarragon sprigs, to garnish
boiled rice and leeks, to serve

For the mushroom sauce
25g/1oz/2 tbsp low-fat spread
175g/6oz/2¼ cups mushrooms, sliced
30ml/2 tbsp plain flour
250ml/8fl oz/1 cup skimmed milk

1 Preheat the oven to 190°C/375°F/Gas 5. Line the bases of four dariole moulds or ramekins with non-stick baking paper. Put the carrots, red pepper and stock in a small pan and bring to the boil. Cover and cook for 5 minutes, or until tender. Drain.

2 Lightly beat the eggs and egg white. Mix with the Quark or cheese. Season to taste. Purée the cooked vegetables in a food processor or blender. Add the cheese mixture and process for a few seconds more, until smooth. Stir in the chopped tarragon.

3 Divide the mixture among the moulds or ramekins and cover with foil. Place in a roasting tin. Pour in boiling water to come halfway up the sides. Bake for 35 minutes, or until set.

4 Make the sauce. Melt 15g/½oz/1 tbsp of the low-fat spread in a frying pan. Sauté the mushrooms for 5 minutes, until soft. Put the remaining low fat spread in a small pan and add the flour and milk. Cook over a medium heat, stirring until the sauce thickens. Stir in the mushrooms and season to taste.

5 Turn out each mousse on to a plate. Spoon over a little sauce and garnish with the tarragon. Serve, with rice and leeks.

Spinach & Potato Galette

Creamy layers of potato, spinach and herbs make a warming supper dish.

Serves 6
900g/2lb large potatoes, peeled
450g/1lb fresh spinach
2 eggs
400g/14oz/1¾ cups low-fat cream cheese
15ml/1 tbsp grainy mustard
50g/2oz chopped fresh herbs (chives, parsley, chervil or sorrel)
salt and ground black pepper
salad, to serve

1 Preheat the oven to 180°C/350°F/Gas 4. Line a deep 23cm/9in round cake tin with non-stick baking paper.

2 Place the potatoes in a large pan and cover with cold water. Bring to the boil and cook for 10 minutes. Drain well and allow to cool slightly before slicing thinly.

3 Wash the spinach and place it in a large pan with only the water that still clings to the leaves. Cover and cook over a low heat, stirring once, until the spinach has just wilted. Drain well in a sieve and squeeze out the excess moisture with your hands. Chop finely.

4 Beat the eggs with the cream cheese and mustard, then stir in the chopped spinach and fresh herbs.

5 Place a layer of the sliced potatoes in the lined tin, arranging them in concentric circles. Top with a spoonful of the cream cheese mixture and spread out.

6 Continue layering, seasoning to taste with salt and pepper as you go, until all the potatoes and the cream cheese mixture have been used. Cover the cake tin with foil and place it in a roasting tin.

7 Fill the roasting tin with enough boiling water to come halfway up the sides of the cake tin and cook in the oven for 45–50 minutes. Turn out on to a plate and serve hot or cold, with a salad of dressed leaves and tomatoes.

Broccoli & Chestnut Terrine

Served hot or cold, this versatile terrine is equally suitable for a dinner party or a picnic.

Serves 4–6

450g/1lb broccoli, cut into small florets
225g/8oz cooked chestnuts, roughly chopped
50g/2oz/1 cup fresh wholemeal breadcrumbs
60ml/4 tbsp low-fat natural yogurt
30ml/2 tbsp freshly grated Parmesan cheese
freshly grated nutmeg
2 eggs, beaten
salt and ground black pepper
steamed new potatoes and dressed leaves, to serve

1 Preheat the oven to 180°C/350°F/Gas 4. Line a 900g/2lb loaf tin with non-stick baking paper.

2 Blanch or steam the broccoli for 3–4 minutes, until just tender. Drain well. Reserve one-quarter of the florets (choosing the smallest ones) and chop the rest finely.

3 Put the chestnuts in a bowl and stir in breadcrumbs, yogurt and Parmesan. Season with nutmeg, salt and pepper to taste, then stir in the chopped broccoli, and the beaten eggs. Fold in the reserved broccoli florets.

4 Spoon the broccoli mixture into the prepared tin and level the surface. Place the loaf tin in a roasting tin. Pour in boiling water to come halfway up the sides of the loaf tin. Bake for 20–25 minutes.

5 Remove from the oven and invert onto a plate or tray. Serve in slices, with new potatoes and dressed leaves.

> **Cook's Tip**
> To cook chestnuts, nick the shells, roast in the oven for about 5 minutes, peel and then steam or boil.

Ratatouille Pancakes

Pretty enough to serve for a dinner party, and packed with juicy vegetables, these pancakes make a tasty treat.

Serves 4

75g/3oz/²⁄₃ cup plain flour
25g/1oz/¼ cup medium oatmeal
1 egg, lightly beaten
300ml/½ pint/1¼ cups skimmed milk
light oil cooking spray, for greasing
mixed salad, to serve

For the filling

1 large aubergine, cut into 2.5cm/1in cubes
1 garlic clove, crushed
2 medium courgettes, sliced
1 green pepper, seeded and sliced
1 red pepper, seeded and sliced
75ml/5 tbsp vegetable stock
200g/7oz can chopped tomatoes
5ml/1 tsp cornflour, mixed to a paste with 10ml/2 tsp water
salt and ground black pepper

1 Sift the flour and a pinch of salt into a bowl. Stir in the oatmeal. Make a well in the centre, add the egg and half the milk and mix to a smooth batter. Gradually beat in the remaining milk. Cover the bowl and set aside for 30 minutes.

2 Spray an 18cm/7in crêpe pan with cooking spray. Heat the pan, then pour in just enough batter to cover the base thinly. Cook the pancake for 2–3 minutes, until set and the underside is golden brown. Flip over and cook for 1–2 minutes more. Slide the pancake on to a plate lined with non-stick baking paper. Make more pancakes in the same way, adding them to the stack and interleaving them with baking paper. Keep warm.

3 Make the filling. Put the aubergine cubes in a colander and sprinkle well with salt. Leave to drain in the sink for 30 minutes. Rinse thoroughly and drain again.

4 Put the garlic, courgettes, peppers, stock and tomatoes into a large pan. Simmer, stirring occasionally, for 10 minutes. Add the aubergine and cook for 15 minutes more. Stir in the cornflour paste and simmer for 2 minutes. Season to taste.

5 Spoon the mixture into the middle of each pancake. Fold them in half, then in half again to make cones. Serve with salad.

Red Pepper & Watercress Filo Purses

These crisp pastry purses have a delectable ricotta and vegetable filling. They are perfect for special occasion meals and dinner parties as they can be made in advance.

Makes 8

3 red peppers, halved and seeded
175g/6oz watercress
225g/8oz/1 cup low-fat ricotta cheese
blanched almonds, toasted and chopped
8 sheets of filo pastry, thawed if frozen
30ml/2 tbsp olive oil
salt and ground black pepper
frisée salad, to serve

1 Preheat the oven to 190°C/375°F/Gas 5. Place the pepper halves, skin side up, on a grill rack and grill until the skins have blistered and charred. Transfer to a bowl and cover with crumpled kitchen paper. Leave to cool slightly, then rub off the skins and chop the flesh roughly.

2 Put the peppers and watercress in a food processor and pulse until coarsely chopped. Spoon into a bowl and stir in the ricotta and almonds. Season with salt and pepper to taste.

3 Working with one sheet of filo pastry at a time and keeping the others covered, cut out two 18cm/7in squares and two 5cm/2in squares from each sheet. Brush one large square with a little olive oil and top it with a second large square at an angle of 45 degrees to form a star shape.

4 Place one of the small squares in the centre of the star shape, brush lightly with oil and top with a second small square. Set this aside, covered with clear film, and make more layered pastry shapes in the same way.

5 Divide the red pepper mixture among the pastries. Bring the edges of each together to form a purse shape and twist to seal. Place the purses on a lightly greased baking sheet and cook for 25–30 minutes, until golden. Serve with a frisée salad.

Cheese, Onion & Mushroom Flan

A tasty savoury flan makes great picnic fare and is also ideal for family suppers.

Serves 6

175g/6oz/1½ cups plain wholemeal flour, plus extra for dusting
75g/3oz/6 tbsp low-fat polyunsaturated margarine
1 onion, sliced
1 leek, sliced
175g/6oz/2¼ cups mushrooms, chopped
30ml/2 tbsp vegetable stock
2 eggs
150ml/¼ pint/⅔ cup skimmed milk
115g/4oz/⅔ cup frozen sweetcorn kernels
30ml/2 tbsp snipped fresh chives
15ml/1 tbsp chopped fresh parsley
75g/3oz/¾ cup finely grated reduced-fat mature Cheddar cheese
salt and ground black pepper
chives, to garnish

1 Sift the flour and a pinch of salt into a bowl. Add the margarine and rub in with your fingertips until the mixture resembles fine breadcrumbs, then add enough cold water to make a soft dough. Wrap and chill for 30 minutes.

2 Mix the onion, leek, mushrooms and vegetable stock in a saucepan. Bring to the boil, then cover and cook over a low heat for 10 minutes, until the vegetables are just tender. Drain well and set aside.

3 Preheat the oven to 200°C/400°F/Gas 6. Roll out the pastry on a lightly floured surface and line a 20cm/8in flan tin. Place on a baking sheet. Using a draining spoon, spread the vegetable mixture in the pastry case.

4 Beat the eggs and milk together in a jug. Add the sweetcorn, snipped chives, parsley and cheese and mix well. Season to taste with salt and pepper.

5 Pour the mixture over the vegetables. Bake for 20 minutes, then reduce the oven temperature to 180°C/350°F/Gas 4, and cook for 30 minutes more, until the filling is set and lightly browned. Garnish with chives and serve warm or cold in slices.

Wild Rice Rösti with Carrot & Orange Purée

Rösti is a traditional dish from Switzerland. This variation has the extra nuttiness of wild rice.

Serves 6
50g/2oz/ ¹/₃ cup wild rice
900g/2lb large potatoes
30ml/2 tbsp walnut oil

5ml/1 tsp yellow mustard seeds
1 onion, finely chopped
30ml/2 tbsp fresh thyme leaves
salt and ground black pepper
broccoli and french beans, to serve

For the purée
1 large orange
350g/12oz carrots, chopped

1 Make the purée. Pare two large strips of rind from the orange and put them in a pan with the carrots. Cover with cold water and bring to the boil. Cook for 10 minutes, or until the carrots are tender. Drain well and discard the rind. Squeeze the orange and put 60ml/4 tbsp of the juice in a blender or food processor with the carrots. Process to a purée.

2 Place the wild rice in a clean pan and cover with water. Bring to the boil and cook for 30–40 minutes, until the rice is just starting to split, but is still crunchy. Drain.

3 Put the unpeeled potatoes in a large pan and cover with cold water. Bring to the boil and cook for 15 minutes. Drain well. When they are cool enough to handle, peel them and grate them coarsely into a large bowl. Add the cooked rice.

4 Heat 15ml/1 tbsp of the oil in a non-stick frying pan and stir in the mustard seeds. When they start to pop, add the onion and cook gently for 5 minutes, until softened. Add to the potato mixture, then stir in the thyme leaves. Season to taste.

5 Heat the remaining oil in the frying pan and add the potato mixture. Press down well and cook for 10 minutes. Cover the pan with an inverted plate. Flip over, then slide the rösti back into the pan. Cook for 10 minutes more. Meanwhile, reheat the purée. Serve the rösti, with broccoli, beans and the purée.

Mixed Mushroom & Parmesan Risotto

A brown rice risotto of mixed mushrooms, herbs and fresh Parmesan cheese, this is beautifully moist and full of flavour.

Serves 4
10g/ ¹/₄ oz/ 2 tbsp dried porcini mushrooms
150ml/ ¹/₄ pint/²/₃ cup hot water
15ml/1 tbsp olive oil
4 shallots, finely chopped

2 garlic cloves, crushed
450g/1lb/6 cups mixed cultivated and wild mushrooms, sliced
250g/9oz/1¹/₄ cups long grain brown rice
900ml/1¹/₂ pints/3³/₄ cups hot vegetable stock
45ml/3 tbsp chopped fresh flat leaf parsley
60ml/4 tbsp freshly grated Parmesan cheese
salt and ground black pepper

1 Soak the porcini mushrooms in the hot water for 20 minutes. Heat the oil in a large, heavy-based pan. Add the shallots and garlic and cook over a low heat, stirring occasionally, for about 5 minutes, until softened. Drain the porcini, reserving their liquid, and chop them roughly.

2 Add all the mushrooms to the pan, with the strained porcini soaking liquid. Stir in the brown rice and one-third of the hot stock. (Keep the stock simmering in a pan.)

3 Bring to the boil, lower the heat and simmer gently, stirring frequently, until all the liquid has been absorbed. Add a ladleful of hot stock and stir until it, too, has been absorbed.

4 Continue in this way, adding a ladleful of hot stock at a time and stirring frequently, until the rice is cooked and creamy, but still retains "bite" at the centre of the grain. This should take about 35 minutes and it may not be necessary to add all the vegetable stock.

5 Season with plenty of salt and pepper, stir in the chopped parsley and grated Parmesan and transfer to a warmed serving dish. Serve immediately.

Lentil Risotto with Vegetables

Although purists may blanch at the concept of adding lentils to a risotto, this actually works very well. The lentils benefit from soaking, but if you are in a hurry, use red split lentils, which don't need to be soaked.

Serves 4
225g/8oz/generous 1 cup brown basmati rice, washed and drained
20ml/4 tsp sunflower oil
1 large onion, thinly sliced
2 garlic cloves, crushed
1 large carrot, cut into matchsticks
115g/4oz/ ½ cup green or brown lentils, soaked and drained
5ml/1 tsp ground cumin
5ml/1 tsp ground cinnamon
20 black cardamom seeds
6 cloves
600ml/1 pint/2½ cups vegetable stock
2 bay leaves
2 celery sticks
1 large avocado
3 plum tomatoes
salt and ground black pepper
green salad, to serve

1 Rinse the rice several times in cold water. If there is sufficient time, leave it to soak for 30 minutes in the water used for the final rinse. Drain well.

2 Heat the oil in a large, heavy-based pan. Add the onion, garlic and carrot and fry over a low heat, stirring occasionally, for 5–6 minutes, until the onion is softened.

3 Add the drained rice and lentils, with the spices, and cook the mixture over a low heat for 5 minutes more, stirring to prevent it from sticking to the pan.

4 Pour in the stock. Add the bay leaves and bring to the boil, then lower the heat, cover the pan and simmer for 15 minutes more, or until the liquid has been absorbed and the rice and lentils are tender.

5 Meanwhile, chop the celery into half-rounds and dice the avocado and tomatoes. Add the fresh ingredients to the rice and lentils and mix well. Season to taste. Spoon into a large serving bowl and serve immediately with a green salad.

Red Pepper Risotto

Several different types of risotto rice are available, and it is worth experimenting to find the one your family prefers. Look out for arborio, carnaroli and Vialone Nano.

Serves 6
3 large red peppers
30ml/2 tbsp olive oil
3 large garlic cloves, thinly sliced
1½ x 400g/14oz cans chopped tomatoes
2 bay leaves
450g/1lb/2½ cups arborio or other risotto rice
about 1.5 litres/2½ pints/6 cups hot vegetable stock
6 fresh basil leaves, snipped
salt and ground black pepper

1 Put the peppers in a grill pan and grill until the skins are charred and blistered all over. Put them in a bowl, cover with crumpled kitchen paper and leave for 10 minutes. Peel off the skins, then slice the flesh, discarding the cores and seeds.

2 Heat the oil in a wide, shallow pan. Add the garlic and tomatoes and cook over a low heat, stirring occasionally, for 5 minutes. Stir in the pepper slices and bay leaves and cook for 15 minutes more.

3 Stir the rice into the vegetable mixture and cook, stirring constantly, for 2 minutes, then add a ladleful of the hot stock. Cook, stirring constantly, until it has been absorbed. (Keep the stock simmering in a pan adjacent to the risotto.)

4 Continue to add stock in this way, making sure that each addition has been absorbed before ladling in the next. When the rice is tender, season with salt and pepper to taste. Remove the pan from the heat, cover and leave to stand for 10 minutes before stirring in the basil and serving.

Variation
Both yellow and orange peppers are also suitable for this recipe, but green peppers are too acerbic.

Mushroom, Leek & Cashew Nut Risotto

Because this risotto is made with brown rice instead of the traditional Italian arborio rice, it has a delicious nutty flavour and interesting texture.

Serves 4
225g/8oz/1⅓ cups long grain
   brown rice
900ml/1½ pints/3¾ cups
   vegetable stock
15ml/1 tbsp walnut or
   hazelnut oil
2 leeks, sliced

225g/8oz/3 cups mixed wild or
   cultivated mushrooms, sliced
50g/2oz/½ cup cashew nuts
grated rind of 1 lemon
30ml/2 tbsp chopped fresh thyme
25g/1oz/scant ¼ cup
   pumpkin seeds
salt and ground black pepper

For the garnish
fresh thyme leaves
lemon wedges

1 Place the brown rice in a large pan, pour in the stock and bring to the boil over a medium heat. Lower the heat and cook gently for about 30 minutes, until all the stock has been absorbed and the rice grains are tender.

2 About 5 minutes before the rice will be ready, heat the oil in a large, heavy-based frying pan. Add the leeks and mushrooms and fry over a low heat, stirring occasionally, for 3 minutes, until the leeks are softened.

3 Add the cashews, grated lemon rind and chopped thyme to the vegetable mixture and cook over a low heat, stirring frequently, for 1–2 minutes more. Season to taste with salt and pepper.

4 Drain off any excess stock from the cooked rice and stir the rice into the vegetable mixture. Turn the mixture into a warmed serving dish. Scatter the pumpkin seeds over the top and garnish with the fresh thyme sprigs and lemon wedges. Serve the risotto at once.

Risotto Primavera

Celebrate springtime with this quick and easy rice dish. Use organic vegetables, if possible, so that you can really savour the flavour.

Serves 4
250g/9oz mixed spring vegetables
10ml/2 tsp olive oil
1 medium onion, sliced

250g/9oz/1¼ cups risotto rice
2.5ml/½ tsp ground turmeric
about 600ml/1 pint/2½ cups
   vegetable stock
45ml/3 tbsp chopped
   fresh parsley
salt and ground black pepper

1 Prepare the vegetables according to type, cutting them to more or less the same size and leaving small ones whole so that they cook evenly.

2 Heat the oil in a large, non-stick pan. Add the onion and fry over a low heat, stirring occasionally, for 10 minutes until softened and golden.

3 Stir in the rice and cook, stirring constantly, for 1–2 minutes, until the grains are all coated with oil and glistening. Add the turmeric and cook, stirring constantly, for 1 minute, then add the vegetable stock. Season well with salt and pepper. Bring to the boil, then add the vegetables.

4 Bring back to the boil, then lower the heat, cover and cook gently, stirring occasionally, for 20 minutes, or until the rice is tender and most of the liquid has been absorbed. Add more stock if necessary.

5 Stir in the parsley. Transfer the risotto to a warmed serving dish and serve immediately.

Variation
Use this risotto to stuff lightly grilled, halved red peppers, but chop the vegetables finely in step 1.

Lemon & Herb Risotto Cake

This unusual rice dish can be served as a main course with a mixed salad, or as a satisfying side dish. It's also good served cold and packs well for picnics.

Serves 4
light oil cooking spray
1 small leek, thinly sliced
600ml/1 pint/2½ cups
   vegetable stock
225g/8oz/generous 1 cup
   risotto rice
finely grated rind of 1 lemon
30ml/2 tbsp chopped fresh chives
30ml/2 tbsp chopped
   fresh parsley
75g/3oz/ ¾ cup grated half-fat
   mozzarella cheese
salt and ground black pepper

For the garnish
fresh flat leaf parsley sprigs
lemon wedges

1 Preheat the oven to 200°C/400°F/Gas 6. Thinly coat a 21cm/8½in loose-based round cake tin with light oil cooking spray and set aside.

2 Put the slices of leek in a large pan with 45ml/3 tbsp of the vegetable stock. Cook over a moderate heat, stirring occasionally, for about 5 minutes, until softened. Add the rice and the remaining stock.

3 Bring to the boil. Lower the heat, cover the pan and simmer gently, stirring occasionally, for about 20 minutes, or until all the liquid has been absorbed.

4 Stir in the lemon rind, chives, chopped parsley and grated mozzarella and season with salt and pepper to taste. Spoon into the tin, cover with foil and bake for 30–35 minutes, or until lightly browned. Turn out and cut into slices. Serve immediately, garnished with parsley and lemon wedges.

> **Cook's Tip**
> If you cannot obtain risotto rice, use short grain rice – the type normally used for puddings – instead.

Low-fat Vegetable Paella

A delicious change from the more traditional seafood- or chicken-based paella, this vegetarian version is full of flavour and includes plenty of healthy fibre.

Serves 6
1 onion, chopped
2 garlic cloves, crushed
225g/8oz leeks, sliced
3 celery sticks, chopped
1 red pepper, seeded and sliced
2 courgettes, sliced
175g/6oz/2¼ cups brown cap
   mushrooms, sliced
175g/6oz/1½ cups frozen peas
450g/1lb/2½ cups long grain
   brown rice
400g/14oz can cannellini beans,
   drained and rinsed
900ml/1½ pints/3¾ cups
   vegetable stock
60ml/4 tbsp dry white wine
a few saffron strands
225g/8oz cherry tomatoes, halved
45–60ml/3–4 tbsp chopped fresh
   mixed herbs
salt and ground black pepper
lemon wedges, whole cherry
   tomatoes and celery leaves, to
   garnish

1 Mix the onion, garlic, leeks, celery, red pepper, courgettes and mushrooms in a large, heavy-based pan or flameproof casserole. Add the peas, rice, cannellini beans, stock, wine and saffron. Bring to the boil over a moderate heat, stirring constantly, then lower the heat and simmer, stirring occasionally, for about 35 minutes, until almost all the liquid has been absorbed and the rice is tender.

2 Stir in the tomatoes and chopped herbs, season to taste with salt and pepper and heat through for 1–2 minutes. Serve garnished with lemon wedges, tomatoes and celery leaves.

> **Cook's Tips**
> • Paella, which originated in Valencia, is not actually the name of the dish, but the heavy, two-handled, cast-iron pan in which it is traditionally cooked.
> • Long grain rice works very well in this recipe, but for a more authentic texture, try to obtain a Spanish rice, such as calasparra, or even use risotto rice.

Vegetable Biryani

The most everyday ingredients can be transformed into an exotic dish with a bit of imagination and flair.

Serves 4–6
175g/6oz/scant 1 cup long grain rice
2 whole cloves
seeds of 2 cardamom pods
450ml/ ³/₄ pint/scant 2 cups vegetable stock
2 garlic cloves
1 small onion, roughly chopped
5ml/1 tsp cumin seeds
5ml/1 tsp ground coriander
2.5ml/ ¹/₂ tsp ground turmeric
2.5ml/ ¹/₂ tsp mild chilli powder
1 large potato, peeled and cut into 2.5cm/1 in cubes
2 carrots, sliced
¹/₂ cauliflower, broken into florets
50g/2oz French beans, cut into short lengths
90ml/6 tbsp water
30ml/2 tbsp chopped fresh coriander
30ml/2 tbsp freshly squeezed lime juice
salt and ground black pepper
fresh coriander sprigs, to garnish

1 Put the rice, cloves and cardamom seeds into a large, heavy-based saucepan. Pour over the stock and bring to the boil, then lower the heat, cover and simmer for 20 minutes, or until all the stock has been absorbed.

2 Meanwhile, put the garlic, onion and remaining spices into a spice mill. Grind to a powder, then tip into a bowl and stir in enough water to make a paste.

3 Preheat the oven to 180°C/350°F/Gas 4. Spoon the spicy paste into a flameproof casserole and cook over a low heat, stirring frequently, for 2 minutes.

4 Add the vegetables and measured water. Cover and cook over a low heat for 12 minutes, stirring occasionally. Add the chopped coriander.

5 Spoon the rice over the vegetables. Sprinkle over the lime juice and season to taste. Cover and cook in the oven for 25 minutes, or until the vegetables are tender. Fluff up the rice with a fork before serving. Garnish with coriander sprigs.

Tomato, Pistachio & Sesame Seed Pilau

Nuts and seeds can really lift the flavour of a simple vegetable and rice dish. The spicing is subtle but essential in this tasty pilau.

Serves 4
225g/8oz/generous 1 cup brown basmati rice
600ml/1 pint/2¹/₂ cups vegetable stock
pinch of saffron strands soaked in 15ml/1 tbsp boiling water
3 tomatoes, peeled and chopped
1 red pepper, seeded and finely diced
seeds from 4–5 cardamom pods
25g/1oz/ ¹/₄ cup pistachio nuts, roughly chopped
30ml/2 tbsp sesame seeds, toasted
salt

1 Rinse the rice several times in cold water. If there is sufficient time, leave it to soak for 30 minutes in the water used for the final rinse. Drain well.

2 Drain the rice and tip it into a large pan. Add the stock, saffron soaking liquid and a pinch of salt. Bring to the boil, then lower the heat, cover and simmer for 25 minutes.

3 Add the tomatoes and red pepper to the rice. Stir in the cardamom seeds. Cook for 5–10 minutes more, until the rice is tender and all the liquid has been absorbed.

4 Tip the rice into a warmed serving dish and scatter the pistachio nuts and sesame seeds over the top. Serve.

Variations
• You can substitute other nuts for the pistachios; unsalted peanuts, almonds and cashews all work well.
• To make a more substantial dish or to provide extra servings for unexpected guests, you can add either fresh or frozen finely chopped vegetables, such as carrots, peas and sweetcorn, with the tomatoes and peppers in step 3.

Herby Rice Pilaff

The difference between a pilau and a pilaff is largely one of origin. Both are rice dishes, usually with spices and often including a mixture of vegetables for colour and extra flavour. This delightful dish is a simple herb mixture.

Serves 4
225g/8oz/scant 1 cup mixed
   brown basmati and wild rice
15ml/1 tbsp olive oil
1 onion, chopped
1 garlic clove, crushed
5ml/1 tsp ground cumin
5ml/.1 tsp ground turmeric
50g/2oz/ 1/3 cup sultanas
750ml/1 1/4 pints/3 cups
   vegetable stock
45ml/3 tbsp chopped fresh
   mixed herbs
salt and ground black pepper
fresh herb sprigs and 25g/1oz/
   1/4 cup chopped nuts,
   to garnish

1 Rinse the rice mixture several times in cold water. If there is sufficient time, leave it to soak for 30 minutes in the water used for the final rinse. Drain well.

2 Heat the oil in a large, heavy-based saucepan. Add the chopped onion and garlic and fry over a low heat, stirring occasionally, for about 5 minutes, until the onion is softened but not coloured.

3 Stir in the ground cumin, turmeric and rice and cook over a moderate heat, stirring constantly, for about 1 minute, until the rice grains are well coated.

4 Stir in the sultanas and vegetable stock. Bring to the boil, stirring frequently. Lower the heat, cover and simmer, stirring occasionally to prevent the rice from sticking, for 20–25 minutes, until the rice is cooked and just tender and almost all the liquid has been absorbed.

5 Stir in the chopped mixed herbs and season to taste with salt and pepper. Spoon the pilaff into a warmed serving dish and garnish with fresh herb sprigs and a scattering of chopped nuts. Serve immediately.

Fried Rice with Mushrooms

Sesame oil adds a hint of nutty flavour to this tasty and substantial rice dish.

Serves 4
225g/8oz/generous 1 cup long
   grain rice
15ml/1 tbsp vegetable oil
1 egg, lightly beaten
2 garlic cloves, crushed
175g/6oz/2 1/4 cups button
   mushrooms, sliced
15ml/1 tbsp light soy sauce
1.5ml/ 1/4 tsp salt
2.5ml/ 1/2 tsp sesame oil
cucumber matchsticks, to garnish

1 Rinse the rice until the water runs clear, then drain it thoroughly. Place it in a saucepan. Measure the depth of the rice against your index finger, then bring the tip of your finger up to just above the surface of the rice and add cold water to the same depth above the rice as the rice depth.

2 Bring the water to the boil. Stir, boil for a few minutes, then cover the pan. Lower the heat to a simmer and cook the rice gently for 5–8 minutes, until all the water has been absorbed. Remove the pan from the heat and, without lifting the lid, leave for 10 minutes more.

3 Meanwhile, heat 5ml/1 tsp of the vegetable oil in a non-stick frying pan or wok. Add the beaten egg and cook, stirring with chopsticks or a wooden spoon until lightly scrambled. Remove from the pan or wok and set aside.

4 Heat the remaining vegetable oil in the pan or wok. Add the garlic and stir-fry for a few seconds, then add the mushrooms and stir-fry for 2 minutes, adding a little water, if needed, to prevent them from burning.

5 Fork up the cooked rice. Add it to the pan or wok. Toss to mix with the mushrooms, then cook for about 4 minutes, or until the rice is hot, stirring from time to time.

6 Add the scrambled egg, soy sauce, salt and sesame oil. Cook for 1 minute to heat through. Serve at once, garnished with the cucumber matchsticks.

Aubergine & Chick-pea Tagine

Spiced with coriander, cumin, cinnamon, turmeric and a dash of chilli sauce, this Moroccan-style stew makes a filling supper dish.

Serves 4

1 small aubergine, cut into 1cm/½in dice
2 courgettes, thickly sliced
30ml/2 tbsp olive oil
1 large onion, sliced
2 garlic cloves, chopped
150g/5oz/2 cups brown cap mushrooms, halved
15ml/1 tbsp ground coriander
10ml/2 tsp cumin seeds
15ml/1 tbsp ground cinnamon
10ml/2 tsp ground turmeric
225g/8oz new potatoes, quartered
600ml/1 pint/2½ cups passata
15ml/1 tbsp tomato purée
150ml/¼ pint/⅔ cup water
15ml/1 tbsp chilli sauce
8 ready-to-eat dried apricots
400g/14oz can chick-peas, drained and rinsed
salt and ground black pepper
15ml/1 tbsp chopped fresh coriander, to garnish
rice, to serve

1 Put the aubergine and courgettes in a colander, sprinkling salt over each layer. Leave to stand in the sink for 30 minutes. Rinse very well, drain and pat dry with kitchen paper.

2 Preheat the grill. Arrange the courgettes and aubergine on a baking sheet and toss in half the olive oil. Grill for 20 minutes, turning occasionally, until tender and golden.

3 Meanwhile, heat the remaining oil in a large heavy-based pan and cook the onion and garlic until softened. Add the mushrooms and sauté for 3 minutes, until tender. Add the spices and stir over the heat for 1 minute more.

4 Add the potatoes and cook for 3 minutes, stirring. Pour in the passata, tomato purée and water and cook for 10 minutes, or until the sauce begins to thicken.

5 Add the aubergine, courgettes, chilli sauce, apricots and chick-peas. Season to taste with salt and pepper and cook, partially covered, for 10–15 minutes, until the potatoes are tender. Sprinkle with chopped fresh coriander and serve with rice.

Purée of Lentils with Baked Eggs

This unusual dish makes an excellent vegetarian supper. If you prefer, and have one big enough, bake the purée and eggs in a single large ovenproof dish.

Serves 4

450g/1lb/2 cups split red lentils
3 leeks, thinly sliced
10ml/2 tsp coriander seeds, finely crushed
15ml/1 tbsp chopped fresh coriander
30ml/2 tbsp chopped fresh mint
15ml/1 tbsp red wine vinegar
1 litre/1¾ pints/4 cups vegetable stock
oil, for greasing
4 eggs
salt and ground black pepper
generous handful of fresh parsley, chopped, to garnish

1 Put the lentils in a deep saucepan. Add the leeks, coriander seeds, fresh coriander, mint, vinegar and stock. Bring to the boil over a moderate heat. Lower the heat, cover and simmer for 30–40 minutes, or until the lentils are cooked and have absorbed all the liquid.

2 Preheat the oven to 180°C/350°F/Gas 4. Lightly grease four individual ovenproof dishes. Season the lentil mixture to taste with salt and pepper and mix thoroughly. Divide the mixture among the prepared dishes and spread out.

3 Using the back of a tablespoon, make a fairly small depression in the centre of the lentil mixture in each dish. Break an egg into each hollow. Season the eggs lightly with salt and pepper. Cover the dishes with foil and bake for 15–20 minutes, or until the eggs are set. Sprinkle with plenty of chopped parsley and serve immediately.

Variation

Tip a 400g/14oz can of unsweetened chestnut purée into a bowl and beat well until softened. Stir the purée into the lentil mixture in step 2, with a little extra vegetable stock if required. Proceed as in the main recipe.

Bulgur & Lentil Pilaff

Many of the ingredients for this tasty, aromatic dish can be found in a well-stocked store cupboard.

Serves 4
5ml/1 tsp olive oil
1 large onion, thinly sliced
2 garlic cloves, crushed
5ml/1 tsp ground coriander
5ml/1 tsp ground cumin
5ml/1 tsp ground turmeric
2.5ml/ $^{1}/_{2}$ tsp ground allspice
225g/8oz/1 $^{1}/_{3}$ cups bulgur wheat
about 750ml/1 $^{1}/_{4}$ pints/3 cups
   vegetable stock
115g/4oz/1 $^{1}/_{2}$ cups button
   mushrooms, sliced
115g/4oz/ $^{1}/_{2}$ cup green lentils
salt and ground black pepper
cayenne pepper
fresh parsley sprigs, to garnish

1 Heat the oil in a non-stick saucepan. Add the onion, garlic, ground coriander, cumin, turmeric and allspice and fry over a low heat, stirring constantly, for 1 minute.

2 Stir in the bulgur wheat and cook, stirring constantly, for about 2 minutes, until lightly browned. Add the vegetable stock, mushrooms and lentils.

3 Bring to the boil, cover, then simmer over a very low heat for 25–30 minutes, until the bulgur wheat and lentils are tender and all the liquid has been absorbed. Add more stock or water during cooking, if necessary.

4 Season the mixture with salt, pepper and cayenne. Transfer to a warmed serving dish and serve, garnished with fresh parsley.

Cook's Tips
• *Bulgur wheat is very easy to cook and can be used in almost any way you would normally use rice – hot or cold. Some of the finer grades need hardly any cooking, so check the packet instructions for cooking times.*
• *Green lentils keep their shape well during cooking, but, if you can find them, use Puy lentils, which not only retain their texture, but have a distinctive and delicious flavour.*

Balti Toor Dhal with Cherry Tomatoes

When cooked, toor dhal has a wonderfully rich texture, best appreciated if served with plain boiled rice. Fresh fenugreek leaves, available from Asian grocers, impart a stunning aroma.

Serves 4
115g/4oz/ $^{1}/_{2}$ cup toor dhal
45ml/3 tbsp corn oil
1.5ml/ $^{1}/_{4}$ tsp onion seeds
1 bunch spring onions,
   roughly chopped
5ml/1 tsp crushed garlic
1.5ml/ $^{1}/_{4}$ tsp ground turmeric
7.5ml/1 $^{1}/_{2}$ tsp grated fresh
   root ginger
5ml/1 tsp mild chilli powder
30ml/2 tbsp fresh fenugreek or
   spinach leaves
5ml/1 tsp salt
6–8 cherry tomatoes
30ml/2 tbsp fresh
   coriander leaves
$^{1}/_{2}$ green pepper, seeded
   and sliced
15ml/1 tbsp lemon juice
shredded spring onion tops
   and fresh coriander leaves,
   to garnish

1 Cook the dhal in a pan of boiling water, stirring frequently, until soft and mushy. Set aside.

2 Heat the oil with the onion seeds in a non-stick wok. Add the dhal and stir-fry for about 3 minutes. Add the spring onions, garlic, turmeric, ginger, chilli powder, fenugreek or spinach leaves and salt and continue to stir-fry for 5–7 minutes.

3 Pour in enough water to loosen the mixture. Stir and add the cherry tomatoes, fresh coriander, green pepper and lemon juice. Serve immediately, garnished with shredded spring onion tops and coriander leaves.

Cook's Tip
• *Toor dhal, also known as red gram, consists of split pigeon peas. Ask for it at your local health-food shop or Asian grocer. If it is not available, substitute green or brown lentils.*

Balti Urad Dhal with Chillies

The creamy urad dhal used in this recipe needs to be soaked overnight, as this makes it easier to cook. Serve with freshly made chapatis or naan.

Serves 4

115g/4oz urad dhal
10ml/2 tsp low-fat olive oil spread
10ml/2 tsp corn oil
1 bay leaf
2 onions, sliced
1 piece of cinnamon bark or stick
15ml/1 tbsp shredded fresh root ginger
2 garlic cloves, peeled but left whole
2 fresh green chillies, seeded and sliced lengthways
2 fresh red chillies, seeded and sliced lengthways
15ml/1 tbsp chopped fresh mint

1 Place the dhal in a bowl and add enough cold water to cover. Set aside to soak overnight. Drain, tip into a pan and pour in cold water to cover by about 2.5cm/1in. Bring to the boil and cook until the individual pulses are soft enough to break into two. Set aside.

2 Heat the low-fat spread with the oil in a non-stick wok or large, heavy-based frying pan over a medium heat. Add the bay leaf with the onions and cinnamon bark or stick.

3 Add the shredded ginger, whole garlic cloves and half the green and red chillies.

4 Drain almost all the water from the dhal. Add to the wok or frying pan, then stir in the remaining green and red chillies and the fresh mint. Heat through briefly, transfer to a warm serving dish and serve immediately.

Cook's Tip
Urad dhal, a creamy white lentil with a dark hull, is just one of several different pulses familiar to Indian cooks, but lesser known in the West. It is worth getting to know, so seek out an Asian grocer that stocks it.

Aromatic Chick-pea & Spinach Curry

High in fibre, this flavourful curry tastes great and boosts vitality. Serve it with brown rice or naan bread and mango chutney.

Serves 3–4

15ml/1 tbsp sunflower oil
1 large onion, finely chopped
2 garlic cloves, crushed
2.5cm/1in piece of fresh root ginger, finely chopped
1 fresh green chilli, seeded and finely chopped
30ml/2 tbsp medium curry paste
10ml/2 tsp ground cumin
5ml/1 tsp ground turmeric
225g/8oz can chopped tomatoes
1 green or red pepper, seeded and chopped
300ml/½ pint/1¼ cups vegetable stock
15ml/1 tbsp tomato purée
450g/1lb fresh spinach
425g/15oz can chick-peas, drained
45ml/3 tbsp chopped fresh coriander
5ml/1 tsp garam masala (optional)
salt

1 Heat the oil in a large pan and cook the onion, garlic, ginger and chilli over a gentle heat for about 5 minutes, or until the onion has softened, but not browned. Stir in the curry paste, cook for 1 minute, then stir in the cumin and turmeric. Stir over a low heat for 1 minute more.

2 Add the tomatoes and pepper and stir to coat with the spice mixture. Pour in the stock and stir in the tomato purée. Bring to the boil, lower the heat, cover and simmer for 15 minutes.

3 Remove any coarse stalks from the spinach, then rinse the leaves thoroughly, drain them and tear them into large pieces. Add them to the pan, in batches, adding more as each batch cooks down and wilts.

4 Stir in the chick-peas, cover and cook gently for 5 minutes more. Add the fresh coriander, season with salt to taste and stir well. Spoon into a warmed bowl and sprinkle with the garam masala, if using. Serve at once.

Lemon & Ginger Spicy Beans

An extremely quick and delicious dish, made with canned beans for speed. You probably won't need extra salt, as canned beans tend to be already salted.

Serves 4
5cm/2in piece of fresh root ginger, roughly chopped
3 garlic cloves, roughly chopped
250ml/8fl oz/1 cup cold water
15ml/1 tbsp sunflower oil
1 large onion, thinly sliced
1 fresh red chilli, seeded and finely chopped
1.5ml/¼ tsp cayenne pepper
10ml/2 tsp ground cumin
5ml/1 tsp ground coriander
2.5ml/½ tsp ground turmeric
30ml/2 tbsp lemon juice
45ml/3 tbsp chopped fresh coriander
400g/14oz can black-eyed beans, drained and rinsed
400g/14oz can aduki beans, drained and rinsed
400g/14oz can haricot beans, drained and rinsed
ground black pepper
crusty bread, to serve

1 Place the ginger, garlic and 60ml/4 tbsp of the cold water in a blender and blend until smooth.

2 Heat the oil in a pan. Add the onion and chilli and cook over a low heat, stirring occasionally, for 5 minutes, until softened. Add the cayenne, cumin, ground coriander and turmeric and stir-fry for 1 minute.

3 Stir in the ginger and garlic paste and cook for 1 minute more. Pour in the remaining water, with the lemon juice and fresh coriander, stir well and bring to the boil. Cover the pan tightly and cook for 5 minutes.

4 Add all the beans and cook for 10 minutes until they are hot. Season with pepper and serve immediately with crusty bread.

Variation
You can use almost any combination of canned beans – red kidney, pinto, cannellini, broad or butter beans, for example.

Vegetable Chilli

This alternative to chilli con carne is delicious served with brown rice.

Serves 4
2 onions, chopped
1 garlic clove, crushed
3 celery sticks, chopped
1 green pepper, seeded and diced
225g/8oz/3 cups mushrooms, sliced
2 courgettes, diced
400g/14oz can red kidney beans, drained and rinsed
400g/14oz can chopped tomatoes
150ml/¼ pint/⅔ cup passata
30ml/2 tbsp tomato purée
15ml/1 tbsp tomato ketchup
5ml/1 tsp hot chilli powder
5ml/1 tsp ground cumin
5ml/1 tsp ground coriander
salt and ground black pepper
fresh coriander, to garnish
low-fat natural yogurt, dusted with cayenne, to serve

1 Put the onions, garlic, celery, pepper, mushrooms and courgettes in a large saucepan and mix together.

2 Stir in the kidney beans, tomatoes, passata, tomato purée, tomato ketchup and spices. Season to taste and mix well.

3 Bring to the boil, then lower the heat, cover and simmer for 20–30 minutes, stirring occasionally, until the vegetables are tender. Garnish with fresh coriander sprigs. Serve with the yogurt, dusted with cayenne.

Simply Red Beans

What to do when you want a quick snack and haven't got much in the store cupboard or fridge.

Serves 2
15ml/1 tbsp sunflower or groundnut oil
1 onion or leek, finely chopped
1 red pepper or fresh red chilli, seeded and sliced
1 garlic clove, crushed
2.5cm/1in piece of fresh root ginger, grated
400g/14oz can red kidney beans, drained and rinsed
30ml/2 tbsp tomato purée, thinned with 60ml/4 tbsp water
generous dash of vegetarian Worcestershire sauce or Tabasco sauce
salt and ground black pepper
lime wedges, to serve

1 Heat the oil in a heavy-based pan. Add the onion or leek with the pepper or chilli and fry over a low heat, stirring occasionally, for 3 minutes.
2 Add the garlic and ginger and cook, stirring constantly, for 2 minutes more.
3 Add the beans and tomato purée mixture, stir well and spike with vegetarian Worcestershire sauce or Tabasco. Heat for about 10 minutes, until the beans are piping hot. Season to taste with salt and pepper and serve with the lime wedges.

Cook's Tip
If you have time to cook your own beans make extra as they freeze very well. There is no need to thaw them before use.

Jamaican Black Bean Pot

Molasses imparts a rich treacly flavour to the spicy sauce, which includes black beans, vibrant red and yellow peppers and melting butternut squash.

Serves 4

225g/8oz/1¼ cups dried black
   beans, soaked overnight in
   water to cover
1 bay leaf
5ml/1 tsp vegetable
   bouillon powder
15ml/1 tbsp sunflower oil
1 large onion, chopped

1 garlic clove, chopped
5ml/1 tsp English
   mustard powder
15ml/1 tbsp blackstrap molasses
30ml/2 tbsp soft dark
   brown sugar
5ml/1 tsp dried thyme
2.5ml/½ tsp dried chilli flakes
1 red pepper, seeded and diced
1 yellow pepper, seeded and diced
675g/1½ lb butternut squash,
   seeded and cut into 1cm/
   ½in dice
salt and ground black pepper
fresh thyme sprigs, to garnish
cooked rice, to serve

1 Drain the beans, rinse them well and drain them again. Place them in a large pan, cover with fresh water and add the bay leaf. Bring to the boil, then boil rapidly for 10 minutes. Lower the heat, cover, and simmer for 30 minutes, until tender.

2 Drain the beans, reserving the cooking liquid in a large measuring jug. Stir in the bouillon powder, then make the liquid up to 400ml/14fl oz/1⅔ cups with water. Preheat the oven to 180°C/350°F/Gas 4.

3 Heat the oil in the pan. Add the onion and garlic and sauté over a low heat, stirring occasionally, for about 5 minutes, until softened. Stir in the mustard powder, molasses, sugar, dried thyme and chilli flakes. Cook for 1 minute, stirring.

4 Stir in the black beans and reserved bouillon. Spoon the mixture into a flameproof casserole. Cover and bake for 25 minutes, then add the peppers and squash. Season to taste with salt and pepper and mix well. Replace the lid and bake for 45 minutes more, until the vegetables are tender. Serve at once, garnished with thyme sprigs, accompanied by the rice.

Sweet & Sour Bean Hot-pot

An appetizing mixture of mixed beans and vegetables in a tasty sweet and sour sauce, topped with a golden potato crust.

Serves 6

450g/1lb potatoes
15ml/1 tbsp olive oil
40g/1½ oz/3 tbsp half-fat spread
40g/1½ oz/6 tbsp plain
   wholemeal flour
300ml/½ pint/1¼ cups passata
150ml/¼ pint/⅔ cup
   unsweetened apple juice
60ml/4 tbsp light brown sugar
60ml/4 tbsp tomato ketchup
60ml/4 tbsp dry sherry

60 ml/4 tbsp cider vinegar
60ml/4 tbsp light soy sauce
400g/14oz can butter beans
400g/14oz can red kidney beans
400g/14oz can flageolet beans
400g/14oz can chick-peas
175g/6oz green beans, chopped
   and blanched
225g/8oz shallots, sliced
   and blanched
225g/8oz/3 cups
   mushrooms, sliced
15ml/1 tbsp chopped fresh thyme
15ml/1 tbsp chopped
   fresh marjoram
salt and ground black pepper
fresh herb sprigs, to garnish

1 Preheat the oven to 200°C/400°F/Gas 6. Bring a pan of water to the boil and par-boil the potatoes for 4 minutes. Drain well, toss in the oil to coat all over and set them aside.

2 Mix the half-fat spread, flour, passata, apple juice, sugar, tomato ketchup, sherry, vinegar and soy sauce in a saucepan. Heat gently, whisking continuously, until the sauce comes to the boil and thickens. Simmer gently for 3 minutes, stirring.

3 Rinse and drain the canned pulses and add to the sauce with the remaining ingredients, except the herb garnish. Mix, then tip into an ovenproof dish and level the surface.

4 Arrange the potato slices over the top, overlapping them slightly and covering the bean mixture completely.

5 Cover with foil and bake for 40 minutes. Remove the foil and bake for 20 minutes more, until the potatoes have begun to brown around the edges. Serve, garnished with fresh herbs.

Bean Feast

A medley of mushrooms, beans and tomatoes, this richly flavoured dish is perfect for a casual party, as quantities can easily be doubled or trebled.

Serves 4

15ml/1 tbsp sunflower oil
2 onions, sliced
1 garlic clove, crushed
15ml/1 tbsp red wine vinegar
400g/14oz can
  chopped tomatoes
15ml/1 tbsp tomato purée
15ml/1 tbsp vegetarian
  Worcestershire sauce
15ml/1 tbsp wholegrain mustard
15ml/1 tbsp dark brown sugar
250ml/8fl oz/1 cup
  vegetable stock
400g/14oz can red kidney
  beans, drained
400g/14oz can cannellini
  beans, drained
1 bay leaf
75g/3oz/½ cup raisins
225g/8oz/3 cups
  mushrooms, chopped
salt and ground black pepper
chopped fresh parsley, to garnish
wholemeal bread, to serve

1 Heat the oil in a large saucepan or flameproof casserole. Add the onions and garlic and fry over a gentle heat, stirring occasionally, for 10 minutes until softened and golden.

2 Add the red wine vinegar, tomatoes, tomato purée, vegetarian Worcestershire sauce, mustard and sugar, then stir in the vegetable stock. Mix thoroughly.

3 Rinse and drain the canned beans and add them to the pan, with the bay leaf and raisins. Bring to the boil, then lower the heat and simmer for 10 minutes, stirring frequently.

4 Add the mushrooms and simmer for 5 minutes more. Season with salt and pepper to taste. Transfer to a warmed dish, sprinkle with chopped parsley and serve immediately with bread.

> **Cook's Tip**
> *Wipe mushrooms clean with damp kitchen paper before using.*

Spicy Bean & Lentil Loaf

This appetizing high fibre savoury loaf is ideal for picnics or packed lunches. It uses canned beans, so takes very little time to prepare.

Serves 12

10ml/2 tsp olive oil
1 onion, finely chopped
1 garlic clove, crushed
2 celery sticks, finely chopped
400g/14oz can red kidney beans
400g/14oz can lentils
1 egg
1 carrot, coarsely grated
50g/2oz/½ cup hazelnuts,
  finely chopped
50g/2oz/½ cup reduced-fat
  mature Cheddar cheese,
  finely grated
50g/2oz/1 cup fresh
  wholemeal breadcrumbs
15ml/1 tbsp tomato purée
15ml/1 tbsp tomato ketchup
5ml/1 tsp ground cumin
5ml/1 tsp ground coriander
5ml/1 tsp hot chilli powder
salt and ground black pepper
salad and vegetables, to serve

1 Preheat the oven to 180°C/350°F/Gas 4. Lightly grease a 900g/2lb loaf tin. Heat the oil in a saucepan, add the onion, garlic and celery and cook gently for 5 minutes, stirring occasionally. Remove the pan from the heat and cool slightly.

2 Rinse and drain the beans and lentils. Put them in a blender or food processor with the onion mixture and egg and process until smooth.

3 Scrape the mixture into a bowl. Mix in the carrot, hazelnuts, Cheddar, breadcrumbs, tomato purée, tomato ketchup, cumin, coriander and chilli. Season with salt and pepper to taste.

4 Spoon the mixture into the prepared tin and level the surface. Bake for about 1 hour, then remove from the tin and serve hot or cold in slices, accompanied by salad and vegetables.

> **Cook's Tip**
> *You'll find it easier to remove the loaf from the tin if you line it with non-stick baking paper first.*

Wild Mushroom Gratin with Beaufort Cheese, New Potatoes & Walnuts

This is one of the simplest and most delicious ways of cooking mushrooms. Serve this dish as the Swiss do, with gherkins.

Serves 4
900g/2lb small new or
   salad potatoes
50g/2oz/ ¼ cup butter or 60ml/
   4 tbsp olive oil
350g/12oz/4½ cups assorted
   wild and cultivated mushrooms,
   thinly sliced

175g/6oz Beaufort or Fontina
   cheese, thinly sliced
50g/2oz/ ½ cup broken
   walnuts, toasted
salt and ground black pepper
fresh flat leaf parsley,
   roughly chopped, to garnish
12 gherkins, sliced, to serve

1 Bring a large pan of lightly salted water to the boil over a medium heat and cook the potatoes for about 20 minutes, until tender. Drain well and return them to the pan. Add a knob of butter or a splash of oil and cover to keep warm.

2 Heat the remaining butter or olive oil in a heavy-based frying pan that can safely be used under the grill. (Cover a wooden handle with foil to protect it.) Add the sliced mushrooms and fry over a low heat, stirring occasionally, until their juices begin to run, then increase the heat and fry until most of the juices have been absorbed again. Season to taste with salt and pepper.

3 Meanwhile, preheat the grill. Arrange the slices of cheese on top of the mushrooms. Place the pan under the grill and cook until the cheese is bubbly and golden brown.

4 Scatter the gratin with the toasted walnuts, garnish with parsley, and serve at once with the buttered potatoes and sliced gherkins.

Courgette Fritters with Pistou

The sauce is the French equivalent of pesto. It provides a lovely contrast to these delicious fritters.

Serves 4
450g/1lb courgettes, trimmed
75g/3oz/ ¾ cup plain flour
1 egg, separated
15ml/1 tbsp olive oil
75ml/5 tbsp water
vegetable oil, for frying
salt and ground black pepper

For the pistou
15g/ ½ oz/ ½ cup fresh
   basil leaves
4 garlic cloves, roughly chopped
75g/3oz/1 cup freshly grated
   Parmesan cheese
finely grated rind of 1 lemon
150ml/ ¼ pint/ ⅔ cup olive oil

1 Start by making the pistou. Put the basil leaves and garlic in a mortar and crush with a pestle to a fairly fine paste. Work in the grated Parmesan and lemon rind. Gradually blend in the olive oil, a little at a time, until fully incorporated, then transfer the pistou to a small serving dish.

2 Grate the courgettes into a sieve. Sprinkle with plenty of salt. Place the sieve over a bowl, leave for 1 hour, then rinse thoroughly. Drain, then dry well on kitchen paper.

3 Sift the flour into a bowl and make a well in the centre, then add the egg yolk, olive oil and water to the well. Whisk, gradually incorporating the surrounding flour to make a smooth batter. Season to taste with salt and pepper and set aside to rest for 30 minutes.

4 Stir the courgettes into the batter. Whisk the egg white until stiff, then fold it into the batter.

5 Heat the vegetable oil in a large, heavy-based frying pan. Add tablespoons of batter to the oil and fry for about 2 minutes, until golden. Lift the fritters out and drain well on kitchen paper. Keep warm while you are frying the remainder. Serve immediately with the sauce.

Vegetable Rösti with Whisky

A splash of Scotch whisky turns a familiar favourite into a special occasion dish, which is perfect for a celebration lunch.

Serves 4

3 medium carrots, grated
1 celeriac, about 275g/
 10oz, grated
1 large potato, grated
2 medium parsnips, grated
45ml/3 tbsp chopped
 fresh parsley
115g/4oz/1½ cups
 mushrooms, chopped
50g/2oz/½ cup grated
 Cheddar cheese
30ml/2 tbsp whisky
50g/2oz/¼ cup butter
30ml/2 tbsp olive oil
salt and ground black pepper
flat leaf parsley and cherry
 tomatoes, to garnish

1 Mix the grated vegetables with the chopped parsley in a large bowl. Season with salt and pepper. In another bowl, combine the mushrooms, grated cheese and whisky.

2 Heat the butter and most of the oil in a large, non-stick frying pan that can safely be used under the grill. (Cover a wooden handle with foil to protect it.) Add half the vegetables and press down in an even layer. Cover with the cheese mixture and top with the remaining grated vegetables. Press down firmly.

3 Cook over a high heat for 5 minutes, then cover, lower the heat and cook for about 10 minutes more, or until the vegetables are soft.

4 Meanwhile, preheat the grill. Brush the top of the rösti with the remaining oil, slide the pan under the hot grill and cook until the topping is golden brown. Serve in generous wedges, garnished with the parsley and cherry tomatoes.

Variation
Instead of cooking the rösti on top of the stove, press the mixture into an ovenproof dish and cook in a hot oven for 40 minutes.

Potato Cakes with Goat's Cheese

Grilled goat's cheese makes a tangy topping for these herby potato cakes.

Serves 2–4

450g/1lb floury potatoes
10ml/2 tsp chopped fresh thyme
1 garlic clove, crushed
2 spring onions, white and green
 parts, finely chopped
30ml/2 tbsp olive oil
50g/2oz/¼ cup butter
2 x 65g/2½ oz firm
 goat's cheeses
salt and ground black pepper
fresh thyme sprigs, to garnish
salad leaves, tossed in walnut
 dressing, to serve

1 Peel the potatoes, then grate them coarsely into a colander. Using your hands, squeeze out as much of the thick starchy liquid as possible, then tip them into a bowl and mix them with the chopped thyme, garlic and spring onions. Season well with salt and pepper. Preheat the oven to 150°C/300°F/Gas 2.

2 Heat half the oil and butter in a non-stick frying pan. Add two large spoonfuls of the potato mixture (about half the mixture), spacing them well apart, and press down firmly with a spatula. Cook for 3–4 minutes on each side, until golden.

3 Remove the potato cakes from the pan, drain on kitchen paper and keep them warm in the oven. Heat the remaining oil and butter and use the remaining mixture to make two more potato cakes.

4 Preheat the grill. Cut each goat's cheese in half horizontally and place one half, cut side up, on each potato cake. Grill for 2–3 minutes, until lightly golden. Serve, garnished with the fresh thyme sprigs, on individual plates, surrounded by the dressed salad leaves.

Cook's Tip
These potato cakes make great party snacks. Make them half the size and serve warm on a large platter.

Layered Vegetable Terrine

With its jacket of green, this spinach, pepper and potato terrine looks very pretty.

Serves 6

3 red peppers, halved and seeded
450g/1lb waxy potatoes, peeled
   and halved
1 medium courgette,
   sliced lengthways
115g/4oz spinach
   leaves, trimmed
25g/1oz/2 tbsp butter
pinch of freshly grated nutmeg
115g/4oz/1 cup grated
   Cheddar cheese
salt and ground black pepper
torn lettuce leaves and tomato
   wedges, to serve

1 Place the pepper halves, skin side up, on a grill rack and grill until the skins have blistered and charred. Transfer to a bowl, cover with crumpled kitchen paper and leave to cool.

2 Meanwhile, bring a pan of lightly salted water to the boil. Cook the potatoes for 15 minutes. Drain and set aside. Bring a separate pan of water to the boil and add the courgette slices. Blanch them for 1 minute, then lift out with a draining spoon. Add the spinach to the boiling water, blanch for a few seconds, then drain and pat dry on kitchen paper.

3 Preheat the oven to 180°C/350°F/Gas 4. Line the base and sides of a 900g/2lb loaf tin with the spinach, overlapping the leaves slightly. Slice the potatoes thinly. Lay one-third of them over the base of the tin, dot with a little butter and season with salt, pepper and nutmeg. Sprinkle some cheese over.

4 Peel the peppers, leaving the halves intact. Arrange half of them on top of the potatoes. Sprinkle with a little cheese and add a layer of courgettes. Lay a further third of the potatoes on top with the remaining peppers and more cheese, seasoning as you go. Top with the final layer of potatoes and scatter over any remaining cheese. Fold the spinach leaves over. Cover with foil.

5 Place the loaf tin in a roasting tin and pour in boiling water to come halfway up the sides. Bake for about 1 hour. Turn out the terrine and serve sliced, with lettuce and tomatoes.

Courgette, Mushroom & Pesto Panino

Packed with delectable vegetables, cheese and pesto, this picnic loaf is certain to impress. It is easy to transport, slices beautifully and tastes very good indeed.

Serves 6

1 medium country-style loaf
30ml/2 tbsp olive oil
3 courgettes, sliced lengthways
250g/9oz/3½ cups brown cap
   mushrooms, thickly sliced
1 garlic clove, chopped
5ml/1 tsp dried oregano
45ml/3 tbsp pesto
250g/9oz Taleggio cheese, sliced
50g/2oz/2 cups green
   salad leaves
salt and ground black pepper

1 Slice off the top third of the loaf and invert it on a board. Remove most of the crumb from the inside of both the lid and base, leaving a shell about 1cm/½in thick.

2 Brush a ridged grill pan with oil and grill the courgettes until they are tender and browned.

3 Meanwhile, heat the remaining oil in a frying pan and fry the mushrooms, garlic and oregano for 3 minutes. Season well.

4 Arrange half the courgettes in the base of the hollow loaf, then spread with half the pesto. Top with half the cheese and salad leaves and all the mushroom mixture. Add one more layer each of the remaining cheese, salad leaves and courgettes. Spread the rest of the pesto over the inside of the bread lid and place it on top.

5 Press the lid down gently, wrap the loaf in clear film and leave to cool. Chill overnight. Serve cut into wedges.

Cook's Tip
The courgettes can be grilled conventionally, if you prefer.

Summer Herb Ricotta Flan

Made without pastry, this delicate flan, infused with aromatic herbs, is ideal for a light lunch.

Serves 4
olive oil, for greasing and glazing
800g/1³⁄₄lb/3¹⁄₂ cups
   ricotta cheese
75g/3oz/1 cup freshly grated
   Parmesan cheese
3 eggs, separated
60ml/4 tbsp torn fresh
   basil leaves
60ml/4 tbsp snipped fresh chives
45ml/3 tbsp fresh oregano leaves
2.5ml/ ¹⁄₂ tsp salt
2.5ml/ ¹⁄₂ tsp paprika
ground black pepper
fresh herb leaves, to garnish

For the black olive purée
400g/14oz/3¹⁄₂ cups stoned
   black olives, rinsed and halved
5 garlic cloves, crushed
75ml/5 tbsp olive oil

1 Preheat the oven to 180°C/350°F/Gas 4. Lightly grease a 23cm/9in springform cake tin with oil. Mix the ricotta, Parmesan and egg yolks in a food processor. Add the fresh herbs, with the salt, and a little pepper. Process until smooth and creamy, then scrape into a bowl.

2 Whisk the egg whites in a large bowl until they form soft peaks. Gently fold the egg whites into the ricotta mixture. Spoon the mixture into the prepared tin and smooth the surface with a palette knife.

3 Bake for 1 hour 20 minutes, or until the flan has risen and the top is golden. Remove from the oven and brush lightly with olive oil, then sprinkle with paprika. Leave the flan to cool before removing it from the tin.

4 Make the olive purée. Set aside a few olives for garnishing, if you like. Place the remainder in a food processor, add the garlic and process until finely chopped. With the motor running, gradually add the olive oil through the feeder tube, until the mixture forms a coarse paste. Transfer it to a serving bowl. Garnish the flan with the herb leaves. Serve with the black olive purée.

Wild Mushroom Brioche with Orange Butter Sauce

A butter-rich brioche, ribboned with a mushroom duxelles would make an impressive centrepiece for a sophisticated dinner party.

Serves 4
5ml/1 tsp easy-blend dried yeast
45ml/3 tbsp milk, at
   room temperature
400g/14oz/3¹⁄₂ cups strong white
   bread flour
5ml/1 tsp salt
15ml/1 tbsp caster sugar
3 eggs
finely grated rind of ¹⁄₂ lemon
200g/7oz/scant 1 cup
   butter, diced

For the filling
50g/2oz/ ¹⁄₄ cup butter
2 shallots, chopped
350g/12oz/4 cups assorted wild
   and cultivated mushrooms,
   roughly chopped
¹⁄₂ garlic clove, crushed
75ml/5 tbsp chopped
   fresh parsley
salt and ground black pepper

For the sauce
30ml/2 tbsp frozen concentrated
   orange juice
175g/6oz/ ³⁄₄ cup butter, diced
cayenne pepper

1 Dissolve the yeast in the milk, add 115g/4oz/1 cup of the flour and mix to form a dough. Fill a large bowl with hand-hot water, then place the bowl of dough in the water. Set aside for 30 minutes.

2 Place the remaining flour in a food processor fitted with the dough blade. Add the salt, caster sugar, eggs, lemon rind and the risen dough and process briefly to mix. Add the butter, in small pieces, and process until the dough is silky smooth and very slack. Wrap it in clear film and chill for 2 hours, until firm.

3 Make the filling. Melt the butter in a large, heavy-based frying pan. Add the shallots and fry over a low heat, stirring occasionally, until softened but not browned.

4 Add the mushrooms and garlic and fry, stirring occasionally, until the juices begin to run. Increase the heat to medium to reduce the moisture. When dry, tip the mixture into a bowl, add the parsley and season to taste with salt and pepper.

5 Grease and line a 900g/2lb loaf tin. Roll out the dough to a 15 x 30cm/6 x 12in rectangle. Spoon the cooked mushroom mixture over the dough and roll up to make a fat sausage. Drop this into the loaf tin, cover with a damp dish towel and set aside in a warm place for 50 minutes, or until the dough has risen above the level of the rim.

6 Preheat the oven to 190°C/375°F/Gas 5, then bake the brioche for 40 minutes.

7 Meanwhile, make the sauce. Place the orange juice concentrate in a heatproof glass bowl and heat by standing in a pan of simmering water. Off the heat, gradually whisk in the butter until creamy. Season to taste with cayenne pepper, cover and keep warm. When the brioche is cooked, turn it out, slice thickly and serve with the sauce.

Roasted Gem Squash

Gem squash has a sweet, subtle flavour that contrasts well with black olives and sun-dried tomatoes. The rice adds substance and texture.

Serves 2–4
4 whole gem squashes
225g/8oz/2 cups cooked white
* long grain rice*
4 pieces sun-dried tomatoes, in
* oil, drained and chopped, plus*
* 30ml/2 tbsp oil from the jar*
50g/2oz/ ¹/₂ cup stoned black
* olives, chopped*
15ml/1 tbsp chopped fresh basil
* leaves, plus fresh basil sprigs,*
* to serve*
60ml/4 tbsp soft goat's cheese
tzatziki, to serve

1 Preheat the oven to 180°C/350°F/Gas 4. Trim away the base of each squash, slice off the top, scoop out the seeds with a spoon and discard.

2 Mix together the rice, sun-dried tomatoes, olives, basil and cheese in a bowl. Stir in half the oil from the jar.

3 Use a little of the remaining oil to grease a shallow ovenproof dish that is just large enough to hold the squash side by side. Divide the rice mixture among the squash and place them in the dish. Drizzle any remaining oil over.

4 Cover with foil and bake for 45–50 minutes, until tender. Garnish with basil sprigs. Serve with tzatziki.

Cook's Tip
225g/8oz/2 cups cooked rice is the equivalent of 65g/2¹/₂oz/ generous ¹/₃ cup raw rice.

Variations
• *If you are not keen on olives, use raisins instead.*
• *If gem squashes are not available, serve half an acorn squash per person instead.*

Stuffed Vegetables

Cooking for friends is fun when there are colourful dishes such as this with its interesting selection of different vegetables

Serves 4
45ml/3 tbsp olive oil, plus extra
* for greasing*
1 aubergine
1 green pepper
2 beefsteak tomatoes
1 onion, chopped
2 garlic clove, crushed
115g/4oz/1¹/₂ cups button
* mushrooms, chopped*
1 carrot, grated
225g/8oz/2 cups cooked white
* long grain rice*
15ml/1 tbsp chopped fresh dill
90g/3¹/₂oz/scant ¹/₂ cup feta
* cheese, crumbled*
75g/3oz/1 cup pine nuts,
* lightly toasted*
30ml/2 tbsp currants
salt and ground black pepper

1 Preheat the oven to 190°C/375°F/Gas 5. Lightly grease a shallow ovenproof dish. Cut the aubergine in half, through the stalk, and scoop out the flesh from each half to leave two hollow "boats". Dice the aubergine flesh. Cut the pepper in half lengthways and remove the seeds.

2 Cut off the tops from the tomatoes and hollow out the centres. Chop the flesh and add it to the diced aubergine. Drain the tomatoes upside down on kitchen paper.

3 Bring a pan of water to the boil, add the aubergine halves and blanch for 3 minutes. Add the pepper halves and blanch for 3 minutes more. Drain, then place all the vegetables, hollow side up, in the prepared dish.

4 Heat 30ml/2 tbsp of the oil in a pan and fry the onion and garlic for about 5 minutes. Stir in the diced aubergine and tomato mixture with the mushrooms and carrot. Cover, cook for 5 minutes, until softened, then mix in the rice, dill, feta, pine nuts and currants. Season to taste with salt and pepper.

5 Divide the mixture among the vegetable shells, drizzle the remaining olive oil over and bake for 20 minutes, until the topping has browned. Serve hot or cold.

Kohlrabi Stuffed with Peppers

If you haven't sampled kohlrabi, or have eaten it only in stews where its flavour is lost, do try this delectable dish.

Serves 4
4 small kohlrabi, about 175g/
  6oz each
about 400ml/14fl oz/1²⁄₃ cups
  hot vegetable stock

15ml/1 tbsp sunflower oil
1 onion, chopped
1 small red pepper, seeded
  and sliced
1 small green pepper, seeded
  and sliced
salt and ground black pepper

1 Preheat the oven to 180°C/350°F/Gas 4. Trim, then top and tail the kohlrabi. Arrange them in a single layer in the base of an ovenproof dish.

2 Pour over the hot stock to come about halfway up the kohlrabi. Cover and braise in the oven for about 30 minutes, until tender. Transfer to a plate, reserving the stock, and allow to cool. Leave the oven on.

3 Heat the sunflower oil in a large, heavy-based frying pan. Add the onion and fry over a low heat, stirring occasionally, for 3–4 minutes, until softened. Add the red and green pepper slices and cook, stirring occasionally, for 2–3 minutes more, until the onion is lightly browned.

4 Add the reserved vegetable stock and season to taste with salt and pepper, then simmer, uncovered, until most of the stock has evaporated.

5 Scoop out the flesh from the kohlrabi and chop it roughly. Stir the flesh into the onion and pepper mixture, taste and adjust the seasoning, if necessary. Arrange the shells in a shallow ovenproof dish.

6 Spoon the filling into the kohlrabi shells. Place in the oven for about 10 minutes to heat through, then serve.

Cabbage Roulades with Lemon Sauce

Cabbage or chard leaves, filled with a rice and red lentil stuffing, and served with a light egg and lemon sauce make a light and tasty main course.

Serves 4–6
12 large cabbage or chard leaves,
  stalks removed
25ml/2 tbsp sunflower oil
1 onion, chopped
1 large carrot, grated
115g/4oz/1½ cups
  sliced mushrooms

600ml/1 pint/2½ cups
  vegetable stock
115g/4oz/generous ½ cup long
  grain rice
60ml/4 tbsp red lentils
5ml/1 tsp dried oregano
90g/3½ oz soft cheese
  with garlic
25g/1oz/¼ cup plain flour
juice of 1 lemon
3 eggs, beaten
salt and ground black pepper

1 Bring a large pan of lightly salted water to the boil. Add the cabbage or chard leaves, in batches if necessary, and blanch briefly until they are just beginning to wilt. Drain thoroughly, reserving the cooking water. Pat the leaves dry with kitchen paper and set aside.

2 Heat the oil in a large pan. Add the onion, carrot and mushrooms and fry over a low heat, stirring occasionally, for 5 minutes, until the onion is softened but not coloured.

3 Pour the stock into the pan, then stir in the rice, lentils and oregano. Bring to the boil over a medium heat. Cover, lower the heat and simmer gently for 15 minutes. Remove the pan from the heat and stir in the cheese. Season to taste.

4 Preheat the oven to 190°C/375°F/Gas 5. Lay each leaf in turn on a board, rib side down, and spoon a little of the filling on to the stalk end. Fold in the sides and roll up.

5 Place the roulades in a small roasting tin, seam side down, and pour in the reserved cabbage water. Cover with foil and bake for 30–45 minutes, until the leaves are tender. Lift out the roulades with a draining spoon and place them on a warmed serving dish. Reserve the cooking liquid. Keep the roulades warm while you make the sauce.

6 Strain 600ml/1 pint/2½ cups of the cooking liquid into a pan and bring to the boil. Blend the flour to a paste with a little cold water and whisk into the boiling liquid, together with the lemon juice.

7 Beat the eggs with about 60ml/4 tbsp of the hot liquid in a heatproof jug. Gradually pour the mixture back into the pan of thickened liquid, whisking constantly. Continue to whisk over a very low heat until smooth and thick. Do not allow the sauce to boil or it will curdle.

8 Serve the roulades with some of the sauce poured over and the rest handed separately.

Festive Lentil & Nut Loaf

For a special celebration, serve this with all the trimmings, including a vegetarian gravy. Garnish it with fresh cranberries and flat leaf parsley for a really festive effect.

Serves 6–8
115g/4oz/ ½ cup red lentils
115g/4oz/1 cup hazelnuts
115g/4oz/1 cup walnuts
1 large carrot
2 celery sticks
1 large onion
115g/4oz/1½ cups mushrooms
50g/2oz/ ¼ cup butter, plus extra
   for greasing
10ml/2 tsp mild curry powder
30ml/2 tbsp tomato ketchup
30ml/2 tbsp vegetarian
   Worcestershire sauce
1 egg, beaten
10ml/2 tsp salt
60ml/4 tbsp chopped
   fresh parsley
150ml/ ¼ pint/ ⅔ cup water

1 Put the lentils in a bowl and add sufficient cold water to cover. Set aside for 1 hour to soak. Grind the nuts in a food processor until quite fine but not too smooth. Tip the nuts into a large bowl. Coarsely chop the carrot, celery, onion and mushrooms, add them to the food processor and process until finely chopped.

2 Heat the butter in a saucepan. Add the vegetables and fry gently over a low heat, stirring occasionally, for 5 minutes. Stir in the curry powder and cook for 1 minute more. Remove from the heat and set aside to cool.

3 Drain the soaked lentils and stir them into the ground nuts. Add the vegetables, ketchup, vegetarian Worcestershire sauce, egg, salt, parsley and water.

4 Preheat the oven to 190°C/375°F/Gas 5. Grease a 1kg/2¼lb loaf tin and line with greaseproof paper or a sheet of foil. Press the mixture into the tin.

5 Bake for 1–1¼ hours, until just firm, covering the top with foil if it starts to burn. Leave to stand for 15 minutes before you turn it out and peel off the paper. It will be fairly soft when cut.

Mushroom & Mixed Nut Roast

The seed topping on this roast, visible when you turn it out, looks very attractive and is a good contrast to the tender loaf.

Serves 4
30ml/2 tbsp sunflower oil, plus
   extra for greasing
45ml/3 tbsp sunflower seeds
45ml/3 tbsp sesame seeds
1 onion, roughly chopped
2 celery sticks, roughly chopped
1 green pepper, seeded
   and chopped
225g/8oz/3 cups mixed
   mushrooms, chopped
1 garlic clove, crushed
115g/4oz/2 cups fresh
   wholemeal breadcrumbs
115g/4oz/1 cup chopped
   mixed nuts
50g/2oz/ ⅓ cup sultanas
small piece of fresh root ginger,
   finely chopped
10ml/2 tsp coriander
   seeds, crushed
30ml/2 tbsp light soy sauce
1 egg, beaten
salt and ground black pepper
celery and coriander leaves,
   to garnish
tomato sauce, to serve

1 Brush a 675g/1½lb loaf tin with sunflower oil and line with greaseproof paper. Sprinkle the sunflower and sesame seeds evenly over the base.

2 Preheat the oven to 190°C/375°F/Gas 5. Heat the oil in a large frying pan. Add the onion, celery, green pepper, mushrooms and garlic and fry over a low heat, stirring occasionally, for about 5 minutes, until the onion has softened but not coloured. Remove the pan from the heat and set aside.

3 Mix together the breadcrumbs and nuts in a large bowl. Tip in the contents of the frying pan, then stir in the sultanas, ginger, coriander seeds and soy sauce. Bind with the egg, then season to taste with salt and pepper.

4 Press the mixture evenly into the prepared tin and bake for 45 minutes. Loosen the sides of the loaf with a knife, then leave it to cool for 2–3 minutes. Turn out on to a serving dish and garnish with the celery and coriander leaves. Serve immediately with the tomato sauce.

Fonduta

Fondues are coming back into fashion. They are perfect for casual entertaining. This variation is rich and tasty.

Serves 4
250g/9oz Fontina or Gruyère cheese, diced
250ml/8fl oz/1 cup milk
15g/ ½ oz/1 tbsp butter
2 eggs, lightly beaten
ground black pepper
1 loaf ciabatta or focaccia, cut in large cubes, to serve

1 Put the cheese in a bowl, pour over the milk and leave to soak for 2–3 hours. Transfer to a double boiler or a heatproof bowl set over a pan of simmering water.

2 Add the butter and eggs and cook gently, stirring until the cheese has melted and the sauce is smooth and thick, with the consistency of custard. Remove from the heat and season with pepper. Transfer to a serving dish and serve immediately with the bread.

Dutch Fondue

This is an amazingly easy, yet delicious supper dish.

Serves 4
250ml/8fl oz/1 cup white wine
15 ml/1 tbsp lemon juice
450g/1lb Gouda cheese, grated
15 ml/1 tbsp cornflour
30 ml/2 tbsp water
30 ml/2 tbsp gin
ground black pepper
cauliflower florets, carrot batons, chicory leaves and bread cubes, to serve

1 Bring the wine and lemon juice to the boil in a pan over a low heat. Gradually stir in the cheese until melted.
2 Mix the cornflour and water to a paste and stir into the fondue. Bring to the boil, stirring constantly, add the gin and season with pepper.
3 Transfer to a fondue. Serve with the vegetables and bread.

Leek Soufflé

Some people think a soufflé is a rather tricky dish for a dinner party, but it is really quite easy.

Serves 2–3
40g/1½ oz/3 tbsp butter, plus extra for greasing
15ml/1 tbsp sunflower oil
2 leeks, thinly sliced
about 300ml/ ½ pint/ 1¼ cups milk
25g/oz/ ¼ cup plain flour
4 eggs, separated
75g/3oz/ ¾ cup grated Gruyère or Emmenthal cheese
salt and ground black pepper

1 Preheat the oven to 180°C/350°F/Gas 4. Butter a 1.2 litre/ 2 pint/5 cup soufflé dish. Heat the oil and 15g/ ½oz/1 tbsp of the butter in a small pan and fry the leeks gently, stirring occasionally, for 4–5 minutes, until soft but not brown.

2 Stir in the milk and bring to the boil. Cover, then simmer for 4–5 minutes, until the leeks are tender. Drain, reserving the liquid. Set the leeks aside and strain the liquid into a measuring jug. Add extra milk to make it up to 300ml/ ½ pint/1¼ cups.

3 Melt the remaining butter in a pan, stir in the flour and cook for 1 minute. Gradually add the milk, whisking constantly until the mixture boils and thickens to a smooth sauce.

4 Remove it from the heat. Cool slightly, then beat in the egg yolks, cheese and reserved leeks. Season to taste.

5 Whisk the egg whites until stiff. Using a large metal spoon, fold them into the leek and egg mixture. Pour into the prepared soufflé dish and bake in the oven for about 30 minutes, until golden and puffy. Serve immediately.

Cook's Tip
Everything except whisking the egg whites can be done in advance. Finish making the soufflé when your guests arrive, and half an hour later you'll be sitting down to a superb light meal.

Classic Cheese Soufflé

A melt-in-the-mouth cheese soufflé makes one of the most delightful light lunches imaginable. All you need to go with it is salad and a glass of good wine.

Serves 2–3

50g/2oz/ ¼ cup butter
30–45ml/2–3 tbsp fine,
   dried breadcrumbs
30g/1¼oz/5 tbsp plain flour
pinch of cayenne pepper
2.5ml/ ½ tsp English
   mustard powder
250ml/8fl oz/1 cup milk
50g/2oz/ ½ cup grated mature
   Cheddar cheese
25g/1oz/ ⅓ cup freshly grated
   Parmesan cheese
4 eggs, separated, plus
   1 egg white
salt and ground black pepper

1 Preheat the oven to 190°C/375°F/Gas 5. Melt 15g/ ½oz/ 1 tbsp of the butter and grease a 1.2 litre/2 pint/5 cup soufflé dish. Coat the inside of the dish with the breadcrumbs.

2 Melt the remaining butter in a saucepan, stir in the flour, cayenne and mustard and cook for 1 minute. Add the milk, whisking constantly, until the mixture boils and thickens to a smooth sauce. Simmer the sauce for 1–2 minutes, then remove from the heat and whisk in all the Cheddar, half the Parmesan and season to taste. Cool a little, then beat in the egg yolks.

3 Whisk the egg whites to soft, glossy peaks. Add a few spoonfuls to the sauce to lighten it. Beat well, then gently fold in the rest of the whites.

4 Pour the mixture into the prepared soufflé dish, level the surface and sprinkle the remaining Parmesan over. Place the dish on a baking sheet and bake for about 25 minutes, until the soufflé has risen and is golden brown. Serve immediately.

Cook's Tip
To help the soufflé rise evenly, run your finger around the inside rim of the dish before baking.

Spinach & Wild Mushroom Soufflé

A variety of wild mushrooms combine especially well with eggs and spinach in this sensational soufflé.

Serves 4

50g/2oz/ ¼ cup butter, plus extra
   for greasing
30ml/2 tbsp freshly grated
   Parmesan cheese
225g/8oz fresh spinach leaves
1 garlic clove, crushed
175g/6oz/2¼ cups assorted
   wild mushrooms, chopped
200ml/7fl oz/scant 1 cup milk
25g/1oz/ ¼ cup plain flour
6 eggs, separated
pinch of freshly grated nutmeg
salt and ground black pepper

1 Preheat the oven to 190°C/375°F/Gas 5. Butter a 900ml/ 1½ pint/3¾ cup soufflé dish, paying particular attention to the sides. Sprinkle with a little of the cheese. Set aside.

2 Steam the spinach over a medium heat for 3–4 minutes. Cool under cold running water, then drain. Press out as much liquid as you can with the back of a large spoon, squeeze with your hands and then chop finely.

3 Melt the butter in a pan and gently soften the garlic and mushrooms. Increase the heat and cook until the mixture is quite dry. Add the spinach and transfer to a bowl. Cover and keep warm.

4 Measure 45ml/3 tbsp of the milk into a bowl and stir in the flour and egg yolks. Bring the remaining milk to the boil, whisk it into the egg and flour mixture until smooth, then pour the mixture back into the pan and whisk over the heat until the sauce thickens. Stir in the spinach mixture. Season to taste with salt, pepper and grated nutmeg.

5 Whisk the egg whites to form soft peaks. Stir a spoonful into the spinach mixture to lighten it, then fold in the rest.

6 Pour the mixture into the soufflé dish, level the surface, scatter with the remaining cheese and bake for about 25 minutes, until well risen and golden. Serve immediately.

Celeriac & Blue Cheese Roulade

Celeriac adds a subtle flavour to this attractive dish. Be sure to roll up the roulade while it is still warm and pliable.

Serves 6
15g/½oz/1 tbsp butter
225g/8oz cooked spinach, drained and chopped
150ml/¼ pint/⅔ cup single cream
4 large eggs, separated
60ml/4 tbsp freshly grated Parmesan cheese
pinch of freshly grated nutmeg
salt and ground black pepper

For the filling
1 large celeriac, about 225g/8oz
lemon juice, to taste
75g/3oz St Agur cheese
115g/4oz/½ cup fromage frais

1 Preheat the oven to 200°C/400°F/Gas 6. Line a 33 × 23cm/13 × 9in Swiss roll tin with non-stick baking paper.

2 Melt the butter in a pan and add the spinach. Cook gently until all the liquid has evaporated, stirring frequently. Off the heat, stir in the cream, egg yolks, Parmesan and nutmeg. Season to taste with salt and pepper.

3 Whisk the egg whites until stiff, fold them gently into the spinach mixture and then spoon into the prepared tin. Spread the mixture evenly and smooth the surface.

4 Bake for 10–15 minutes until the roulade is firm to the touch and lightly golden on top. Carefully turn out on to a sheet of non-stick baking paper and peel away the lining paper. Roll it up with the paper inside and leave to cool slightly.

5 Make the filling. Peel the celeriac, grate it into a bowl and sprinkle well with lemon juice. Blend the blue cheese and fromage frais together and mix with the celeriac. Season with a little black pepper.

6 Carefully unroll the roulade, spread the filling evenly over the surface and roll up again. Serve at once, cut into slices, or wrap loosely and chill in the refrigerator.

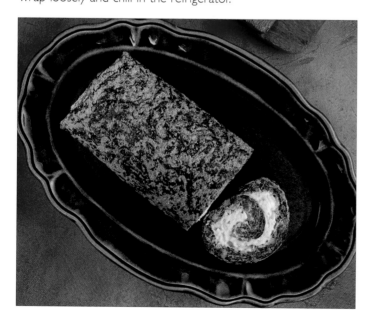

Twice-baked Spinach, Mushroom & Goat's Cheese Roulade

A roulade is really a Swiss roll soufflé. Because it has air trapped inside, it magically rises again on reheating and becomes quite crisp on the outside. It is ideal for a dinner party.

Serves 4
150g/5oz/⅔ cup butter, plus extra, for greasing
50g/2oz/½ cup plain flour
300ml/½ pint/1¼ cups milk
100g/3¾oz chèvre (goat's cheese), chopped
40g/1½ oz/½ cup freshly grated Parmesan cheese, plus extra for sprinkling
4 eggs, separated
225g/8oz/3 cups fresh shiitake mushrooms, stalks discarded, sliced
275g/10oz young spinach leaves, wilted
45ml/3 tbsp crème fraîche
salt and ground black pepper

1 Preheat the oven to 190°C/375°F/Gas 5. Line a 30 × 20cm/12 × 8in Swiss roll tin with non-stick baking paper, making sure that the paper rises well above the sides of the tin. Grease lightly with butter.

2 Melt 50g/2oz/¼ cup of the butter in a large, heavy-based saucepan. Stir in the plain flour and cook over a low heat, stirring constantly with a wooden spoon, for 1 minute, then gradually whisk in the milk. Bring the mixture to the boil, whisking constantly, and continue cooking, until the mixture thickens to a smooth sauce.

3 Simmer for 2 minutes, then mix in the chèvre and half the Parmesan. Cool for 5 minutes, then beat in the egg yolks and plenty of salt and pepper.

4 Whisk the egg whites until they form soft peaks. Stir a spoonful of the egg whites into the chèvre mixture to lighten it, then fold in the remainder. Spoon the mixture into the prepared tin, spread gently with a palette knife to level, then bake for 15–17 minutes, until the top feels just firm.

5 Remove the roulade from the oven and cool for a few minutes, then invert it on to a sheet of non-stick baking paper dusted with the remaining Parmesan. Carefully remove and discard the lining paper. Roll the roulade up with the baking paper inside and leave to cool completely.

6 Make the filling. Melt the remaining butter in a heavy-based frying pan and set aside 30ml/2 tbsp. Add the mushrooms to the pan and fry over a low heat, stirring occasionally, for about 3 minutes. Stir in the spinach and heat through briefly. Drain well, then stir in the crème fraîche. Season to taste with salt and pepper, then set aside to cool.

7 Preheat the oven to 190°C/375°F/Gas 5. Carefully unroll the roulade and spread the filling over the surface. Roll it up again and place, join side down, in an ovenproof dish. Brush with the reserved melted butter and sprinkle with the remaining Parmesan. Bake for 15 minutes, or until risen and golden brown. Serve immediately.

Leek Roulade with Cheese, Walnuts & Peppers

This is surprisingly easy to prepare and makes a good main course.

Serves 4–6
50g/2oz/4 tbsp butter, plus extra
    for greasing
30ml/2 tbsp fine dried
    white breadcrumbs
75g/3oz/1 cup freshly grated
    Parmesan cheese
2 leeks, thinly sliced
40g/1½oz/6 tbsp plain flour
250ml/8fl oz/1 cup milk
5ml/1 tsp Dijon mustard
about 2.5ml/½ tsp freshly
    grated nutmeg

2 large eggs, separated, plus
    1 egg white
2.5ml/½ tsp cream of tartar
salt and ground black pepper

For the filling
2 large red peppers, halved
    and seeded
350g/12oz/1½ cups
    ricotta cheese
75g/3oz/¾ cup
    walnuts, chopped
4 spring onions, finely chopped
15g/½ oz/½ cup fresh
    basil leaves

1 Preheat the oven to 190°C/375°F/Gas 5. Grease a 30 × 23cm/12 × 9in Swiss roll tin and line it with baking paper. Sprinkle the breadcrumbs and 30ml/2 tbsp of the Parmesan evenly over the paper.

2 Melt the butter in a saucepan and fry the leeks gently for 5 minutes, until softened but not browned. Stir in the flour and cook for 1 minute, stirring. Add the milk, whisking constantly until the mixture boils and thickens.

3 Stir in the mustard and nutmeg and season. Reserve 30–45ml/2–3 tbsp of the remaining Parmesan, then stir the rest into the sauce. Cool slightly, then beat in the egg yolks.

4 Whisk the egg whites and cream of tartar until stiff. Stir 2–3 spoonfuls of the egg white into the leek mixture to lighten it, then carefully fold in the rest.

5 Pour the mixture into the tin and level the surface. Bake for 15–18 minutes, until risen and just firm.

6 Make the filling. Grill the peppers, skin side uppermost, until black and blistered. Place in a bowl, cover with crumpled kitchen paper and leave for 10 minutes. Peel off the skin and cut the peppers into long strips.

7 Beat the cheese with the walnuts and spring onions. Chop half the basil and beat it into the mixture. Season to taste.

8 Scatter a large sheet of baking paper with the remaining Parmesan. Turn out the roulade on to it. Strip off the lining paper and cool slightly. Spread the cheese mixture over and top with the red pepper strips. Tear the remaining basil leaves and sprinkle them over the top.

9 Using the paper as a guide, roll up the roulade and roll it on to a serving platter. Serve warm or cold.

Pancakes with Butternut Filling

These melt-in-the-mouth pancakes are wonderful served with a green salad and a rich tomato sauce.

Serves 4
115g/4oz/1 cup plain flour
50g/2oz/scant ½ cup polenta
    or cornmeal
2.5ml/½ tsp mild chilli powder
2 large eggs, beaten
about 450ml/¾ pint/scant
    2 cups milk
25g/1oz/2 tbsp butter, melted
vegetable oil, for greasing
salt and ground black pepper

For the filling
45ml/3 tbsp olive oil
450g/1lb/3½ cups seeded and
    diced butternut squash
pinch of dried red chilli flakes
2 large leeks, thickly sliced
2.5ml/½ tsp chopped
    fresh thyme
3 chicory heads, thickly sliced
115g/4oz goat's cheese, cubed
75g/3oz/¾ cup walnuts,
    roughly chopped
30ml/2 tbsp chopped fresh
    parsley, plus extra to garnish
45ml/3 tbsp freshly grated
    Parmesan cheese

1 Mix the flour, polenta, chilli powder and a pinch of salt and make a well in the centre. Add the eggs and a little of the milk. Whisk, gradually incorporating the flour mixture and adding enough milk to make a creamy batter. Set aside for 1 hour.

2 Whisk the melted butter into the batter. Heat a lightly greased crêpe pan. Pour in about 60ml/4 tbsp of the batter, cook for 2–3 minutes, turn over and cook for 1–2 minutes, then slide out. Make more pancakes in the same way.

3 Make the filling. Heat 30ml/2 tbsp of the oil in a frying pan and cook the squash, stirring frequently, for 10 minutes. Stir in the chilli flakes, leeks and thyme and cook for 5 minutes. Add the chicory and cook, stirring frequently, for 4–5 minutes. Cool, then stir in the goat's cheese, walnuts and parsley. Season well.

4 Preheat the oven to 200°C/400°F/Gas 6. Lightly grease an ovenproof dish. Stuff each pancake with 30–45ml/2–3 tbsp of the filling and place in the dish. Scatter with the Parmesan and drizzle with the remaining olive oil. Bake for 10–15 minutes, until the cheese is bubbling and the pancakes are hot.

Baked Herb Crêpes

A spinach, cheese and pine nut filling turns pancakes into party food.

Serves 4
25g/1oz/1 cup chopped fresh herbs
15ml/1 tbsp sunflower oil, plus extra for frying and greasing
120ml/4fl oz/ ½ cup milk
3 eggs
25g/1oz/ ¼ cup plain flour

For the sauce
30ml/2 tbsp olive oil
1 small onion, chopped
2 garlic cloves, crushed
400g/14oz can chopped tomatoes
pinch of soft light brown sugar

For the filling
450g/1lb fresh spinach, cooked and drained
175g/6oz/¾ cup ricotta cheese
25g/1oz pint nuts, toasted
5 pieces of sun-dried tomato in oil, drained and chopped
4 egg whites
30ml/2 tbsp shredded fresh basil
salt and ground black pepper

1 Process the herbs and oil in a food processor until smooth. Add the milk, eggs and flour, with a pinch of salt. Process again until smooth. Leave to rest for 30 minutes.

2 Heat a lightly greased crêpe pan. Pour in one-eighth of the batter. Cook for 2 minutes, turn over and cook for 1–2 minutes more. Slide the crêpe out of the pan. Make seven more crêpes.

3 Make the sauce. Heat the oil in a small pan, and cook the onion and garlic gently for 5 minutes. Add the tomatoes and sugar and cook for about 10 minutes, until thickened. Purée in a blender or food processor, then sieve into a pan and set aside.

4 Mix all the filling ingredients except the egg whites, seasoning with salt and pepper. Whisk the egg whites until stiff. Stir one-third into the spinach mixture, then fold in the rest.

5 Preheat the oven to 190°C/375°F/Gas 5. Place one crêpe at a time on a lightly oiled baking sheet, add a spoonful of filling and fold into quarters. Bake for 12 minutes, until set. Reheat the sauce and serve with the crêpes.

Moroccan Pancakes

An unusual and tasty dish which makes a good talking point at the dinner table.

Serves 4–6
15ml/1 tbsp olive oil
1 large onion, chopped
250g/9oz fresh spinach leaves
400g/14oz can chick-peas
2 courgettes, grated
30ml/2 tbsp chopped fresh coriander
2 eggs, beaten
salt and ground black pepper
fresh coriander leaves, to garnish

For the pancakes
150g/5oz/1¼ cups plain flour
1 egg
about 350ml/12fl oz/ 1½ cups milk
75ml/5 tbsp water
15ml/1 tbsp sunflower oil, plus extra for greasing

For the sauce
25g/1oz/2 tbsp butter
30ml/2 tbsp plain flour
about 300ml/ ½ pint/ 1¼ cups milk

1 Make the batter by blending the flour, egg, milk and water until smooth in a blender. Stir in the oil and a pinch of salt. Heat a lightly greased frying pan and ladle in about one-eighth of the batter. Cook for 2–3 minutes, without turning, then slide the pancake out of the pan. Make seven more pancakes.

2 Heat the olive oil in a small pan and fry the onion until soft. Set aside. Wash the spinach, place it in a pan and cook until wilted, shaking the pan occasionally. Chop the spinach roughly.

3 Drain the chick-peas, place in a bowl of cold water and rub them until the skins float to the surface. Drain the chick-peas and mash roughly with a fork. Add the onion, courgettes, spinach and coriander. Stir in the eggs, season and mix well.

4 Preheat the oven to 180°C/350°F/Gas 4. Place the pancakes, cooked side up, on a board and spoon the filling down the centres. Roll up and place in a large oiled ovenproof dish. Make the sauce. Melt the butter in a pan, stir in the flour and cook for 1 minute. Gradually whisk in the milk until the mixture boils. Season and pour over the pancakes. Bake for 15 minutes, until golden. Serve garnished with the coriander leaves.

Artichoke & Leek Pancakes

Fill thin pancakes with a
mouth-watering soufflé
mixture of Jerusalem
artichokes and leek.

Serves 4
115g/4oz/1 cup plain flour
pinch of salt
1 egg
300ml/ 1/2 pint/1 1/4 cups milk
vegetable oil, for greasing
fresh flat leaf parsley, to garnish

For the filling
50g/2oz/ 1/4 cup butter
450g/1lb Jerusalem
   artichokes, diced
1 large leek, thinly sliced
30ml/2 tbsp self-raising flour
30ml/2 tbsp single cream
75g/3oz/ 3/4 cup grated mature
   Cheddar cheese
30ml/2 tbsp chopped
   fresh parsley
freshly grated nutmeg
2 eggs, separated
salt and ground black pepper

1 Make the batter by blending the flour, salt, egg and milk to a
smooth batter in a blender or food processor. Heat a lightly
greased frying pan and add one-eighth of the batter. Cook for
2–3 minutes, then turn over and cook the other side for
2 minutes. Slide the pancake out of the pan. Make seven more
pancakes in the same way.

2 Make the filling. Melt the butter in a pan, add the artichokes
and leek, cover and cook gently for about 12 minutes, until very
soft. Mash with the back of a wooden spoon. Season well.

3 Stir the flour into the vegetables and cook for 1 minute. Take
the pan off the heat and beat in the cream, cheese, parsley and
nutmeg to taste. Cool, then add the egg yolks.

4 Preheat the oven to 190°C/375°F/Gas 5. Lightly grease a
small ovenproof dish. Whisk the egg whites to soft peaks and
carefully fold them into the leek and artichoke mixture.

5 Fold each pancake in four, hold the top open and spoon the
mixture into the centre. Arrange the pancakes in the prepared
dish with the filling uppermost, if possible. Bake for 15 minutes,
until risen and golden. Serve immediately, garnished with parsley.

Roast Asparagus Crêpes

Roast asparagus is truly
delicious – good enough to
eat just as it is. However, for
a really splendid dish, try
this simple recipe.

Serves 3
175g/6oz/1 1/2 cups plain flour
2 eggs
350ml/12fl oz/1 1/2 cups milk
vegetable oil, for frying

For the filling
90–120ml/6–8 tbsp olive oil
450g/1lb fresh asparagus
175g/6oz/ 3/4 cup
   mascarpone cheese
60ml/4 tbsp single cream
25g/1oz/ 1/3 cup freshly grated
   Parmesan cheese
sea salt

1 Make the pancake batter by blending the flour, eggs, milk and
a pinch of salt in a blender or food processor.

2 Heat a 20cm/8in frying pan, grease it lightly with vegetable oil
and add one-sixth of the batter to make a pancake. Cook for
2–3 minutes, then turn over and cook the other side until
golden. Slide out of the pan and set aside. Cook five more
pancakes in the same way.

3 Preheat the oven to 180°C/350°F/Gas 4. Lightly grease a
large, shallow ovenproof dish. Arrange the asparagus in a single
layer in the dish, trickle over the remaining olive oil and gently
shake the dish to coat each asparagus spear.

4 Sprinkle the asparagus with a little sea salt, then roast for
8–12 minutes, until tender.

5 Mix the mascarpone with the cream and Parmesan, beating
well to combine, and spread a generous tablespoonful of the
mixture over each pancake, reserving little for the topping.
Preheat the grill.

6 Divide the asparagus spears among the pancakes, roll up and
arrange in a single layer in an ovenproof dish. Spoon over the
remaining cheese mixture and grill for 4–5 minutes, until heated
through and golden brown. Serve at once.

Garganelli with Asparagus & Cream

A lovely recipe for late spring, when bunches of fresh young asparagus are on sale everywhere.

Serves 4
1 bunch fresh young asparagus, about 275g/10oz
350g/12oz/3 cups dried garganelli
25g/1oz/2 tbsp butter
250ml/8fl oz/1 cup double cream
30ml/2 tbsp dry white wine
115g/4oz/1⅓ cups freshly grated Parmesan cheese
30ml/2 tbsp chopped fresh mixed herbs
salt and ground black pepper

1 With your fingers, snap off and discard the woody ends of the asparagus. Cut off the tips and set them aside. Cut the stalks diagonally into pieces that are about the same length and shape as the garganelli.

2 Bring a large pan of lightly salted water to the boil and blanch the asparagus stalks for 1 minute. Add the tips and blanch for 1 minute more. Transfer to a colander with a draining spoon. Rinse under cold water, drain again and set aside.

3 Bring the water in the pan back to the boil, add the pasta and cook until it is *al dente*. Meanwhile, mix the butter and cream in a pan, season to taste and bring to the boil. Simmer for a few minutes, until the cream thickens, then add the asparagus, wine and about half the grated Parmesan. Taste for seasoning and leave over a low heat.

4 Drain the cooked pasta and tip it into a warmed bowl. Pour the sauce over, sprinkle with the fresh herbs and toss well. Serve immediately, topped with the remaining grated Parmesan.

Cook's Tip
When buying asparagus, look for thin, unwrinkled stalks, which will be sweet and tender. The buds should be tight and the stalks should be an even colour.

Fusilli with Wild Mushrooms

A very rich dish with an earthy flavour and lots of garlic, this makes an ideal main course, especially if it is followed by a crisp green salad in the French manner.

Serves 4
½ x 275g/10oz jar wild mushrooms in olive oil
25g/1oz/2 tbsp butter
225g/8oz/3 cups fresh wild mushrooms, sliced if large
5ml/1 tsp each finely chopped fresh thyme, marjoram or oregano, plus extra herbs, to garnish
4 garlic cloves, crushed
350g/12oz/3 cups fresh or dried fusilli
250ml/8fl oz/1 cup double cream
salt and ground black pepper

1 Drain about 15ml/1 tbsp of the oil from the jar of wild mushrooms into a large, heavy-based frying pan. Slice or chop the bottled mushrooms into bite-size pieces, if they are large.

2 Add the butter to the oil in the pan and place over a low heat until sizzling. Add the bottled and the fresh mushrooms, the chopped herbs and the garlic. Season with salt and pepper to taste. Cook over a low heat, stirring occasionally, for about 10 minutes, until the fresh mushrooms are soft and tender.

3 Bring a large saucepan of lightly salted water to the boil and cook the pasta until it is *al dente*.

4 Meanwhile, increase the heat under the pan of mushrooms to medium and toss the mixture until all the excess liquid has been driven off.

5 Pour in the cream and bring to the boil, stirring constantly, then taste and add more salt and pepper if needed.

6 Drain the pasta and tip it into a warmed serving bowl. Pour the mushroom sauce over the pasta and toss thoroughly to mix. Serve the fusilli immediately, sprinkled with extra fresh herb leaves to garnish.

Tagliarini with White Truffle

There is nothing quite like the fragrance and flavour of rare Italian white truffles.

Serves 4
350g/12oz fresh tagliarini
75g/3oz/6 tbsp butter, diced

60ml/4 tbsp freshly grated
  Parmesan cheese
freshly grated nutmeg
1 small white truffle, about
  25–40g/1–1½oz
salt and ground black pepper

1 Bring a large pan of lightly salted water to the boil and cook the pasta until it is *al dente*. Immediately, drain it well and tip it into a large, warmed bowl.

2 Add the diced butter, grated Parmesan and a little freshly grated nutmeg. Season with salt and pepper to taste. Toss well until all the strands are coated in melted butter.

3 Divide the pasta equally among four warmed, individual bowls and shave paper-thin slivers of the white truffle on top. Serve immediately.

Farfalle with Dolcelatte Cream

Sweet and simple, this sauce has a light nutty tang from the blue cheese.

Serves 4
350g/12oz/3 cups dried farfalle
175g/6oz dolcelatte cheese, diced

150ml/¼ pint/⅓ cup
  double cream
10ml/2 tsp chopped fresh sage
salt and ground black pepper
fresh sage leaves, to garnish

1 Bring a large pan of lightly salted water to the boil and cook the pasta until it is *al dente*.
2 Meanwhile, melt the cheese with the double cream in a pan, stirring frequently.
3 Drain the pasta and return to the pan. Pour in the sauce with the chopped sage and toss to coat. Serve garnished with sage.

Sardinian Ravioli

With their unusual mashed potato and mint filling, these ravioli are certainly special.

Serves 4–6
1 quantity Pasta Dough
flour, for dusting
50g/2oz/¼ cup butter
50g/2oz/⅔ cup freshly grated
  Pecorino cheese

For the filling
400g/14oz potatoes, diced
65g/2½ oz/generous ⅔ cup
  grated mature Pecorino cheese
75g/3oz soft fresh
  Pecorino cheese
1 egg yolk
leaves from 1 large bunch fresh
  mint, chopped
good pinch of saffron powder
salt and ground black pepper

1 Make the filling. Bring a pan of lightly salted water to the boil and cook the potatoes for 15–20 minutes, or until soft. Drain, tip into a bowl, then mash until smooth. Cool, then stir in the cheeses, egg yolk, mint, saffron and salt and pepper to taste.

2 Using a pasta machine, roll out one-quarter of the pasta into a 90cm/36in strip. Cut the strip into two 45cm/18in lengths.

3 With a fluted 10cm/4in biscuit cutter, cut out 4–5 discs from one of the strips. Using a heaped teaspoon, put a mound of filling on one side of each disc. Brush a little water around the edge of each disc, then fold the plain side of the disc over the filling to make a half-moon shape. Pleat the curved edge to seal.

4 Put the ravioli on floured dish towels, sprinkle with flour and leave to dry. Repeat the process with the remaining dough to make 32–40 ravioli altogether.

5 Preheat the oven to 190°C/375°F/Gas 5. Bring a large pan of lightly salted water to the boil and cook the ravioli for 4–5 minutes. Meanwhile, melt the butter in a small pan.

6 Drain the ravioli, transfer to a large ovenproof dish and pour the melted butter over. Sprinkle with the grated Pecorino and bake in the oven for 10–15 minutes, until golden and bubbly. Allow to stand for 5 minutes before serving.

Grilled Polenta with Caramelized Onions

Slices of grilled polenta topped with caramelized onions and bubbling Taleggio cheese are extremely tasty.

Serves 4
900ml/1½ pints/3¾ cups water
5ml/1 tsp salt
150g/5oz/generous 1 cup polenta
　or cornmeal
50g/2oz/ ⅔ cup freshly grated
　Parmesan cheese
5ml/1 tsp chopped fresh thyme
90ml/6 tbsp olive oil
675g/1½ lb onions, halved
　and sliced
2 garlic cloves, chopped
a few fresh thyme sprigs
5ml/1 tsp soft light brown sugar
30ml/2 tbsp balsamic vinegar
2 heads radicchio, cut into thick
　slices or wedges
225g/7oz Taleggio cheese, sliced
salt and ground black pepper

1 Pour the water into a large saucepan, add the salt and bring to the boil. Adjust to a simmer. Stirring constantly, add the polenta in a steady stream, then bring to the boil. Immediately, reduce the heat to the lowest setting and cook, stirring frequently, for 30–40 minutes, until thick and smooth.

2 Beat in the Parmesan and chopped thyme, then tip the mixture on to a large tray. Spread evenly, then leave to set.

3 Heat 30ml/2 tbsp of the oil in a frying pan and cook the onions over a very low heat for 15 minutes, stirring occasionally. Add the garlic and some thyme sprigs. Cook for 10 minutes more, until golden and very soft. Add the sugar and half the vinegar. Season to taste. Cook for 10 minutes, until browned.

4 Preheat the grill. Thickly slice the polenta and brush with a little oil, then grill until crusty and lightly browned. Turn over. Add the radicchio to the grill rack, season and brush with a little oil. Grill for 5 minutes, until the polenta and radicchio are browned. Drizzle a little vinegar over the radicchio.

5 Heap the onions on the polenta. Scatter with the cheese and thyme sprigs. Grill until the cheese is bubbling. Serve at once.

Layered Polenta Bake

When you are entertaining, it's good to serve something a little out of the ordinary. This combination of polenta, tomatoes, spinach and beans fits the bill very well.

Serves 6
2 litres/3½ pints/9 cups water
5ml/1 tsp salt
375g/13oz/3 cups fine polenta
　or cornmeal
olive oil, for greasing and brushing
25g/1oz/ ⅓ cup freshly grated
　Parmesan cheese
salt and ground black pepper

For the tomato sauce
15ml/1 tbsp olive oil
2 garlic cloves, chopped
400g/14oz can
　chopped tomatoes
15ml/1 tbsp chopped fresh sage
2.5ml/ ½ tsp soft light
　brown sugar
200g/7oz can cannellini beans,
　drained and rinsed

For the spinach sauce
250g/9oz spinach, tough
　stalks removed
150ml/ ¼ pint/ ⅔ cup
　single cream
115g/4oz Gorgonzola
　cheese, cubed
large pinch of freshly
　grated nutmeg

1 Pour the water into a large, heavy-based pan and add the salt. Bring to the boil. Remove the pan from the heat and gradually whisk in the polenta.

2 Return the pan to the heat and simmer over a low heat, stirring constantly, for 15–20 minutes, until the polenta is thick and comes away from the side of the pan. Remove the pan from the heat.

3 Season the polenta to taste with pepper, then spoon it on to a wet work surface and spread it out evenly with a wet spatula until it is about 1cm/ ½in thick. Leave to cool for about 1 hour, or until set.

4 Preheat the oven to 190°C/375°F/Gas 5. To make the tomato sauce, heat the oil in a pan, then fry the garlic for 1 minute. Add the tomatoes, sage and sugar and season to taste with salt and pepper. Simmer, stirring occasionally, for 10 minutes, until slightly reduced. Stir in the beans and cook for 2 minutes more.

5 Meanwhile, wash the spinach thoroughly and place in a large pan with only the water that clings to the leaves. Cover the pan tightly and cook over a medium heat, stirring occasionally, for about 3 minutes, or until tender. Drain in a colander, squeezing out as much water as possible.

6 Put the cream, cheese and nutmeg in a small pan. Bring to the boil over a medium heat, stir in the spinach and season to taste with salt and pepper. Lower the heat and simmer gently, stirring frequently, until slightly thickened.

7 Cut the polenta into triangles, then place a layer of polenta in an oiled deep ovenproof dish. Spoon over the tomato sauce, then top with another layer of polenta. Cover with the spinach sauce and then the remaining polenta triangles. Brush with olive oil, sprinkle with Parmesan and bake for 35–40 minutes. Brown the top under a hot grill before serving, if you like.

Gnocchi with Gorgonzola Sauce

A simple potato dough is used to make these ridged dumplings, which are delicious with a creamy cheese sauce.

Serves 4
450g/1lb potatoes, unpeeled
1 large egg
about 115g/4oz/1 cup plain flour
salt and ground black pepper
fresh thyme sprigs, to garnish
60ml/4 tbsp freshly shaved
 Parmesan cheese, to serve

For the sauce
115g/4oz Gorgonzola cheese
60ml/4 tbsp double cream
15ml/1 tbsp chopped fresh thyme

1 Put the potatoes in a pan of cold water. Bring to the boil, add salt and cook the potatoes for about 20 minutes, until tender. Drain and, when cool enough to handle, remove the skins.

2 Tip the potatoes into a sieve placed over a mixing bowl. Press through with the back of a spoon. Season, then beat in the egg. Add the flour, a little at a time, stirring after each addition until you have a smooth dough. (You may not need all the flour.)

3 Knead the dough on a floured surface for 3 minutes, adding more flour if necessary, until smooth, soft and no longer sticky.

4 Divide the dough into six equal pieces. Gently roll each piece between floured hands into a 2.5cm/1in wide log shape that is 15cm/6in long. Cut each log into six equal pieces, then gently roll each piece in the flour. Form into gnocchi by gently pressing each piece with the tines of a fork to leave ridges in the dough.

5 Bring a large pan of water to the boil. Drop in the gnocchi, about 12 at a time. After about 2 minutes, they will rise to the surface. Cook for 4–5 minutes more, then lift out with a draining spoon. Drain and keep hot while you cook the rest.

6 Make the sauce. Place the Gorgonzola, cream and thyme in a large frying pan and heat gently until the cheese melts to a thick, creamy consistency. Add the drained gnocchi and toss well to combine. Garnish with thyme and serve with Parmesan.

Semolina & Pesto Gnocchi

These gnocchi are cooked rounds of semolina paste, which are brushed with melted butter, topped with cheese and baked. They taste wonderful with a home-made tomato sauce.

Serves 4–6
750ml/1¼ pints/3 cups milk
200g/7oz/1¼ cups semolina
45ml/3 tbsp pesto sauce
60ml/4 tbsp finely chopped
 sun-dried tomatoes, patted
 dry if oily
50g/2oz/¼ cup butter, plus extra
 for greasing
75g/3oz/1 cup freshly grated
 Pecorino cheese
2 eggs, beaten
freshly grated nutmeg
salt and ground black pepper
fresh basil sprigs, to garnish
tomato sauce, to serve

1 Heat the milk in a large non-stick saucepan. When it is on the point of boiling, sprinkle in the semolina, stirring constantly until the mixture is smooth and very thick. Lower the heat and simmer for 2 minutes.

2 Remove the pan from the heat and stir in the pesto and sun-dried tomatoes, with half the butter and half the Pecorino. Beat in the eggs, with nutmeg, salt and pepper to taste. Spoon into a clean shallow ovenproof dish or tin to a depth of 1cm/½in and level the surface. Leave to cool, then chill.

3 Preheat the oven to 190°C/375°F/Gas 5. Lightly grease a shallow ovenproof dish. Using a 4cm/1½in scone cutter, stamp out as many rounds as possible from the semolina paste.

4 Place the leftover semolina paste on the base of the greased dish and arrange the rounds on top in overlapping circles. Melt the remaining butter and brush it over the gnocchi. Sprinkle over the remaining Pecorino. Bake for 30–40 minutes, until golden. Garnish with the basil and serve with the tomato sauce.

Variation
Use Parmesan instead of Pecorino, if you prefer.

Pumpkin Gnocchi with Chanterelle Cream

Very much a gourmet dish, this is perfect for occasions when you really want to impress your guests.

Serves 4
450g/1lb peeled
   pumpkin, chopped
450g/1lb potatoes, unpeeled
2 egg yolks
200g/7oz/1¾ cups plain flour,
   plus extra for dredging
pinch of ground allspice
1.5ml/¼ tsp ground cinnamon
pinch of freshly grated nutmeg

finely grated rind of ½ orange
50g/2oz/⅔ cup freshly shaved
   Parmesan cheese
salt and ground black pepper

For the sauce
30ml/2 tbsp olive oil
1 shallot, chopped
175g/6oz/2 cups fresh
   chanterelles, sliced
150ml/¼ pint/⅔ cup
   crème fraîche
a little milk or water
75ml/5 tbsp chopped
   fresh parsley

1 Preheat the oven to 180°C/350°F/Gas 4. Wrap the pumpkin in foil and bake for 30 minutes. Meanwhile, put the potatoes in a pan of cold water, add salt and bring to the boil. Cook for about 20 minutes, until tender. Drain, peel and set aside.

2 Add the pumpkin to the potato and pass through a potato ricer. Alternatively, press through a sieve. Mix in the egg yolks, flour, spices, orange rind and seasoning to make a soft dough.

3 Bring a pan of lightly salted water to the boil. Dredge a work surface with flour. Spoon the dough into a piping bag with a 1cm/½in plain nozzle. Pipe a 15cm/6in sausage on the surface. Roll in flour and cut into 2.5cm/1in pieces. Mark each lightly with a fork and cook for 3–4 minutes in the boiling water.

4 Make the sauce. Heat the oil in a pan and fry the shallot until soft. Add the chanterelles and cook briefly, then stir in the crème fraîche. Simmer and add milk or water, if required. Add the parsley and season. Transfer the gnocchi to bowls. Spoon all the sauce over the top. Scatter with Parmesan and serve.

Radicchio Pizza

A scone dough base and an interesting radicchio, leek and tomato topping make this a quick and easy dish.

Serves 2
25ml/5 tsp olive oil, plus
   extra for greasing and dipping
½ x 400g/14oz can
   chopped tomatoes
2 garlic cloves, crushed
pinch of dried basil
2 leeks, sliced
90g/3½ oz radicchio,
   roughly chopped

20g/¾oz/¼ cup freshly grated
   Parmesan cheese
115g/4oz mozzarella
   cheese, sliced
10–12 stoned black olives
salt and ground black pepper
fresh basil leaves, to garnish

For the dough
225g/8oz/2 cups self-raising flour,
   plus extra for dusting
2.5ml/½ tsp salt
50g/2oz/¼ cup butter
about 120ml/4fl oz/½ cup milk

1 Preheat the oven to 220°C/425°F/Gas 7. Grease a baking sheet. Make the dough by mixing the flour and salt in a bowl, rubbing in the butter and gradually stirring in the milk. Roll the dough out on a lightly floured surface to a 25–28cm/10–11in round. Place this on the baking sheet.

2 Tip the tomatoes into a small pan. Stir in half the crushed garlic, together with the dried basil and a little seasoning. Simmer over a medium heat until the mixture is thick and has reduced by about half.

3 Heat the olive oil in a large frying pan and fry the leeks and remaining garlic until slightly softened. Add the radicchio and cook, stirring constantly, for 2–3 minutes, then cover and simmer gently for 5–10 minutes. Stir in the Parmesan cheese and season to taste with salt and pepper.

4 Cover the dough base with the tomato mixture, then spoon the leek and radicchio mixture on top. Arrange the mozzarella slices over the vegetables and scatter over the olives. Dip a few basil leaves in olive oil and arrange them on top. Bake the pizza for 15–20 minutes, until the base and top are golden brown.

Spring Vegetable & Pine Nut Pizza

Here's a chance to practise your artistic skills. With its colourful topping of tender young vegetables, the pizza looks like an artist's palette and it tastes wonderful.

Serves 2–3
25–30cm/10–12in pizza base
45ml/3 tbsp olive oil
1 garlic clove, crushed
4 spring onions, sliced
2 courgettes, thinly sliced
1 leek, thinly sliced
115g/4oz asparagus tips, sliced
15ml/1 tbsp chopped
  fresh oregano

30ml/2 tbsp pine nuts
50g/2oz/½ cup grated
  mozzarella, cheese
30ml/2 tbsp freshly grated
  Parmesan cheese
salt and ground black pepper

For the tomato sauce
15ml/1 tbsp olive oil
1 onion, finely chopped
1 garlic clove, crushed
400ml/14oz can
  chopped tomatoes
15ml/1 tbsp tomato purée
15ml/1 tbsp chopped fresh herbs
pinch of sugar

1 Make the tomato sauce. Heat the oil in a pan and fry the onion and garlic over a low heat, stirring occasionally, for about 5 minutes, until softened but not browned. Add the remaining ingredients, stir well and simmer for 15–20 minutes, until the mixture is thick and flavoursome.

2 Preheat the oven to 220°C/425°F/Gas 7. Brush the pizza base with 15ml/1 tbsp of the olive oil, then spread the tomato sauce evenly over the top to within 1cm/½in of the edge.

3 Heat half the remaining olive oil in a frying pan and stir-fry the garlic, spring onions, courgettes, leek and asparagus over a medium heat for 3–5 minutes.

4 Arrange the vegetables over the tomato sauce, then sprinkle the oregano and pine nuts over the top.

5 Mix the cheeses and sprinkle over. Drizzle with the remaining olive oil and season well. Bake for 15–20 minutes until crisp and golden. Serve immediately.

Roasted Vegetable & Goat's Cheese Pizza

This pizza incorporates the smoky flavours of roasted vegetables and the unique taste of goat's cheese.

Serves 3
1 aubergine, cut into thick chunks
2 courgettes, sliced lengthways
1 red pepper, quartered
  and seeded
1 yellow pepper, quartered
  and seeded

1 small red onion, cut into wedges
90ml/6 tbsp olive oil
25–30cm/10–12in pizza base
400g/14oz can chopped
  tomatoes, well drained
115g/4oz goat's cheese, cubed
15ml/1 tbsp chopped fresh thyme
ground black pepper
green olive tapenade (see Cook's
  Tip), to serve

1 Preheat the oven to 220°C/425°F/Gas 7. Place the vegetables in a roasting tin. Brush with 60ml/4 tbsp of the oil. Roast for 30 minutes, until charred, turning the peppers once. Remove the vegetables but leave the oven on.

2 Put the peppers in a bowl and cover with crumpled kitchen paper. When cool enough to handle, peel off the skins and cut the flesh into thick strips. Brush the pizza base with half the remaining oil and spread over the drained tomatoes. Arrange the roasted vegetables on top of the pizza. Dot with the goat's cheese and scatter over the thyme.

3 Drizzle over the remaining oil and season. Bake for 15–20 minutes, until crisp. Spoon the tapenade over to serve.

Cook's Tip
For vegetarian green olive tapenade, put 40 stoned green olives and 5ml/1 tsp capers in a food processor. Add four pieces of drained sun-dried tomatoes in oil, 5ml/1 tsp ground almonds, one chopped garlic clove and a pinch of ground cumin. Process briefly, add 60ml/4 tbsp olive oil and process to a paste.

Wild Mushroom Pizzettes

Serve these extravagant pizzas as a starter for special guests, or make miniature versions for serving with glasses of champagne or cocktails.

Serves 4
45ml/3 tbsp olive oil
350g/12oz/4½ cups fresh wild
   mushrooms, sliced

2 shallots, chopped
2 garlic cloves, finely chopped
30ml/2 tbsp chopped fresh mixed
   thyme and flat leaf parsley
1 quantity pizza dough
40g/1½ oz/scant ½ cup grated
   Gruyère cheese
30ml/2 tbsp freshly grated
   Parmesan cheese
salt and ground black pepper

1 Preheat the oven to 220°C/425°F/Gas 7. Heat 30ml/2 tbsp of the oil in a frying pan. Add the mushrooms, shallots and garlic and fry over a medium heat, stirring occasionally, until all the juices have evaporated.

2 Stir in half the mixed herbs and season to taste with salt and pepper, then set aside to cool.

3 Divide the dough into four pieces and roll out each one on a lightly floured surface to a 13cm/5in circle. Place well apart on two greased baking sheets, then push up the dough edges on each to form a thin rim. Brush the pizza bases with the remaining oil and top with the wild mushroom mixture, leaving a small rim all the way around.

4 Mix the Gruyère and Parmesan cheeses, then sprinkle one-quarter of the mixture over each of the pizzettes. Bake for 15–20 minutes until crisp and golden. Remove from the oven and scatter over the remaining herbs to serve.

> **Cook's Tip**
> *Fresh wild mushrooms add a distinctive flavour to the topping, but a mixture of cultivated mushrooms, such as shiitake, oyster and chestnut mushrooms, would do just as well.*

Feta, Pimiento & Pine Nut Pizzettes

Perk up a party with these tempting mini pizzas. They take only minutes to make, a short time to cook and will be eaten even quicker.

Makes 24
Double quantity pizza dough
60ml/4 tbsp olive oil

30ml/2 tbsp vegetarian green
   olive tapenade
175g/6oz feta cheese
1 large canned or bottled
   pimiento, drained
30ml/2 tbsp chopped fresh thyme
30ml/2 tbsp pine nuts
ground black pepper
fresh thyme sprigs, to garnish

1 Preheat the oven to 220°C/425°F/Gas 7. Divide the pizza dough into 24 pieces and roll out each one on a lightly floured surface to a small oval, about 3mm/⅛in thick.

2 Place well apart on greased baking sheets and prick all over with a fork. Brush with 30ml/2 tbsp of the oil.

3 Spread a thin layer of the tapenade on each oval and crumble over the feta. Cut the pimiento into thin strips and pile on top of the cheese.

4 Sprinkle each pizzette with thyme and pine nuts. Drizzle over the remaining oil and grind over plenty of black pepper. Bake for 10–15 minutes, until crisp and golden. Garnish with thyme sprigs and serve immediately.

> **Cook's Tip**
> *Try to find ewe's milk feta, which has the best flavour.*

> **Variations**
> • *Substitute goat's cheese for the feta.*
> • *The tapenade can be made with stoned black, rather than green olives, if you prefer.*

Spinach & Ricotta Panzerotti

These make great party nibbles for serving with drinks or as appetizers.

Makes 20–24
115g/4oz frozen chopped spinach, thawed, drained and squeezed dry
50g/2oz/ 1/4 cup ricotta cheese
50g/2oz/ 2/3 cup freshly grated Parmesan cheese
good pinch of freshly grated nutmeg
Double quantity pizza dough
flour, for dusting
1 egg white, lightly beaten
oil for deep-frying
salt and ground black pepper

1 Place the spinach, ricotta, Parmesan and nutmeg in a bowl. Season to taste with salt and pepper and beat well with a wooden spoon until smooth.

2 Roll out the dough on a lightly floured surface to a thickness of about 3mm/ 1/8in. Using a 7.5cm/3in plain round cutter, stamp out 20–24 circles.

3 Spread a teaspoon of spinach mixture over one half of each circle, then brush the edges of the dough with a little egg white, fold the dough over and press the edges firmly together to seal.

4 Heat the oil in a large heavy-based pan or deep-fat fryer to 180°C/350°F or until a cube of day-old bread, added to the oil, browns in 45–60 seconds. Deep-fry the panzerotti, a few at a time, for 2–3 minutes until golden. Drain on kitchen paper and serve immediately.

Cook's Tips
• *Make sure the spinach is squeezed as dry as possible.*
• *It is important to ensure that oil for deep-frying is heated to the right temperature before adding the panzerotti.*
• *Do not crowd the pan, as this not only drastically lowers the temperature of the oil, but can also cause it to splash.*
• *Do serve these as soon as possible after frying, as they taste nowhere near so good if left to cool.*

Aubergine & Sun-dried Tomato Calzone

Aubergines, shallots and sun-dried tomatoes make an unusual filling for calzone – pizza "turnovers".

Serves 2
45ml/3 tbsp olive oil
3 shallots, chopped
4 baby aubergines, cut into small cubes
1 garlic clove, chopped
6 pieces of sun-dried tomatoes in oil, drained and chopped
1.5ml/ 1/4 tsp dried red chilli flakes
10ml/2 tsp chopped fresh thyme
1 quantity pizza dough
flour, for dusting
75g/3oz mozzarella, cubed
salt and ground black pepper
15–30ml/1–2 tbsp freshly grated Parmesan cheese, to serve

1 Preheat the oven to 220°C/425°F/Gas 7. Heat 30ml/2 tbsp of the oil in a heavy-based frying pan. Add the shallots and fry over a low heat, stirring occasionally, for 5 minutes, until softened but not browned.

2 Add the aubergines, garlic, sun-dried tomatoes, chilli flakes and thyme and season with salt and pepper to taste. Cook for 4–5 minutes, stirring frequently, until the aubergines are beginning to soften.

3 Divide the dough in half and roll out each piece on a lightly floured surface to an 18cm/7in circle. Spread the aubergine mixture over half of each circle, leaving a 2.5cm/1in border, then scatter over the mozzarella.

4 Dampen the edges with water, then fold the dough over to enclose the filling. Press the edges firmly together to seal. Place the calzones on two greased baking sheets.

5 Brush with half the remaining oil and make a small hole in the top of each to allow the steam to escape. Bake the calzone for 15–20 minutes, until golden. Remove from the oven and brush with the remaining olive oil. Sprinkle over the grated Parmesan and serve immediately.

Parsnip & Pecan Gougères

These nutty puffs conceal a sweet parsnip centre.

Makes 18
115g/4oz/ 1/2 cup butter, plus extra for greasing
300ml/ 1/2 pint/1 1/4 cups water
75g/3oz/ 2/3 cup plain flour
50g/2oz/ 1/2 cup wholemeal flour
3 eggs, beaten
30ml/2 tbsp finely grated Cheddar cheese
pinch of cayenne pepper
75g/3oz/ 3/4 cup pecan nuts, chopped
1 parsnip, cut into 18 x 2cm/ 3/4in pieces
15ml/1 tbsp milk
10ml/2 tsp sesame seeds
fresh watercress sprigs, to garnish
Watercress & Rocket Sauce to serve (optional)

1 Preheat the oven to 200°C/400°F/Gas 6. Place the butter and water in a pan. Bring to the boil, then add both the flours. Beat vigorously until the mixture leaves the sides of the pan.

2 Remove from the heat and cool for 10 minutes. Beat in the eggs, a little at a time, until the mixture is shiny with a soft dropping consistency. Beat in the Cheddar, cayenne and pecans.

3 Lightly grease a large baking sheet and drop 18 heaped tablespoons of the mixture on to it. Place a piece of parsnip on each and top with another heaped tablespoon of the mixture.

4 Brush the gougères with a little milk and sprinkle with sesame seeds. Bake for 25–30 minutes, until firm and golden. Garnish with the watercress. Serve with the watercress sauce, if you like.

> **Cook's Tip**
> The secret of making successful choux pastry is to let the flour and butter mixture cool before beating in the eggs to prevent them from setting.

Watercress & Rocket Sauce

This fresh-tasting sauce can be served with either of these gougères and is also good with pasta.

Serves 4
150g/5oz watercress, trimmed
150g/5oz rocket, trimmed
175ml/6fl oz/ 3/4 cup natural low-fat yogurt
freshly grated nutmeg
salt and ground black pepper

1 Bring a pan of water to the boil and blanch the watercress and rocket for 2–3 minutes. Drain, refresh under cold water, drain again and chop roughly.
2 Place the watercress and rocket in a blender or food processor with the yogurt and process until smooth. Add a pinch of nutmeg and season to taste with salt and pepper.
3 Just before serving, place in the top of a double boiler or in a heatproof bowl set over a pan of barely simmering water. Heat gently, taking care not to let the sauce curdle.

Mushroom Gougère

A savoury choux pastry ring makes a marvellous main course dish that can be made ahead then baked when required.

Serves 4
75g/3oz/6 tbsp butter
115g/4oz/1 cup strong plain flour
2.5ml/ 1/2 tsp salt
200ml/7fl oz/scant 1 cup water
3 eggs, beaten
75g/3oz/ 3/4 cup diced Gruyère cheese

For the filling
40g/1 1/2oz/3 tbsp butter
1 small onion, sliced
1 carrot, coarsely grated
225g/8oz/3 cups button mushrooms, sliced
5ml/1 tsp mild curry paste
25g/1oz/ 1/4 cup plain flour
300ml/ 1/2 pint/1 1/4 cups milk
30ml/2 tbsp chopped fresh parsley
30ml/2 tbsp flaked almonds
salt and ground black pepper

1 Preheat the oven to 200°C/400°F/Gas 6. Use a little butter to grease a shallow 23cm/9in round ovenproof dish. Sift the flour and salt on to a sheet of greaseproof paper.

2 Heat the remaining butter and water in a large saucepan until the butter just melts, then add all the flour. Beat vigorously until the mixture leaves the sides of the pan and forms a ball.

3 Remove from the heat and cool for 10 minutes. Beat in the eggs, a little at a time, until the mixture is shiny and soft enough to fall gently from a spoon.

4 Stir in the cheese, then spoon the mixture around the sides of the ovenproof dish.

5 Make the filling. Melt the butter in a pan and sauté the onion, carrot and mushrooms for 5 minutes. Stir in the curry paste, then the flour. Gradually add the milk, stirring until the mixture boils and thickens. Mix in the parsley, season to taste with salt and pepper, then pour into the centre of the choux ring.

6 Bake for 35–40 minutes, until risen and golden brown, sprinkling on the almonds for the last 5 minutes. Serve at once.

Party Purses

Filo "money bags" filled with creamy leeks make a very attractive dinner party dish.

Serves 4

115g/4oz/ ½ cup butter
225g/8oz leeks, trimmed and
    finely chopped
225g/8oz/1 cup cream cheese
15ml/1 tbsp finely chopped
    fresh dill
15ml/1 tbsp finely chopped
    fresh parsley
2 spring onions, finely chopped
pinch of cayenne pepper
1 garlic clove, finely chopped
1 egg yolk
9 sheets filo pastry, thawed
    if frozen
salt and ground black pepper
lightly cooked leeks, to serve

1 Preheat the oven to 200°C/400°F/Gas 6. Melt 25g/1oz/2 tbsp of the butter in a frying pan and fry the leeks for 4–5 minutes, until soft. Drain off any liquid.

2 Put the cream cheese in a bowl and stir in the dill, parsley, spring onions, cayenne and garlic. Stir in the egg yolk and leeks and season well. Melt the remaining butter.

3 Place one sheet of filo pastry on a board, brush with a little of the melted butter and place another sheet on top. Brush again with butter and top with a third sheet of filo.

4 Cut the layered filo into four squares and place 20ml/4 tsp of the cheese mixture in the centre of each square. Gather up the edges into a "bag", twisting the top to seal. Repeat with the remaining filo to make 12 bags. Brush them with a little butter.

5 Place the bags on a greased baking sheet and bake for 20–25 minutes, until golden brown. Serve on a bed of lightly cooked leeks.

> **Cook's Tip**
> For an attractive effect, tie each bag with a strip of blanched leek before serving.

Ratatouille & Fontina Strudel

Mix a colourful jumble of ratatouille vegetables with chunks of creamy cheese, wrap in filo and bake for a summery party pastry.

Serves 6

1 small aubergine, diced
45ml/3 tbsp extra virgin olive oil
1 onion, sliced
2 garlic cloves, crushed
1 red pepper, seeded and sliced
1 yellow pepper, seeded
    and sliced
2 courgettes, cut into
    small chunks
generous pinch of dried
    mixed herbs
30ml/2 tbsp pine nuts
30ml/2 tbsp raisins
8 filo pastry sheets, each about
    30 x 18cm/12 x 7in, thawed
    if frozen
50g/2oz/¼ cup butter, melted
130g/4½ oz Fontina or Bel Paese
    cheese, cut into small cubes
salt and ground black pepper
dressed mixed salad, to serve

1 Layer the aubergine in a colander, sprinkling each layer with salt. Drain for 20 minutes, then rinse, drain and pat dry.

2 Heat the oil in a large frying pan and gently fry the onion, garlic, peppers and aubergine for about 10 minutes. Add the courgettes and herbs and season with salt and pepper to taste. Cook for 5 minutes, until softened. Cool to room temperature, then stir in the pine nuts and raisins.

3 Preheat the oven to 180°C/350°F/Gas 4. To assemble the strudel, brush two sheets of filo pastry lightly with a little of the melted butter. Lay the filo sheets side by side, overlapping them by about 5cm/2in, to make a large rectangle.

4 Cover with the remaining filo, in the same way, brushing each layer with a little of the melted butter. Spoon the vegetable mixture down one long side of the filo.

5 Scatter the cheese over, then roll up to a long sausage. Transfer to a non-stick baking sheet and curl round to form a ring. Brush with the remaining melted butter and bake for 30 minutes, until golden. Cool for 10 minutes, then slice and serve with a mixed salad.

Potato & Leek Filo Pie

This makes an attractive and unusual centrepiece for a vegetarian buffet.

Serves 8
800g/1¾lb new potatoes, thinly sliced
75g/3oz/6 tbsp butter
400g/14oz leeks, sliced
15g/½oz/½ cup parsley, finely chopped
60ml/4 tbsp chopped mixed fresh herbs
12 sheets filo pastry, thawed if frozen
150g/5oz white Cheshire, Lancashire or Cantal cheese, sliced
2 garlic cloves, finely chopped
250ml/8fl oz/1 cup double cream
2 large egg yolks
salt and ground black pepper

1 Preheat the oven to 190°C/375°F/Gas 5. Bring a saucepan of lightly salted water to the boil and cook the potato slices for 3–4 minutes. Drain carefully.

2 Melt 25g/1oz/2 tbsp of the butter in a frying pan and fry the leeks gently, stirring occasionally, until softened. Remove from the heat, season with pepper and stir in half the parsley and half the mixed herbs.

3 Melt the remaining butter. Line a 23cm/9in round loose-based cake tin with six or seven sheets of filo, brushing each layer with butter. Let the edges of the pastry overhang the tin.

4 Layer the potatoes, leeks and cheese in the pastry-lined tin, scattering a few herbs and the garlic between the layers. Season with a little salt and pepper. Flip the overhanging pastry over the filling and cover with two sheets of filo, tucking in the sides to fit and brushing with melted butter as before. Cover the pie loosely with foil and bake for 35 minutes.

5 Meanwhile, beat the cream, egg yolks and remaining herbs together. Make a hole in the centre of the pie and gradually pour in the eggs and cream. Arrange the remaining pastry on top, teasing it into swirls, then brush with melted butter. Reduce the oven temperature to 180°C/350°F/Gas 4 and bake the pie for another 25–30 minutes. Allow to cool before serving.

Spanakopitta

This popular spinach and filo pastry pie comes from Greece. There are several ways of making it, but feta or Kefalotiri cheese is inevitably included.

Serves 6
1kg/2¼lb fresh spinach
4 spring onions, chopped
300g/11oz feta or Kefalotiri cheese, crumbled or coarsely grated
2 large eggs, beaten
30ml/2 tbsp chopped fresh parsley
15ml/1 tbsp chopped fresh dill
about 8 filo pastry sheets, each about 30 x 18cm/12 x 7in, thawed if frozen
150ml/¼ pint/⅔ cup olive oil
ground black pepper

1 Preheat the oven to 190°C/375°F/Gas 5. Break off any thick stalks from the spinach, then wash the leaves and cook them in just the water that clings to the leaves in a heavy-based pan. As soon as they have wilted, drain them, refresh under cold water and drain again. Squeeze dry and chop roughly.

2 Place the spinach in a bowl. Add the spring onions and cheese, then pour in the eggs. Mix in the herbs and season the filling with pepper.

3 Brush a filo sheet with oil and fit it into a 23cm/9in pie dish, allowing it to hang over the edge. Top with three or four more sheets; place these at different angles and brush each one with more oil, to make a roughly shaped pie case.

4 Spoon in the filling, then top with all but one of the remaining filo sheets. Brush each filo sheet with oil. Fold in the over-hanging filo to seal in the filling. Brush the reserved filo with oil and scrunch it over the top of the pie.

5 Brush the pie with oil. Sprinkle with a little water to stop the filo edges from curling, then place on a baking sheet. Bake for about 40 minutes, until golden and crisp. Cool the pie for 15 minutes before serving.

Asparagus Filo Wraps

For a taste sensation, try tender asparagus spears wrapped in crisp filo pastry. The buttery herb sauce makes the perfect partner.

Serves 2
4 sheets of filo pastry, thawed
    if frozen
50g/2oz/ ¼ cup butter, melted
16 young asparagus
    spears, trimmed
salad leaves, to garnish (optional)

For the sauce
2 shallots, finely chopped
1 bay leaf
150ml/ ¼ pint/ ⅔ cup dry
    white wine
175g/6oz/ ¾ cup butter, softened
15ml/1 tbsp chopped fresh herbs
salt and ground black pepper
snipped chives, to garnish

1 Preheat the oven to 200°C/400°F/Gas 6. Keeping the rest of the filo covered with a damp dish towel, brush each sheet with melted butter and fold one corner down to the bottom edge to create a wedge shape.

2 Lay four asparagus spears on top at the longest edge and roll up towards the shortest edge. Using the remaining filo and asparagus spears, make three more rolls in the same way.

3 Lay the rolls on a greased baking sheet. Brush with the remaining melted butter. Bake the rolls for 8 minutes, until the pastry is golden.

4 Meanwhile, make the sauce. Mix the shallots, bay leaf and wine in a pan. Cook over a high heat until the wine is reduced to about 45–60ml/3–4 tbsp.

5 Strain the wine mixture into a bowl. Whisk in the butter, a little at a time, until the sauce is smooth and glossy.

6 Stir in the herbs and add salt and pepper to taste. Return to the pan and warm through gently. Serve the rolls on individual plates with salad, if liked. Serve the butter sauce separately, sprinkled with a few snipped chives.

Asparagus & Ricotta Tart

The melt-in-the-mouth filling in this summery tart has a much more delicate texture than a quiche – and tastes absolutely wonderful.

Serves 4
175g/6oz/1½ cups plain flour,
    plus extra for dusting
75g/3oz/6 tbsp butter

For the filling
225g/8oz asparagus
2 eggs, beaten
225g/8oz/1 cup ricotta cheese
30ml/2 tbsp Greek-style yogurt
40g/1½oz/ ½ cup freshly grated
    Parmesan cheese
salt and ground black pepper

1 Preheat the oven to 200°C/400°F/Gas 6. Mix the flour and a pinch of salt in a bowl and rub in the butter with your fingertips or a pastry blender until the mixture resembles fine breadcrumbs. Stir in enough cold water to form a smooth dough and knead lightly on a floured surface.

2 Roll out the pastry on a lightly floured surface and then use to line a 23cm/9in flan ring. Prick the base all over with a fork. Bake the tart case for 10 minutes, until the pastry is pale but firm. Remove from the oven and reduce the temperature to 180°C/350°F/Gas 4.

3 Make the filling. Snap the asparagus and discard the woody ends. Cut off the tips and chop the remaining stalks into 2.5cm/1in pieces. Bring a pan of water to the boil. Blanch the stalks for 1 minute, then add the asparagus tips. Simmer for 4–5 minutes, until almost tender, then drain and refresh under cold water. Drain again. Separate the chopped stalks from the asparagus tips.

4 Beat the eggs, ricotta, yogurt and Parmesan in a bowl. Stir in the asparagus stalks, season to taste with salt and pepper and pour the mixture into the pastry case.

5 Arrange the asparagus tips on top, pressing them down slightly into the ricotta mixture. Bake for 35–40 minutes, until golden. Serve warm or cold.

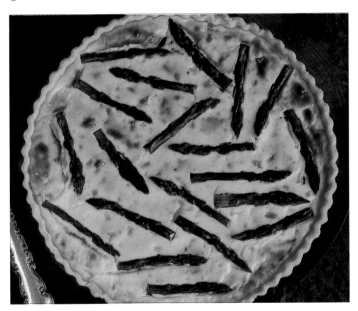

Leek & Onion Tartlets

Individual tartlets are easy to serve and look pretty on the plate when garnished with lettuce and tomato.

Serves 6

25g/1oz/2 tbsp butter
1 onion, thinly sliced
2.5ml/ 1/2 tsp dried thyme
450g/1lb leeks, thinly sliced
50g/2oz/ 1/2 cup grated Gruyère
   or Emmenthal cheese
3 eggs

300ml/ 1/2 pint/1 1/4 cups
   single cream
pinch of freshly grated nutmeg
salt and ground black pepper
lettuce, parsley and cherry
   tomatoes, to serve

For the pastry

175g/6oz/1 1/2 cups plain flour
2.5ml/ 1/2 tsp salt
75g/3oz/6 tbsp cold butter
1 egg yolk
30–45ml/2–3 tbsp cold water

1 Make the pastry. Sift the flour and salt into a bowl and rub in the butter until the mixture resembles fine breadcrumbs. Make a well in the centre. Add the egg yolk and water and, using a fork, mix lightly to a dough. Wrap and chill for 30 minutes.

2 Lightly butter six 10cm/4in tartlet tins. On a lightly floured surface, roll out the dough thinly, cut into 13cm/5in rounds and line the tins. Prick the bases and chill for 30 minutes.

3 Preheat the oven to 190°C/375°F/Gas 5. Line the tartlets with foil and fill with baking beans. Place on a baking sheet and bake for 6–8 minutes, until the edges are golden. Remove the foil and beans and bake for 2 minutes more. Transfer to a wire rack. Reduce the oven temperature to 180°C/350°F/Gas 4.

4 Melt the butter in a frying pan and cook the onion with the thyme for 3–5 minutes, until softened. Add the leeks and cook for 10–12 minutes, until they are soft and tender. Divide the mixture among the pastry cases and sprinkle each with cheese.

5 Beat the eggs with the cream, nutmeg and seasoning. Place the tartlets on a baking sheet and pour in the egg mixture. Bake for 20 minutes until set. Cool slightly, then remove from the tins. Serve with lettuce, parsley and cherry tomatoes.

Pissaladière

A Provençal classic, this is a delicious and colourful tart full of punchy flavour. The classic version includes anchovies, but it is just as good without.

Serves 6

225g/8oz/2 cups plain flour
115g/4oz/ 1/2 cup butter
5ml/1 tsp dried mixed herbs
pinch of salt

For the filling

45ml/3 tbsp olive oil
2 large onions, thinly sliced
2 garlic cloves, crushed
400g/14oz can
   chopped tomatoes
5ml/1 tsp granulated sugar
leaves from small sprig of thyme
freshly grated nutmeg
75g/3oz/ 3/4 cup stoned black
   olives, sliced
30ml/2 tbsp rinsed capers
salt and ground black pepper
chopped fresh parsley, to garnish

1 Preheat the oven to 190°C/375°F/Gas 5. Put the flour in a bowl and rub in the butter until the mixture resembles fine breadcrumbs, then stir in the herbs and salt. Mix to a firm dough with cold water.

2 Roll out the pastry and line a 23cm/9in round flan dish. Line the pastry case with non-stick baking paper and add baking beans. Bake for 20 minutes, then lift out the paper and beans and bake the empty case for 5–7 minutes more. Leave to cool.

3 Make the filling. Heat the oil in a frying pan and fry the onions and garlic gently for about 10 minutes, until quite soft. Stir in the tomatoes, sugar, thyme and nutmeg. Season and simmer for 10 minutes.

4 Leave the filling to cool. Mix in the olives and capers, then spoon into the flan case. Sprinkle with parsley and serve.

Variation
To serve Pissaladière hot, top with grated cheese and grill until the cheese is golden and bubbling.

Cheese & Spinach Flan

This flan freezes well and can be reheated once it has been defrosted. It makes an excellent addition to a party buffet table.

Serves 8
225g/8oz/2 cups plain flour, plus
   extra for dusting
115g/4oz/ 1/2 cup butter
2.5ml/ 1/2 tsp English
   mustard powder
2.5ml/ 1/2 tsp paprika
large pinch of salt
115g/4oz/1 cup grated
   Cheddar cheese

45–60ml/3–4 tbsp cold water
beaten egg, to glaze

For the filling
450g/1lb frozen spinach
1 onion, finely chopped
pinch of grated nutmeg
225g/8oz/1 cup cottage cheese
2 large eggs
50g/2oz/ 2/3 cup freshly grated
   Parmesan cheese
150ml/ 1/4 pint/ 2/3 cup
   single cream
salt and ground black pepper

1 Put the flour in a bowl and rub in the butter until the mixture resembles fine breadcrumbs. Stir in the mustard powder, paprika, salt and cheese. Bind to a dough with the cold water. Knead until smooth, wrap and chill for 30 minutes.

2 Make the filling. Put the spinach and onion in a pan, cover and cook gently until the spinach has thawed and the onion is tender. Increase the heat and stir until the mixture is dry. Season with salt, pepper and nutmeg. Spoon the spinach into a bowl and cool slightly. Add the remaining filling ingredients.

3 Preheat the oven to 200°C/400°F/Gas 6. Cut one-third off the pastry and set it aside for the lid. On a lightly floured surface, roll out the rest and line a 23cm/9in loose-based flan tin. Pour the filling into the flan case.

4 Roll out the reserved pastry and cut a lid with a lattice pastry cutter. Carefully open the lattice. With the help of a rolling pin, lay it over the flan. Press the edges together and neaten the joins. Brush the pastry lattice with egg to glaze. Bake for 35–40 minutes, or until golden brown. Serve hot or cold.

Wild Mushroom Pie

Wild mushrooms give this pie a really rich flavour.

Serves 6
225g/8oz/2 cups plain flour
2.5ml/ 1/2 tsp salt
115g/4oz/ 1/2 cup butter
10ml/2 tsp lemon juice
150ml/ 1/4 pint/ 2/3 cup iced water
beaten egg, to glaze

For the filling
150g/5oz/ 2/3 cup butter
2 shallots, finely chopped
2 garlic cloves, crushed
450g/1lb/6 cups mixed wild
   mushrooms, sliced
45ml/3 tbsp chopped
   fresh parsley
30ml/2 tbsp double cream
salt and ground black pepper

1 Sift the flour and salt into a bowl. Rub in half the butter until the mixture resembles breadcrumbs. Cut the remaining butter into cubes and put these in the fridge to chill. Add the lemon juice to the flour mixture with enough iced water to make a soft but not sticky dough. Cover and chill for 20 minutes.

2 Roll the pastry out into a rectangle on a lightly floured surface. With a narrow end facing you, mark the dough horizontally into three equal sections. Arrange half the butter cubes over the top two sections of the dough. Fold the bottom section up and the top section down. Seal the edges with a rolling pin. Give the dough a quarter turn and roll it out again. Mark it into thirds and dot with the remaining butter cubes in the same way. Chill for 20 minutes, then repeat the rolling, folding and chilling three times, without the butter.

3 Make the filling. Melt the butter and fry the shallots and garlic until soft. Add the mushrooms and cook for 35–40 minutes. Drain off any excess liquid and stir in the remaining ingredients. Leave to cool. Preheat the oven to 230°C/450°F/Gas 8.

4 Divide the pastry in two. Roll out one half and line a 23cm/9in round tin. Pile the filling into the centre. Roll out the remaining pastry to a round large enough to cover the top. Brush the edge of the case with water and then lay the second circle on top. Press the edges together and decorate the top. Brush with egg. Bake for 45 minutes, or until the pastry is golden.

Mediterranean One-crust Pie

This free-form pie encases a rich tomato, aubergine and kidney bean filling. If your pastry cracks, just patch it up – it adds to the pie's rustic character.

Serves 4
500g/1¼lb aubergine, cubed
1 red pepper
30ml/2 tbsp olive oil, plus extra
    for greasing
1 large onion, finely chopped
1 courgette, sliced
2 garlic cloves, crushed
15ml/1 tbsp chopped fresh
    oregano or 5ml/1 tsp dried,
plus extra fresh oregano
    to garnish
200g/7oz can red kidney beans,
    drained and rinsed
115g/4oz/1 cup stoned black
    olives, rinsed
150ml/¼ pint/⅔ cup passata
beaten egg, for brushing
30ml/2 tbsp semolina
salt and ground black pepper

For the pastry
75g/3oz/⅔ cup plain white flour
75g/3oz/⅔ cup wholemeal flour
75g/3oz/6 tbsp
    vegetable margarine
50g/2oz/⅔ cup freshly grated
    Parmesan cheese

1 Preheat the oven to 220°C/425°F/Gas 7. Make the pastry. Sift both types of flour into a large bowl and tip the bran remaining in the sieve into the bowl. Rub in the margarine with a pastry blender or your fingertips until the mixture resembles fine breadcrumbs, then stir in the grated Parmesan. Mix in enough cold water to form a soft dough. Shape into a ball, wrap and chill for 30 minutes.

2 Place the aubergine cubes in a colander, sprinkle with salt, then leave to drain in the sink for about 30 minutes. Rinse well, drain and pat dry with kitchen paper.

3 Meanwhile, grill the red pepper until blistered and charred all over. Put in a small bowl, cover with crumpled kitchen paper and leave to cool slightly. Rub off the skin, remove the core and seeds and dice the flesh. Set it aside.

4 Heat the oil in a large, heavy-based frying pan. Add the onion and fry over a low heat, stirring occasionally, for 5 minutes, until softened. Add the aubergine cubes and fry for about 5 minutes, until tender.

5 Stir in the courgette slices, garlic and oregano, and cook for a further 5 minutes, stirring frequently. Add the kidney beans and olives, stir well to mix, then add the passata and diced red pepper. Season to taste with salt and pepper. Cook over a medium heat, stirring occasionally, until heated through, then set aside to cool.

6 Roll out the pastry to a rough 30cm/12in round. Place on a lightly oiled baking sheet. Brush with some beaten egg, then sprinkle over the semolina, leaving a 4cm/1½in border. Spoon over the filling.

7 Gather up the edges of the pastry to partly cover the filling – it should remain open in the middle. Brush with the remaining egg and bake for 30–35 minutes, until golden. Transfer to a warmed serving plate, garnish with oregano and serve.

Chestnut, Stilton & Ale Pie

This hearty winter dish has a rich stout gravy and a herb pastry top.

Serves 4
30ml/2 tbsp sunflower oil
2 large onions, chopped
500g/1¼lb/8 cups button
    mushrooms, halved
3 carrots, sliced
1 parsnip, thickly sliced
15ml/1 tbsp chopped fresh thyme
2 bay leaves
250ml/8fl oz/1 cup stout
120ml/4fl oz/½ cup
    vegetable stock
5ml/1 tsp yeast extract
5ml/1 tsp soft dark brown sugar
350g/12oz/3 cups drained
    canned chestnuts, halved
30ml/2 tbsp cornflour, mixed to
    a paste with 30ml/2 tbsp
    cold water
150g/5oz Stilton cheese, cubed
beaten egg, to glaze
salt and ground black pepper

For the pastry
115g/4oz/1 cup wholemeal flour
a pinch of salt
50g/2oz/¼ cup butter
15ml/1 tbsp chopped fresh thyme

1 Make the pastry. Put the flour and salt in a bowl. Rub in the butter until the mixture resembles fine breadcrumbs. Add the thyme and enough water to form a soft dough. Knead it lightly, wrap and chill for 30 minutes.

2 Make the filling. Heat the oil in a pan and fry the onions until softened. Add the mushrooms and cook for 3 minutes. Stir in the carrots, parsnip and herbs. Cover and cook for 3 minutes.

3 Pour in the stout and stock then stir in the yeast extract and sugar. Simmer, covered, for 5 minutes. Add the chestnuts and season to taste. Stir in the cornflour paste until the sauce thickens. Stir in the cheese and heat until melted, stirring.

4 Preheat the oven to 220°C/425°F/Gas 7. Spoon the chestnut mixture into a 1.5 litre/2½ pint/6¼ cup pie dish. Roll out the pastry to make a lid. Dampen the edges of the dish and cover with the pastry. Seal, trim and crimp the edges. Cut a small slit in the top of the pie and use any surplus pastry to make pastry leaves. Brush with egg and bake for 30 minutes.

Shallot & Garlic Tarte Tatin

Savoury versions of the famous apple tarte tatin have been popular for some years. Here, caramelized shallots are baked beneath a layer of Parmesan pastry.

Serves 4–6
300g/11oz puff pastry, thawed if frozen
50g/2oz/¼ cup butter
75g/3oz/1 cup freshly grated Parmesan cheese

For the topping
40g/1½oz/3 tbsp butter
500g/1¼lb shallots, peeled but left whole
12–16 large garlic cloves, peeled but left whole
15ml/1 tbsp golden caster sugar
15ml/1 tbsp balsamic vinegar
45ml/3 tbsp water
5ml/1 tsp chopped fresh thyme
salt and ground black pepper

1 Roll out the pastry into a rectangle. Spread the butter over it, leaving a 2.5cm/1in border. Scatter the Parmesan on top. Fold the bottom third of the pastry up to cover the middle and the top third down. Seal the edges, give a quarter turn and roll out to a rectangle, then fold as before. Chill for 30 minutes.

2 Make the topping. Melt the butter in a 23–25cm/9–10in heavy-based frying pan that can safely be used in the oven. Add the shallots and garlic and cook until lightly browned all over.

3 Scatter the sugar over the top and increase the heat a little. Cook until the sugar begins to caramelize, then turn the shallots and garlic in the buttery juices. Add the vinegar, water and thyme and season to taste. Partially cover the pan and cook for 5–8 minutes, until the garlic cloves are just tender. Cool.

4 Preheat the oven to 190°C/375°F/Gas 5. Roll out the pastry to a round slightly larger than the pan and lay it over the shallots and garlic. Tuck the pastry overlap down inside the pan, then prick the pastry with a sharp knife. Bake the tart for 25–35 minutes, or until it is risen and golden.

5 Cool for 5–10 minutes, then turn the tart out on to a serving platter. Serve, cut in wedges.

Red Onion Tart with a Polenta Crust

Mild red onions go well with Fontina cheese and thyme in this tasty tart.

Serves 5–6
60ml/4 tbsp olive oil
1kg/2¼lb red onions, thinly sliced
2–3 garlic cloves, thinly sliced
5ml/1 tsp chopped fresh thyme, plus a few whole sprigs
5ml/1 tsp soft dark brown sugar
10ml/2 tsp sherry vinegar
225g/8oz Fontina cheese, thinly sliced
salt and ground black pepper

For the pastry
115g/4oz/1 cup plain flour
75g/3oz/¾ cup fine polenta
5ml/1 tsp soft dark brown sugar
5ml/1 tsp chopped fresh thyme
90g/3½oz/7 tbsp butter
1 egg yolk
about 30ml/2 tbsp iced water

1 Make the pastry. Mix the flour and polenta in a bowl and add salt, pepper, the sugar and thyme. Rub in the butter until the mixture resembles breadcrumbs. Beat the egg yolk with the water and use to bind the pastry, adding more water, if needed. Gather the dough into a ball, wrap and chill for 30–40 minutes.

2 Heat 45ml/3 tbsp of the oil in a frying pan. Add the onions, cover and cook gently, stirring occasionally, for 20–30 minutes.

3 Add the garlic and chopped thyme. Cook, stirring occasionally, for 10 minutes. Increase the heat slightly, then add the sugar and sherry vinegar. Cook, uncovered, for 5–6 minutes more, until the onions start to caramelize slightly. Season to taste. Cool.

4 Preheat the oven to 190°C/375°F/Gas 5. Roll out the pastry thinly and use to line a 25cm/10in loose-based flan tin. Prick the pastry with a fork and support the sides with foil. Bake for 12–15 minutes, until lightly coloured.

5 Spread the onions over the base of the pastry. Add the cheese and most of the thyme sprigs and season. Drizzle over the remaining oil, then bake for 15–20 minutes, until the cheese is bubbling. Serve immediately, garnished with thyme sprigs.

Leek & Roquefort Tart with Walnut Pastry

Mild leeks go exceptionally well with the salty flavour of Roquefort cheese.

Serves 4–6

25g/1oz/2 tbsp butter
450g/1lb leeks (trimmed weight), sliced
175g/6oz Roquefort cheese, sliced
2 large eggs
250ml/8fl oz/1 cup double cream
10ml/2 tsp chopped fresh tarragon
salt and ground black pepper

For the pastry

175g/6oz/1½ cups plain flour
5ml/1 tsp soft dark brown sugar
50g/2oz/¼ cup butter
75g/3oz/¾ cup walnuts, ground
15ml/1 tbsp lemon juice
30ml/2 tbsp iced water

1 First make the pastry: sift the flour and 2.5ml/ ½ tsp salt into a bowl. Add some pepper and the sugar. Rub in the butter until the mixture resembles breadcrumbs, then stir in the ground walnuts. Bind with the lemon juice and iced water. Form the dough into a ball, wrap and chill for 30–40 minutes.

2 Preheat the oven to 190°C/375°F/Gas 5. Roll out the pastry and line a 23cm/9in loose-based metal flan tin. Protect the sides of the pastry with foil, prick the base with a fork and bake for 15 minutes. Remove the foil and bake the flan for a further 5–10 minutes, until just firm to the touch. Reduce the oven temperature to 180°C/350°F/Gas 4.

3 Meanwhile, melt the butter in a pan, add the leeks, cover and cook for 10 minutes. Season with salt and pepper to taste, stir and cook for a further 10 minutes. Cool.

4 Arrange the leeks and slices of Roquefort in the pastry case. Whisk the eggs with the cream and season with black pepper. Beat in the tarragon and pour the mixture into the tart.

5 Bake for 30–40 minutes, until the filling has risen and browned and feels firm when gently touched. Allow to cool for 10 minutes before serving.

Mushroom, Nut & Prune Jalousie

A stunning dish for Sunday lunch, this comprises a nutty filling in a pastry case.

Serves 6

75g/3oz/1/3 cup green lentils, rinsed
5ml/1 tsp vegetable bouillon powder
15ml/1 tbsp sunflower oil
2 large leeks, sliced
2 garlic cloves, chopped
10ml/2 tsp dried mixed herbs
200g/7oz/3 cups field mushrooms, finely chopped
75g/3oz/ ¾ cup chopped mixed nuts
75g/3oz/ 1/3 cup ready-to-eat stoned prunes
25g/1oz/ ½ cup fresh white breadcrumbs
2 eggs, beaten
2 sheets pre-rolled puff pastry, about 425g/15oz, thawed
flour, for dusting
salt and ground black pepper

1 Put the lentils in a pan and cover with cold water. Bring to the boil, lower the heat and stir in the bouillon powder. Partially cover and simmer for 20 minutes, until the lentils are tender.

2 Heat the oil in a large, heavy-based frying pan and fry the leeks and garlic for 5 minutes, until softened. Add the herbs and mushrooms and cook for 5 minutes more. Transfer the mixture to a bowl. Stir in the nuts, prunes, breadcrumbs and lentils.

3 Preheat the oven to 220°C/425°F/Gas 7. Add two-thirds of the eggs to the filling mixture and season. Set aside to cool.

4 Meanwhile, unroll one pastry sheet. Cut off and discard a 2.5cm/1in border, then lay it on a dampened baking sheet. Unroll the second sheet, dust lightly with flour, then fold in half lengthways. Make a series of cuts across the fold, 1cm/ ½in apart, leaving a 2.5cm/1in border around the edge of the pastry.

5 Spoon the filling mixture evenly over the pastry base, leaving a 2.5cm/1in border. Dampen the edges of the base. Open out the folded pastry and lay it over the top of the filling. Trim the edges, then press them together to seal. Crimp the edges. Brush the top with the remaining beaten egg and bake for 25–30 minutes, until golden. Cool slightly before serving.

Puff Pastry Boxes filled with Spring Vegetables in Pernod Sauce

Pernod is the perfect companion for tender vegetables in crisp cases.

Serves 4
225g/8oz puff pastry, thawed if frozen
15ml/1 tbsp freshly grated Parmesan cheese, plus extra
15ml/1 tbsp chopped fresh parsley
beaten egg, to glaze
175g/6oz/1 cup broad beans
115g/4oz baby carrots, scraped

8 spring onions, sliced
75g/3oz/generous ½ cup peas
50g/2oz/½ cup mangetouts
salt and ground black pepper
fresh dill sprigs, to garnish

For the sauce
200g/7oz can chopped tomatoes
25g/1oz/2 tbsp butter
25g/1oz/¼ cup plain flour
pinch of granulated sugar
45ml/3 tbsp chopped fresh dill
300ml/½ pint/1¼ cups water
15ml/1 tbsp Pernod

1 Preheat the oven to 220°C/425°F/Gas 7. Grease a baking sheet. Roll out the pastry. Sprinkle with Parmesan and parsley, fold and roll out, then cut out four 7.5 x 10cm/3 x 4in rectangles. Lift them on to the baking sheet. Cut an inner oblong 1cm/½in from the edge on each, cutting halfway through. Score criss-cross lines on top of the inner rectangles, brush with egg and bake for 12–15 minutes, until golden.

2 Meanwhile, make the sauce. Press the tomatoes through a sieve into a pan, add the remaining ingredients and bring to the boil, stirring. Season, lower the heat and simmer until required.

3 Bring a pan of salted water to the boil. Cook the beans for 8 minutes. Add the carrots, onions and peas, cook for 5 minutes more, then add the mangetouts. Cook for 1 minute. Drain well.

4 Cut out the inner pieces from the pastry boxes. Swirl a little sauce on to four plates. Half-fill each box with vegetables, spoon over some sauce, then top up with vegetables. Sprinkle with Parmesan and place on the plates. Garnish with dill and set the lids at an angle. Serve with the remaining sauce.

Courgette & Dill Tart

It is worth making your own pastry for this tart. Using a mixture of wholemeal flour and self-raising white flour gives very good results.

Serves 4
115g/4oz/1 cup plain wholemeal flour
115g/4oz/1 cup self-raising white flour
115g/4oz/½ cup chilled butter, diced

75ml/5 tbsp iced water
fresh dill sprigs, to garnish

For the filling
15ml/1 tbsp sunflower oil
3 courgettes, thinly sliced
2 egg yolks
150ml/¼ pint/⅔ cup double cream
1 garlic clove, crushed
15ml/1 tbsp finely chopped fresh dill
salt and ground black pepper

1 Mix the flours in a food processor. Add a pinch of salt and the butter and pulse until the mixture resembles fine breadcrumbs. Gradually add the water until the mixture forms a dough. Wrap and chill for 30 minutes.

2 Preheat the oven to 200°C/400°F/Gas 6. Grease a 20cm/8in flan tin. Roll out the pastry and ease it into the tin. Prick the base with a fork and bake for 10–15 minutes until golden.

3 Meanwhile, make the filling. Heat the oil in a frying pan and sauté the courgettes for 2–3 minutes, until lightly browned. Mix the egg yolks, cream, garlic and dill in a small bowl. Season to taste with salt and pepper.

4 Layer the courgette slices in concentric circles in the pastry case. Pour over the cream mixture. Bake for 25–30 minutes, or until the filling is firm and lightly golden. Cool in the tin, then transfer to a board or plate. Garnish with dill and serve.

> **Cook's Tip**
> If you don't have a food processor, rub the butter into the flour mixture by hand.

Upside-down Vegetable Tart

This is a Mediterranean variation of the tarte tatin.

Serves 2–4

30ml/2 tbsp sunflower oil
about 25ml/1½ tbsp olive oil
1 aubergine, sliced lengthways
1 large red pepper, seeded and
  cut into long strips
5 tomatoes
2 red shallots, finely chopped
1–2 garlic cloves, crushed
150ml/¼ pint/⅔ cup
  white wine
10ml/2 tsp chopped fresh basil
225g/8oz/2 cups long grain rice
40g/1½ oz/⅓ cup stoned black
  olives, chopped
350g/12oz puff pastry, thawed
  if frozen
ground black pepper
lamb's lettuce, to garnish

1 Cook the rice. Preheat the oven to 190°C/375°F/Gas 5. Heat the sunflower oil with 15ml/1 tbsp of the olive oil in a frying pan and fry the aubergine slices for 4–5 minutes on each side, until golden brown. Lift out and drain on kitchen paper.

2 Add the red pepper to the pan, turning to coat. Cover and sweat over a medium heat for 5–6 minutes, stirring occasionally, until soft and flecked with brown.

3 Slice two of the tomatoes and set them aside. Plunge the remaining tomatoes briefly into boiling water, then peel, cut into quarters and remove the core and seeds. Chop them roughly.

4 Heat the remaining oil in the frying pan. Fry the shallots and garlic until softened. Add the chopped tomatoes and cook for 3 minutes. Stir in the wine and basil, with pepper to taste. Bring to the boil, remove from the heat and stir in the rice and olives.

5 Arrange the tomatoes slices, aubergine slices and peppers in a single layer over the base of a heavy, 30cm/12in shallow ovenproof dish. Spread the rice mixture on top.

6 Roll out the pastry to a circle slightly larger than the dish and place on top of the rice, tucking in the overlap. Bake for 25–30 minutes, until risen and golden. Cool slightly, then invert on to a large, warmed serving plate. Garnish with lamb's lettuce.

Greek Picnic Pie

Aubergines layered with spinach, feta and rice make a marvellous filling for a pie.

Serves 6

375g/13oz shortcrust pastry,
  thawed if frozen
45–60ml/3–4 tbsp olive oil
1 large aubergine, sliced
  into rounds
1 onion, chopped
1 garlic clove, crushed
175g/6oz spinach
4 eggs
75g/3oz feta cheese
40g/1½oz/½ cup freshly grated
  Parmesan cheese
60ml/4 tbsp natural yogurt
90ml/6 tbsp creamy milk
225g/8oz/2 cups cooked
  long grain rice
salt and ground black pepper

1 Preheat the oven to 180°C/350°F/Gas 4. Roll out the pastry thinly and line a 25cm/10in flan ring. Prick the pastry all over and bake the unfilled case in the oven for 10–12 minutes, until the pastry is pale golden.

2 Heat 30–45ml/2–3 tbsp of the oil in a frying pan and fry the aubergine slices for 6–8 minutes on each side, until golden. Lift out and drain on kitchen paper.

3 Add the onion and garlic to the oil remaining in the pan and fry gently until soft, adding a little extra oil if necessary.

4 Chop the spinach finely, by hand or in a food processor. Beat the eggs in a large mixing bowl, then add the spinach, feta, Parmesan, yogurt, milk and the onion mixture. Season well with salt and pepper and stir thoroughly.

5 Spread the rice in an even layer over the base of the partially cooked pastry case. Reserve a few aubergine slices for the top, and arrange the rest in an even layer over the rice.

6 Spoon the spinach and feta mixture over the aubergines and place the remaining aubergine slices on top. Bake for 30–40 minutes, until lightly browned. Serve the pie warm, or cool completely before transferring to a serving plate or wrapping and packing for a picnic.

Risotto with Four Cheeses

This is a very rich dish. Serve it as a starter for a special dinner party – preferably with a light, dry, sparkling white wine.

Serves 4
40g/1½oz/3 tbsp butter
1 small onion, finely chopped
1.2 litres/2 pints/5 cups well-
    flavoured vegetable stock
350g/12oz/1¾ cups risotto rice
200ml/7fl oz/scant 1 cup dry
    white wine

50g/2oz/½ cup grated
    Gruyère cheese
50g/2oz/½ cup diced
    Taleggio cheese
50g/2oz/½ cup diced
    Gorgonzola cheese
50g/2oz/⅔ cup freshly grated
    Parmesan cheese
salt and ground black pepper
chopped fresh flat leaf parsley,
    to garnish

1 Melt the butter in a large, heavy-based saucepan. Add the onion and fry over a low heat, stirring occasionally, for about 8 minutes, until softened and lightly browned. Pour the stock into another pan and heat it to simmering point. Lower the heat so that the stock is barely simmering.

2 Add the rice to the onion mixture, stir until all the grains start to swell and burst, then stir in the white wine. When most of it has been absorbed, pour in a little of the hot stock. Season with salt and pepper to taste. Stir over a low heat until the stock has been absorbed.

3 Gradually add the remaining stock, a little at a time, allowing the rice to absorb the liquid before adding more, and stirring constantly. After 20–25 minutes the rice will be *al dente* and the risotto creamy.

4 Turn off the heat under the pan, then add the Gruyère, Taleggio, Gorgonzola and half the Parmesan cheese. Stir gently until the cheeses have melted, then taste and adjust the seasoning, if necessary. Spoon the risotto into a warmed serving bowl and garnish with parsley. Serve immediately and hand the remaining Parmesan separately.

Risotto with Asparagus

Fresh farm asparagus is only in season for a short time. Make the most of it by inviting friends to share this elegant risotto.

Serves 3–4
225g/8oz fresh asparagus
750ml/1¼ pints/3 cups well-
    flavoured vegetable stock
65g/2½ oz/5 tbsp butter
1 small onion, finely chopped
275g/10oz/1½ cups risotto rice
75g/3oz/1 cup freshly grated
    Parmesan cheese
salt and ground black pepper

1 Snap the asparagus stalks and discard the woody ends. Bring a pan of water to the boil, add the asparagus and cook for 5 minutes. Drain, reserving the cooking water, refresh under cold water and drain well again. Cut the asparagus stalks diagonally into 4cm/1½in pieces. Keep the tips separate from the rest of the stalks.

2 Pour the stock into a pan and add 450ml/¾ pint/scant 2 cups of the reserved asparagus cooking water. Heat to simmering point.

3 Melt two-thirds of the butter in a large, heavy-based pan and fry the onion until soft and golden. Stir in all the asparagus except the tips. Cook for 2–3 minutes. Add the rice and cook for 1–2 minutes, stirring to coat the grains with butter. Add a ladleful of the hot stock and stir until it has been absorbed.

4 Gradually add the remaining hot stock, a little at a time, allowing the rice to absorb each addition before adding more and stirring all the time.

5 After 15 minutes of adding stock, mix in the asparagus tips. Continue to cook as before, for 5–10 minutes, until the rice is *al dente* and the risotto is creamy.

6 Off the heat, stir in the remaining butter and the Parmesan. Grind in a little black pepper and salt, if needed. Serve at once.

Porcini & Parmesan Risotto

The success of a good risotto depends on both the quality of the rice used and the technique. Add the stock gradually and stir constantly to create a creamy texture.

Serves 4

15g/½ oz/¼ cup dried porcini mushrooms
150ml/¼ pint/⅔ cup warm water
1 litre/1¾ pints/4 cups well-flavoured vegetable stock
generous pinch of saffron strands
30ml/2 tbsp olive oil
1 onion, finely chopped
1 garlic clove, crushed
350g/12oz/1¾ cups risotto rice
150ml/¼ pint/⅔ cup dry white wine
25g/1oz/2 tbsp butter
50g/2oz/⅔ cup freshly grated Parmesan cheese
salt and ground black pepper
pink and yellow oyster mushrooms, to serve (optional)

1 Put the dried porcini in a bowl and pour over the warm water. Leave to soak for 20 minutes, then lift out the mushrooms with a slotted spoon. Filter the soaking water through a sieve lined with kitchen paper, then place it in a pan with the stock. Bring the liquid to a gentle simmer.

2 Spoon about 45ml/3 tbsp of the hot stock into a cup and stir in the saffron strands. Set aside. Finely chop the porcini. Heat the oil in a separate pan and lightly sauté the onion, garlic and mushrooms for 5 minutes. Add the rice and stir to coat the grains in oil. Cook for 2 minutes, stirring constantly. Season with salt and pepper.

3 Pour in the white wine. Cook, stirring until it has been absorbed, then ladle in one-quarter of the stock. Cook, stirring, until that has been absorbed, then gradually add the remaining stock, a little at a time. Allow the rice to absorb each batch of liquid before adding more and stir constantly.

4 After about 20 minutes, when all the stock has been absorbed and the rice is *al dente*, stir in the butter, saffron water (with the strands) and half the Parmesan. Serve, sprinkled with the remaining Parmesan and with oyster mushrooms, if you like.

Champagne Risotto

This may seem rather extravagant, but it makes a beautifully flavoured risotto, perfect for that special celebratory dinner.

Serves 3–4

25g/1oz/2 tbsp butter
2 shallots, finely chopped
275g/10oz/1½ cups risotto rice
½ bottle or 300ml/½ pint/1¼ cups champagne
750ml/1¼ pints/3 cups simmering light vegetable stock
150ml/¼ pint/⅔ cup double cream
40g/1½ oz/½ cup freshly grated Parmesan cheese
10ml/2 tsp very finely chopped fresh chervil
salt and ground black pepper
black truffle shavings, to garnish (optional)

1 Melt the butter in a large, heavy-based pan. Add the shallots and fry over a low heat, stirring occasionally, for 2–3 minutes, until softened. Add the rice and cook, stirring constantly, until the grains are coated in butter.

2 Carefully pour in about two-thirds of the champagne so that it doesn't bubble over, and cook over a high heat, stirring constantly, until all the liquid has been absorbed.

3 Add the stock, a ladleful at a time, stirring constantly and making sure that each addition has been completely absorbed before adding more. The risotto should gradually become creamy and velvety and all the stock should be absorbed.

4 When the rice is tender but retains a bit of "bite", stir in the remaining champagne with the double cream and Parmesan. Adjust the seasoning. Remove from the heat, cover and leave to stand for a few minutes. Stir in the chervil. If you want to enhance the flavour, garnish with a few truffle shavings.

Cook's Tip
When cooking a risotto of this calibre, it is especially important to use the correct type of rice. Carnaroli would be perfect.

Barley Risotto with Roasted Squash & Leeks

This is more like a nutty pilaff than a classic risotto. Sweet leeks and roasted squash are superb with pearl barley.

Serves 4–5
200g/7oz/scant 1 cup
   pearl barley
1 butternut squash, peeled,
   seeded and cut into chunks
10ml/2 tsp chopped fresh thyme
60ml/4 tbsp olive oil
25g/1oz/2 tbsp butter
4 leeks, cut diagonally into fairly
   thick slices

2 garlic cloves, finely chopped
175g/6oz/2¼ cups chestnut
   mushrooms, sliced
2 carrots, coarsely grated
about 120ml/4fl oz/ ½ cup
   vegetable stock
30ml/2 tbsp chopped fresh
   flat leaf parsley
50g/2oz Pecorino cheese, grated
   or shaved
45ml/3 tbsp pumpkin
   seeds, toasted
salt and ground black pepper

1 Rinse and drain the barley. Bring a pan of water to simmering point, add the barley and half-cover. Cook for 35–45 minutes, or until tender. Drain. Preheat the oven to 200°C/400°F/Gas 6.

2 Place the squash in a roasting tin with half the thyme. Season with pepper and toss with half the oil. Roast, stirring once, for 30–35 minutes, until tender and beginning to brown.

3 Heat half the butter with the remaining oil in a large frying pan. Cook the leeks and garlic gently for 5 minutes. Add the mushrooms and remaining thyme, then cook until the liquid from the mushrooms evaporates and they begin to fry.

4 Stir in the carrots and cook for 2 minutes, then add the barley and most of the stock. Season and partially cover. Cook for 5 minutes. Pour in the remaining stock if necessary. Stir in the parsley, the remaining butter and half the Pecorino, then the squash, with salt and pepper to taste. Serve, sprinkled with pumpkin seeds and the remaining Pecorino.

Risotto-stuffed Aubergines with Spicy Tomato Sauce

Dramatic good looks, plenty of substance and an interesting flavour make aubergines an excellent choice when entertaining.

Serves 4
4 small aubergines
105ml/7 tbsp olive oil
1 small onion, chopped
175g/6oz/scant 1 cup risotto rice
750ml/1¼ pints/3 cups hot
   vegetable stock

15ml/1 tbsp white wine vinegar
25g/1oz/ ⅓ cup freshly grated
   Parmesan cheese
30ml/2 tbsp pine nuts

For the tomato sauce
300ml/ ½ pint/1¼ cups thick
   passata or puréed tomatoes
5ml/1 tsp mild curry paste
pinch of salt

1 Preheat the oven to 200°C/400°F/Gas 6. Cut the aubergines in half lengthways, cross-hatch the flesh, then remove it with a small knife. Brush the shells with 30ml/2 tbsp of the oil and place on a baking sheet, supported by crumpled foil. Bake for 6–8 minutes. Set aside.

2 Chop the aubergine flesh. Heat the remaining oil in a large, heavy-based pan. Add the aubergine flesh and the onion and cook over a low heat, stirring occasionally, for 3–4 minutes, until softened but not coloured.

3 Stir in the rice and stock, and leave to simmer, uncovered, for about 15 minutes. Add the vinegar.

4 Increase the oven temperature to 230°C/450°F/Gas 8. Spoon the rice mixture into the aubergine skins, top with the cheese and pine nuts, return to the oven and brown for 5 minutes.

5 Meanwhile, make the sauce. Mix the passata or puréed tomatoes with the curry paste in a small pan. Heat through and add salt to taste. Spoon the sauce on to four individual serving plates and arrange two aubergine halves on each one.

Courgette Roulade

This makes an impressive buffet supper or dinner party dish.

Serves 6
40g/1½oz/3 tbsp butter
50g/2oz/½ cup plain flour
300ml/½ pint/1¼ cups milk
4 eggs, separated
3 courgettes, grated
25g/1oz/⅓ cup freshly grated
   Parmesan cheese, plus 30ml/
   2 tbsp for sprinkling
salt and ground black pepper

herb and green leaf salad,
   to serve

For the filling
75g/3oz/ scant ½ cup soft
   goat's cheese
60ml/4 tbsp fromage frais
225g/8oz/2 cups cooked rice
15ml/1 tbsp chopped mixed
   fresh herbs
15ml/1 tbsp olive oil
15g/½oz/1 tbsp butter
75g/3oz/generous 1 cup button
   mushrooms, very finely chopped

1 Preheat the oven to 200°C/400°F/Gas 6. Line a 33 × 23cm/13 × 9in Swiss roll tin with non-stick baking paper.

2 Melt the butter in a saucepan, stir in the flour and cook for 1–2 minutes, stirring. Gradually stir in the milk until the mixture forms a smooth sauce. Remove from the heat and cool. Stir in the egg yolks, add the courgettes and the Parmesan and season.

3 Whisk the egg whites until stiff, fold them into the courgette mixture and scrape into the prepared tin. Spread evenly. Bake for 10–15 minutes, until firm and lightly golden. Carefully turn out on to a sheet of non-stick baking paper sprinkled with 30ml/2 tbsp grated Parmesan. Peel away the lining paper. Roll the roulade up, using the paper as a guide, and leave it to cool.

4 To make the filling, mix the goat's cheese, fromage frais, rice and herbs in a bowl. Season with salt and pepper. Heat the oil and butter in a small pan and fry the mushrooms until soft.

5 Unwrap the roulade, spread with the rice filling and lay the mushrooms along the centre. Roll up again. Serve with a herb and green leaf salad.

Wild Rice with Grilled Vegetables

The mixture of wild rice and long grain rice in this dish works very well, and makes an extremely tasty vegetarian meal.

Serves 4
225g/8oz/generous 1 cup mixed
   wild and long grain rice
1 large aubergine, thickly sliced
1 red pepper, seeded and cut
   into quarters
1 yellow pepper, seeded and cut
   into quarters
1 green pepper, seeded and cut
   into quarters
2 red onions, sliced
225g/8oz/3 cups brown cap or
   shiitake mushrooms
2 small courgettes, cut in
   half lengthways
olive oil, for brushing
30ml/2 tbsp chopped fresh
   thyme, plus whole sprigs to
   garnish (optional)

For the dressing
90ml/6 tbsp extra virgin olive oil
30ml/2 tbsp balsamic vinegar
2 garlic cloves, crushed
salt and ground black pepper

1 Put the wild and long grain rice in a large pan of cold salted water. Bring to the boil, then lower the heat, cover and cook gently for 30–40 minutes (or according to the instructions on the packet), until tender.

2 Preheat the grill. Make the dressing by whisking together the olive oil, vinegar and garlic in a bowl, then season to taste with salt and pepper.

3 Arrange all the vegetables on a grill rack. Brush with olive oil and grill for about 5 minutes.

4 Turn the vegetables over, brush them with more olive oil and grill for 5–8 minutes more, or until tender and beginning to char in places.

5 Drain the rice, tip into a bowl and toss in half the dressing. Spoon on to individual plates and arrange the grilled vegetables on top. Pour over the remaining dressing, scatter over the chopped thyme and serve. Whole thyme sprigs can be used as a garnish, if you like.

Californian Citrus Fried Rice

As with all fried rice dishes, the important thing here is to make sure the rice is cold. Add it after cooking all the other ingredients, and stir to heat it through.

Serves 4–6

4 eggs
10ml/2 tsp Japanese rice vinegar
30ml/2 tbsp light soy sauce
about 45ml/3 tbsp groundnut oil
50g/2oz/ ½ cup cashew nuts
2 garlic cloves, crushed
6 spring onions, diagonally sliced
2 small carrots, cut into
    matchstick strips
225g/8oz asparagus, each spear
    cut diagonally into 4 pieces
175g/6oz/2¼ cups button
    mushrooms, halved
30ml/2 tbsp rice wine
30ml/2 tbsp water
450g/1lb/4 cups cooked white
    long grain rice
about 10ml/2 tsp sesame oil
1 pink grapefruit or
    orange, segmented
strips of orange rind, to garnish

For the hot dressing

5ml/1 tsp grated orange rind
30ml/2 tbsp Japanese rice wine
45ml/3 tbsp vegetarian
    "oyster" sauce
30ml/2 tbsp freshly squeezed
    pink grapefruit or orange juice
5ml/1 tsp medium chilli sauce

1 Beat the eggs with the vinegar and 10ml/2 tsp of the soy sauce. Heat 15ml/1 tbsp of the oil in a wok and cook the eggs until lightly scrambled. Transfer to a plate and set aside.

2 Add the cashew nuts to the wok and stir-fry for 1–2 minutes. Set aside. Heat the remaining oil and add the garlic and spring onions. Cook until the onions begin to soften, then add the carrots and stir-fry for 4 minutes.

3 Add the asparagus and cook for 2–3 minutes, then stir in the mushrooms and stir-fry for a further 1 minute. Stir in the rice wine, the remaining soy sauce and the water. Simmer for a few minutes until the vegetables are crisp-tender.

4 Mix the ingredients for the dressing, then add to the wok and bring to the boil. Add the rice, scrambled eggs and cashews. Toss over a low heat for 3–4 minutes. Stir in the sesame oil and the citrus segments. Garnish with the orange rind and serve.

Provençal Rice

Colourful and bursting with flavour, this is a substantial lunch or supper dish.

Serves 3–4

2 onions
90ml/6 tbsp olive oil
175g/6oz/scant 1 cup brown long
    grain rice
10ml/2 tsp mustard seeds
475ml/16fl oz/2 cups
    vegetable stock
1 large or 2 small red peppers,
    seeded and cut into chunks
1 small aubergine, cut into cubes
2–3 courgettes, sliced
about 12 cherry tomatoes
5–6 fresh basil leaves, torn
2 garlic cloves, finely chopped
60ml/4 tbsp white wine
60ml/4 tbsp passata
2 hard-boiled eggs, cut
    into wedges
8 stuffed green olives, sliced
15ml/1 tbsp drained and
    rinsed capers
butter, to taste
sea salt and ground black pepper
garlic bread, to serve

1 Preheat the oven to 200°C/400°F/Gas 6. Finely chop one onion. Heat 30ml/2 tbsp of the oil in a pan and fry the chopped onion gently until softened.

2 Add the rice and mustard seeds. Cook, stirring, for 2 minutes. Pour in the stock with a little salt. Bring to the boil, lower the heat, cover and simmer for 35 minutes, until the rice is tender.

3 Meanwhile, cut the remaining onion into wedges. Put these in a roasting tin with the peppers, aubergine, courgettes and cherry tomatoes. Scatter over the torn basil leaves and chopped garlic. Pour over the remaining olive oil and sprinkle with sea salt and black pepper. Roast for 15–20 minutes, until the vegetables begin to char, stirring halfway through cooking. Reduce the oven temperature to 180°C/350°F/Gas 4.

4 Spoon the rice into an earthenware casserole. Put the roasted vegetables on top, together with any vegetable juices from the roasting tin, then pour over the wine and passata. Arrange the egg wedges on top, with the sliced olives and capers. Dot with butter, cover and cook for 15–20 minutes until heated through. Serve with garlic bread.

Kedgeree of Oyster & Chanterelle Mushrooms

Special occasion breakfasts and brunches call for something a little out of the ordinary, such as this luxurious dish.

Serves 4
25g/1oz/2 tbsp butter
1 onion, chopped
400g/14oz/2 cups long grain rice
1 small carrot, cut into matchstick strips
900ml/1½ pints/3¾ cups boiling vegetable stock
pinch of saffron strands
225g/8oz/3 cups oyster and chanterelle mushrooms, trimmed and halved
1 floury potato, about 115g/4oz, peeled and grated
450ml/¾ pint/scant 2 cups milk
½ vegetable stock cube
2.5ml/½ tsp curry paste
30ml/2 tbsp double cream
4 hard-boiled eggs, quartered
60ml/4 tbsp chopped fresh parsley, plus a whole sprig

1 Melt the butter in a large saucepan. Add the onion and fry over a low heat, stirring occasionally, for about 5 minutes, until softened but not coloured.

2 Spoon about half the softened onion into a medium pan and set it aside until required.

3 Add the rice, carrot and stock to the large pan, with the saffron. Heat to simmering point and cook, uncovered, for 15 minutes. Remove the pan from the heat, cover and leave to stand for 5 minutes.

4 Add the oyster and chanterelle mushrooms to the smaller pan and mix them with the onion. Cook over a low heat for a few minutes to soften. Stir in the grated potato, milk, stock cube, curry paste and cream and simmer for 15 minutes, until the potatoes have thickened the liquid.

5 Fork the rice on to a warmed serving platter. Spoon the mushrooms and sauce into the centre and garnish with the egg quarters and chopped parsley. Garnish and serve immediately.

Pilaff with Saffron & Pickled Walnuts

Pickled walnuts have a warm, tangy flavour that is lovely in rice and bulgur wheat dishes. This Eastern Mediterranean pilaff is interesting enough to serve on its own.

Serves 4
5ml/1 tsp saffron strands
15ml/1 tbsp boiling water
40g/1½oz/½ cup pine nuts
45ml/3 tbsp olive oil
1 large onion, chopped
3 garlic cloves, crushed
1.5ml/¼ tsp ground allspice
5cm/2in piece of fresh root ginger, grated
225g/8oz/generous 1 cup long grain rice
300ml/½ pint/1¼ cups vegetable stock
50g/2oz/½ cup pickled walnuts, drained and roughly chopped
40g/1½oz/¼ cup raisins
45ml/3 tbsp roughly chopped fresh parsley or coriander, plus whole leaves, to garnish
salt and ground black pepper
natural yogurt, to serve

1 Put the saffron in a bowl with the boiling water and leave to stand. Heat a large frying pan and dry-fry the pine nuts until they turn golden. Set them aside.

2 Heat the oil in the pan and fry the onion, garlic and allspice for 3 minutes. Stir in the ginger and rice and cook for 1 minute.

3 Add the stock and bring to the boil. Lower the heat, cover and simmer gently for 15 minutes, until the rice is just tender.

4 Stir in the saffron and liquid, the pine nuts, pickled walnuts, raisins and parsley or coriander. Season to taste with salt and pepper. Heat through gently for 2 minutes. Garnish with the parsley or coriander leaves and serve with natural yogurt.

> **Variation**
> Use one small aubergine, chopped and fried in a little olive oil, instead of the pickled walnuts, if you prefer.

Brussels Sprouts with Chestnuts

A Christmas classic, Brussels sprouts braised with chestnuts are delicious at any time of year.

Serves 4–6
225g/ ½lb/2–3 cups chestnuts
120ml/4fl oz/ ½ cup milk

500g/1 ¼lb/5 cups small tender Brussels sprouts
25g/1oz/2 tbsp butter
1 shallot, finely chopped
30–45ml/2–3 tbsp dry white wine or water

1 Using a small knife, score a cross in the base of each chestnut. Bring a pan of water to the boil and cook them for 6–8 minutes. Remove from the heat. Remove a few chestnuts from the pan with a draining spoon. Holding them in a dish towel, remove the outer shell with a knife, then peel off the inner skin. Repeat with the remaining chestnuts, a few at a time.

2 Rinse the pan, return the peeled chestnuts to it and add the milk. Pour in enough water to cover the chestnuts completely. Simmer for 12–15 minutes, until the chestnuts are just tender. Drain and set aside.

3 Trim the Brussels sprouts and score a cross in the base of each. Melt the butter in a large, heavy frying pan, and cook the chopped shallot until just softened. Add the Brussels sprouts and wine or water. Cover the pan and cook over a medium heat for 6–8 minutes, shaking the pan occasionally, and adding a little more water if necessary.

4 Add the poached chestnuts and toss gently to combine, then cover and cook for 3–5 minutes more, until the chestnuts and Brussels sprouts are tender. Serve at once.

Cook's Tip
Fresh chestnuts have a wonderful texture and flavour, but bottled or canned unsweetened whole chestnuts make an adequate substitute.

Artichoke Rösti

A traditional Swiss dish, rösti is usually made from potatoes alone. The addition of Jerusalem artichokes provides a subtle variation of the flavour.

Serves 4–6
450g/1lb potatoes
juice of 1 lemon
450g/1lb Jerusalem artichokes
about 50g/2oz/ ¼ cup butter
salt

1 Peel the potatoes and place them in a pan of lightly salted water. Bring to the boil and cook until barely tender – they will take 15–20 minutes.

2 Meanwhile, fill a pan with cold water and add the lemon juice. Peel the Jerusalem artichokes and add them to the pan, with a pinch of salt. Bring to the boil and cook for about 5 minutes, until barely tender.

3 Drain and cool both the potatoes and the artichokes, then grate them into a bowl. Mix them with your fingers, without breaking them up too much.

4 Melt the butter in a large, heavy-based frying pan. Add the artichoke mixture, spreading it out with the back of a spoon. Cook over a low heat for about 10 minutes.

5 Invert the "cake" on to a plate and then slide back into the pan. Cook the underside for about 10 minutes, until golden. Serve at once.

Cook's Tips
• If there is time, chill the cooled par-boiled potatoes and Jerusalem artichokes in the fridge for 15–30 minutes before peeling. This makes them easier to grate and they will be less likely to break up.
• Jerusalem artichokes discolour very quickly once they have been peeled. Dropping them in a bowl of cold water acidulated with a little lemon juice or vinegar helps to prevent this.

Broad Beans with Cream

Tiny new broad beans can be eaten raw with a little salt, just like radishes. More mature beans taste wonderful when cooked and skinned to reveal the bright green kernel inside.

Serves 4–6
450g/1lb shelled broad beans
(from about 2kg/4½lb broad
beans in the pod)
90ml/6 tbsp crème fraîche or
whipping cream
salt and ground black pepper
finely snipped chives, to garnish

1 Bring a large pan of lightly salted water to the boil over a medium heat. Add the beans. Bring the water back to the boil, then lower the heat slightly and cook the beans gently for about 8 minutes, until just tender. Drain and rinse under cold water, then drain again.

2 To remove the skins, make a slit along one side of each bean with the tip of a sharp knife and then gently squeeze out the kernel with your fingers.

3 Put the skinned beans in a pan with the crème fraîche or whipping cream, season with salt and pepper to taste, cover and heat through gently. Transfer to a warmed serving dish, sprinkle with the snipped chives and serve at once.

> **Variation**
> If you can find them, fresh flageolet or lima beans may be served in the same way.

Asparagus with Vermouth Sauce

Coating grilled young asparagus spears with a vermouth and parsley sauce creates a sensational dish.

Serves 4
20 asparagus spears
5ml/1 tsp olive oil
50g/2oz/⅔ cup freshly grated
Parmesan cheese
salt and ground black pepper

For the sauce
45ml/3 tbsp dry white vermouth
250ml/8fl oz/1 cup well-flavoured
vegetable stock
15ml/1 tbsp chopped
fresh parsley
25g/1oz/2 tbsp chilled
butter, cubed

1 Brush the asparagus spears with olive oil and seasoning. Place on a grill rack, sprinkle with the Parmesan and grill slowly, under a moderately hot grill, until the asparagus is just tender when pierced with the tip of a knife and lightly charred.
2 Meanwhile, make the sauce. Pour the vermouth and stock into a saucepan. Boil over a high heat until reduced by half. Stir in the parsley and season with salt and pepper.
3 Lower the heat and stir in the chilled butter cubes, two at a time. Continue to stir over a gentle heat until all the butter has melted and the sauce has thickened. Arrange the asparagus spears in a serving dish, pour the sauce over and serve at once.

Runner Beans with Garlic

Flageolet beans and garlic add a distinct French flavour to this simple side dish.

Serves 4
225g/8oz/1¼ cups dried
flageolet beans, soaked
overnight and drained
15ml/1 tbsp olive oil
25g/1oz/2 tbsp butter
1 onion, finely chopped

1–2 garlic cloves, crushed
3–4 tomatoes, peeled
and chopped
350g/12oz runner beans, sliced
150ml/¼ pint/⅔ cup
white wine
150ml/¼ pint/⅔ cup
vegetable stock
30ml/2 tbsp chopped
fresh parsley
salt and ground black pepper

1 Place the flageolet beans in a large saucepan of water, bring to the boil over a medium heat, then lower the heat and simmer for 45 minutes–1 hour until tender. Drain thoroughly and set aside.

2 Heat the oil and butter in a large, heavy-based frying pan. Add the onion and garlic and fry over a low heat, stirring occasionally, for 3–4 minutes, until soft.

3 Add the chopped tomatoes to the pan and cook over a gentle heat until they are soft.

4 Stir the flageolet beans into the onion and tomato mixture, then add the runner beans, wine and stock and season with a little salt. Stir well. Cover and simmer for 5–10 minutes, until the runner beans are tender.

5 Increase the heat to medium to reduce the liquid, then stir in the chopped parsley. Check the seasoning, adding a little more salt, if necessary, and pepper. Transfer to a warmed serving dish and serve immediately.

> **Cook's Tip**
> Flageolets are also known as green haricot beans.

Courgettes in Citrus Sauce

Courgettes are so attractive, especially the brightly coloured varieties, that their bland taste can sometimes be horribly disappointing. This spicy and piquant sauce ensures that will not be the case here.

Serves 4

350g/12oz baby courgettes
4 spring onions, finely sliced
2.5cm/1in piece of fresh root
     ginger, grated
30ml/2 tbsp cider vinegar
15ml/1 tbsp light soy sauce
5ml/1 tsp soft light brown sugar
45ml/3 tbsp vegetable stock
finely grated rind and juice of
     ½ lemon and ½ orange
5ml/1 tsp cornflour
10ml/2 tsp water

1 Bring a pan of lightly salted water to the boil. Add the courgettes, bring back to the boil and simmer for 3–4 minutes, until just tender.

2 Meanwhile, combine the onions, ginger, vinegar, soy sauce, sugar, stock and orange and lemon juice and rind in a small pan. Bring to the boil, lower the heat and simmer for 2 minutes.

3 Mix the cornflour to a paste with the water, then stir the paste into the sauce. Bring to the boil, stirring constantly until the sauce has thickened.

4 Drain the courgettes well and tip them into a warmed serving dish. Spoon over the hot sauce. Shake the dish gently to coat the courgettes and serve at once.

Cook's Tip
If you can't find baby courgettes – about 7.5cm/3in long – use larger ones, but cook them whole so that they don't absorb too much water and become soggy. Halve them lengthways after cooking and then cut the halves into 10cm/4in lengths before coating them in the sauce.

Red Cabbage in Port & Red Wine

A sweet and sour, spicy red cabbage dish, with the added juiciness of pears and extra crunch of walnuts.

Serves 6

15ml/1 tbsp walnut oil
1 onion, sliced
2 whole star anise
5ml/1 tsp ground cinnamon
pinch of ground cloves

450g/1lb red cabbage,
     finely shredded
25g/1oz/2 tbsp soft dark
     brown sugar
45ml/3 tbsp red wine vinegar
300ml/½ pint/1¼ cups red wine
150ml/¼ pint/⅔ cup port
2 pears, cut into 1cm/½in cubes
115g/4oz/⅔ cup raisins
115g/4oz/1 cup walnut halves
salt and ground black pepper

1 Heat the oil in a large, heavy-based pan. Add the onion and cook over a low heat, stirring occasionally, for about 5 minutes, until softened.

2 Add the star anise, cinnamon, cloves and cabbage and cook for about 3 minutes more.

3 Stir in the sugar, vinegar, red wine and port. Cover the pan and simmer gently for 10 minutes, stirring occasionally.

4 Stir in the cubed pears and raisins and cook for 10 minutes more, without replacing the lid, or until the cabbage is tender. Season to taste with salt and pepper. Mix in the walnut halves and serve immediately.

Cook's Tip
The vinegar and wine help to preserve the beautiful colour of the cabbage as well as adding to the flavour.

Variation
Juniper berries taste wonderful with red cabbage. Omit the star anise and cinnamon and add 15ml/1 tbsp juniper berries with the ground cloves.

Baked Cabbage

This healthy and economical dish uses the whole cabbage, including the flavoursome core.

Serves 4

1 green or white cabbage, about 675g/1½lb
15ml/1 tbsp light olive oil
30ml/2 tbsp water
45–60ml/3–4 tbsp vegetable stock
4 firm, ripe tomatoes, peeled and chopped
5ml/1 tsp mild chilli powder
15ml/1 tbsp chopped fresh parsley or fennel, to garnish (optional)

For the topping

3 firm ripe tomatoes, thinly sliced
15ml/1 tbsp olive oil
salt and ground black pepper

1 Preheat the oven to 180°C/350°F/Gas 4. Shred the leaves and the core of the cabbage finely. Heat the oil in a frying pan with the water and add the cabbage. Cover and cook over a very low heat, to allow the cabbage to sweat, for 5–10 minutes. Stir occasionally.

2 Pour in the vegetable stock, then stir in the tomatoes. Cook over a low heat for a further 10 minutes. Season with the chilli powder and a little salt.

3 Tip the cabbage mixture into a large square ovenproof dish. Level the surface and arrange the sliced tomatoes on top. Brush with the oil then sprinkle with salt and pepper to taste.

4 Bake for 30–40 minutes, or until the tomatoes are just starting to brown. Serve hot, with a little parsley or fennel sprinkled over the top, if you like.

Cook's Tips

To vary the taste, add seeded, diced red or green peppers to the cabbage with the tomatoes. If you have a shallow flameproof casserole, you could cook the cabbage in it on the hob and then simply transfer the casserole to the oven.

Broccoli & Cauliflower with Cider & Apple Mint Sauce

The cider sauce is also ideal for other vegetables, such as celery or beans.

Serves 4

15ml/1 tbsp olive oil
1 large onion, chopped
2 large carrots, chopped
1 large garlic clove
15ml/1 tbsp dill seeds
4 large fresh apple mint sprigs
30ml/2 tbsp plain flour
300ml/½ pint/1¼ cups dry cider
500g/1¼ lb/4 cups broccoli florets
500g/1¼ lb/4 cups cauliflower florets
30ml/2 tbsp tamari
10ml/2 tsp mint jelly
salt

1 Heat the olive oil in a large, heavy-based frying pan. Add the onion, carrots, garlic, dill seeds and apple mint leaves and cook over a low heat, stirring occasionally, for about 5 minutes, until the vegetables are soft.

2 Stir in the flour and cook, stirring constantly, for 1 minute, then stir in the cider. Bring to the boil, then simmer until the sauce looks glossy. Remove the pan from the heat and set aside to cool slightly.

3 Bring two small pans of lightly salted water to the boil and cook the broccoli and cauliflower separately until just tender.

4 Meanwhile, pour the sauce into a food processor and add the tamari and mint jelly. Process to a fine purée.

5 Drain the broccoli and cauliflower well and mix them in a warmed serving dish. Pour over the sauce, mix lightly to coat and serve immediately.

Cook's Tip

Tamari is a Japanese soy sauce. It is dark and thick and tastes less salty than Chinese soy.

Baked Fennel with a Crumb Crust

The delicate aniseed flavour
of baked fennel makes it a
very good accompaniment
to pasta dishes and risottos.

Serves 4
*3 fennel bulbs, cut lengthways
    into quarters
30ml/2 tbsp olive oil
50g/2oz/1 cup day-old
    wholemeal breadcrumbs
1 garlic clove, chopped
30ml/2 tbsp chopped fresh
    flat leaf parsley
salt and ground black pepper
fennel leaves, to garnish*

1 Bring a saucepan of lightly salted water to the boil over a
medium heat. Add the fennel quarters, bring back to the boil,
then lower the heat and simmer for about 10 minutes, or until
just tender.

2 Preheat the oven to 190°C/375°F/Gas 5. Drain the fennel
and place the pieces in an ovenproof dish or roasting tin. Brush
with half of the olive oil.

3 Put the breadcrumbs, garlic and parsley in a separate bowl
and drizzle over the remaining olive oil. Season to taste with
salt and pepper. Mix lightly, then sprinkle the mixture evenly
over the fennel.

4 Bake for 30 minutes, or until the fennel is tender and the
breadcrumbs are crisp and golden. Serve hot, garnished with
feathery fennel leaves.

> **Variations**
> • *Add 60ml/4 tbsp finely grated, strongly flavoured cheese, such
> as mature Cheddar, Red Leicester or Parmesan, to the
> breadcrumb topping.*
> • *Add two or three cored and sliced red eating apples to the
> dish with the cooked fennel quarters.*

Spinach with Raisins & Pine Nuts

Wilted spinach benefits
from a touch of sweetness,
as this delicious Spanish dish
amply illustrates.

Serves 4
*50g/2oz/1/3 cup raisins
1 thick slice crusty white bread
45ml/3 tbsp olive oil
25g/1oz/1/3 cup pine nuts
500g/1 1/4lb young spinach leaves,
    stalks removed
2 garlic cloves, crushed
salt and ground black pepper*

1 Put the raisins in a small bowl. Cover with boiling water and
leave to soak for 10 minutes.

2 Cut off the crusts from the bread and discard. Cut the bread
into small cubes.

3 Heat 30ml/2 tbsp of the oil in a large, heavy-based frying pan.
Add the bread cubes and fry over a medium heat, stirring and
turning frequently, until golden all over. Lift out with a draining
spoon and drain well on kitchen paper.

4 Add the remaining oil to the pan. When it is hot, fry the pine
nuts until beginning to colour. Add the spinach and garlic and
cook quickly, turning the spinach until it has just wilted.

5 Drain the raisins, toss them into the pan and season lightly
with salt and black pepper. Transfer to a warmed serving dish.
Scatter with the croûtons and serve.

> **Variation**
> *Swiss chard or spinach beet can be used instead of the
> spinach, but will need to be cooked a little more.*

Courgettes in Rich Tomato Sauce

Serve this colourful dish hot
or cold. Cut the courgettes
fairly thickly, so they stay
slightly crunchy.

Serves 4
*15ml/1 tbsp olive oil
1 onion, chopped
1 garlic clove, chopped
4 courgettes, thickly sliced*

*400g/14oz can chopped
    tomatoes, drained
2 tomatoes, peeled, seeded
    and chopped
5ml/1 tsp vegetable
    bouillon powder
15ml/1 tbsp tomato purée
salt and ground black pepper*

1 Heat the oil in a heavy pan and sauté the onion and garlic
until softened, stirring occasionally. Add the courgettes and cook
for 5 minutes more.
2 Tip in the canned and fresh tomatoes, then stir in the
bouillon powder and tomato purée. Simmer for 10–15 minutes,
until the sauce has thickened and the courgettes are just
tender. Season to taste with salt and pepper and serve.

Braised Leeks with Carrots

Sweet carrots and leeks go well together, especially when married with a little chopped mint, chervil or flat leaf parsley.

Serves 6
65g/2¹/₂oz/5 tbsp butter
675g/1¹/₂lb carrots, thickly sliced
2 bay leaves
2.5ml/¹/₂ tsp caster sugar
75ml/5 tbsp water
675g/1¹/₂lb leeks, cut into
  5cm/2in lengths
120ml/4fl oz/¹/₂ cup white wine
30ml/2 tbsp chopped fresh mint
salt and ground black pepper

1 Melt 25g/1oz/2 tbsp of the butter in a pan and cook the carrots gently for 4–5 minutes. Do not let them brown.

2 Add the bay leaves, caster sugar and water. Season with salt and pepper to taste. Bring to the boil, cover tightly and cook for 10–15 minutes, or until the carrots are tender, shaking the pan frequently to stop the carrots from sticking. Remove the lid, then boil until the juices have evaporated, leaving the carrots moist and glazed.

3 Meanwhile, melt 25g/1oz/2 tbsp of the remaining butter in a pan that is wide enough to hold the leeks in a single layer. Add the leeks, stir to coat them in butter, then fry over a low heat for 4–5 minutes, without letting them brown.

4 Stir in the wine and half the mint, then season to taste. Heat until simmering, then cover and cook gently for 5–8 minutes, or until the leeks are tender, but have not collapsed.

5 Uncover the leeks and turn them in the buttery juices. Increase the heat, then boil the liquid rapidly until reduced to a few tablespoons.

6 Add the carrots to the leeks and reheat them gently, then swirl in the remaining butter. Adjust the seasoning, if necessary. Transfer to a warmed serving dish and serve sprinkled with the remaining mint.

Caramelized Shallots

Wonderful with well-flavoured nut roasts or lentil loaves, these also taste good with other braised or roasted vegetables, such as chunks of butternut squash.

Serves 4–6
50g/2oz/¹/₄ cup butter
500g/1¹/₄lb shallots or small
  onions, peeled, with root
  ends intact
15ml/1 tbsp golden caster sugar
30ml/2 tbsp red or white wine
150ml/¹/₄ pint/²/₃ cup
  vegetable stock
2–3 fresh bay leaves
salt and ground black pepper
fresh thyme sprigs, to garnish

1 Melt the butter in a large frying pan and add the shallots or onions in a single layer. Fry over a low heat, turning occasionally, for about 10 minutes, until lightly browned.

2 Sprinkle the sugar over the shallots or onions and cook gently, turning them in the juices, until the sugar begins to caramelize. Add the red or white wine and let the mixture bubble for 4–5 minutes.

3 Pour in the stock and add the bay leaves. Season with salt and pepper to taste. Cover and cook for 5 minutes, then remove the lid and cook until the liquid evaporates and the shallots are tender and glazed.

4 Adjust the seasoning, if necessary, and spoon into a serving bowl. Garnish with the sprigs of thyme and serve.

> **Variation**
> *Shallots with Chestnuts: Cook the shallots as above, but toss in 250g/9oz/2–3 cups partially cooked chestnuts just before adding the stock. Cook the two vegetables together for about 5–10 minutes, then serve sprinkled with plenty of chopped flat leaf parsley.*

Okra with Coriander & Tomatoes

When combined with tomatoes and mild spices, okra makes a very good side dish and is particularly good with potato strudel or a courgette and dill tart.

Serves 4
450g/1lb tomatoes or 400g/14oz
   can chopped tomatoes
450g/1lb fresh okra
45ml/3 tbsp olive oil
2 onions, thinly sliced
10ml/2 tsp coriander
   seeds, crushed
3 garlic cloves, crushed
about 2.5ml/ $\frac{1}{2}$ tsp caster sugar
finely grated rind and juice
   of 1 lemon
salt and ground black pepper

1 If using fresh tomatoes, cut a cross in the skin at the top of each one with a sharp knife, then plunge them into boiling water for 30 seconds. Drain and refresh in cold water. Peel away the skins and chop the flesh.

2 With a sharp knife, trim off any stalks from the okra and leave the pods whole. Avoid piercing the pods or the sticky juice they contain will leak out.

3 Heat the oil in a large, heavy-based frying pan. Add the onions with the coriander seeds and fry over a medium heat, stirring occasionally, for 3–4 minutes, until the onions are softened and beginning to colour.

4 Add the okra and garlic and fry for 1 minute. Carefully stir in the tomatoes and sugar, without breaking up the okra, then lower the heat and simmer gently for about 20 minutes, or until the okra is tender, stirring once or twice.

5 Stir in the lemon rind and juice. Season to taste with salt and pepper. Taste the mixture and add a little more sugar, if necessary. Transfer to a warmed serving dish and serve immediately. Alternatively, set aside to cool and then serve at room temperature.

Braised Lettuce & Peas

This dish is based on the traditional French way of braising peas with lettuce and spring onions in butter.

Serves 4
50g/2oz/ $\frac{1}{4}$ cup butter
4 Little Gem lettuces,
   halved lengthways
2 bunches spring onions, trimmed
5ml/1 tsp caster sugar
400g/14oz/3 $\frac{1}{2}$ cups shelled peas
   (about 1kg/2 $\frac{1}{4}$ lb in pods)
4 fresh mint sprigs
120ml/4fl oz/ $\frac{1}{2}$ cup
   vegetable stock
15ml/1 tbsp fresh mint leaves
salt and ground black pepper

1 Melt half the butter in a wide, heavy-based saucepan over a low heat. Add the lettuces and spring onions. Turn the vegetables in the butter, then sprinkle in the sugar, 2.5ml/ $\frac{1}{2}$ tsp salt and plenty of black pepper. Cover, and cook very gently for 5 minutes, stirring once.

2 Add the peas and mint sprigs. Turn the peas in the buttery juices and pour in the stock, then cover and cook over a gentle heat for 5 minutes more. Uncover and increase the heat to reduce the liquid to a few tablespoons.

3 Stir in the remaining butter and adjust the seasoning, if necessary. Transfer to a warmed serving dish and sprinkle with the mint leaves. Serve immediately.

Variations
• Braise about eight baby carrots with the lettuce.
• Use 1 lettuce, shredding it coarsely, and omit the mint. Towards the end of cooking, stir in about 150g/5oz rocket (preferably the stronger-flavoured wild rocket) and cook briefly until the leaves are just wilted.
• Any of the smaller cos-type lettuces, such as Sucrine and Winter Density, would work well in this recipe. Equally, you could use shredded cos or Webb's Wonder leaves.
• For a different flavour, omit the mint and season with freshly grated nutmeg to taste.

Celeriac Gratin

It may not look very handsome, but celeriac has a delicious sweet and nutty flavour, which is accentuated in this dish by the addition of Emmenthal cheese.

Serves 4
juice of ½ lemon
450g/1lb celeriac
25g/1oz/2 tbsp butter

1 small onion, finely chopped
30ml/2 tbsp plain flour
300ml/½ pint/1¼ cups milk
25g/1oz/¼ cup grated
   Emmenthal cheese
15ml/1 tbsp capers, rinsed
   and drained
salt and cayenne pepper

1 Preheat the oven to 190°C/375°F/Gas 5. Fill a pan with water and add the lemon juice. Peel the celeriac and cut it into 5mm/¼in slices, immediately adding them to the pan of acidulated water. This prevents them from discolouring.

2 Bring the water to the boil, then lower the heat and simmer the celeriac for 10–12 minutes, until just tender. Drain the celeriac and arrange the slices, overlapping them slightly, in a shallow ovenproof dish.

3 Melt the butter in a small pan. Add the onion and fry over a low heat, stirring occasionally, for 5 minutes, until soft but not browned. Stir in the flour, cook for 1 minute and then gradually add the milk, stirring constantly until the mixture thickens, to make a smooth sauce.

4 Stir in the grated cheese and capers and season with salt and cayenne to taste. Pour the mixture over the celeriac. Bake for 15–20 minutes, until the top is golden brown.

> **Variation**
> For a less strongly flavoured dish, alternate the layers of celeriac with potato. Slice the potato, cook until almost tender, then drain well before assembling the dish.

Baked Peppers & Tomatoes

The juices from this vegetable medley are absolutely delicious, so serve it with a pasta or rice dish or just crusty bread to soak them up.

Serves 8
2 red peppers, seeded
2 yellow peppers, seeded
1 red onion, sliced
2 garlic cloves, halved
6 plum tomatoes, quartered
50g/2oz/¼ cup black olives
5ml/1 tsp soft light brown sugar
45ml/3 tbsp sherry
3–4 fresh rosemary sprigs
30ml/2 tbsp olive oil
salt and ground black pepper

1 Preheat the oven to 200°C/400°F/Gas 6. Cut each pepper into 12 strips and place them in a large roasting tin. Add the onion, garlic, tomatoes and olives.

2 Sprinkle over the sugar, then drizzle over the sherry. Season well, cover with foil and bake for 45 minutes.

3 Remove the foil from the tin and stir the mixture well. Add the rosemary sprigs.

4 Drizzle over the olive oil. Return the tin to the oven and roast for 30 minutes more, until the vegetables are tender. Serve hot.

> **Cook's Tip**
> For the best flavour, buy tomatoes on the vine, if possible.

> **Variation**
> Use four or five well-flavoured beef tomatoes instead of plum tomatoes, if you prefer. Cut them into thick wedges instead of quarters.

Corn with Jalapeños & Cheese

When you tire of plain corn on the cob, try this creamy vegetable dish, spiked with pickled chillies.

Serves 6
4 sweetcorn cobs
50g/2oz/ 1/4 cup butter
1 small onion, finely chopped
115g/4oz/ 2/3 cup drained pickled jalapeño chilli slices
130g/4 1/2oz/ 2/3 cup full-fat soft cheese
25g/1oz/ 1/3 cup freshly grated Parmesan cheese, plus shavings, to garnish
salt and ground black pepper

1 Strip off the husks from the corn and pull off the silks. Place the cobs in a bowl of water and use a vegetable brush to remove any remaining silks. Stand each cob in turn on a board and slice off the kernels, cutting as close to the cob as possible.

2 Melt the butter in a saucepan, add the onion and fry, stirring occasionally, for 4–5 minutes, until softened and translucent.

3 Add the corn kernels and cook for 4–5 minutes, until they are just tender. Chop the jalapeños finely and stir them into the corn mixture.

4 Stir in the soft cheese and the grated Parmesan. Cook over a low heat until both cheeses have melted and the corn kernels are coated in the mixture. Season to taste, tip into a heated dish and serve, topped with shaved Parmesan.

> **Variations**
> • Whole cooked corn cobs may be dipped in cream, then sprinkled with crumbled fresh cheese.
> • Put whole corn cobs in a shallow ovenproof dish and bake them in an oven preheated to 200°C/400°F/Gas 6 for 30 minutes, until tender and golden. Pour over 120ml/4fl oz/ 1/2 cup soured cream or crème fraîche, then sprinkle the cobs with 30ml/2 tbsp freshly grated Parmesan cheese and serve. Alternatively grill the cobs, brushed with butter, on a barbecue.

Spiced Pumpkin with Tomato Salsa

Roasted pumpkin has a wonderful, rich flavour, especially when served with a salsa and a dollop of crème fraîche.

Serves 6
1kg/2 1/4lb pumpkin
50g/2oz/ 1/4 cup butter, melted
10ml/2 tsp hot chilli sauce
2.5ml/ 1/2 tsp salt
2.5ml/ 1/2 tsp ground allspice
5ml/1 tsp ground cinnamon
chopped fresh herbs, to garnish
crème fraîche, to serve

For the tomato salsa
3 fresh serrano chillies
1 large onion, finely chopped
grated rind and juice of 2 limes, plus strips of lime rind, to garnish
8 ripe, firm tomatoes, peeled and diced
large bunch of fresh coriander, finely chopped
pinch of caster sugar

1 Make the salsa about 3 hours in advance. Grill the chillies until the skins are blistered and charred. Place in a bowl, cover with crumpled kitchen paper and set aside for 20 minutes. Meanwhile, marinate the onion in the lime rind and juice.

2 Add the tomatoes to the marinated onion. Peel the chillies, remove the core and seeds from each, then chop the flesh finely. Add it to the bowl with the coriander and the sugar. Mix well, garnish with extra lime rind, cover and chill.

3 Preheat the oven to 220°F/425°F/Gas 7. Cut the pumpkin into large pieces. Scoop out and discard the fibre and seeds, then put the pumpkin pieces in a roasting tin.

4 Mix the melted butter and chilli sauce and drizzle the mixture evenly over the pumpkin pieces. Mix the salt, allspice and cinnamon in a bowl. Sprinkle the mixture over the pumpkin.

5 Roast for 30–40 minutes, or until the pumpkin flesh yields when pressed gently. Transfer the pumpkin to a heated serving platter, garnish with the chopped herbs and serve with the salsa and crème fraîche.

Roasted Mediterranean Vegetables with Pecorino

Aubergines, courgettes, peppers and tomatoes make a marvellous medley when roasted and served drizzled with fragrant olive oil. Shavings of ewe's milk Pecorino add the perfect finishing touch.

Serves 4–6
1 aubergine, sliced
2 courgettes, sliced
2 peppers (red or yellow or one of
   each), quartered and seeded
1 large onion, thickly sliced
2 large carrots, cut in sticks
4 firm plum tomatoes, halved
extra virgin olive oil, for brushing
   and sprinkling
45ml/3 tbsp chopped
   fresh parsley
45ml/3 tbsp pine nuts,
   lightly toasted
115g/4oz piece of
   Pecorino cheese
salt and ground black pepper

1 Layer the aubergine slices in a colander, sprinkling each layer with a little salt. Leave to drain over a sink for about 20 minutes, then rinse thoroughly under cold running water, drain well and pat dry with kitchen paper. Preheat the oven to 220°C/425°F/Gas 7.

2 Spread out aubergine slices, courgettes, peppers, onion, carrots and tomatoes in one or two large roasting tins. Brush them lightly with olive oil and roast them for 20–30 minutes, or until they are lightly browned and the skins on the peppers have begun to blister.

3 Transfer the vegetables to a large serving platter. If you like, peel the peppers and discard the skins. Trickle over any vegetable juices from the pan and season to taste with salt and pepper. As the vegetables cool, sprinkle them with more olive oil. When they are at room temperature, mix in the fresh parsley and toasted pine nuts.

4 Using a swivel vegetable peeler, shave the Pecorino and scatter the shavings over the vegetables.

Lemony Vegetable Parcels

What could be prettier – or more convenient – than these handy packages of winter vegetables? They're guaranteed to brighten up even the dreariest day.

Serves 4
2 medium carrots, cubed
1 small swede, cubed
1 large parsnip, cubed
1 leek, sliced
finely grated rind of ½ lemon
15ml/1 tbsp lemon juice
15ml/1 tbsp wholegrain mustard
5ml/1 tsp walnut or sunflower oil
salt and ground black pepper

1 Preheat the oven to 190°C/375°F/Gas 5. Place the carrot, swede and parsnip cubes in a large bowl, then add the sliced leek. Stir in the lemon rind and juice and the mustard. Season to taste with salt and pepper.

2 Cut four 30cm/12in squares of non-stick baking paper and brush them lightly with the oil. Divide the vegetable mixture among them. Roll up the paper from one side, then twist the ends firmly to seal.

3 Transfer the parcels to a baking sheet and bake them for 50–55 minutes, or until the vegetables are just tender.

4 Serve on heated plates, opening each parcel slightly to reveal the contents.

Cook's Tip
If you haven't got any baking paper, use greaseproof paper, but foil is not suitable for these parcels.

Variation
Substitute the same quantity of curry or tikka paste for the mustard and omit the lemon rind and juice.

Radicchio & Chicory Gratin

Creamy béchamel sauce, with its delicate flavour, is the perfect foil for these bitter-tasting leaves.

Serves 4
oil, for greasing
2 heads radicchio
2 heads chicory
4 pieces of sun-dried tomatoes in
    oil, drained and roughly

chopped, plus 30ml/2 tbsp oil
    from the jar
25g/1oz/2 tbsp butter
15ml/1 tbsp plain flour
250ml/8fl oz/1 cup milk
pinch of freshly grated nutmeg
50g/2oz/ ½ cup grated
    Emmenthal cheese
salt and ground black pepper
chopped fresh parsley, to garnish

1 Preheat the oven to 180°C/350°F/Gas 4. Grease a 1.2 litre/ 2 pint/5 cup ovenproof dish. Trim the radicchio and chicory and pull away and discard any damaged or wilted leaves. Quarter them lengthways and arrange them in the dish.

2 Scatter over the sun-dried tomatoes and brush the leaves liberally with the oil from the jar. Sprinkle with salt and pepper and cover with foil. Bake for 15 minutes, then remove the foil and bake for 10 minutes more, until the vegetables are soft.

3 Meanwhile, make the sauce. Melt the butter in a small pan, stir in the flour and cook for 1 minute. Gradually add the milk, whisking until the sauce boils and thickens. Lower the heat and simmer for 2–3 minutes. Season to taste and add the nutmeg.

4 Pour the sauce over the vegetables and sprinkle with the cheese. Bake for 20 minutes more, until the topping is golden. Serve immediately, garnished with parsley.

Cook's Tip
In Italy radicchio and chicory are often grilled on a barbecue. To do this, prepare the vegetables as above and brush with olive oil. Place cut side down on the grill for 7–10 minutes, until browned. Turn and grill until the other side is browned.

Mixed Vegetables with Aromatic Seeds

A tantalizing aroma is the first indication of how tasty this vegetable medley will be. Fresh ginger and three different types of seeds create a wonderful flavour.

Serves 4–6
675g/1½lb small new potatoes
1 small cauliflower
175g/6oz French beans

115g/4oz/1 cup frozen peas
a small piece of fresh root ginger
30ml/2 tbsp sunflower oil
10ml/2 tsp cumin seeds
10ml/2 tsp black mustard seeds
30ml/2 tbsp sesame seeds
juice of 1 lemon
salt and ground black pepper

1 Scrub the potatoes but do not peel them. Cut the cauliflower into small florets, then trim and halve the French beans.

2 Cook the vegetables in separate pans of lightly salted boiling water until tender, allowing 15–20 minutes for the potatoes, 8–10 minutes for the cauliflower and 4–5 minutes for the beans and peas. Drain thoroughly.

3 Using a small, sharp knife, peel and finely chop the ginger.

4 Heat the oil in a wide, shallow pan. Add the ginger and seeds. Cover the pan and fry until the seeds start to pop.

5 Add the cooked vegetables and toss over the heat for another 2–3 minutes. Sprinkle over the lemon juice and season with pepper.

Cook's Tip
Other vegetables could be used, such as courgettes, leeks or broccoli. Buy whatever looks freshest and do not store vegetables for long periods, as their vitamin content, flavour and texture will deteriorate.

Oven Chip Roasties

This easy alternative to fried chips tastes just as good and is much easier to cook. They also make very popular canapés to serve with pre-dinner drinks.

Serves 4–6
150ml/ ¼ pint/ ⅔ cup olive oil
4 medium to large
    baking potatoes
5ml/1 tsp mixed dried
    herbs (optional)
sea salt flakes
mayonnaise, to serve

1 Preheat the oven to the highest temperature; this is generally 240°C/475°F/Gas 9. Lightly oil a large shallow roasting tin and place it in the oven to get really hot while you are preparing the potatoes.

2 Cut the potatoes in half lengthwise, then into long thin wedges, or thicker ones if you prefer. Brush each side lightly with olive oil.

3 When the oven is really hot, remove the roasting tin carefully and scatter the potato wedges over it, spreading them out in a single layer over the hot oil.

4 Sprinkle the potato wedges with the herbs and sea salt flakes and then roast for about 20 minutes, or longer if they are thicker, turning once so that they brown evenly, until they are golden brown, crisp and lightly puffy. Remove from the oven, drain thoroughly on kitchen paper and serve with a dollop of mayonnaise.

> **Variations**
> • Sweet potatoes also make fine oven chips. Prepare and roast as for regular potatoes, although you may find they do not take so long to cook.
> • You can flavour the roasties with mild paprika instead of mixed herbs.
> • Serve with lemon juice instead of mayonnaise.

Garlic Sweet Potato Mash

Orange-fleshed sweet potatoes not only look good; they taste delicious mashed with garlicky butter.

Serves 4
900g/2lb sweet potatoes
45ml/3 tbsp butter
3 garlic cloves, crushed
salt and ground black pepper

1 Bring a large pan of lightly salted water to the boil. Add the sweet potatoes and cook for about 15 minutes, or until tender. Drain very well, return to the pan and cover tightly.

2 Melt the butter in a frying pan and sauté the garlic over a low heat, stirring constantly, for 1–2 minutes, until light golden.

3 Pour the garlic butter over the potatoes, season with salt and pepper, and mash until smooth and creamy. Serve immediately.

Perfect Creamed Potatoes

Smooth mashed potatoes taste very good and are the ideal accompaniment for other vegetarian dishes.

Serves 4
900g/2lb firm but not waxy
    potatoes, diced
45ml/3 tbsp extra virgin olive oil

about 150ml/¼ pint/⅔ cup
    hot milk
freshly grated nutmeg
a few fresh basil leaves or parsley
    sprigs, chopped
salt and ground black pepper
fresh basil leaves, to garnish

1 Put the potatoes in a pan of cold water and bring to the boil. Cook until just tender. Drain very well. Press the potatoes through a potato ricer or mash with a potato masher.
2 Beat in the olive oil and enough hot milk to give a smooth, thick purée.
3 Flavour to taste with the nutmeg and seasoning, then stir in the chopped fresh herbs. Spoon into a warm serving dish and serve at once, garnished with the basil leaves.

Potato Pan Gratin

Baked potatoes layered with mustard butter are perfect to serve with a green salad for supper, or as an accompaniment to a vegetable or nut roast.

Serves 4

4 large potatoes, total weight
   about 1kg/2¼ lb
25g/1oz/2 tbsp butter
15ml/1 tbsp olive oil
2 large garlic cloves, crushed
30ml/2 tbsp plain or herbed
   Dijon mustard
15ml/1 tbsp lemon juice
15ml/1 tbsp fresh thyme leaves,
   plus extra to garnish
60ml/4 tbsp well-flavoured
   vegetable stock
salt and ground black pepper

1 Peel the potatoes and slice them thinly, using a knife or the slicing attachment on a food processor. Place the slices in a bowl of cold water to prevent them from discolouring.

2 Preheat the oven to 200°C/400°F/Gas 6. Heat the butter and oil in a deep frying pan that can safely be used in the oven. Add the garlic and cook gently for 3 minutes, until light golden, stirring constantly. Stir in the mustard, lemon juice and thyme. Remove from the heat and pour the mixture into a jug.

3 Drain the potatoes and pat them dry with kitchen paper. Place a layer of potatoes in the frying pan, season and pour over one-third of the butter mixture. Place another layer of potatoes on top, season, and pour over another third of the butter mixture. Arrange a final layer of potatoes on top, pour over the remainder of the butter mixture and then the stock. Season and sprinkle with the extra thyme.

4 Cover with non-stick baking paper and bake for 1 hour. Remove the paper and bake for 15 minutes more, until golden.

> **Variation**
> Any root vegetables can be used: try celery sticks, parsnips, carrots or a mixture.

Lyonnaise Potatoes

Two simple ingredients are prepared separately and then tossed together to create the perfect combination. These potatoes go very well with grilled beef tomatoes and lightly cooked French beans.

Serves 6

900g/2lb floury potatoes,
   scrubbed but not peeled
vegetable oil, for shallow frying
25g/1oz/2 tbsp butter
15ml/1 tbsp olive oil
2 medium onions, sliced into rings
sea salt
15ml/1 tbsp chopped
   fresh parsley

1 Bring a large pan of lightly salted water to the boil and cook the potatoes for 10 minutes. Drain them in a colander and leave to cool slightly. When the potatoes are cool enough to handle, peel them and slice them finely.

2 Heat the vegetable oil in a large, heavy-based pan. Add half the potato slices and fry over a low heat, turning occasionally, for about 10 minutes, until crisp. Remove from the pan with a draining spoon and drain on kitchen paper. Set aside and keep hot while you fry the remaining potato slices.

3 Meanwhile, melt the butter with the olive oil in a frying pan. Add the onions and fry over a low heat, stirring occasionally, for about 10 minutes, until golden. Drain on kitchen paper.

4 Remove the second batch of potato slices with a draining spoon and drain on kitchen paper. Mix the two batches together in a warmed serving dish, toss with sea salt and carefully mix with the onions. Sprinkle with the parsley and serve.

> **Variation**
> For garlic-flavoured Lyonnaise potatoes, add about six unpeeled garlic cloves when you par-boil the potatoes in step 1. Then either leave them whole or squeeze out the flesh and spread it over the potatoes.

Potato Latkes

These traditional Jewish potato pancakes taste wonderful with apple sauce and soured cream.

Serves 4
2 medium floury potatoes
1 onion
1 large egg, beaten
30ml/2 tbsp medium-ground matzo meal
vegetable oil, for frying
salt and ground black pepper

1 Peel the potatoes and grate them coarsely. Grate the onion in the same way. Mix the potatoes and onion in a large colander in the sink, but do not rinse them. Press them down, squeezing out as much of the thick starchy liquid as possible. Tip the potato mixture into a large bowl.

2 Immediately stir in the beaten egg. Add the matzo meal, stirring gently to mix. Season with salt and plenty of pepper.

3 Preheat the oven to 150°C/300°F/Gas 2. Pour oil to a depth of 1cm/ ½in into a heavy-based frying pan. Heat it until a small piece of day-old bread, added to the oil, sizzles. Take a spoonful of the potato mixture and lower it carefully into the oil. Continue adding spoonfuls, leaving space between each one.

4 Flatten the pancakes slightly with the back of a spoon. Fry for a few minutes until the latkes are golden brown on the underside, then turn them over carefully and continue frying until golden brown all over.

5 Drain the latkes on kitchen paper, then transfer to an ovenproof serving dish and keep warm in the oven while frying the remainder. Serve hot.

> **Variation**
> *Try using equal quantities of potatoes and Jerusalem artichokes for a really distinct flavour.*

New Potatoes with Shallot Butter

New potatoes are always a treat and are superb with this delicate butter.

Serves 6
500g/1¼lb small new potatoes
25g/1oz/2 tbsp butter

3 shallots, finely chopped
2 garlic cloves, crushed
5ml/1 tsp chopped fresh tarragon
5ml/1 tsp chopped fresh chives
5ml/1 tsp chopped fresh parsley
salt and ground black pepper

1 Bring a pan of lightly salted water to the boil. Add the potatoes and cook for 15–20 minutes, until just tender. Drain them well.

2 Melt the butter in a large frying pan. Fry the shallots and garlic over a low heat, stirring occasionally, for 5 minutes. Add the potatoes to the pan and mix with the shallot butter. Season to taste with salt and pepper. Cook, stirring constantly, until the potatoes are heated through.

3 Transfer the potatoes to a warmed serving bowl. Sprinkle with the chopped herbs and serve at once.

New Potatoes with Soured Cream

This is a traditional Russian way of serving potatoes. The soured cream may be flavoured with spring onions, as here, or snipped fresh chives.

Serves 6
900g/2lb new potatoes
150ml/¼ pint/⅔ cup soured cream
4 spring onions, thinly sliced
salt and ground black pepper
15ml/1 tbsp chopped fresh dill, to garnish

1 Bring a pan of lightly salted water to the boil. Add the potatoes and cook for 15–20 minutes, until just tender. Drain.
2 Mix the soured cream and spring onions and season to taste with salt and pepper. Place the potatoes in a warm serving dish, add the cream mixture and toss lightly. Garnish with dill.

Marquis Potatoes

Swirled potato nests filled with a tangy tomato mixture look wonderfully appetizing and taste superb. As a side dish, this recipe will serve six, but could also make a tasty lunch for two or three people.

Makes 6 nests

4 large floury potatoes, total
    weight about 900g/2lb
15ml/1 tbsp olive oil, plus extra
    for greasing
2 shallots, finely chopped
450g/1lb ripe tomatoes, peeled,
    seeded and diced
25g/1oz/2 tbsp butter
60ml/4 tbsp milk
3 egg yolks
salt and ground black pepper
chopped fresh parsley, to garnish

1 Peel the potatoes and cut them into small chunks. Put them in a pan of cold water. Add salt, bring to the boil and cook for 20 minutes, or until very tender.

2 Heat the olive oil in a large frying pan. Add the shallots and fry, stirring constantly, for 2 minutes.

3 Add the diced tomatoes and fry over a low heat, stirring occasionally, for 10 minutes more, until all the moisture has evaporated. Keep warm over a low heat.

4 Drain the potatoes in a colander, then return them to the pan so that they can dry off. Cool slightly, then mash with the butter, the milk and two of the egg yolks. Season to taste with salt and pepper.

5 Preheat the grill and grease a baking sheet. Spoon the potato mixture into a piping bag fitted with a medium star nozzle. Pipe six oval nests on to the baking sheet. Beat the remaining egg yolk with a little water and carefully brush over the potato. Grill for 5 minutes or until golden.

6 Spoon the tomato mixture inside the nests and top with a little parsley. Serve them immediately.

Gratin Dauphinois

This popular bake is a good alternative to traditional roast potatoes, particularly as it needs no last-minute attention.

Serves 8
butter, for greasing
1.6kg/3½lb potatoes
2–3 garlic cloves, crushed

115g/4oz/1 cup grated
    Cheddar cheese
2.5ml/½ tsp freshly
    grated nutmeg
600ml/1 pint/2½ cups milk
300ml/½ pint/1¼ cups
    single cream
2 large eggs, beaten
salt and ground black pepper

1 Preheat the oven to 180°C/350°F/Gas 4. Generously grease a 2.4 litre/4 pint/10 cup shallow ovenproof dish with butter. Peel the potatoes and slice them thinly.

2 Layer the potatoes in the dish, with the garlic and two-thirds of the grated cheese. Season each layer with salt and pepper to taste and a little grated nutmeg.

3 Whisk the milk, cream and eggs in a jug, then pour the mixture over the potatoes. If necessary, prick the layered potatoes with a skewer so that the liquid goes all the way to the bottom of the dish.

4 Scatter the remaining grated cheese on top and bake for 45–50 minutes, or until golden brown. Test the potatoes with a sharp knife; they should be very tender. Serve immediately.

Variations
• For a lower-fat version, substitute skimmed milk for the full-cream milk. Omit the cheese and cream and use 150g/5oz fromage blanc instead.
• For gratin savoyarde, omit the milk, cream and eggs. Substitute Beaufort cheese for the Cheddar. Layer the potatoes with the cheese and knobs of butter, then pour in 900ml/1½ pints/3¾ cups vegetable stock. Bake as above.

Swiss Soufflé Potatoes

A fabulous combination of rich and satisfying ingredients – cheese, eggs, cream, butter and potatoes. This is perfect for cold-weather entertaining.

Serves 4
4 floury baking potatoes, total
    weight about 900g/2lb
115g/4oz/1 cup grated
    Gruyère cheese
115g/4oz/ ½ cup herb butter
60ml/4 tbsp double cream
2 eggs, separated
salt and ground black pepper
snipped fresh chives, to garnish
mayonnaise, to serve (optional)

1 Preheat the oven to 220°C/425°F/Gas 7. Prick the potatoes all over with a fork. Bake for 1–1½ hours, until tender. Remove them from the oven and reduce the temperature to 180°C/350°F/Gas 4.

2 Cut each potato in half and scoop out the flesh into a bowl. Place the potato shells on a baking sheet and return them to the oven to crisp up while you are making the filling.

3 Mash the potato flesh, then add the Gruyère, herb butter, cream and egg yolks. Beat well until smooth, then taste and add salt and pepper if needed.

4 Whisk the egg whites to stiff peaks, then carefully fold them into the potato mixture. Pile the mixture into the potato shells and bake for 20–25 minutes until risen and golden brown.

5 Transfer the potatoes to a warm serving dish, garnish with chives and serve with mayonnaise, if you like.

> **Cook's Tip**
> To make the herb butter, mix 45ml/3 tbsp finely chopped fresh parsley and 10ml/2 tsp finely chopped fresh dill with 115g/4oz/ ½ cup softened butter. Season with a little salt.

Caribbean Roasted Sweet Potatoes, Onions & Beetroot

An aromatic coconut, ginger and garlic paste makes a medley of root vegetables truly memorable.

Serves 4
30ml/2 tbsp groundnut oil
450g/1lb sweet potatoes, peeled
    and cut into thick strips
    or chunks
4 freshly cooked beetroot, peeled
    and cut into wedges
450g/1lb small red or yellow
    onions, halved
5ml/1 tsp coriander seeds,
    lightly crushed
3–4 small whole fresh red chillies

salt and ground black pepper
chopped fresh coriander,
    to garnish

For the paste
2 large garlic cloves, chopped
1–2 fresh green chillies, seeded
    and chopped
15ml/1 tbsp chopped fresh
    root ginger
45ml/3 tbsp chopped
    fresh coriander
76ml/5 tbsp coconut milk
30ml/2 tbsp groundnut oil
grated rind of ½ lime
2.5ml/ ½ tsp light
    muscovado sugar

1 Preheat the oven to 200°C/400°F/Gas 6. Make the paste. Process the garlic, chillies, ginger, coriander and coconut milk in a food processor or blender. Scrape the paste into a small bowl and beat in the oil, lime rind and muscovado sugar.

2 Heat the oil in a roasting tin in the oven for 5 minutes. Add the sweet potatoes, beetroot, onions and coriander seeds, tossing them in the hot oil. Roast for 10 minutes.

3 Stir in the paste and the whole red chillies. Season to taste with salt and pepper and toss the vegetables to coat them thoroughly with the paste.

4 Roast the vegetables for a further 25–35 minutes, or until the sweet potatoes and onions are fully cooked and tender. Stir occasionally to prevent the paste from sticking to the tin. Transfer to a warmed platter and serve immediately, sprinkled with a little chopped fresh coriander.

Pilau Rice with Whole Spices

This fragrant rice dish makes a perfect accompaniment to any Indian vegetarian dish.

Serves 4
600ml/1 pint/2½ cups hot vegetable stock
generous pinch of saffron strands
250g/9oz/1⅓ cups basmati rice
50g/2oz/¼ cup butter
1 onion, chopped
1 garlic clove, crushed
½ cinnamon stick
6 green cardamom pods
1 bay leaf
50g/2oz/⅓ cup sultanas
15ml/1 tbsp sunflower oil
50g/2oz/½ cup cashew nuts
naan bread and tomato and onion salad, to serve (optional)

1 Pour the stock into a jug and stir in the saffron strands. Set aside to infuse. Rinse the rice several times in cold water. If there is time, leave it to soak for 30 minutes in the water used for the final rinse.

2 Heat the butter in a saucepan and fry the onion and garlic for 5 minutes. Stir in the cinnamon stick, cardamoms and bay leaf and cook for 2 minutes.

3 Drain the rice thoroughly, add it to the pan and cook, stirring, for 2 minutes more. Pour in the saffron-flavoured stock and add the sultanas. Bring to the boil, stir, then lower the heat, cover and cook gently for about 10 minutes, or until the rice is tender and all the liquid has been absorbed.

4 Meanwhile, heat the oil in a frying pan and fry the cashew nuts until browned. Drain well on kitchen paper. Scatter the cashew nuts over the rice. Serve with naan bread and a tomato and onion salad, if you like.

> **Cook's Tip**
> Don't be tempted to use black cardamoms in this dish. They are coarser and more strongly flavoured than green cardamoms and are only used in dishes that are cooked for a long time.

Indonesian Coconut Rice

This way of cooking rice is very popular throughout the whole of South-east Asia.

Serves 4–6
350g/12oz/1¾ cups Thai fragrant rice
400ml/14fl oz can coconut milk
300ml/½ pint/1¼ cups water
2.5ml/½ tsp ground coriander
5cm/2in piece of cinnamon stick
1 lemon grass stalk, bruised
1 bay leaf
salt
deep-fried onions (see Cook's Tip), to garnish

1 Put the rice in a strainer and rinse thoroughly under cold water. Drain well, then put in a pan. Pour in the coconut milk and water. Add the coriander, cinnamon stick, lemon grass and bay leaf. Season with salt. Bring to the boil, then lower the heat, cover and simmer for 8–10 minutes.

2 Lift the lid and check that all the liquid has been absorbed, then fork the rice through carefully, removing the cinnamon stick, lemon grass and bay leaf.

3 Cover the pan with a tight-fitting lid and continue to cook over the lowest possible heat for 3–5 minutes more.

4 Pile the rice on to a warm serving dish and serve garnished with the crisp, deep-fried onions.

> **Cook's Tips**
> • Deep-fried onions are a traditional Indonesian garnish. You can buy them ready-prepared from Oriental food stores, but they are easy to make at home. Slice 450g/1lb onions very thinly, then spread the slices in a single layer on kitchen paper. Leave to dry for at least 1 hour, preferably longer. Deep-fry in batches in hot oil until crisp and golden. Drain on kitchen paper and use at once, or cool, then store in an airtight container.
> • If you have access to a well-stocked Oriental supermarket, substitute a pandan leaf for the bay leaf. Pull the tines of a fork through the leaf to release its flavour.

Tomato Rice

Proof positive that you don't need elaborate ingredients or complicated cooking methods to make a delicious dish.

Serves 4
400g/14oz/2 cups basmati rice
30ml/2 tbsp sunflower oil
2.5ml/ ½ tsp onion seeds
1 onion, sliced
2 tomatoes, chopped
1 orange or yellow pepper,
  seeded and sliced
5ml/1 tsp crushed fresh
  root ginger
1 garlic clove, crushed
5ml/1 tsp hot chilli powder
1 potato, diced
7.5ml/1 ½ tsp salt
750ml/1 ¼ pints/3 cups water
30–45ml/2–3 tbsp chopped
  fresh coriander

1 Rinse the rice several times in cold water. If there is sufficient time, leave it to soak for about 30 minutes in the water used for the final rinse.

2 Heat the oil in a large, heavy-based pan and fry the onion seeds for about 30 seconds, until they are giving off their aroma. Add the sliced onion and fry over a low heat, stirring occasionally, for 5 minutes, then increase the heat slightly.

3 Stir in the tomatoes, orange or yellow pepper, ginger, garlic, chilli powder, diced potato and salt. Stir-fry over a medium heat for about 5 minutes more.

4 Drain the rice thoroughly. Add it to the pan, then stir for about 1 minute until the grains are well coated in the spicy vegetable mixture.

5 Pour in the water and bring it to the boil, then lower the heat, cover the pan with a tight-fitting lid and cook the rice for 12–15 minutes. Remove from the heat, without lifting the lid, and leave the rice to stand for 5 minutes.

6 Gently fork through the rice to fluff up the grains, stir in the chopped coriander and transfer to a warmed serving dish. Serve immediately.

Wild Rice Pilaff

Wild rice isn't a rice at all, but is actually a type of wild grass. Call it what you will, it has a wonderful nutty flavour and makes a fine addition to this fruity, Middle-Eastern mixture.

Serves 6
200g/7oz/1 cup wild rice
40g/1 ½oz/3 tbsp butter
½ onion, finely chopped
200g/7oz/1 cup long grain rice
475ml/16fl oz/2 cups
  vegetable stock
75g/3oz/ ¾ cup flaked almonds
115g/4oz/ ⅔ cup sultanas
30ml/2 tbsp chopped
  fresh parsley
salt and ground black pepper

1 Bring a large pan of lightly salted water to the boil. Add the wild rice and 5ml/1 tsp salt. Lower the heat, cover and simmer gently for 45–60 minutes, until the rice is tender. Drain well.

2 Meanwhile, melt 15g/ ½oz/1 tbsp of the butter in another pan and fry the onion until it is just softened. Stir in the long grain rice and cook for 1 minute more.

3 Stir in the stock and bring to the boil. Lower the heat, cover tightly and simmer gently for about 30 minutes, until the rice is tender and the liquid has been absorbed.

4 Melt the remaining butter in a small pan. Add the almonds and cook until they are just golden. Set aside.

5 Tip both types of rice into a warmed serving dish and stir in the almonds, sultanas and half the parsley. Adjust the seasoning if necessary. Sprinkle with the remaining parsley and serve.

> **Cook's Tip**
> Like all pilaff dishes, this one must be made with well-flavoured stock. Make your own, if possible, and let it reduce so that the flavour intensifies.

Minted Couscous Castles

These pretty little timbales are perfect for serving as part of a summer lunch. They're virtually fat-free, so you can indulge yourself with impunity.

Makes 4
225g/8oz/1¼ cups couscous
475ml/16fl oz/2 cups boiling
   vegetable stock
15ml/1 tbsp lemon juice
2 tomatoes, diced
30ml/2 tbsp chopped fresh mint
vegetable oil, for brushing
salt and ground black pepper
fresh mint sprigs, to garnish

1 Put the couscous in a bowl and pour over the boiling stock. Cover and leave to stand for 30 minutes, until all the stock has been absorbed and the grains are tender.

2 Stir in the lemon juice with the tomatoes and chopped mint. Season to taste with salt and pepper.

3 Brush the insides of four cups or individual moulds lightly with oil. Spoon in the couscous mixture and pack down firmly. Chill for several hours.

4 Invert the castles on a platter and serve cold, garnished with mint. Alternatively, cover and heat gently in a low oven, then turn out and serve hot.

Cook's Tip
Moroccan couscous, the kind most commonly seen in Western supermarkets, is produced in fairly small grains, whereas the grains of Israeli couscous are about the size of peppercorns, and Lebanese couscous resembles small chick-peas in appearance. All three types may be cooked in the slow, traditional manner. Only Moroccan couscous is produced in an "instant", ready-cooked form, but this is not immediately distinguishable from traditional couscous, so always check the instructions on the packet.

Stir-fried Noodles with Beansprouts

A classic Chinese noodle dish that makes a marvellous accompaniment. In China, noodles are served at virtually every meal – even breakfast.

Serves 4
175g/6oz dried egg noodles
15ml/1 tbsp vegetable oil
1 garlic clove, finely chopped
1 small onion, halved and sliced
225g/8oz/2 cups beansprouts
1 small red pepper, seeded and
   cut into strips
1 small green pepper, seeded and
   cut into strips
2.5ml/½ tsp salt
1.5ml/¼ tsp ground
   white pepper
30ml/2 tbsp light soy sauce

1 Bring a large pan of water to the boil. Add the noodles and remove the pan from the heat. Cover and leave to stand for about 4 minutes, until the noodles are just tender.

2 Heat the oil in a wok. When it is very hot, add the garlic, stir briefly, then add the onion slices. Cook, stirring, for 1 minute, then add the beansprouts and peppers. Stir-fry for 2–3 minutes.

3 Drain the noodles thoroughly, then add them to the wok. Toss over the heat, using two spatulas or wooden spoons, for 2–3 minutes, or until the ingredients are well mixed and have heated through.

4 Add the salt, white pepper and soy sauce and stir thoroughly before serving the noodle mixture in heated bowls.

Variations
This is a useful, basic noodle dish that not only makes a good accompaniment, but can also be easily adapted to make a more substantial main course. For example, add carrot batons, quartered button mushrooms and mangetouts with the beansprouts and peppers in step 2, or ½ cucumber, cut into batons, with the vegetables in step 2 and 115g/4oz/2 cups shredded spinach just before adding the noodles in step 3.

Warm Dressed Salad with Poached Eggs

Soft poached eggs, hot croûtons and cool, crisp salad leaves with a warm dressing make a lively and unusual combination.

Serves 2

½ small loaf Granary bread
45ml/3 tbsp walnut oil
2 eggs
115g/4oz mixed salad leaves
45ml/3 tbsp extra virgin olive oil
2 garlic cloves, crushed
15ml/1 tbsp balsamic or
   sherry vinegar
50g/2oz piece of Parmesan
   cheese, shaved
ground black pepper (optional)

1 Carefully cut off the crust from the Granary loaf and discard it. Cut the bread into 2.5cm/1in cubes.

2 Heat the walnut oil in a large, heavy-based frying pan. Add the bread cubes and cook over a low heat for about 5 minutes, turning and tossing the cubes occasionally, until they are crisp and golden brown all over.

3 Bring a pan of water to the boil. Break each egg into a jug, one at a time, and carefully slide each one into the water. Gently poach the eggs over a low heat for about 4 minutes, until lightly cooked and the whites have just set.

4 Meanwhile, divide the salad leaves among two plates. Arrange the croûtons over the leaves.

5 Wipe the frying pan clean with kitchen paper. Heat the olive oil in the pan, add the garlic and vinegar and cook over a high heat for 1 minute. Pour the warm dressing over the salad on each plate.

6 Lift out each poached egg, in turn, with a draining spoon and place one on top of each of the salads. Top with thin shavings of Parmesan and a little freshly ground black pepper, if you like. Serve immediately.

Springtime Salad with Quail's Eggs

Enjoy some of the best early season garden vegetables in this crunchy green salad. Quail's eggs add a touch of sophistication and elegance.

Serves 4

175g/6oz broad beans
175g/6oz fresh peas
175g/6oz asparagus
175g/6oz very small new
   potatoes, scrubbed
45ml/3 tbsp good lemon
   mayonnaise (see Cook's Tip)
45ml/3 tbsp soured cream or
   crème fraîche
½ bunch fresh mint, chopped,
   plus whole leaves for garnishing
8 quail's eggs, soft-boiled
   and peeled
salt and ground black pepper

1 Cook the broad beans, peas, asparagus and new potatoes in separate pans of lightly salted boiling water until just tender. Drain, refresh under cold water and drain again.

2 When the vegetables are cold, mix them lightly in a bowl.

3 Mix the mayonnaise with the soured cream or crème fraîche and chopped mint in a jug. Stir in salt and pepper, if needed.

4 Pour the dressing over the salad and toss to coat. Add the quail's eggs and whole mint leaves and toss very gently to mix. Serve immediately.

Cook's Tip
To make your own lemon mayonnaise, combine two egg yolks, 5ml/1 tsp Dijon mustard, and the grated rind and juice of half a lemon in a blender or food processor. Add salt and pepper to taste. Process to combine. With the motor running, add about 250ml/8fl oz/1 cup mild olive oil (or a mixture of olive oil and sunflower oil) through the lid or feeder tube, until the mixture emulsifies. Trickle the oil in at first, then add it in a steady stream. For a glossy mayonnaise, beat in about 15ml/1 tbsp boiling water at the end.

Leek & Grilled Pepper Salad with Goat's Cheese

This is a perfect dish for entertaining, as the salad actually benefits from being made in advance.

Serves 6
4 x 1cm/ 1/2in slices goat's cheese
75g/3oz/ 1 cup fine dry
    white breadcrumbs
675g/1 1/2 lb young leeks
15ml/1 tbsp olive oil
2 large red peppers, halved
    and seeded

few fresh thyme sprigs, chopped
vegetable oil, for shallow frying
45ml/3 tbsp chopped fresh flat
    leaf parsley
salt and ground black pepper

For the dressing
75ml/5 tbsp extra virgin olive oil
1 small garlic clove,
    finely chopped
5ml/1 tsp Dijon mustard
15ml/1 tbsp red wine vinegar

1 Roll the cheese slices in the breadcrumbs, pressing them in so that the cheese is well coated. Chill the cheese for 1 hour.

2 Preheat the grill. Bring a saucepan of lightly salted water to the boil and cook the leeks for 3–4 minutes. Drain, cut into 10cm/4in lengths and place in a bowl. Add the olive oil, toss to coat, then season to taste. Place the leeks on a grill rack and grill for 3–4 minutes on each side.

3 Set the leeks aside. Place the peppers on the grill rack, skin side up, and grill until blackened and blistered. Place them in a bowl, cover with crumpled kitchen paper and leave for 10 minutes. Rub off the skin and cut the flesh into strips. Place in a bowl and add the leeks, thyme and a little pepper.

4 Make the dressing by shaking all the ingredients together in a jar, adding seasoning to taste. Pour the dressing over the leek mixture, cover and chill for several hours.

5 Heat a little oil and fry the cheese until golden on both sides. Drain and cool, then cut into bite-size pieces. Toss the cheese and parsley into the salad and serve at room temperature.

Butternut Salad with Feta Cheese

This is especially good served with a grain or starchy salad, based on rice or couscous. The salad is best served warm or at room temperature, rather than chilled.

Serves 4–6
75ml/5 tbsp olive oil
15ml/1 tbsp balsamic vinegar,
    plus a little extra if needed
15ml/1 tbsp sweet soy sauce
    (kecap manis)

350g/12oz shallots, peeled but
    left whole
3 fresh red chillies, chopped
1 butternut squash, peeled,
    seeded and cut into chunks
5ml/1 tsp finely chopped
    fresh thyme
15g/ 1/2 oz/ 1/2 cup flat
    leaf parsley
1 small garlic clove,
    finely chopped
75g/3oz/3/4 cup walnuts, chopped
150g/5oz feta cheese
salt and ground black pepper

1 Preheat the oven to 200°C/400°F/Gas 6. Put the olive oil, balsamic vinegar and soy sauce in a large bowl and beat until thoroughly incorporated.

2 Toss the shallots and two of the chillies in the oil mixture and tip into a large, shallow roasting tin. Roast, uncovered, for about 25 minutes, stirring once or twice.

3 Add the butternut squash and roast for 35–40 minutes more, stirring once, until the squash is tender and browned. Remove from the oven, stir in the chopped thyme and set the vegetables aside to cool.

4 Chop the parsley and garlic together and mix with the walnuts. Seed and finely chop the remaining chilli.

5 Stir the parsley, garlic and walnut mixture into the cooled vegetables. Add the remaining chopped chilli. Taste and season with salt and pepper, if necessary, and add a little extra balsamic vinegar. Crumble the feta and add it to the salad.

6 Transfer to a serving dish and serve immediately, at room temperature, rather than chilled.

Roasted Plum Tomato & Rocket Salad

This is a good side salad to accompany a cheese flan or a fresh herb pizza.

Serves 4

450g/1lb ripe baby Italian plum
   tomatoes, halved lengthways
75ml/5 tbsp extra virgin olive oil
2 garlic cloves, cut into thin slivers
225g/8oz/2 cups dried
   pasta shapes
30ml/2 tbsp balsamic vinegar
2 pieces sun-dried tomato in olive
   oil, drained and chopped
large pinch of granulated sugar
1 handful rocket leaves
salt and ground black pepper

1 Preheat the oven to 190°C/375°F/Gas 5. Arrange the halved tomatoes, cut side up, in a roasting tin. Drizzle 30ml/ 2 tbsp of the oil over them and sprinkle with the slivers of garlic and salt and pepper to taste. Roast for 20 minutes, turning once.

2 Meanwhile, bring a large pan of lightly salted water to the boil and cook the pasta until it is al dente.

3 Put the remaining oil in a large bowl with the vinegar, sun-dried tomatoes and sugar with salt and pepper to taste.

4 Drain the pasta, add it to the bowl of dressing and toss to mix. Add the roasted tomatoes and mix gently.

5 Just before serving, add the rocket leaves, toss lightly and taste for seasoning. Serve at room temperature or chilled.

Variations
• If you are in a hurry and don't have time to roast the tomatoes, you can make the salad with halved raw tomatoes instead, but make sure that they are really ripe.
• If you like, add 150g/5oz mozzarella cheese, drained and diced, with the rocket.

Chargrilled Pepper Salad with Pesto

The ingredients of this colourful salad are simple and few, but the overall flavour is quite intense.

Serves 4

1 large red pepper, halved
   and seeded
1 large green pepper, halved
   and seeded
250g/9oz/2¼ cups dried fusilli
   tricolore or other pasta shapes
1 handful fresh basil leaves
1 handful fresh coriander leaves
1 garlic clove
salt and ground black pepper

For the dressing
30ml/2 tbsp bottled pesto
juice of ½ lemon
60ml/4 tbsp extra virgin olive oil

1 Place the red and green pepper halves, skin side up, on a grill rack and grill until the skins have blistered and are beginning to char. Transfer the peppers to a bowl, cover with crumpled kitchen paper and leave to cool slightly. When they are cool enough to handle, rub off the skins and discard.

2 Bring a large pan of lightly salted water to the boil and cook the pasta until it is al dente.

3 Meanwhile, whisk together the pesto, lemon juice and olive oil in a large bowl. Season to taste with salt and pepper.

4 Drain the cooked pasta well and tip it into the bowl of dressing. Toss thoroughly to mix and set aside to cool.

5 Chop the pepper flesh and add it to the pasta. Put most of the basil and coriander and all the garlic on a board and chop them. Add the herb mixture to the pasta and toss, then season to taste, if necessary, and serve, garnished with the herb leaves.

Cook's Tip
Serve the salad at room temperature or lightly chilled, whichever you prefer.

Gado Gado

The peanut sauce on this traditional Indonesian salad owes its flavour to galangal, an aromatic rhizome that resembles ginger.

Serves 4
250g/9oz white
    cabbage, shredded
4 carrots, cut into
    matchstick strips
4 celery sticks, cut into
    matchstick strips
225g/8oz/2 cups beansprouts
1/2 cucumber, cut into
    matchstick strips
fried onion, salted peanuts and
    sliced fresh chilli, to garnish

For the peanut sauce
15ml/1 tbsp vegetable oil
1 small onion, finely chopped
1 garlic clove, crushed
1 small piece galangal, grated
5ml/1 tsp ground cumin
1.5ml/ 1/4 tsp mild chilli powder
5ml/1 tsp tamarind paste or
    freshly squeezed lime juice
60ml/4 tbsp crunchy
    peanut butter
5ml/1 tsp soft light brown sugar

1 Steam the cabbage, carrots and celery for 3–4 minutes, until just tender. Cool. Spread out the beansprouts on a serving dish. Top with the cabbage, carrots, celery and cucumber.

2 Make the sauce. Heat the oil in a saucepan, add the onion and garlic and cook gently for 5 minutes, until soft. Stir in the galangal, cumin and chilli powder and cook for 1 minute more. Stir in the tamarind paste or lime juice, peanut butter and sugar.

3 Heat gently, stirring occasionally and adding a little hot water, if necessary, to make a coating sauce. Spoon a little of the sauce over the vegetables and garnish with fried onions, peanuts and sliced chilli. Serve the rest of the sauce separately.

> **Variations**
> As long as the sauce remains the same, the vegetables can be altered at the whim of the cook and the season.

Couscous Salad

Couscous has become an extremely popular salad ingredient, and there are many variations on the classic theme. This salad comes from Morocco.

Serves 4
275g/10oz/1 2/3 cups couscous
550ml/18fl oz/2 1/2 cups boiling
    vegetable stock
16–20 stoned black olives, halved
2 small courgettes, cut in
    matchstick strips

25g/1oz/ 1/4 cup flaked
    almonds, toasted
60ml/4 tbsp olive oil
15ml/1 tbsp lemon juice
15ml/1 tbsp chopped
    fresh coriander
15ml/1 tbsp chopped
    fresh parsley
good pinch of ground cumin
good pinch of cayenne pepper
salt

1 Place the couscous in a bowl and pour over the boiling stock. Stir with a fork, then set aside for 10 minutes for the stock to be absorbed. Fluff up with a fork.

2 Add the olives, courgettes and almonds to the couscous and mix in gently.

3 Whisk the olive oil, lemon juice, coriander, parsley, cumin, cayenne and a pinch of salt in a jug. Pour the dressing over the salad and toss to mix.

> **Cook's Tip**
> This salad benefits from being made several hours ahead, so that the flavours can blend.

> **Variations**
> • You can substitute 1/2 cucumber for the courgettes and pistachios for the almonds.
> • For extra heat, add a pinch of chilli powder to the dressing.

Tabbouleh

The classic bulgur wheat salad, this remains a winner. Serve it with roasted or barbecued vegetables.

Serves 4

150g/5oz/scant 1 cup
   bulgur wheat
600ml/1 pint/2½ cups water
3 spring onions, finely chopped
2 large garlic cloves, crushed
4 firm tomatoes, peeled
   and chopped
90ml/6 tbsp chopped
   fresh parsley
60ml/4 tbsp chopped fresh mint
90ml/6 tbsp fresh lemon juice
75ml/5 tbsp extra virgin olive oil
salt and ground black pepper

1 Place the bulgur wheat in a bowl and pour over the water. Leave to soak for 20 minutes.

2 Line a colander with a clean dish towel. Tip the soaked bulgur wheat into the centre, let it drain, then gather up the sides of the dish towel and squeeze out any remaining liquid. Tip the bulgur wheat into a large bowl.

3 Add the spring onions, garlic, tomatoes, parsley and mint. Mix well, then pour over the lemon juice and olive oil. Season generously with salt and pepper, then toss so that all the ingredients are combined. Cover and chill in the fridge for several hours before serving.

Ratatouille

Wonderfully versatile, ratatouille can be served hot or cold. Apart from being a good side dish, it makes an excellent filling for baked potatoes and warm tortillas and a good sauce for pasta.

Serves 4–6

60ml/4 tbsp olive oil
2 large onions, chopped
2 garlic cloves, crushed
2 large aubergines, cut into
   large cubes
3 courgettes, thickly sliced
2 peppers (red and green),
   seeded and sliced
3 large tomatoes, peeled, seeded
   and chopped
15ml/1 tbsp sun-dried tomato
   purée dissolved in 30ml/2 tbsp
   boiling water
30ml/2 tbsp chopped
   fresh coriander
salt and ground black pepper

1 Heat the oil in a large pan and fry the onions and garlic until softened. Add the aubergines and fry for 10 minutes, stirring frequently. Stir in the courgettes, peppers and tomatoes, with the diluted tomato purée and plenty of salt and pepper.
2 Bring to the boil, then lower the heat and simmer for about 30 minutes, stirring occasionally and adding a little water if needed, until the vegetables are just tender. Stir in the coriander and serve hot or cold.

Cook's Tip
If you have time, salt the aubergine cubes in a colander over the sink for 20 minutes. Rinse well and pat dry before using.

Cracked Wheat Salad with Oranges & Almonds

The citrus flavours of lemon and orange really come through in this tasty salad, which can be made several hours before serving.

Serves 4

150g/5oz/scant 1 cup
   bulgur wheat
600ml/1 pint/2½ cups water
1 small green pepper, seeded
   and diced
¼ cucumber, diced
15g/½oz/½ cup chopped
   fresh mint
60ml/4 tbsp flaked
   almonds, toasted
grated rind and juice of 1 lemon
2 seedless oranges
salt and ground black pepper
fresh mint sprigs, to garnish

1 Place the bulgur wheat in a bowl, pour over the water and leave to soak for 20 minutes.

2 Line a colander with a clean dish towel. Tip the soaked bulgur wheat into the centre, let it drain, then gather up the sides of the dish towel and squeeze out any remaining liquid. Tip the bulgur wheat into a large bowl.

3 Add the green pepper, diced cucumber, mint, toasted almonds and grated lemon rind. Pour in the lemon juice and toss thoroughly to mix.

4 Cut the rind from the oranges, then, working over a bowl to catch the juice, cut both oranges into neat segments. Add the segments and the juice to the bulgur mixture, then season to taste with salt and pepper and toss lightly. Garnish with the mint sprigs and serve.

Cook's Tip
Bulgur is also known as cracked wheat because the grains are cracked after hulling and steaming and before drying.

Spanish Rice Salad

Ribbons of green and yellow pepper add colour and flavour to this simple salad.

Serves 6

275g/10oz/1½ cups white
   long grain rice
1 bunch spring onions,
   thinly sliced
1 green pepper, seeded
   and sliced
1 yellow pepper, seeded
   and sliced

3 tomatoes, peeled, seeded
   and chopped
30ml/2 tbsp chopped
   fresh coriander

For the dressing

45ml/3 tbsp mixed sunflower
   and olive oil
15ml/1 tbsp rice vinegar
5ml/1 tsp Dijon mustard
salt and ground black pepper

1 Bring a large pan of lightly salted water to the boil and cook the rice for 10–12 minutes, until tender but still slightly firm at the centre of the grain. Do not overcook. Drain, rinse under cold water and drain again. Leave until cold.

2 Place the rice in a large serving bowl. Add the spring onions, peppers, tomatoes and coriander.

3 Make the dressing. Mix the oils, vinegar and mustard in a jar with a tight-fitting lid and season to taste with salt and pepper. Shake vigorously. Stir 60–75ml/4–5 tbsp of the dressing into the rice and adjust the seasoning, if necessary.

4 Cover and chill for about 1 hour before serving. Offer the remaining dressing separately.

> **Variations**
> • Cooked garden peas, cooked diced carrot and drained, canned sweetcorn can be added to this versatile salad.
> • This recipe works well with long grain rice, but if you can obtain Spanish rice, it will be more authentic. This has a rounder grain, a little like risotto rice.

Fruity Brown Rice Salad

An Oriental-style dressing gives this colourful rice salad extra piquancy.

Serves 4–6

115g/4oz/⅔ cup brown rice
1 small red pepper, seeded
   and diced
200g/7oz can sweetcorn
   kernels, drained
45ml/3 tbsp sultanas

225g/8oz can pineapple pieces
   in fruit juice
15ml/1 tbsp light soy sauce
15ml/1 tbsp sunflower oil
15ml/1 tbsp hazelnut oil
1 garlic clove, crushed
5ml/1 tsp finely chopped
   fresh root ginger
salt and ground black pepper
4 spring onions, diagonally sliced,
   to garnish

1 Bring a large pan of lightly salted water to the boil and cook the brown rice for about 30 minutes, or until it is just tender. Drain thoroughly, rinse under cold water and drain again. Set aside to cool.

2 Tip the rice into a bowl and add the red pepper, sweetcorn and sultanas. Drain the pineapple pieces, reserving the juice, then add them to the rice mixture and toss lightly.

3 Pour the reserved pineapple juice into a clean screw-top jar. Add the soy sauce, sunflower and hazelnut oils, garlic and chopped root ginger and season to taste with salt and pepper. Close the jar tightly and shake vigorously.

4 Pour the dressing over the salad and toss well. Scatter the spring onions over the top and serve.

> **Cook's Tips**
> • Hazelnut oil gives a distinctive flavour to any salad dressing and is especially good for leafy salads that need a bit of a lift. It is like olive oil, in that it contains mainly monounsaturated fats.
> • Brown rice is often mistakenly called wholegrain. In fact, the outer husk is completely inedible and is removed from all rice, but the bran layer is left intact on brown rice.

Sesame Noodle Salad

Toasted sesame oil adds a nutty flavour to this salad, which is at its best when served warm.

Serves 2–4
250g/9oz medium egg noodles
200g/7oz/1¾ cups sugar snap
   peas or mangetouts,
   sliced diagonally
2 carrots, cut into
   matchstick strips
2 tomatoes, seeded and diced
30ml/2 tbsp chopped fresh
   coriander, plus coriander sprigs,
   to garnish

15ml/1 tbsp sesame seeds
3 spring onions, shredded

For the dressing
10ml/2 tsp light soy sauce
30ml/2 tbsp toasted sesame
   seed oil
15ml/1 tbsp sunflower oil
4cm/1½in piece of fresh root
   ginger, finely grated
1 garlic clove, crushed

1 Bring a large pan of water to the boil, add the noodles and remove the pan from the heat. Cover and leave to stand for about 4 minutes, until the noodles are just tender.

2 Meanwhile, bring a second, smaller saucepan of water to the boil. Add the sugar snap peas or mangetouts, bring back to the boil and cook for 2 minutes. Drain and refresh under cold water, then drain again.

3 Make the dressing. Put the soy sauce, sesame seed and sunflower oils, ginger and garlic in a screw-top jar. Close tightly and shake vigorously to mix.

4 Drain the noodles thoroughly and tip them into a large bowl. Add the peas or mangetouts, carrots, tomatoes and coriander. Pour the dressing over the top, and toss thoroughly with your hands to combine.

5 Sprinkle the salad with the sesame seeds, top with the shredded spring onions and coriander sprigs and serve while the noodles are still warm.

Japanese Salad

Delicate and refreshing, this is based on a mild-flavoured, sweet-tasting seaweed, combined with radishes, cucumber and beansprouts.

Serves 4
15g/½oz/½ cup dried hijiki
250g/9oz/1¼ cups radishes,
   sliced into very thin rounds
1 small cucumber, cut into
   thin sticks
75g/3oz/¾ cup beansprouts

For the dressing
15ml/1 tbsp sunflower oil
15ml/1 tbsp toasted sesame oil
5ml/1 tsp light soy sauce
30ml/2 tbsp rice vinegar or
   15ml/1 tbsp wine vinegar
15ml/1 tbsp mirin or dry sherry

1 Place the hijiki in a bowl and add cold water to cover. Soak for 10–15 minutes, until it is rehydrated, then drain, rinse under cold running water and drain again. It should have almost trebled in volume.

2 Place the hijiki in a saucepan of water. Bring to the boil, then lower the heat and simmer for about 30 minutes, or until tender. Drain well.

3 Meanwhile, make the dressing. Place the sunflower and sesame oils, soy sauce, vinegar and mirin or sherry in a screw-top jar. Shake vigorously to combine.

4 Arrange the hijiki in a shallow bowl or platter with the radishes, cucumber and beansprouts. Pour over the dressing and toss lightly.

Cook's Tip
Hijiki is a type of seaweed. A rich source of minerals, it comes from Japan, where it has a distinguished reputation for enhancing beauty and adding lustre to hair. Look for hijiki in Oriental food stores.

Fragrant Lentil & Spinach Salad

This earthy salad is great for a picnic or barbecue.

Serves 6
225g/8oz/1 cup Puy lentils
1 fresh bay leaf
1 celery stick
1 fresh thyme sprig
30ml/2 tbsp olive oil
1 onion, finely sliced
10ml/2 tsp crushed toasted
 cumin seeds
400g/14oz young spinach leaves
30–45ml/2–3 tbsp chopped fresh

parsley, plus a few extra sprigs
 for garnishing
salt and ground black pepper
toasted French bread, to serve

For the dressing
45ml/3 tbsp extra virgin olive oil
5ml/1 tsp Dijon mustard
15–25ml/3–5 tsp red
 wine vinegar
1 small garlic clove,
 finely chopped
2.5ml/ 1/2 tsp finely grated
 lemon rind

1 Rinse the lentils and place them in a large saucepan. Add water to cover. Tie the bay leaf, celery and thyme into a bundle and add to the pan, then bring to the boil. Lower the heat to a steady boil. Cook the lentils for 30–45 minutes, until just tender.

2 Meanwhile, make the dressing. Mix the oil and mustard with 15ml/1 tbsp of the vinegar. Add the garlic and lemon rind, and whisk to mix. Season well with salt and pepper.

3 Drain the lentils and discard the herbs. Tip them into a bowl, add most of the dressing and toss. Set aside and stir occasionally.

4 Heat the oil in a pan and cook the onion for 4–5 minutes, until it starts to soften. Add the cumin and cook for 1 minute.

5 Add the spinach and season to taste, then cover and cook for 2 minutes. Stir, then cook again briefly until wilted.

6 Stir the spinach into the lentils and leave the salad to cool to room temperature. Stir in the remaining dressing and chopped parsley. Adjust the seasoning, adding more vinegar if necessary. Spoon on to a serving platter, scatter some parsley sprigs over, and serve at room temperature with toasted French bread.

White Bean Salad with Roasted Red Pepper Dressing

The speckled herb and red pepper dressing adds a wonderful colour contrast to this salad, which is best served warm.

Serves 4
1 large red pepper, halved
 and seeded
30ml/2 tbsp olive oil

1 large garlic clove, crushed
25g/1oz/1 cup fresh oregano
 leaves or flat leaf parsley
10ml/2 tsp balsamic vinegar
400g/14oz/3 cups drained
 canned flageolet beans, rinsed
200g/7oz/1 1/2 cups drained
 canned cannellini beans, rinsed
salt and ground black pepper

1 Preheat the grill. Place the red pepper in a grill pan and cook under a medium heat until the skin is blistered and blackened all over. Place in a bowl and cover with crumpled kitchen paper. Set aside to cool slightly.

2 When the pepper is cool enough to handle, rub off the skin. Carefully pull away the core and seeds, saving any juices, then dice the flesh.

3 Heat the olive oil in a saucepan. Add the garlic and fry over a low heat, stirring constantly, for 1 minute, until softened. Remove the pan from the heat, then add the oregano or parsley. Stir in the diced red pepper and any reserved juices, then stir in the balsamic vinegar.

4 Put the beans in a large bowl and pour over the dressing. Season to taste with salt and pepper, then stir gently until thoroughly combined. Serve immediately.

> **Cook's Tip**
> Cannellini beans are always a creamy white, but flageolets may be green or white. The salad will look attractive either way, but if you prefer white beans, you could substitute haricots.

Sweet-&-sour Artichoke Salad

Beetroot & Red Onion Salad

This salad looks especially attractive when it is made with a mixture of red and yellow beetroot.

Serves 6
500g/1¼lb small beetroot
75ml/5 tbsp water
60ml/4 tbsp olive oil
90g/3½ oz/scant 1 cup
    walnut halves
5ml/1 tsp caster sugar, plus a
    little extra for the dressing
30ml/2 tbsp walnut oil
15ml/1 tbsp sherry vinegar
5ml/1 tsp soy sauce
5ml/1 tsp grated orange rind
2.5ml/½ tsp ground roasted
    coriander seeds
5–10ml/1–2 tsp orange juice
1 red onion, halved and very
    thinly sliced
15–30ml/1–2 tbsp chopped
    fresh fennel
75g/3oz watercress or
    mizuna leaves
handful of baby red chard or
    beetroot leaves (optional)
salt and ground black pepper

1 Preheat the oven to 180°C/350°F/Gas 4. Place the beetroot in an ovenproof dish in a single layer and add the water. Cover tightly and roast for 1–1½ hours, or until they are just tender.

2 Cool, then peel the beetroot. Slice or cut them into strips and toss with 15ml/1 tbsp of the olive oil in a bowl. Set aside.

3 Heat 15ml/1 tbsp of the remaining olive oil in a small frying pan. Fry the walnuts until starting to brown. Add the sugar and cook, stirring, until starting to caramelize. Season with pepper and 2.5ml/½ tsp salt, then tip them on to a plate to cool.

4 In a jug, whisk together the remaining olive oil, the walnut oil, sherry vinegar, soy sauce, orange rind and coriander seeds. Season with salt and pepper and add a pinch of caster sugar. Whisk in orange juice to taste.

5 Separate the red onion slices into half-rings and add them to the beetroot. Pour over the dressing and toss well. When ready to serve, toss the salad with the fennel, watercress or mizuna and red chard or beetroot leaves, if using. Transfer to individual bowls or plates and sprinkle with the caramelized nuts.

This Italian salad combines spring vegetables with a deliciously piquant sauce called *agrodolce*.

Serves 4
juice of 1 lemon
6 small globe artichokes
30ml/2 tbsp olive oil
2 medium onions,
    roughly chopped
175g/6oz/1 cup fresh or frozen
    broad beans (shelled weight)
300ml/½ pint/1¼ cups water
175g/6oz/1½ cups fresh or
    frozen peas (shelled weight)
salt and ground black pepper
fresh mint leaves, to garnish

For the sauce
120ml/4fl oz/½ cup white
    wine vinegar
15ml/1 tbsp caster sugar
a handful of fresh mint leaves,
    roughly torn

1 Fill a bowl with cold water and add the lemon juice. Peel the outer leaves from the artichokes and discard them. Cut the artichokes into quarters and place them in the bowl of acidulated water to prevent them from discolouring.

2 Heat the oil in a large, heavy-based pan. Add the onions and fry over a low heat, stirring occasionally, until they are golden.

3 Stir in the beans, then drain the artichokes and add them to the pan. Pour in the measured water. Bring the water to the boil, lower the heat, cover and cook for 10–15 minutes.

4 Add the peas, season to taste with salt and pepper and cook for 5 minutes more, stirring from time to time, until the vegetables are tender. Drain them thoroughly, place them in a bowl, leave to cool, then cover and chill.

5 Make the sauce. Mix all the ingredients in a small pan. Heat gently for 2–3 minutes, until the sugar has dissolved. Simmer for about another 5 minutes, stirring occasionally. Remove from the heat and leave to cool.

6 To serve, drizzle the sauce over the vegetables and garnish with the fresh mint leaves.

Feta & Mint Potato Salad

The oddly named pink fir apple potatoes are perfect for this salad, and taste great with feta cheese, yogurt and fresh mint.

Serves 4
500g/1¼ lb pink fir
    apple potatoes
90g/3½ oz feta cheese, crumbled

For the dressing
225g/8oz/1 cup natural yogurt
15g/1/2oz/ ½ cup fresh
    mint leaves
30ml/2 tbsp mayonnaise
salt and ground black pepper

1 Steam the potatoes over a pan of boiling water for about 20 minutes, until tender.

2 Meanwhile, make the dressing. Mix the yogurt and mint in a food processor and pulse until the mint leaves are finely chopped. Scrape the mixture into a small bowl, stir in the mayonnaise and season to taste with salt and pepper.

3 Drain the potatoes well and tip them into a large bowl. Spoon the dressing over and scatter the feta cheese on top. Serve immediately.

Cook's Tip
Pink fir apple potatoes have a smooth waxy texture and retain their shape when cooked, making them ideal for salads. Charlotte, Belle de Fontenay and other special salad potatoes could be used instead.

Variations
• *Crumbled Kefalotiri or young Manchego could be used instead of the feta.*
• *For a richer dressing, use Greek-style yogurt.*

Baked Sweet Potato Salad

This salad has a truly tropical taste and is ideal served with Asian or Caribbean dishes.

Serves 4–6
1kg/2¼lb sweet potatoes
1 red pepper, seeded and
    finely diced
3 celery sticks, finely diced
¼ red skinned onion,
    finely chopped

1 fresh red chilli, finely chopped
salt and ground black pepper
coriander leaves, to garnish

For the dressing
45ml/3 tbsp chopped
    fresh coriander
juice of 1 lime
150ml/ ¼ pint/ ⅔ cup
    natural yogurt

1 Preheat the oven to 200°C/400°F/Gas 6. Wash the potatoes, pierce them all over with a fork and bake for about 40 minutes, or until tender.

2 Meanwhile, make the dressing. Whisk together the coriander, lime juice and yogurt in a small bowl and season to taste with salt and pepper. Chill in the fridge while you prepare the remaining salad ingredients.

3 In a large bowl, mix the diced red pepper, celery, chopped onion and chilli together.

4 Remove the potatoes from the oven. As soon as they are cool enough to handle, peel them and cut them into cubes. Add them to the bowl. Drizzle the dressing over and toss carefully. Taste and adjust the seasoning, if necessary. Serve, garnished with coriander leaves.

Cook's Tip
It is generally thought that the seeds are the hottest part of a chilli. In fact, they contain no capsaicin – the hot element – but it is intensely concentrated in the flesh surrounding them. Removing the seeds usually removes this extra hot flesh.

Grilled Onion & Aubergine Salad with Tahini

Deliciously smoky, this dish balances sweet and sharp flavours. It tastes good with crisp lettuce and sweet, sun-ripened tomatoes.

Serves 6
3 aubergines, cut into 1cm/
    ½in thick slices
675g/1½lb onions, thickly sliced
75–90ml/5–6 tbsp olive oil
45ml/3 tbsp roughly chopped flat
    leaf parsley
45ml/3 tbsp pine nuts, toasted
salt and ground black pepper

For the dressing
2 garlic cloves, crushed
150ml/ ¼ pint/ ⅔ cup light tahini
juice of 1–2 lemons
45–60ml/3–4 tbsp water

1 Place the aubergines in a colander, sprinkling each layer generously with salt. Leave to stand in the sink for about 45 minutes, then rinse thoroughly under cold running water and pat dry with kitchen paper.

2 Thread the onion slices on to skewers (soaked in cold water if wooden or bamboo), to keep them together.

3 Heat a ridged cast-iron griddle pan. Brush the aubergine slices and onions with about 45ml/3 tbsp of the oil and cook for 6–8 minutes on each side, brushing with more oil, as necessary. The vegetables should be browned and soft when cooked. The onions may need a little longer than the aubergines.

4 Arrange the vegetables on a serving dish and season to taste with salt and pepper. Sprinkle with the remaining olive oil if they look a bit dry.

5 To make the dressing, put the garlic and a pinch of salt in a mortar and crush with a pestle. Gradually work in the tahini. When it has been fully incorporated, gradually work in the juice of 1 lemon, then the water. Taste and add more lemon juice if you think the dressing needs it. Thin with more water, if necessary, so that the dressing is fairly runny.

6 Drizzle the dressing over the salad and set aside for 30–60 minutes for the flavours to mingle. Sprinkle with the chopped parsley and pine nuts. Serve the salad at room temperature, not chilled.

Cook's Tips
• *If you haven't got a cast-iron griddle pan, cook the vegetables under the grill.*
• *Tahini is a thick, smooth, oily paste made from sesame seeds. It is available from Middle Eastern stores, wholefood shops and from some supermarkets.*

Variation
Use red rather than yellow onions.

Oriental Salad

Ribboned vegetables and crisp beansprouts look very attractive, and taste good together. Serve this salad with samosas or Thai tempeh cakes.

Serves 4
225g/8oz/2 cups beansprouts
1 cucumber
2 carrots
1 small mooli (daikon) radish
1 small red onion, thinly sliced
2.5cm/1in piece of fresh root
    ginger, cut into thin matchsticks
1 small fresh red chilli, seeded
    and thinly sliced
a handful of fresh coriander
    leaves or mint leaves

For the oriental dressing
15ml/1 tbsp rice vinegar
15ml/1 tbsp light soy sauce
10ml/2 tsp vegetarian "oyster"
    sauce, or to taste
1 garlic clove, finely chopped
15ml/1 tbsp sesame oil
45ml/3 tbsp groundnut oil
30ml/2 tbsp sesame seeds,
    lightly toasted

1 Make the dressing. Put the vinegar, soy sauce, "oyster" sauce, garlic, sesame and groundnut oils and sesame seeds in a screw-top jar. Close the lid tightly and shake vigorously.

2 Wash the beansprouts under cold running water and drain thoroughly in a colander.

3 Peel the cucumber and cut it in half lengthways. Scoop out the seeds with a teaspoon and discard. Using a vegetable peeler, peel the cucumber flesh into long ribbon strips. Peel the carrots and mooli radish into similar strips.

4 Place the carrot, radish and cucumber strips in a large shallow serving dish. Add the beansprouts, onion, ginger, chilli and fresh coriander or mint and toss to mix. Pour the dressing over just before serving and toss lightly.

Cook's Tip
If you have difficulty tracking down the vegetarian version of oyster sauce, use more soy sauce instead.

Avocado, Red Onion & Spinach Salad with Polenta Croûtons

The simple lemon dressing gives a sharp tang to this sophisticated salad, while the croûtons, with their crunchy golden exterior and soft centre, add a contrast.

Serves 4

1 large red onion, cut into wedges
300g/11oz ready-made polenta,
    cut into 1cm/½in cubes
olive oil, for brushing
225g/8oz baby spinach leaves
1 avocado
5ml/1 tsp lemon juice

For the dressing
60ml/4 tbsp extra virgin olive oil
juice of ½ lemon
salt and ground black pepper

1 Preheat the oven to 200°C/400°F/Gas 6. Place the onion wedges and polenta cubes on a lightly oiled baking sheet and bake for 25 minutes, or until the onion is tender and the polenta is crisp and golden, turning everything frequently to prevent sticking. Leave to cool slightly.

2 Meanwhile, make the dressing. Place the olive oil and lemon juice in a screw-top jar. Add salt and pepper to taste, close the jar tightly and shake vigorously to combine.

3 Place the spinach in a serving bowl. Peel, stone and slice the avocado, then toss the slices in the lemon juice to prevent them from discolouring. Add them to the spinach with the onions.

4 Pour the dressing over the salad and toss gently. Sprinkle the polenta croûtons on top or hand them separately.

Cook's Tip
If you can't find ready-made polenta, you can make your own using instant polenta grains. Simply cook 115g/4oz/1 cup according to the instructions on the packet, then pour into a tray and leave to cool and set.

Watercress, Pear, Walnut & Roquefort Salad

Sharp-tasting blue Roquefort and peppery leaves are complemented in this salad by sweet fruit and crunchy nuts.

Serves 4
75g/3oz/¾ cup shelled
    walnuts, halved
2 red Williams' pears
15ml/1 tbsp lemon juice
1 large bunch watercress,
    about 150g/5oz, tough
    stalks removed
200g/7oz Roquefort cheese, cut
    into chunks

For the dressing
45ml/3 tbsp extra virgin olive oil
30ml/2 tbsp lemon juice
2.5ml/½ tsp clear honey
5ml/1 tsp Dijon mustard
salt and ground black pepper

1 Toast the walnuts in a dry frying pan over a low heat for about 2 minutes, until golden, tossing frequently to prevent them from burning.

2 Meanwhile, make the dressing. Put the olive oil, lemon juice, honey and mustard into a screw-top jar and season to taste with salt and pepper. Close the lid tightly and shake vigorously until thoroughly combined.

3 Core and slice the pears then toss them in the lemon juice to prevent them from discolouring. Place the slices in a bowl and add the watercress, walnuts and Roquefort. Pour the dressing over the salad, toss well and serve immediately.

Cook's Tip
For a special dinner party, fan the pears on a bed of the dressed watercress. Cut the pears in half, remove the cores, then, keeping them intact at the top, slice them lengthways. Brush them with lemon juice to prevent discoloration, then place one half, cut side down, on each salad. Press down gently to fan the slices. Sprinkle the toasted walnuts over.

Fattoush

This simple salad has been served for centuries in the Middle East. It has been adopted by restaurateurs all over the world, and you are as likely to encounter it in San Francisco as in Syria.

Serves 4

1 yellow or red pepper, seeded and sliced
1 large cucumber, roughly chopped
4–5 tomatoes, chopped
1 bunch spring onions, sliced
30ml/2 tbsp finely chopped fresh parsley
30ml/2 tbsp finely chopped fresh mint
30ml/2 tbsp finely chopped fresh coriander
2 garlic cloves, crushed
juice of 1 1/2 lemons
45ml/3 tbsp olive oil
salt and ground black pepper
2 pitta breads

1 Place the yellow or red pepper, cucumber and tomatoes in a large salad bowl. Add the spring onions, with the finely chopped parsley, mint and coriander.

2 Make the dressing. Mix the garlic with the lemon juice in a jug. Gradually whisk in the olive oil, then season to taste with salt and black pepper. Pour the dressing over the salad and toss lightly to mix.

3 Toast the pitta bread, in a toaster or under a hot grill until crisp. Serve with the salad.

> **Cook's Tip**
> People either love or hate fresh coriander. If you hate it, omit it and double the quantity of parsley.

> **Variation**
> If you prefer, make this salad in the traditional way. After toasting the pitta breads until crisp, crush them in your hand and sprinkle over the salad before serving.

Radish, Mango & Apple Salad

Clean, crisp tastes and mellow flavours make this salad a good choice at any time, although it is at its best with fresh garden radishes in early summer.

Serves 4

10–15 radishes
1 eating apple
2 celery stalks, thinly sliced
1 small ripe mango
fresh dill sprigs, to garnish

For the dressing

120ml/4fl oz/ 1/2 cup low fat crème fraîche
10ml/2 tsp creamed horseradish
15ml/1 tbsp chopped fresh dill
salt and ground black pepper

1 Make the dressing by mixing the crème fraîche with the creamed horseradish and dill in a small jug. Season with a little salt and pepper.

2 Top and tail the radishes, then slice them thinly. Place them in a bowl. Cut the apple into quarters, remove the core from each wedge, then slice them thinly and add it to the bowl with the celery.

3 Cut through the mango lengthways either side of the stone. Leaving the skin on each section, cross hatch the flesh, then bend it back so that the cubes stand proud of the skin. Slice them off with a small knife and add them to the bowl.

4 Pour the dressing over the vegetables and fruit and stir gently to coat. When ready to serve, spoon the salad into a salad bowl and garnish with the dill.

> **Cook's Tip**
> Radishes are members of the mustard family and may be red or white, round or elongated. They vary considerably in their strength of flavour; small, slender French radishes are especially mild and sweet. Whatever type you are buying, look for small, firm, brightly coloured specimens, with no sign of limpness.

Romanian Pepper Salad

Try to locate authentic long sweet peppers for this salad.

Serves 4

8 long green and/or orange
    peppers, halved and seeded
1 garlic clove, crushed
60ml/4 tbsp wine vinegar
75ml/5 tbsp olive oil
4 tomatoes, sliced
1 red onion, thinly sliced
salt and ground black pepper
fresh coriander sprigs, to garnish
black bread, to serve

1 Place the pepper halves, skin side up, on a grill rack and grill until the skins have blistered and charred. Transfer to a bowl and cover with crumpled kitchen paper. Leave to cool slightly, then rub off the skins and cut each piece in half lengthways.

2 Mix the garlic and vinegar in a bowl, then whisk in the olive oil. Arrange the peppers, tomatoes and onion on four serving plates and pour over the garlic dressing. Season to taste with salt and pepper, garnish with fresh coriander sprigs and serve with black bread.

Simple Pepper Salad

Peppers are perfect for making refreshing salads.

Serves 4

4 large mixed peppers, halved
    and seeded
60ml/4 tbsp olive oil
1 medium onion, thinly sliced
2 garlic cloves, crushed
4 tomatoes, peeled and chopped
pinch of sugar
5ml/1 tsp lemon juice
salt and ground black pepper

1 Place the peppers, skin side up, on a grill rack and grill until blistered. Transfer to a bowl and cover with crumpled kitchen paper. Cool slightly, then rub off the skins and slice thinly.
2 Heat the oil and fry the onion and garlic until softened. Add the peppers and tomatoes and fry for 10 minutes more.
3 Remove from the heat, stir in the sugar and lemon juice and season. Leave to cool and serve at room temperature.

Cucumber & Tomato Salad

Yogurt cools the dressing for this salad; fresh chilli hots it up. The combination works very well and is delicious with fresh bread.

Serves 4
450g/1lb firm ripe tomatoes
½ cucumber
1 onion
1 small hot chilli, seeded and
    chopped and snipped chives,
    to garnish
country bread or tomato toasts
    (see Cook's Tip), to serve

For the dressing
60ml/4 tbsp olive oil
90ml/6 tbsp thick
    Greek-style yogurt
30ml/2 tbsp chopped fresh
    parsley or snipped chives
2.5ml/ ½ tsp white wine vinegar
salt and ground black pepper

1 Peel the tomatoes by first cutting a cross in the base of each tomato. Place in a bowl and cover with boiling water for 1–2 minutes, or until the skin starts to curl back from the crosses. Drain, plunge into cold water and drain again. Peel, cut the tomatoes into quarters, seed and chop.

2 Chop the cucumber and onion into pieces that are the same size as the tomatoes and put them all in a bowl.

3 Make the dressing. Whisk together the oil, yogurt, parsley or chives and vinegar in a bowl and season to taste with salt and pepper. Pour over the salad and toss all the ingredients together. Sprinkle over black pepper and the chopped chilli and chives to garnish. Serve with crusty bread or tomato toasts.

> **Cook's Tip**
> To make tomato toasts, cut a French loaf diagonally into thin slices. Mix together a crushed garlic clove, a peeled and chopped tomato and 30ml/2 tbsp olive oil. Season. Spread on the bread and bake at 220°C/425°F/Gas 7 for 10 minutes.

Grated Beetroot & Celery Salad

Raw beetroot has a lovely crunchy texture. In this Russian salad, its flavour is brought out by marinating it in a cider dressing.

Serves 4–6
450g/1lb uncooked beetroot, peeled and grated
4 celery sticks, finely chopped
30ml/2 tbsp apple juice
fresh herbs, to garnish

For the dressing
15ml/1 tbsp cider vinegar
4 spring onions, finely sliced
30ml/2 tbsp chopped fresh parsley
45ml/3 tbsp sunflower oil
salt and ground black pepper

1 Toss the beetroot and celery with the apple juice in a bowl until well mixed.

2 Make the dressing. Put the vinegar, spring onions and parsley in a small bowl and whisk in the oil until well blended. Season with salt and pepper to taste, then stir half the dressing into the beetroot mixture.

3 Drizzle the remaining dressing over the salad, cover it and chill for 2 hours. Garnish with fresh herbs and serve.

Beetroot & Orange Salad

This is a classic combination for a refreshing salad.

Serves 4
1 small lettuce, shredded
8 cooked baby beetroot, halved
2 oranges, peeled and segmented
30ml/2 tbsp orange juice
15ml/1 tbsp lemon juice
30ml/2 tbsp olive oil
5ml/1 tsp sugar
10ml/2 tsp snipped fresh chives, plus extra to garnish

1 Place the lettuce on a serving plate and top with the beetroot and orange segments in a circle.
2 Whisk together the remaining ingredients and pour over the salad. Garnish with extra chives and serve.

Fennel, Orange & Rocket Salad

This light and refreshing salad is ideal for serving with spicy or rich foods.

Serves 4
2 oranges
1 fennel bulb
115g/4oz rocket leaves
50g/2oz/½ cup stoned black olives

For the dressing
15ml/1 tbsp balsamic vinegar
1 small garlic clove, crushed
30ml/2 tbsp extra virgin olive oil
salt and ground black pepper

1 With a vegetable peeler, cut thin strips of rind from the oranges, leaving the pith behind. Cut the pieces into thin matchstick strips. Set them aside.

2 Peel the oranges, removing all the white pith. Slice them into thin rounds and discard any seeds. Bring a small pan of water to the boil, add the strips of rind and cook for 2–3 minutes. Drain and dry on kitchen paper.

3 Cut the fennel bulb in half lengthways and slice across the bulb as thinly as possible, preferably in a food processor fitted with a slicing disc, or using a mandoline.

4 Combine the orange rounds and fennel slices in a serving bowl and toss with the rocket leaves.

5 Make the dressing. Mix the vinegar and garlic in a bowl. Whisk in the oil, then season with salt and pepper to taste. Pour the dressing over the salad, toss well and leave to stand for a few minutes. Sprinkle with the black olives and garnish with the blanched strips of orange rind before serving.

Cook's Tip
Although extra virgin olive oil is expensive, it is worth investing in it for salad dressings, as it has by far the best flavour.

Fruit & Nut Coleslaw

A delicious and nutritious mixture of crunchy vegetables, fruit and nuts, tossed together in a mayonnaise dressing.

Serves 6

225g/8oz white cabbage
1 large carrot
175g/6oz/ ¾ cup ready-to-eat
   dried apricots

50g/2oz/ ½ cup walnuts
50g/2oz/ ½ cup hazelnuts
115g/4oz/ ⅔ cup raisins
30ml/2 tbsp chopped
   fresh parsley
105ml/7 tbsp light mayonnaise
75ml/5 tbsp natural yogurt
salt and ground black pepper
fresh chives, to garnish

1 Finely shred the cabbage, coarsely grate the carrot and place both in a large mixing bowl.

2 Roughly chop the dried apricots, walnuts and hazelnuts. Stir them into the cabbage and carrot mixture with the raisins and chopped parsley.

3 In a separate bowl, mix together the mayonnaise and yogurt and season to taste with salt and pepper.

4 Add the mayonnaise mixture to the cabbage mixture and toss together to mix. Cover and set aside in a cool place for at least 30 minutes before serving, to allow the flavours to mingle. Garnish with a few fresh chives and serve.

Variations
• For a salad that is lower in fat, use low-fat natural yogurt and reduced-calorie mayonnaise.
• Instead of walnuts and hazelnuts, use flaked almonds and chopped pistachios.
• Omit the dried apricots and add a cored and chopped, unpeeled eating apple.
• Substitute other dried fruit or a mixture for the apricots – try nectarines, peaches or prunes.

Panzanella

Open-textured, Italian-style bread is essential for this colourful Tuscan salad.

Serves 6

10 thick slices day-old Italian style
   bread, about 275g/10oz
1 cucumber, peeled and cut
   into chunks
5 tomatoes, seeded and diced

1 large red onion, chopped
175g/6oz/1½ cups stoned black
   or green olives
20 fresh basil leaves, torn

For the dressing
60ml/4 tbsp extra virgin olive oil
15ml/1 tbsp red or white
   wine vinegar
salt and ground black pepper

1 Soak the bread in water to cover for about 2 minutes, then lift it out and squeeze gently, first with your hands and then in a dish towel to remove any excess water.

2 Make the dressing. Place the oil, vinegar and seasoning in a screw-top jar. Close the lid tightly and shake vigorously. Mix the cucumber, tomatoes, onion and olives in a bowl.

3 Break the bread into chunks and add to the bowl with the basil. Pour the dressing over the salad, and toss before serving.

Date, Orange & Carrot Salad

A simple oil-free dressing is perfect on this juicy salad.

Serves 4

1 Little Gem lettuce
2 carrots, finely grated
2 oranges, segmented

115g/4oz/⅔ cup fresh dates,
   stoned and sliced lengthways
30ml/2 tbsp toasted almonds
30ml/2 tbsp lemon juice
5ml/1 tsp caster sugar
1.5ml/¼ tsp salt
15ml/1 tbsp orange flower water

1 Spread out the lettuce leaves on a platter. Place the carrot in the centre. Surround it with the oranges, dates and almonds.

2 Mix the lemon juice, sugar, salt and orange flower water. Sprinkle over the salad and serve chilled.

Mixed Leaf & Herb Salad with Toasted Seeds

This simple salad is the perfect antidote to a rich, heavy meal as it contains fresh herbs that can aid the digestion.

Serves 4
115g/4oz/4 cups mixed salad leaves
50g/2oz/2 cups mixed salad herbs, such as coriander, parsley, basil and rocket

25g/1oz/2 tbsp pumpkin seeds
25g/1oz/2 tbsp sunflower seeds

For the dressing
60ml/4 tbsp extra virgin olive oil
15ml/1 tbsp balsamic vinegar
2.5ml/ ½ tsp Dijon mustard
salt and ground black pepper

1 Start by making the dressing. Combine the olive oil, balsamic vinegar and mustard in a screw-top jar. Add salt and pepper to taste. Close the jar tightly, then shake the dressing vigorously until well combined.

2 Mix the salad and herb leaves in a large bowl.

3 Toast the pumpkin and sunflower seeds in a dry frying pan over a medium heat for 2 minutes, until golden, tossing frequently to prevent them from burning. Allow the seeds to cool slightly before sprinkling them over the salad.

4 Pour the dressing over the salad and toss gently with your hands until the leaves are well coated. Serve at once.

> **Variations**
> • Balsamic vinegar adds a rich, sweet taste to the dressing, but red or white wine vinegar could be used instead.
> • A few nasturtium flowers would look very pretty in this salad, as would borage flowers.
> • Substitute your favourite seeds for those given here.

Caesar Salad

There are few dishes more famous than this popular combination of crisp lettuce leaves and Parmesan in a fresh egg dressing.

Serves 4
2 large garlic cloves, halved
45ml/3 tbsp extra virgin olive oil
4 slices wholemeal bread
1 small cos or 2 romaine or Little Gem lettuces

50g/2oz piece of Parmesan cheese, shaved or coarsely grated

For the dressing
1 egg
10ml/2 tsp French mustard
5ml/1 tsp vegetarian Worcestershire sauce
30ml/2 tbsp fresh lemon juice
30ml/2 tbsp extra virgin olive oil
salt and ground black pepper

1 Preheat the oven to 190°C/375°F/Gas 5. Rub the inside of a salad bowl with one of the half cloves of garlic.

2 Heat the oil gently with the remaining garlic in a frying pan for 5 minutes, then remove and discard the garlic.

3 Remove the crusts from the bread and cut the crumb into small cubes. Toss these in the garlic-flavoured oil, making sure that they are well coated. Spread out the bread cubes on a baking sheet, and bake for about 10 minutes, until crisp. Remove from the oven, then leave to cool.

4 Separate the lettuce leaves, wash and dry them and arrange in a shallow salad bowl. Chill until ready to serve.

5 Make the dressing. Bring a small pan of water to the boil, lower the egg into the water and boil for 1 minute only. Crack it into a bowl. Use a teaspoon to scoop out and discard any softly set egg white. Using a balloon whisk, beat in the French mustard, Worcestershire sauce, lemon juice and olive oil, then season with salt and pepper to taste.

6 Sprinkle the Parmesan over the salad and then drizzle the dressing over. Scatter with the croûtons. Take the salad to the table, toss lightly and serve immediately.

Split Tin Loaf

As its name suggests, this homely loaf is so called because of the centre split. Some bakers mould the dough in two loaves which join together when the dough is proved, but retain the characteristic crack after baking.

Makes 1 loaf

500g/1¼lb/5 cups unbleached white bread flour, plus extra for dusting
10ml/2 tsp salt
15g/½oz fresh yeast
300ml/½ pint/1¼ cups lukewarm water
60ml/4 tbsp lukewarm milk

1 Lightly grease a 900g/2lb loaf tin. Sift the flour and salt into a bowl and make a well in the centre. Mix the yeast with half the lukewarm water in a jug, then stir in the remaining water.

2 Pour the yeast mixture into the centre of the flour. Gradually mix in enough of the surrounding flour to make a thick, smooth batter. Sprinkle a little more flour over the batter and leave in a warm place for about 20 minutes, until bubbles appear in the batter. Add the milk and remaining flour; mix to a firm dough.

3 Knead on a lightly floured surface for 10 minutes, until smooth and elastic. Place in a lightly oiled bowl, cover with lightly oiled clear film and set aside in a warm place for 1–1¼ hours, or until nearly doubled in bulk.

4 Knock back the dough, then shape it into a rectangle the length of the tin. Roll up lengthways, tuck the ends under and place, seam side down, in the tin. Cover and leave in a warm spot to rise for 20–30 minutes, or until nearly doubled in size.

5 Using a sharp knife, make one deep central slash the length of the bread; dust with flour. Leave for 10–15 minutes. Preheat the oven to 230°C/450°F/Gas 8.

6 Bake for 15 minutes, then reduce the oven temperature to 200°C/400°F/Gas 6. Bake for 20–25 minutes more, or until the bread is golden and sounds hollow when tapped on the base. Turn out on to a wire rack to cool.

Grant Loaves

The dough for these quick and easy loaves requires no kneading and takes only a minute to mix. The loaves should keep moist for several days.

Makes 3 loaves
oil, for greasing

1.3kg/3lb/12 cups wholemeal bread flour
15ml/1 tbsp salt
15ml/1 tbsp easy-blend dried yeast
15ml/1 tbsp muscovado sugar
1.2 litres/2 pints/5 cups warm water (35–38°C/95–100°F)

1 Thoroughly grease three loaf tins, each measuring about 21 x 2 x 6cm/8½ x 4½ x 2½in and set aside in a warm place. Sift the flour and salt into a large bowl and warm slightly to take off the chill.

2 Stir in the dried yeast and sugar. Make a well in the centre and pour in the water. Mix for about 1 minute, working the sides into the middle. The dough should be slippery.

3 Divide among the prepared tins, cover with oiled clear film and leave in a warm place, for 30 minutes, or until the dough has risen to within 1cm/½in of the top of the tins.

4 Meanwhile, preheat the oven to 200°C/400°F/Gas 6. Bake for 40 minutes, or until the loaves are crisp and sound hollow when tapped on the base. Cool on a wire rack.

Cook's Tips
• *Most breads require a raising or leavening agent, and yeast is the commonest, although there are a number of others.*
• *Easy-blend dried yeast is widely available. There is no need to mix it with liquid before adding it to the flour and other dry ingredients. Lukewarm liquid is then added.*
• *Ordinary dried yeast must be mixed with a little warm liquid, and sometimes with sugar as well. When it has dissolved and the mixture is frothy it can be added to the dried ingredients.*

Cottage Loaf

Always a good-looking loaf, this makes a good centrepiece for a casual lunch or supper.

Makes I large round loaf

oil, for greasing

675g/1½lb/6 cups unbleached white bread flour, plus extra for dusting
10ml/2 tsp salt
20g/¾oz fresh yeast
400ml/14fl oz/1⅔ cups lukewarm water

I Lightly grease two baking sheets. Sift the flour and salt into a large bowl and make a well in the centre. Dissolve the yeast in 150ml/¼ pint/⅔ cup of the water. Add to the flour, with the remaining water, and mix to a firm dough.

2 Knead the dough on a lightly floured surface for 10 minutes. Place in a lightly oiled bowl, cover with lightly oiled clear film and leave in a warm place to rise for about 1 hour, or until doubled in bulk.

3 Knock back the dough on a lightly floured surface. Knead for 2–3 minutes, then divide the dough into two-thirds and one-third; shape each to a ball.

4 Place the balls of dough on the prepared baking sheets. Cover with inverted bowls and leave in a warm place to rise, for about 30 minutes.

5 Gently flatten the top of the larger ball of dough and cut a cross in the centre, 5cm/2in across. Brush with a little water and place the smaller ball on top. Make small cuts around each ball.

6 Carefully press a hole through both balls, using the thumb and first two fingers of one hand. Cover with lightly oiled clear film and leave to rest in a warm place for about 10 minutes.

7 Heat the oven to 220°C/425°F/Gas 7 and place the baking sheet on the lower shelf. The loaf will finish expanding as the oven heats up. Bake for 35–40 minutes, or until golden brown and sounding hollow when tapped. Cool on a wire rack.

Wholemeal Bread

This seeded loaf looks rustic and is great for picnics and other *al fresco* meals.

Makes 4 rounds
20g/¾oz fresh yeast
300ml/½ pint/1¼ cups lukewarm milk
5ml/1 tsp caster sugar
225g/8oz/2 cups wholemeal bread flour

225g/8oz/2 cups unbleached white bread flour, plus extra for dusting
5ml/1 tsp salt
50g/2oz/¼ cup chilled butter, cubed
1 egg, lightly beaten
oil, for greasing
30ml/2 tbsp mixed seeds

I Mash the yeast with a little of the milk and the sugar until it dissolves to make a paste. Sift both types of flour and the salt into a large warmed mixing bowl. Rub in the butter until the mixture resembles breadcrumbs.

2 Add the yeast mixture, remaining milk and egg and mix into a fairly soft dough. Knead on a floured surface for 15 minutes. Place in a lightly oiled bowl, cover with lightly oiled clear film and leave to rise in a warm place for at least 1 hour, until doubled in bulk.

3 Knock back the dough and knead it for 10 minutes. Divide the dough into four pieces and shape them into flattish rounds. Place them on a floured baking sheet and leave to rise for about 15 minutes more.

4 Preheat the oven to 200°C/400°F/Gas 6. Sprinkle the loaves with the mixed seeds. Bake for about 20 minutes, until golden and firm. Cool on wire racks.

Cook's Tip
15g/½oz fresh yeast is the equivalent of 15ml/1 tbsp dried. It must always be crumbled into a bowl and then mashed with a little lukewarm liquid before adding to the dry ingredients.

Granary Cob

Serve this delicious Granary cob warm, so the house is infused with its welcoming fresh-baked aroma.

Makes 1 round loaf
450g/1lb/4 cups Granary or
    malthouse flour, plus extra
    for dusting
10ml/2 tsp salt
15g/½oz fresh yeast
300ml/½ pint/1¼ cups
    lukewarm water or milk and
    water mixed
oil, for greasing

For the topping
30ml/2 tbsp water
2.5ml/½ tsp salt
wheat flakes or cracked wheat,
    to sprinkle

1 Lightly flour a baking sheet. Sift the flour and salt into a large bowl. Place in a very low oven for 5 minutes to warm.

2 Crumble the yeast into a small bowl and add a little of the water or milk mixture. Mash with a fork, then blend in the remaining liquid. Add the yeast mixture to the flour and mix to form a dough.

3 Knead on a floured surface for about 10 minutes. Place in a lightly oiled bowl, cover with lightly oiled clear film and leave in a warm place for 1¼ hours, or until doubled in bulk.

4 Knock back the dough, knead it for 2–3 minutes, then roll it into a ball. Flatten it slightly so that it resembles a plump round cushion in appearance. Place on the prepared baking sheet, cover with an inverted bowl and leave in a warm place to rise for 30–45 minutes.

5 Preheat the oven to 230°C/450°F/Gas 8. Mix the water and salt for the topping and brush over the bread. Sprinkle with wheat flakes or cracked wheat.

6 Bake for 15 minutes, then reduce the oven temperature to 200°C/400°F/Gas 6 and bake for 20 minutes more, or until the loaf is firm to the touch and sounds hollow when tapped on the base. Cool on a wire rack.

Irish Soda Bread

Traditional Irish soda bread can be prepared in minutes and is excellent served warm, with plenty of butter. You can use all plain white flour, if preferred, to create a bread with a finer texture.

Makes 1 round loaf
oil, for greasing
225g/8oz/2 cups
    unbleached plain flour
225g/8oz/2 cups wholemeal flour,
    plus extra for dusting
5ml/1 tsp salt
10ml/2 tsp bicarbonate of soda
10ml/2 tsp cream of tartar
40g/1½oz/3 tbsp butter
5ml/1 tsp caster sugar
350–375ml/12–13fl oz/
    1½–1⅔ cups buttermilk

1 Preheat the oven to 190°C/375°F/Gas 5. Lightly grease a baking sheet and set aside. Sift both types of flour and the salt into a large bowl.

2 Add the bicarbonate of soda and cream of tartar, then rub in the butter. Stir in the sugar.

3 Pour in sufficient buttermilk to mix to a soft dough. Do not over-mix or the bread will be heavy and tough. Shape into a round on a lightly floured surface.

4 Place on the prepared baking sheet and mark a cross using a sharp knife, cutting deep into the dough.

5 Dust lightly with wholemeal flour and bake the loaf for 35–45 minutes, or until well risen. The bread should sound hollow when tapped on the base. Cool slightly on a wire rack, but serve warm.

Variations
• Shape into two small loaves and bake for 25–30 minutes.
• Soured cream may be used instead of buttermilk, as both have a high lactic acid content and so react with the soda.

Sour Rye Bread

You need to plan ahead to make this loaf, as the starter takes a day or two.

Makes 2 loaves
450g/1lb/4 cups rye flour
450g/1lb/4 cups strong white
    flour, plus extra for dusting
15ml/1 tbsp salt
7g/1/4oz sachet easy-blend
    dried yeast

25g/1oz/2 tbsp butter, softened
600ml/1 pint/2½ cups
    warm water
oil, for greasing
15ml/1 tbsp caraway seeds,
    for sprinkling

For the sourdough starter
60ml/4 tbsp rye flour
45ml/3 tbsp warm milk

1 For the starter, mix the rye flour and milk in a small bowl. Cover with clear film and leave in a warm place for 1–2 days, or until it smells pleasantly sour.

2 Sift both types of flour and the salt into a large bowl and stir in the yeast. Make a well in the centre and add the butter, water and sourdough starter. Mix to a soft dough.

3 Knead the dough on a floured surface for 10 minutes. Put it in a clean bowl, cover with lightly oiled clear film and leave in a warm place to rise for 1 hour, or until doubled in bulk.

4 Knead for 1 minute. Divide the dough in half. Shape each piece into a 15cm/6in round. Place on greased baking sheets. Cover with oiled clear film and leave to rise for 30 minutes.

5 Preheat the oven to 200°C/400°F/Gas 6. Brush the loaves with water, sprinkle with caraway seeds and bake them for 35–40 minutes. The loaves should have browned and sound hollow when tapped on the bottom. Cool on a wire rack.

Cook's Tip
Sour rye bread keeps fresh for up to a week. This recipe can also be made without yeast, but it will be much denser.

Pan de Cebada

This Spanish bread is perfect for serving with chilled soup, or a healthy dip.

Makes 1 large loaf
For the sourdough starter
175g/6oz/1½ cups maize meal
560ml/scant 1 pint/scant
    2½ cups water
225g/8oz/2 cups wholemeal
    bread flour, plus extra

75g/3oz/¾ cup barley flour
oil, for greasing

For the dough
maize meal, for dusting
20g/¾oz fresh yeast
45ml/3 tbsp lukewarm water
225g/8oz/2 cups wholemeal
    bread flour
15ml/1 tbsp salt

1 In a pan, mix the maize meal for the sourdough starter with half the water, then stir in the remainder. Stir over a gentle heat until thickened. Transfer to a large bowl and set aside to cool. Mix in the wholemeal and barley flours. Knead on a lightly floured surface for 5 minutes, then return to the bowl, cover with lightly oiled clear film and leave in a warm place for 36 hours.

2 Make the dough. Dust a baking sheet with maize meal. In a small bowl, cream the yeast with the water, then add to the starter with the wholemeal flour and salt and work to a dough. Knead on a lightly floured surface for 4–5 minutes.

3 Put the dough in a lightly oiled bowl, cover with oiled clear film and leave in a warm place to rise for 1½–2 hours.

4 Knock back the dough, shape it into a plump round and sprinkle with a little maize meal. Put it on the prepared baking sheet and cover with a large upturned bowl. Leave in a warm place to rise, for about 1 hour, or until nearly doubled in bulk.

5 Place an empty roasting tin in the base of the oven. Preheat the oven to 220°C/425°F/Gas 7. Pour 300ml/½ pint/1¼ cups cold water into the tin. Lift the bowl off the loaf and place the baking sheet in the oven. Bake for 10 minutes. Remove the tin of water, reduce the oven temperature to 190°C/375°F/Gas 5 and bake the bread for 20 minutes more. Cool on a wire rack.

Walnut Bread

This delicious enriched wholemeal bread is filled with walnuts. It is the perfect companion for cheese, and also tastes wonderful with salads.

Makes 2 loaves
oil, for greasing
50g/2oz/ 1/4 cup butter
350g/12oz/3 cups wholemeal

bread flour, plus extra
or dusting
115g/4oz/1 cup unbleached
white bread flour
15ml/1 tbsp light brown
muscovado sugar
7.5ml/1 1/2 tsp salt
20g/3/4oz fresh yeast
275ml/9fl oz/1 cup
lukewarm milk
175g/6oz/1 1/2 cups walnut pieces

1 Lightly grease two baking sheets. Melt the butter in a small pan until it starts to turn brown, then set aside to cool. Mix the flours, sugar and salt in a large bowl and make a well in the centre. Cream the yeast with half the milk. Add to the well with the remaining milk. Strain the cool butter into the liquids in the well and mix with your hand, gradually incorporating the surrounding flour to make a batter, then a moist dough.

2 Knead for 6–8 minutes. Place in a lightly oiled bowl, cover with lightly oiled clear film and leave in a warm place to rise for 1 hour, or until doubled in bulk.

3 Gently knock back the dough on a lightly floured surface. Press or roll it flat, then sprinkle over the nuts, press them in and roll up the dough. Return it to the oiled bowl, re-cover and leave, in a warm place, for 30 minutes.

4 Turn out on to a lightly floured surface, divide in half and shape each piece into a ball. Place on the baking sheets, cover with lightly oiled clear film and leave in a warm place to rise for 45 minutes, or until doubled in bulk.

5 Meanwhile, preheat the oven to 220°C/425°F/Gas 7. Using a sharp knife, slash the top of each loaf three times. Bake for about 35 minutes, or until the loaves sound hollow when tapped on the base. Cool on a wire rack.

Focaccia with Green Peppercorns & Rock Salt

There's something irresistible about a loaf of freshly baked focaccia with its dimpled surface and fabulous flavour.

Makes 1 loaf
350g/12oz/3 cups white bread
flour, plus extra for dusting
2.5ml/ 1/2 tsp salt
10ml/2 tsp easy-blend dried yeast

10ml/2 tsp drained green
peppercorns in brine,
lightly crushed
25ml/5 tsp fruity extra virgin
olive oil
about 250ml/8fl oz/1 cup
lukewarm water
20ml/4 tsp roughly crushed rock
salt, for the topping
fresh basil leaves, to garnish

1 Sift the flour and salt into a mixing bowl. Stir in the yeast and peppercorns. Make a well in the centre and add 15ml/1 tbsp of the oil, with half the water. Mix, gradually incorporating the flour and adding more water to make a soft dough.

2 Knead the dough on a lightly floured surface for 10 minutes. Return to the clean, lightly oiled bowl, cover with lightly oiled clear film and leave in a warm place until doubled in bulk.

3 Knock down the dough and knead lightly for 2–3 minutes. Place on an oiled baking sheet and pat out to an oval. Cover with lightly oiled clear film and leave for 30 minutes.

4 Preheat the oven to 190°C/375°F/Gas 5. Make a few dimples in the surface of the dough with your fingers. Drizzle with the remaining oil and sprinkle with the salt. Bake for 25–30 minutes, until pale gold. Scatter with basil leaves and serve warm.

Cook's Tip
Kneading is a vital step in bread-making as it develops the gluten in the flour. Press and stretch the dough, using the heel of your hand and turning the dough frequently.

Ciabatta

This irregular-shaped Italian bread is made with a very wet dough flavoured with olive oil; cooking produces a bread with holes and a wonderfully chewy crust.

Makes 3 loaves
For the biga starter
7g/¼oz fresh yeast
175–200ml/6–7fl oz/ ¾–scant
    1 cup lukewarm water
350g/12oz/3 cups unbleached
    plain flour, plus extra
    for dusting

For the dough
oil, for greasing
15g/ ½oz fresh yeast
400ml/14fl oz/1⅔ cups
    lukewarm water
60ml/4 tbsp lukewarm milk
500g/1¼lb/5 cups unbleached
    white bread flour
10ml/2 tsp salt
45ml/3 tbsp extra virgin olive oil

1 Cream the yeast for the biga starter with a little of the water. Sift the flour into a large bowl. Gradually mix in the yeast mixture and add sufficient of the remaining water to form a firm dough.

2 Knead the dough for about 5 minutes, until smooth and elastic. Return it to the bowl, cover with lightly oiled clear film and leave in a warm place for 12–15 hours, or until the dough has risen and is starting to collapse.

3 Sprinkle three baking sheets with flour. Mix the yeast for the dough with a little of the water until creamy, then mix in the remaining water. Gradually add this yeast mixture to the biga and mix them together.

4 Mix in the milk, beating thoroughly with a wooden spoon. Using your hand, gradually beat in the flour, lifting the dough as you mix. Mixing the dough will take 15 minutes or more and form a very wet mix, impossible to knead on a work surface.

5 Beat in the salt and olive oil. Cover with lightly oiled clear film and leave to rise, in a warm place, for 1½–2 hours, or until doubled in bulk.

6 Using a spoon, carefully tip one-third of the dough at a time on to the prepared baking sheets, trying to avoid knocking back the dough in the process.

7 Using floured hands, shape into rough rectangular loaf shapes, about 2.5cm/1in thick. Flatten slightly with splayed fingers. Sprinkle with flour and leave to rise in a warm place for 30 minutes.

8 Preheat the oven to 220°C/425°F/Gas 7. Bake the loaves for 25–30 minutes, or until golden brown. The loaves should sound hollow when tapped on the base. Cool on a wire rack.

> **Cook's Tip**
> Ciabatta is delicious served warm, but not hot.

Onion Focaccia

This pizza-like flat bread is characterized by its soft dimpled surface, sometimes dredged simply with coarse sea salt, or as here, with red onions.

Makes 2 loaves
675g/1½lb/6 cups strong plain
    flour, plus extra for dusting
2.5ml/ ½ tsp salt
2.5ml/ ½ tsp caster sugar
15ml/1 tbsp easy-blend
    dried yeast
60ml/4 tbsp extra virgin olive oil,
    plus extra for greasing
about 450ml/ ¾ pint/scant
    2 cups lukewarm water

To finish
2 red onions, thinly sliced
45ml/3 tbsp extra virgin olive oil
15ml/1 tbsp coarse salt

1 Sift the flour, salt and sugar into a large bowl. Stir in the yeast, oil and water and mix to a dough using a round-bladed knife. Add a little extra water if the dough is dry.

2 Knead on a lightly floured surface for about 10 minutes, then put the dough in a clean, lightly oiled bowl and cover with lightly oiled clear film. Leave in a warm place for about 1 hour, until doubled in bulk.

3 Preheat the oven to 200°C/400°F/Gas 6. Place two 25cm/10in plain metal flan rings on baking sheets. Oil the insides of the rings and the baking sheets.

4 Halve the dough and roll each piece to a 25cm/10in round. Press into the flan rings, cover each with a dampened dish towel and leave for 30 minutes to rise.

5 With your fingers, make dimples about 2.5cm/1in apart, in the dough. Cover and leave for 20 minutes more.

6 To finish, scatter the surface of the two loaves with the sliced onions and drizzle over the olive oil. Sprinkle with the coarse salt, then a little cold water, to stop a crust from forming. Bake for about 25 minutes, sprinkling with water once during cooking. Cool on a wire rack.

Olive Bread

A mixture of olives combined with olive oil make this wonderful Italian bread.

Makes 1 loaf
oil, for greasing
275g/10oz/2½ cups unbleached white bread flour, plus extra
50g/2oz/½ cup wholemeal bread flour

7g/¼oz sachet easy-blend dried yeast
2.5ml/½ tsp salt
210ml/7½ fl oz/scant 1 cup lukewarm water
15ml/1 tbsp extra virgin olive oil, plus extra for brushing
115g/4oz/1 cup stoned black and green olives, coarsely chopped

1 Lightly grease a baking sheet. Mix the flours, yeast and salt together in a large bowl and make a well in the centre.

2 Add the water and oil to the well in the flour and mix to a soft dough. Knead on a lightly floured surface until smooth and elastic, then place in a lightly oiled bowl, cover with lightly oiled clear film and leave in a warm place to rise for 1 hour, or until doubled in bulk.

3 Knock back the dough on a lightly floured surface. Flatten it and sprinkle over the olives. Fold up and knead to distribute the olives. Leave to rest for 5 minutes, then shape into an oval loaf. Place on the prepared baking sheet.

4 Make six deep cuts in the top of the loaf, and gently push the sections over. Cover with lightly oiled clear film and leave in a warm place to rise for 30–45 minutes, or until doubled in size.

5 Meanwhile, preheat the oven to 200°C/400°F/Gas 6. Brush the bread with olive oil and bake for 35 minutes. Cool on a wire rack.

Variation
Increase the proportion of wholemeal flour to make the loaf more rustic.

Challah

With its plaited shape, light texture and rich flavour, Challah is perfect for every special occasion, not just the Jewish Sabbath.

Makes 1 large loaf
oil, for greasing
500g/1¼lb/5 cups unbleached white bread flour, plus extra
10ml/2 tsp salt

20g/¾oz fresh yeast
200ml/7fl oz/scant 1 cup lukewarm water
30ml/2 tbsp caster sugar
2 eggs
75g/3oz/6 tbsp butter, melted

For the topping
1 egg yolk
15ml/1 tbsp water
10ml/2 tsp poppy seeds

1 Lightly grease a baking sheet. Sift the flour and salt into a bowl and make a well in the centre. Mix the yeast with the water and sugar; add to the well with the eggs and melted butter. Gradually mix in the flour to form a soft dough.

2 Knead on a lightly floured surface for 10 minutes. Place in a lightly oiled bowl, cover with lightly oiled clear film and leave in a warm place to rise for 1 hour, or until doubled in bulk.

3 Knock back, re-cover and leave to rise again in a warm place for about 1 hour. Knock back, turn out on to a lightly floured surface and knead gently. Divide into four equal pieces. Roll each piece into a rope about 45cm/18in long. Line them up next to each other. Pinch the ends together at one end.

4 Starting from the right, lift the first rope over the second and the third over the fourth. Place the fourth rope between the first and second ropes. Repeat, starting from the right, and continue until plaited. Tuck the ends under and place the loaf on the baking sheet. Cover with oiled clear film and leave in a warm place to rise for 30–45 minutes, or until doubled in size.

5 Preheat the oven to 200°C/400°F/Gas 6. Beat the egg yolk and water for the topping together. Gently brush the loaf with the mixture. Sprinkle with the poppy seeds and bake for 35–40 minutes, until deep golden brown. Cool on a wire rack.

Dill Bread

The slightly aniseed flavour of fresh dill works well in this tasty loaf enriched with cottage cheese.

Makes 2 loaves
850g/1lb 14oz/7½ cups white bread flour, plus extra for dusting
20ml/4 tsp easy-blend dried yeast
30ml/2 tbsp granulated sugar
20ml/4 tsp salt
475ml/16fl oz/2 cups lukewarm water
60ml/4 tbsp light olive oil, plus extra for greasing
½ onion, chopped
a large bunch of fresh dill, finely chopped
2 eggs, lightly beaten
115g/4oz/½ cup cottage cheese
milk, for glazing

1 Mix 350g/12oz/3 cups of the flour with the yeast, sugar and salt in a large bowl. Make a well in the centre. Pour in the water. Beat, gradually incorporating the surrounding flour to make a smooth batter. Cover and leave in a warm place to rise for 45 minutes.

2 Meanwhile, heat 15ml/1 tbsp of the oil in a small pan. Add the onion and fry over a low heat, stirring occasionally, for 5 minutes, until soft. Set aside to cool.

3 When the onion is cool, stir it into the risen batter. Stir in the dill, eggs, cottage cheese and remaining oil, then gradually add the remaining flour until the mixture forms a dough.

4 Knead the dough on a floured surface for 10 minutes. Place in a bowl, cover with oiled clear film and leave in a warm place for 1–1½ hours, until doubled in bulk.

5 Grease a large baking sheet. Cut the dough in half and shape into two rounds. Cover again and leave to rise for 30 minutes.

6 Meanwhile, preheat the oven to 190°C/375°F/Gas 5. Score the top of each round, making a criss-cross pattern over the entire surface. Brush with the milk. Bake for about 50 minutes, until the loaves are golden brown and sound hollow when tapped on the base. Cool on wire racks.

Russian Potato Bread

Another extremely good-looking loaf, this keeps very well, thanks to the mashed potato in the dough.

Makes 1 loaf
oil, for greasing
225g/8oz potatoes, peeled and diced
350g/12oz/3 cups unbleached white bread flour
115g/4oz/1 cup wholemeal bread flour, plus extra for sprinkling
7g/¼ oz sachet easy-blend dried yeast
2.5ml/½ tsp caraway seeds, crushed
25g/1oz/2 tbsp butter
salt

1 Lightly grease a baking sheet. Put the potatoes in a pan of lightly salted water and bring to the boil. Cook until tender, then drain, reserving 150ml/¼ pint/⅔ cup of the cooking water. Mash the potatoes and press them through a sieve into a bowl. Leave to cool.

2 Mix both types of flour in a large bowl. Add the yeast, seeds and 10ml/2tsp salt, then rub in the butter. Mix the reserved potato water and sieved potatoes together. Gradually work this mixture into the flour mixture to form a soft dough.

3 Knead on a lightly floured surface for 8–10 minutes. Place in a lightly oiled bowl, cover with lightly oiled clear film and leave in a warm place to rise for 1 hour, or until doubled in bulk.

4 Knock back the dough and knead it gently. Shape into a plump oval loaf, about 18cm/7in long. Place on the prepared baking sheet and sprinkle with a little wholemeal bread flour.

5 Cover the loaf with lightly oiled clear film and leave in a warm place for 30 minutes, or until doubled in size. Meanwhile, preheat the oven to 200°C/400°F/Gas 6.

6 Using a sharp knife, slash the top with 6–8 diagonal cuts to make a criss-cross effect. Bake for 30–35 minutes, or until the bread is golden and sounds hollow when tapped on the base. Cool on a wire rack.

Spiral Herb Bread

When cut, this loaf looks very pretty with its swirls of garlic and herbs. It tastes pretty good, too.

Makes 2 loaves
350g/12oz/3 cups white bread
    flour, plus extra for dusting
350g/12oz/3 cups wholemeal
    bread flour
2 x 7g/¼ oz sachets easy-blend
    dried yeast
600ml/1 pint/2½ cups
    lukewarm water
oil, for greasing
25g/1oz/2 tbsp butter
1 bunch of spring onions,
    finely chopped
1 garlic clove, finely chopped
1 large bunch of fresh parsley,
    finely chopped
1 egg, lightly beaten
salt and ground black pepper
milk, for glazing

1 Mix the flours in a large bowl. Stir in 15ml/1 tbsp salt and the yeast. Make a well in the centre and pour in the water. Beat, gradually incorporating the flour to make a rough dough.

2 Knead the dough on a floured surface for 8–10 minutes. Return it to the bowl, cover with lightly oiled clear film and leave in a warm place to rise for 2 hours, until doubled in bulk.

3 Meanwhile, melt the butter in a pan and cook the spring onions and garlic over a low heat, until softened. Season with salt and pepper, stir in the parsley and set aside.

4 Grease two 23 x 13cm/9 x 5in bread tins. When the dough has risen, cut it in half, then roll each half to a 35 x 23cm/ 14 x 9in rectangle. Brush with the beaten egg and divide the herb mixture between them, spreading it just to the edges.

5 Roll up each dough rectangle from a long side and pinch the short ends together to seal. Place in the tins, seam side down. Cover and leave in a warm place until the dough has risen above the rims of the tins.

6 Preheat the oven to 190°C/375°F/Gas 5. Brush the loaves with milk and bake for 55 minutes, until they are golden and sound hollow when tapped on the base. Cool on a wire rack.

Three-grain Twist

A mixture of grains gives this close-textured bread a delightful nutty flavour.

Makes 1 loaf
30ml/2 tbsp malt extract
475ml/16fl oz/2 cups
    boiling water
225g/8oz/2 cups white bread
    flour, plus extra for dusting
7.5ml/1½ tsp salt
225g/8oz/2 cups malted
    brown flour
225g/8oz/2 cups rye flour
15ml/1 tbsp easy-blend
    dried yeast
pinch of granulated sugar
30ml/2 tbsp linseed
75g/3oz/scant 1 cup
    medium oatmeal
45ml/3 tbsp sunflower seeds
oil, for greasing

1 Stir the malt extract into the boiling water. Let the mixture cool until it is lukewarm.

2 Sift the white flour and salt into a mixing bowl and add the other flours. Stir in the yeast and sugar. Set aside 5ml/1 tsp of the linseed and add the rest to the flour mixture with the oatmeal and sunflower seeds. Make a well in the centre.

3 Pour the malted water into the well and gradually mix in the flour to make a soft dough, adding extra water if necessary. Knead on a floured surface for about 5 minutes, then return to the clean bowl, cover with lightly oiled clear film and leave in a warm place to rise for about 2 hours until doubled in bulk.

4 Flour a baking sheet. Knead the dough again and divide it in half. Roll each half to a 30cm/12in long sausage. Twist them together, dampen the ends and press to seal. Lift the twist on to the prepared baking sheet. Brush it with water, sprinkle with the remaining linseed and cover loosely with a large plastic bag (ballooning it to trap the air inside). Leave in a warm place until well risen. Preheat the oven to 220°C/425°F/Gas 7.

5 Bake the loaf for 10 minutes, then reduce the oven temperature to 200°C/400°F/Gas 6 and cook for 20 minutes more, or until the loaf sounds hollow when it is tapped underneath. Cool on a wire rack.

Sweet Potato Bread with Cinnamon & Walnuts

Spicy and sweet, this tastes great both with savoury dishes and as a teabread, with cream cheese.

Makes I loaf
I medium sweet potato
450g/1lb/4 cups strong white
    flour, plus extra for dusting
5ml/1 tsp ground cinnamon
5ml/1 tsp easy-blend dried yeast
50g/2oz/²/₃ cup walnut pieces
300ml/ ¹/₂ pint/1 ¹/₄ cups
    warmed milk
salt and ground black pepper
oil, for greasing

I Bring a pan of water to the boil and cook the sweet potato whole, without peeling, for 45 minutes, or until tender. Meanwhile, sift the flour and cinnamon into a large bowl. Stir in the dried yeast.

2 Drain the sweet potato, cool it in cold water, then peel it. Mash the flesh with a fork, then mix it into the dry ingredients with the nuts and some salt and pepper.

3 Make a well in the centre of the mixture and pour in the milk. Mix with a round-bladed knife to a rough dough, then knead on a floured surface for 5 minutes.

4 Return the dough to a bowl and cover with oiled clear film. Leave in a warm place to rise for I hour, or until doubled in bulk. Turn the dough out and knock it back to remove any air bubbles. Knead again for a few minutes.

5 Grease a 900g/2lb loaf tin lightly with oil and line the base with non-stick baking paper. Shape the dough to fit the tin. Cover with lightly oiled clear film and leave in a warm place for I hour, or until doubled in size.

6 Preheat the oven to 200°C/400°F/Gas 6. Bake the loaf for 25 minutes. Turn it out and tap the base; if it sounds hollow the bread is cooked. Cool on a wire rack.

Polenta & Pepper Bread

Full of Mediterranean flavours, this satisfying, sunshine-coloured bread is best eaten while it is still warm, drizzled with a little virgin olive oil.

Makes 2 loaves
175g/6oz/scant 1 ¹/₂ cups polenta
5ml/1 tsp salt
350g/12oz/3 cups unbleached
    white bread flour, plus extra
    for dusting
5ml/1 tsp granulated sugar
7g/ ¹/₄ oz sachet easy-blend
    dried yeast
I red pepper, roasted, peeled
    and diced
15ml/1 tbsp olive oil, plus extra
    for greasing
300ml/ ¹/₂ pint/1 ¹/₄ cups
    lukewarm water

I Mix the polenta, salt, flour, sugar and yeast in a large bowl. Stir in the diced red pepper until it is evenly distributed, then make a well in the centre of the mixture. Grease two loaf tins.

2 Add the warm water and the oil to the well in the dry ingredients and mix to a soft dough. Knead for 10 minutes. Place in an oiled bowl, cover with oiled clear film and leave in a warm place to rise for I hour, until doubled in bulk.

3 Knock back the dough, knead it lightly, then divide it in half. Shape each piece into an oblong and place in a tin. Cover with oiled clear film and leave to rise for 45 minutes. Preheat the oven to 220°C/425°F/Gas 7.

4 Bake for 30 minutes, until golden and the loaves sound hollow when tapped underneath. Leave in the tins for about 5 minutes, then cool on a wire rack.

Cook's Tip
Grill the pepper until blistered and beginning to char, then place in a bowl, cover with kitchen paper and set aside until cool enough to peel.

Sun-dried Tomato Bread

This is one bread that absolutely everyone seems to love. Chopped onion and sun-dried tomatoes give it an excellent flavour.

Makes 4 small loaves
675g/1½ lb/6 cups strong plain
    flour, plus extra for dusting
10ml/2 tsp salt
25g/1oz/2 tbsp caster sugar
25g/1oz fresh yeast
400–475ml/14–16fl oz/
    1⅔–2 cups lukewarm milk
15ml/1 tbsp tomato purée
75g/3oz/¾ cup sun-dried
    tomatoes in oil, drained and
    chopped, plus 75ml/5 tbsp oil
    from the jar
75ml/5 tbsp extra virgin olive oil,
    plus extra for greasing
1 large onion, chopped

1 Sift the flour, salt and sugar into a bowl and make a well in the centre. Crumble the yeast into a jug, mix with 150ml/¼ pint/⅔ cup of the milk and pour into the well in the flour.

2 Stir the tomato purée into the remaining milk, then add to the well in the flour, with the tomato oil and olive oil.

3 Mix the liquid ingredients, and gradually incorporate the surrounding flour to make a dough. Knead on a floured surface for about 10 minutes, then return the dough to the clean bowl, cover with lightly oiled clear film and leave to rise in a warm place for about 2 hours.

4 Knock back the dough, and add the tomatoes and onion. Knead until evenly distributed. Shape into four rounds and place on two greased baking sheets. Cover each pair with a dish towel and leave to rise again for about 45 minutes.

5 Preheat the oven to 190°C/375°F/Gas 5. Bake the bread for 45 minutes, or until the loaves sound hollow when you tap them underneath. Cool on a wire rack.

Cook's Tip
Use a pair of sharp kitchen scissors to cut up the tomatoes.

Warm Herb Bread

This mouthwatering Italian-style bread, flavoured with basil, rosemary, olive oil and sun-dried tomatoes, is absolutely delicious served warm with fresh salads.

Makes 3 loaves
1.3kg/3lb/12 cups white bread
    flour, plus extra for dusting
15ml/1 tbsp salt
5ml/1 tsp caster sugar
7g/¼oz sachet easy-blend
    dried yeast
about 900ml/1½ pints/3¾ cups
    lukewarm water
75g/3oz/1½ cups sun-dried
    tomatoes in oil, drained and
    roughly chopped
150ml/¼ pint/⅔ cup virgin
    olive oil, plus extra for greasing
75ml/5 tbsp chopped mixed fresh
    basil and rosemary

To finish
extra virgin olive oil
rosemary leaves
sea salt flakes

1 Sift the flour and salt into a bowl. Stir in the sugar and yeast. Make a well in the centre and add the water, tomatoes, oil and herbs. Beat well, gradually incorporating the surrounding flour.

2 As the mixture becomes stiffer, bring it together with your hands. Mix to a soft but not sticky dough, adding a little extra water if needed.

3 Knead the dough on a lightly floured surface for about 10 minutes, then return it to the bowl, cover loosely with oiled clear film and put in a warm place for 30–40 minutes, or until doubled in bulk.

4 Knead the dough again until smooth and elastic, then cut it into three pieces. Shape each into an oval loaf about 18cm/7in long and place each on an oiled baking sheet. Slash the top of each loaf in a criss-cross pattern. Cover loosely and leave in a warm place for 15–20 minutes, until well risen.

5 Preheat the oven to 220°C/425°F/Gas 7. Brush the loaves with a little olive oil and sprinkle with the rosemary leaves and salt flakes. Cook for about 25 minutes, until golden brown. The bases should sound hollow when tapped.

Cheese & Courgette Cluster Bread

This unusual bread owes its moistness to grated courgettes, and its depth of flavour to freshly grated Parmesan cheese.

Makes 1 loaf
4 courgettes, coarsely grated
675g/1½lb/6 cups strong white bread flour
2 x 7g/¼oz sachets easy-blend dried yeast
50g/2oz/⅔ cup freshly grated Parmesan cheese
30ml/2 tbsp olive oil, plus extra for greasing
milk, to glaze
poppy seeds or sesame seeds, to sprinkle
salt and ground black pepper

1 Put the grated courgettes into a colander and sprinkle with salt. Stand the colander in a sink for about 20 minutes to drain the juices, then rinse the courgettes thoroughly, drain again and pat dry with kitchen paper.

2 Sift the flour into a large bowl and add the yeast, Parmesan, 2.5ml/½ tsp salt and pepper to taste. Stir in the oil and courgettes, then add enough lukewarm water to make a firm but still soft dough.

3 Knead the dough for about 10 minutes, then return it to the bowl, cover with lightly oiled clear film and leave in a warm place for about 1 hour, or until doubled in bulk.

4 Lightly grease a deep 23cm/9in cake tin. Knock back the dough and knead it again. Divide it into eight pieces and roll into smooth balls. Fit these into the tin, placing one in the centre and the remainder around the outside.

5 Glaze the loaf with a little milk and sprinkle over the seeds. Cover lightly with oiled clear film and leave to rise in a warm place until the balls of dough have doubled in size.

6 Meanwhile, preheat the oven to 200°C/400°F/Gas 6. Bake the loaf for 35–45 minutes, until it is golden brown and sounds hollow when tapped on the base. Cool on a wire rack and eat as soon as possible.

Spicy Millet Bread

This is a delicious spicy bread with a golden crust. Cut into wedges and serve warm with a thick soup.

Makes 1 loaf
90g/3½oz/½ cup millet
600g/1lb 6oz/5½ cups strong unbleached plain flour, plus extra for dusting
10ml/2 tsp salt
7g/¼oz sachet easy-blend dried yeast
5ml/1 tsp caster sugar
5ml/1 tsp dried chilli flakes (optional)
25g/1oz/2 tbsp butter
1 onion, roughly chopped
15ml/1 tbsp cumin seeds
5ml/1 tsp ground turmeric

1 Bring 200ml/7fl oz/scant 1 cup water to the boil in a small pan. Add the millet, cover and simmer gently for 20 minutes, until the grains are soft and the water has been absorbed. Remove from the heat and leave to cool until just warm.

2 Mix the flour, salt, yeast, sugar and chilli flakes, if using, in a large bowl. Stir in the millet, then add 350ml/12fl oz/1½ cups warm water and mix to a soft dough.

3 Knead the dough on a floured surface for 10 minutes, then place it in an oiled bowl and cover with oiled clear film. Leave in a warm place for 1 hour, or until doubled in bulk.

4 Meanwhile, melt the butter in a heavy-based frying pan, and fry the onion until softened. Add the cumin seeds and turmeric, and fry for 5–8 minutes more, stirring constantly, until the cumin seeds begin to pop. Set aside.

5 Knock back the dough, knead it briefly again and shape it into a round. Place the onion mixture in the middle of the dough and bring the sides over to cover it. Seal well. Place the loaf on an oiled baking sheet, seam side down, cover with oiled clear film and leave in a warm place for 45 minutes, until doubled in size. Preheat the oven to 220°C/425°F/Gas 7.

6 Bake the bread for 30 minutes, until golden. It should sound hollow when tapped underneath. Cool on a wire rack.

Syrian Onion Bread

These unusual small breads come from Syria and have a spicy topping spiked with fresh mint.

Makes 8 breads
450g/1lb/4 cups unbleached
    white bread flour, plus extra
5ml/1 tsp salt
20g/¾oz fresh yeast
280ml/9fl oz/scant 1¼ cups
    lukewarm water
oil, for greasing

For the topping
60ml/4 tbsp finely chopped onion
5ml/1 tsp ground cumin
10ml/2 tsp ground coriander
10ml/2 tsp chopped fresh mint
30ml/2 tbsp olive oil

1 Lightly flour two baking sheets. Sift the flour and salt together into a large bowl and make a well in the centre. Cream the yeast with a little of the water, then mix in the remainder.

2 Add the yeast mixture to the centre of the flour and mix to a firm dough. Knead on a lightly floured surface for 8–10 minutes, until smooth and elastic. Place in a lightly oiled bowl, cover with lightly oiled clear film and leave in a warm place for about 1 hour, until doubled in bulk.

3 Knock back the dough and turn it out on to a lightly floured surface. Divide into eight equal pieces and roll each into a 13–15cm/5–6in round. Make the rounds slightly concave. Prick them all over and space well apart on the baking sheets. Cover with lightly oiled clear film and leave to rise for 15–20 minutes.

4 Meanwhile, preheat the oven to 200°C/400°F/Gas 6. Mix the chopped onion, ground cumin, ground coriander and chopped mint in a bowl. Brush the breads with the olive oil, sprinkle them evenly with the spicy onion mixture and bake for 15–20 minutes. Serve the onion breads warm.

Cook's Tip
If you haven't any fresh mint, add 15ml/1 tbsp dried mint. Use the freeze-dried variety, if you can, as it has much more flavour.

Spring Onion, Chive & Ricotta Bread

Ricotta cheese and chives make moist, well-flavoured rolls or bread, both of which are excellent for serving with salads, especially ones that are based on rice or bulgur wheat.

Makes 1 loaf or 16 rolls
15g/½oz fresh yeast
5ml/1 tsp caster sugar
270ml/9fl oz/1⅙ cups
    lukewarm water
450g/1lb/4 cups unbleached
    strong white flour, plus a
    little extra
7.5ml/1½ tsp salt
1 large egg, beaten
115g/4oz/½ cup ricotta cheese
30ml/2 tbsp extra virgin olive oil,
    plus extra for greasing
1 bunch spring onions, sliced
45ml/3 tbsp snipped fresh chives
15ml/1 tbsp milk
10ml/2 tsp poppy seeds
coarse sea salt

1 Using a fork, cream the fresh yeast with the sugar and then gradually stir in 120ml/4fl oz/½ cup lukewarm water. Set aside in a warm place for 10 minutes.

2 Sift the flour and salt into a warmed bowl. Make a well in the centre and pour in the yeast liquid and the remaining lukewarm water. Reserve a little of the beaten egg, then add the remainder to the liquid in the bowl. Add the ricotta and mix all the ingredients to form a dough, adding a little more flour if the mixture is very sticky.

3 Knead the dough on a floured work surface for 10 minutes, until smooth and elastic, then return it to the bowl, cover with lightly oiled clear film and set aside in a warm place for 1–2 hours, until doubled in bulk.

4 Meanwhile, heat the oil in a small pan. Add the spring onions and cook over a low heat, stirring occasionally, for 3–4 minutes, until soft but not browned. Set aside to cool.

5 Knock back the risen dough and knead in the onions, with any oil remaining in the pan. Add the chives. Shape the dough into rolls, a large loaf or a plait.

6 Grease a baking sheet or loaf tin and place the rolls or bread in it. Cover with oiled clear film and leave in a warm place to rise for about 1 hour. Preheat the oven to 200°C/400°F/Gas 6.

7 Beat the milk into the reserved beaten egg and use to glaze the rolls or loaf. Sprinkle with poppy seeds and a little coarse sea salt, then bake until golden and well risen. Rolls will need about 15 minutes and a large loaf will require 30–40 minutes. Cool on a wire rack.

Cook's Tip
To make a plait, divide the dough into three equal sausage-shaped pieces about 40cm/16in long. Press them together at one end and then plait, pressing the ends together to seal when completed.

French Baguettes

Baguettes are difficult to reproduce at home as they require a very hot oven and steam. However, by using less yeast and a triple fermentation, you can produce a bread that looks and tastes better than when mass-produced.

Makes 3 loaves
500g/1¼lb/5 cups unbleached white bread flour, plus extra
115g/4oz/1 cup fine French plain flour
10ml/2 tsp salt
15g/½ oz fresh yeast
550ml/18fl oz/2½ cups lukewarm water

1 Sift the flours and salt together into a bowl. Stir the yeast into the water in another bowl. Gradually beat in half the flour mixture to form a batter. Cover with clear film and set aside for 3 hours, or until nearly trebled in size and starting to collapse.

2 Beat in the remaining flour, a little at a time, with your hand. Knead on a lightly floured surface for 8–10 minutes to form a moist dough. Place in a lightly oiled bowl, cover with lightly oiled clear film and leave to rise, in a warm place, for about 1 hour.

3 Knock back the dough and divide it into three equal pieces. Shape each into a ball and then into a rectangle measuring 15 × 7.5cm/6 × 3in. Fold the bottom third of each up lengthways and the top third down and press down. Seal the edges. Repeat two or three more times until each loaf is an oblong.

4 Gently stretch each loaf lengthways to 35cm/14in long. Pleat a floured dish towel on a baking sheet to make three moulds so the loaves hold their shape. Cover with lightly oiled clear film and leave in a warm place for 45–60 minutes.

5 Meanwhile, preheat the oven to 230°C/450°F/Gas 8. Roll the loaves on to a baking sheet, spaced well apart. Using a sharp knife, slash the top of each loaf several times with long diagonal slits. Place at the top of the oven, spray the inside of the oven with water and bake for 20–25 minutes, or until golden. Spray the oven twice more during the first 5 minutes of baking. Cool on a wire rack. Eat on the day of baking.

Cheese & Onion Herb Sticks

These tasty breads are very good with soup or salads. Use an extra-strong cheese to give plenty of flavour.

Makes 2 sticks
15ml/1 tbsp sunflower oil, plus extra for greasing
1 red onion, chopped
450g/1lb/4 cups strong white flour, plus extra for dusting
5ml/1 tsp salt
5ml/1 tsp dry mustard powder
10ml/2 tsp easy-blend dried yeast
pinch of sugar
45ml/3 tbsp chopped mixed fresh herbs
75g/3oz/¾ cup grated reduced-fat Cheddar cheese
about 300ml/½ pint/1¼ cups lukewarm water

1 Heat the oil in a frying pan and fry the onion until well coloured. Lightly grease two baking sheets.

2 Sift the flour, salt and mustard into a mixing bowl. Add the dried yeast, sugar and herbs. Set aside 30ml/2 tbsp of the cheese. Stir the rest into the flour mixture and make a well in the centre. Add the lukewarm water, with the fried onions and oil, then gradually incorporate the flour and mix to a soft dough, adding extra water if necessary.

3 Knead the dough on a floured surface for about 10 minutes. Return the dough to the clean bowl, cover with lightly oiled clear film and set aside in a warm place to rise for about 1 hour, until doubled in bulk.

4 Turn the dough on to a floured surface, knead it briefly, then divide the mixture in half and roll each piece into a 30cm/12in long stick. Place each stick on a baking sheet and make diagonal cuts along the top.

5 Sprinkle the sticks with the reserved cheese. Cover and leave for 30 minutes, until well risen.

6 Preheat the oven to 220°C/425°F/Gas 7. Bake the sticks for 25 minutes, or until they sound hollow when they are tapped underneath. Cool on a wire rack.

Pitta Bread

Although you can buy pitta breads in any corner shop, it is great fun to bake your own. They are delicious filled with ratatouille, roasted Mediterranean vegetables or salad. Make sure the oven is hot or they will not puff up.

Makes 6
225g/8oz/2 cups unbleached white bread flour, plus extra
5ml/1 tsp salt
15g/1/2oz fresh yeast
140ml/scant 1/4 pint/scant 2/3 cup lukewarm water
15ml/3 tsp extra virgin olive oil

1 Sift the flour and salt into a bowl. Dissolve the yeast in the water, then stir in 10ml/2 tsp of the olive oil and pour into a large bowl. Gradually beat in the flour to form a soft dough.

2 Knead on a lightly floured surface for 10 minutes, then return to the clean bowl, cover with lightly oiled clear film and leave in a warm place to rise for about 1 hour, or until doubled in bulk.

3 Knock back the dough. On a lightly floured surface, divide it into six equal pieces and shape into balls. Cover with oiled clear film and leave to rest for 5 minutes. Roll out each ball of dough to an oval, about 5mm/1/4in thick and 15cm/6in long. Place on a floured dish towel and cover with lightly oiled clear film. Leave to rise at room temperature for about 20–30 minutes.

4 Meanwhile, preheat the oven to 230°C/450°F/Gas 8. Place three large baking sheets in the oven to heat.

5 Place the breads on the baking sheets and bake for 4–6 minutes, or until puffed up. Transfer to a wire rack to cool slightly, then cover them with a dish towel to keep them soft.

> **Variations**
> To make wholemeal pitta breads, replace half the white bread flour with wholemeal bread flour. You can also make smaller round pitta breads, about 10cm/4in in diameter, to serve as snack breads and for canapés.

Spiced Naan

Traditionally, Indian naan bread is baked in a fiercely hot tandoori oven, but you can use a combination of a hot oven and a grill.

Makes 6
450g/1lb/4 cups plain flour, plus extra for dusting
5ml/1 tsp baking powder
2.5ml/1/2 tsp salt
7g/1/4oz sachet easy-blend dried yeast
5ml/1 tsp caster sugar
5ml/1 tsp fennel seeds
10ml/2 tsp black onion seeds
5ml/1 tsp cumin seeds
150ml/1/4 pint/2/3 cup lukewarm milk
30ml/2 tbsp oil, plus extra for greasing and brushing
150ml/1/4 pint/2/3 cup natural yogurt
1 egg, beaten

1 Sift the flour, baking powder and salt into a mixing bowl. Stir in the yeast, sugar and seeds. Make a well in the centre. Pour in the milk, oil, yogurt and beaten egg. Beat well, gradually incorporating the surrounding flour to make a dough.

2 Knead the dough on a lightly floured surface for 10 minutes. Place in a lightly oiled bowl, cover with oiled clear film and leave in a warm place for about 1 hour, until doubled in bulk.

3 Put a heavy baking sheet in the oven and preheat the oven to 240°C/475°F/Gas 9. Preheat the grill. Knead the dough lightly again and divide it into six pieces. Cover five pieces. Roll out the sixth to a tear-drop shape, brush lightly with oil and slap on to the hot baking sheet. Repeat with the remaining five pieces.

4 Bake the naan for 3 minutes, until puffed up, then place the baking sheet under the grill for about 30 seconds to brown the naan lightly. Serve hot or warm.

> **Variation**
> Vary the spices used by adding chopped chilli to the mixture, or sprinkling with poppy seeds before baking.

Chapatis

These chewy, unleavened breads from India are the authentic accompaniment to spicy vegetarian dishes.

Makes 6

175g/6oz/1½ cups atta or wholemeal flour, plus extra for dusting

2.5ml/½ tsp salt

110ml/scant 4fl oz/scant ½ cup water

5ml/1 tsp vegetable oil, plus extra for greasing

melted ghee or butter, for brushing (optional)

1 Sift the flour and salt into a bowl. Add the water and mix to a soft dough. Knead in the oil.

2 Knead on a lightly floured surface for 5–6 minutes, until smooth. Place in a lightly oiled bowl, cover with a damp dish towel and leave to rest for 30 minutes. Turn out on to a floured surface. Divide the dough into six equal pieces. Shape each piece into a ball. Press the dough into a larger round with the palm of your hand, then roll into a 13cm/5in chapati. Stack, layered between clear film, to keep moist.

3 Heat a griddle or heavy-based frying pan over a medium heat for a few minutes. Take one chapati, brush off any excess flour, and place on the griddle. Cook for 30–60 seconds, until the top begins to bubble and white specks appear on the underside.

4 Turn the chapati over using a palette knife and cook for 30 seconds more. Remove from the pan and keep warm, layered between a folded dish towel, while cooking the remaining chapatis. If liked, lightly brush the chapatis with melted ghee or butter immediately after cooking. Serve warm.

> **Cook's Tip**
> Atta or ata is a very fine wholemeal flour, which is found only in Indian stores and supermarkets. It is sometimes simply labelled chapati flour.

Bagels

Bagels are great fun to make and taste wonderful with cream cheese, either on its own or with grilled aubergines or courgettes and fresh herbs.

Makes 10

oil, for greasing

350g/12oz/3 cups unbleached white bread flour, plus extra

10ml/2 tsp salt

7g/¼ oz sachet easy-blend dried yeast

5ml/1 tsp malt extract

210ml/7½fl oz/scant 1 cup lukewarm water

For poaching

2.5 litres/4¼ pints/10⅔ cups water

15ml/1 tbsp malt extract

For the topping

1 egg white

10ml/2 tsp cold water

30ml/2 tbsp poppy, sesame or caraway seeds, or a mixture

1 Grease two baking sheets. Sift the flour and salt into a bowl. Stir in the yeast. Mix the malt extract and water, add to the flour and mix to a dough. Knead on a floured surface for 10 minutes. Place in a lightly oiled bowl, cover with lightly oiled clear film and leave in a warm place for about 1 hour, or until doubled in bulk.

2 Knock back, knead for 1 minute, then divide into 10 equal pieces. Shape into balls, cover with clear film and leave to rest for 5 minutes. Gently flatten each ball and make a hole through the centre. Place on a floured tray; re-cover and leave in a warm place, for 10–20 minutes, or until the rings begin to rise.

3 Meanwhile, preheat the oven to 220°C/425°F/Gas 7. Place the water and malt extract for poaching in a large pan, bring to the boil, then reduce to a simmer. Poach two or three bagels at a time for about 1 minute. They will sink and then rise again when first added to the pan. Turn them over and poach the other side for 30 seconds. Remove and drain on a dish towel.

4 Place five bagels on each baking sheet. Beat the egg white with the water and brush over the bagels. Sprinkle with the seeds. Bake for 25 minutes, until golden. Cool on a wire rack.

Shaped Dinner Rolls

These rolls are the perfect choice for entertaining.

Makes 12

oil, for greasing
450g/1lb/4 cups unbleached
    white bread flour, plus extra
10ml/2 tsp salt
2.5ml/½ tsp caster sugar
7g/¼oz sachet easy-blend
    dried yeast

50g/2oz/¼ cup butter
250ml/8fl oz/1 cup
    lukewarm milk
1 egg, beaten

For the topping
1 egg yolk
15ml/1 tbsp water
poppy seeds and sesame seeds,
    for sprinkling

1 Grease two baking sheets. Sift the flour and salt into a bowl. Stir in the sugar and yeast. Rub in the butter. Add the milk and egg and mix to a dough. Knead on a lightly floured surface for 10 minutes. Place in a lightly oiled bowl, cover with oiled clear film and leave in a warm place for 1 hour, until doubled in bulk.

2 Knock back the dough on a lightly floured surface and knead for 2–3 minutes. Divide into 12 equal pieces and make shapes.

3 **Plait:** divide a piece of dough into three sausages. Pinch together at one end, plait, then pinch the ends and tuck under.
Trefoil: make three balls from a piece of dough and fit them together in a triangular shape.
Baton: shape a piece of dough into an oblong. Slash the surface.
Cottage roll: divide a piece of dough into two-thirds and one-third and shape into two rounds. Place the small one on top of the large one and make a hole through the centre.
Knot: shape a piece of dough into a rope and tie a single knot.

4 Place the rolls on the baking sheets, cover with oiled clear film and leave in a warm place for 30 minutes, until doubled in bulk. Meanwhile, preheat the oven to 220°C/425°F/Gas 7.

5 Mix the egg yolk and water and brush the rolls. Sprinkle some with poppy seeds and some with sesame seeds. Bake for 15–18 minutes or until golden. Cool on a wire rack.

Panini All'olio

The Italians adore elaborately shaped rolls.

Makes 16

60ml/4 tbsp extra virgin olive
    oil, plus extra for greasing
    and brushing

450g/1lb/4 cups unbleached
    white bread flour, plus extra
    for dusting
10ml/2 tsp salt
15g/½ oz fresh yeast
250ml/8fl oz/1 cup
    lukewarm water

1 Lightly oil three baking sheets. Sift the flour and salt into a bowl. Cream the yeast with half of the water, then stir in the remainder. Add to the flour with the oil and mix to a dough.

2 Knead the dough on a floured surface for 8–10 minutes. Place in a lightly oiled bowl, cover with lightly oiled clear film and leave in a warm place for about 1 hour, or until the dough has nearly doubled in bulk.

3 Knock back on a lightly floured surface. Divide into 12 equal pieces and shape into rolls as described below.

4 **Tavalli (twisted spirals):** roll each piece of dough into a strip about 30cm/12in long and 4cm/1½in wide. Twist each strip into a loose spiral and join the ends of dough in a circle.
Filoncini (finger-shaped rolls): flatten each piece of dough into an oval and roll to about 23cm/9in long. Make it 5cm/2in wide at one end and 10cm/4in wide at the other. Roll up from the wider end, then stretch to 20–23cm/8–9in long. Cut in half.
Carciofi (artichoke-shaped rolls): shape each piece of dough into a ball.

5 Place the rolls on the baking sheets. Brush with olive oil, cover with oiled clear film and leave in a warm place for 30 minutes. Meanwhile, preheat the oven to 200°C/400°F/Gas 6.

6 To finish the carciofi, snip four or five 5mm/¼in deep cuts in a circle on the top of each ball, then make five larger horizontal cuts around the sides. Bake the rolls for about 15 minutes. Cool on a wire rack.

Tomato Breadsticks

Fresh, healthy and low in fat, these are delectable with dips. Make plenty, as they are very moreish.

Makes 16
225g/8oz/2 cups plain flour, plus extra for dusting
2.5ml/ ½ tsp salt
7.5ml/1½ tsp easy-blend dried yeast
5ml/1 tsp clear honey
10ml/2 tsp olive oil, plus extra about 150ml/ ¼ pint/ ⅔ cup lukewarm water
6 pieces of sun-dried tomatoes in olive oil, drained and chopped
15ml/1 tbsp skimmed milk
10ml/2 tsp poppy seeds

1 Place the flour, salt and yeast in a food processor. Add the honey and 5ml/1 tsp of the olive oil and, with the machine running, gradually pour in enough lukewarm water to make a dough. Process for 1 minute more.

2 Knead the dough on a lightly floured surface for 3–4 minutes. Knead in the chopped sun-dried tomatoes. Form the dough into a ball and place in a lightly oiled bowl. Set aside to rise for 5 minutes.

3 Preheat the oven to 150°C/300°F/Gas 2. Lightly brush a baking sheet with oil.

4 Divide the dough into 16 pieces and roll each piece into a stick about 28 x 1cm/11 x ½in long. Place the breadsticks on the prepared baking sheet and set aside in a warm place to rise for 15 minutes.

5 Brush the sticks with milk and sprinkle with poppy seeds. Bake for 30 minutes. Cool on a wire rack.

> **Cook's Tip**
> Flours vary in their absorbency, so you may not require all the water. Stop adding it as soon as soon as the dough starts to cling together.

Wholemeal Herb Triangles

Stuffed with salad and cheese, these make a good lunchtime snack.

Makes 8
225g/8oz/2 cups wholemeal flour, plus extra for dusting
115g/4oz/1 cup white bread flour
5ml/1 tsp salt
2.5ml/ ½ tsp bicarbonate of soda
5ml/1 tsp cream of tartar
2.5ml/ ½ tsp chilli powder
50g/2oz/ ¼ cup soft margarine
60ml/4 tbsp chopped mixed fresh herbs
250ml/8fl oz/1 cup skimmed milk
15ml/1 tbsp sesame seeds

1 Preheat the oven to 220°C/425°F/Gas 7. Lightly flour a baking sheet. Put the wholemeal flour in a mixing bowl. Sift in the white flour, salt, bicarbonate of soda, cream of tartar and chilli powder, then rub in the soft margarine.

2 Add the herbs and milk and mix quickly to a soft dough. Turn on to a lightly floured surface. Knead only very briefly or the dough will become tough.

3 Roll out to a 23cm/9in round and place on the prepared baking sheet. Brush lightly with water and sprinkle evenly with the sesame seeds.

4 Carefully cut the dough round into 8 wedges, separate them slightly and bake for 15–20 minutes. Cool briefly on a wire rack and serve warm.

> **Variations**
> • For cheese and herb triangles, add 50–115g/2–4oz/½–1 cup grated Gruyère or Emmenthal cheese after rubbing in the margarine in step 1.
> • To make sun-dried tomato triangles, omit the fresh mixed herbs and replace them with 30ml/2 tbsp drained chopped sun-dried tomatoes in oil. Add 15ml/1 tbsp each mild paprika, chopped fresh parsley and chopped fresh marjoram with the milk in step 2.

Brioche

Rich, yet light and airy, this is a classic French bread.

Makes 1 loaf
350g/12oz/3 cups unbleached white bread flour, plus extra for dusting
2.5ml/ 1/2 tsp salt
15g/ 1/2oz fresh yeast
60ml/4 tbsp lukewarm milk
3 eggs, lightly beaten
175g/6oz/ 3/4 cup butter, softened
25g/1oz/2 tbsp caster sugar
oil, for greasing

For the glaze
1 egg yolk
15ml/1 tbsp milk

1 Sift the flour and salt into a large bowl and make a well in the centre. Mash the yeast with the milk in a jug, then add it to the flour, with the eggs. Mix to a soft dough.

2 Using your hand, beat the dough for 4–5 minutes. Cream the butter and sugar together. Add the butter mixture to the dough in small amounts, making sure it is incorporated before adding more. Beat until smooth, shiny and elastic.

3 Cover with lightly oiled clear film and leave in a warm place for 1½ hours, or until the dough has doubled in bulk. Knock it back lightly, cover again and put it in the fridge for 8–10 hours.

4 Lightly grease a brioche mould. Turn the dough out on to a lightly floured surface. Shape three-quarters of the dough into a ball and put it in the mould. Shape the rest into an elongated oval. Make a hole in the centre of the large ball of dough. Gently press a narrow end of the oval dough into the hole.

5 Mix the egg yolk and milk for the glaze, and brush a little over the brioche. Cover with lightly oiled clear film and leave in a warm place, for 1½–2 hours, or until the dough nearly reaches the top of the mould.

6 Meanwhile, preheat the oven to 230°C/450°F/Gas 8. Brush the brioche with the remaining glaze and bake for 10 minutes. Reduce the oven temperature to 190°C/375°F/Gas 5 and bake for 20–25 minutes more, or until golden. Cool on a wire rack.

Croissants

Served with home-made preserves, these melt-in-the-mouth rolls are the ultimate luxury for breakfast.

Makes 18
500g/1 1/4 lb/5 cups plain flour, plus extra for dusting
7.5ml/1 1/2 tsp salt
10ml/2 tsp caster sugar
15ml/1 tbsp easy-blend dried yeast
325ml/11fl oz/1 1/3 cups lukewarm milk
oil, for greasing
225g/8oz/1 cup chilled butter
1 egg, beaten with 10ml/2 tsp water, for the glaze

1 Mix the flour, salt, sugar and yeast in a bowl. Add enough of the milk to make a soft dough. Transfer to a clean bowl, cover with lightly oiled clear film and leave to rise for 1½ hours.

2 Knead the dough until smooth. Wrap in greaseproof paper and chill for 15 minutes. Meanwhile, divide the butter in half and roll each half between two sheets of greaseproof paper to form a 15 × 10cm/6 × 4in rectangle.

3 Roll out the dough on a floured surface to a 30 × 20cm/ 12 × 8in rectangle. Place a sheet of butter in the centre. Fold the bottom third of dough over the butter, press to seal, then place the remaining butter sheet on top. Fold over the top third. Turn the dough so the short side faces you. Roll it gently to a 30 × 20cm/12 × 8in rectangle. Fold in thirds as before, then wrap and chill for 30 minutes. Repeat this process twice more, then wrap and chill for at least 2 hours, or overnight.

4 Roll out the dough to a rectangle, about 33cm/13in wide. Cut in half, then into 18 triangles, 15cm/6in high, with a 10cm/4in base. Roll them slightly to stretch, then roll up from base to point. Place on baking sheets, curving to make crescents. Cover with lightly oiled clear film and leave to rise for 1–1½ hours.

5 Preheat the oven to 240°C/475°F/Gas 9. Brush the croissants with the egg glaze and bake for 2 minutes. Lower the oven temperature to 190°C/375°F/Gas 5 and bake them for 10–12 minutes more, until golden. Serve warm.

Cheese & Potato Scones

The addition of creamy mashed potato gives these wholemeal scones a moist crumb and a crisp crust.

Makes 9

40g/1½oz/3 tbsp butter, plus
    extra for greasing
115g/4oz/1 cup wholemeal flour,
    plus extra for dusting
2.5ml/½ tsp salt
20ml/4 tsp baking powder
2 eggs, beaten
60ml/4 tbsp semi-skimmed milk
115g/4oz/1⅓ cups cooked,
    mashed potato
45ml/3 tbsp chopped fresh sage
50g/2oz/½ cup grated mature
    Cheddar cheese
sesame seeds, for sprinkling

1 Preheat the oven to 220°C/425°F/Gas 7. Grease a baking sheet. Sift the flour, salt and baking powder into a bowl. Rub in the butter, then mix in half the beaten eggs and all the milk. Add the mashed potato, sage and half the Cheddar, and mix to a soft dough.

2 Knead the dough lightly on a floured surface until smooth. Roll it out to 2cm/¾in thick, then stamp out nine scones using a 6cm/2½in fluted cutter.

3 Place the scones on the prepared baking sheet and brush the tops with the remaining beaten egg. Sprinkle the rest of the cheese and the sesame seeds on top and bake for 15 minutes, until golden. Cool on a wire rack.

Cook's Tip
Use a sharp cutter to avoid compressing the edges of the scones, which would prevent them from rising evenly.

Variations
• *Use unbleached self-raising flour instead of wholemeal flour and baking powder, if you wish.*
• *Fresh rosemary or basil can be used in place of the sage.*

Caramelized Onion & Walnut Scones

These are very good buttered and served with mature Cheddar or Lancashire cheese. They are also excellent with soup or a robust vegetable stew.

Makes 10–12

90g/3½oz/7 tbsp butter
15ml/1 tbsp olive oil
1 Spanish onion, chopped
2.5ml/½ tsp cumin seeds, lightly
    crushed, plus a few extra
200g/7oz/1⅔ cups self-
    raising flour, plus extra
5ml/1 tsp baking powder
25g/1oz/¼ cup oatmeal
5ml/1 tsp light muscovado sugar
90g/3½ oz/scant 1 cup
    chopped walnuts
5ml/1 tsp chopped fresh thyme
120–150ml/4–5fl oz/½–⅔ cup
    buttermilk or smetana
a little milk
salt and ground black pepper
coarse sea salt

1 Melt 15g/½oz/1 tbsp of the butter with the oil in a small pan and cook the onion over a low heat, covered, until softened but not browned. Uncover, then continue to cook gently until it begins to brown.

2 Add the crushed cumin seeds and increase the temperature slightly. Cook, stirring occasionally, until the onion browns and begins to caramelize around the edges. Cool. Preheat the oven to 200°C/400°F/Gas 6.

3 Sift the flour and baking powder into a large bowl and add the oatmeal, 2.5ml/½ tsp salt, a generous grinding of black pepper and the muscovado sugar. Rub in the remaining butter, then add the onion, walnuts and thyme. Stir in enough of the buttermilk or smetana to make a soft dough.

4 Roll or pat out the mixture to just over 1cm/½in thick and stamp out 5–6cm/2–2½in round scones. Place on a floured baking sheet, brush with milk and scatter with a little coarse sea salt and a few extra cumin seeds. Bake for 12–15 minutes, until well-risen and golden brown. Cool the scones briefly on a wire rack and serve warm.

Cheese & Mustard Scones

Depending on their size, these cheese scones can be served as little canapé bases, tea-time treats or even as a quick pie topping.

Makes 12
250g/9oz/2¼ cups self-raising flour, plus extra for dusting
5ml/1 tsp baking powder
2.5ml/½ tsp salt
40g/1½ oz/3 tbsp butter or

sunflower margarine
175g/6oz/1½ cups grated mature Cheddar cheese, plus extra for sprinkling
10ml/2 tsp wholegrain mustard
about 150ml/¼ pint/⅔ cup milk
ground black pepper

To serve (optional)
garlic-flavoured cream cheese
chopped fresh chives
sliced radishes

1 Preheat the oven to 220°C/425°F/Gas 7. Sift the flour, baking powder and salt into a large bowl, then rub in the butter or sunflower margarine. Season to taste with pepper and stir in the grated cheese.

2 Mix the mustard with the milk until thoroughly combined. Add the mixture to the dry ingredients and mix quickly until the mixture just comes together.

3 Knead the dough lightly on a lightly floured surface, then pat it out to a depth of 2cm/¾in. Use a 5cm/2in cutter to stamp out rounds. Place on a non-stick baking sheet and sprinkle with extra grated cheese.

4 Bake for about 10 minutes until risen and golden. You can test scones by pressing the sides, which should spring back. Cool on a wire rack. Serve spread with garlic-flavoured cream cheese, topped with chopped chives and sliced radishes, if you like.

> **Cook's Tip**
> Do not over-mix the dough, or the scones will be heavy, tough and chewy.

Sunflower & Almond Sesame Crackers

Full of flavour, these slim savoury biscuits taste great with cheese and celery, or could be served with hummus or a similar dip.

Makes about 24
130g/4½oz/1 cup ground sunflower seeds
90g/3½oz/scant 1 cup ground almonds
5ml/1 tsp baking powder
30ml/2 tbsp milk
1 egg yolk
25g/1oz/2 tbsp butter, melted
25g/1oz/¼ cup sesame seeds

1 Preheat the oven to 190°C/375°F/Gas 5. Reserve 25g/1oz/¼ cup of the ground sunflower seeds for rolling out and mix the remaining ground seeds with the ground almonds and baking powder in a bowl.

2 Mix the milk and egg yolk in a cup, then stir the mixture into the dry ingredients, with the melted butter, mixing well. Gently work the mixture with your hands to form a moist dough.

3 On a cool surface that has been lightly dusted with some of the reserved ground sunflower seeds, roll out the dough to a thickness of about 5mm/¼in, sprinkling more ground seeds on top to prevent sticking.

4 Sprinkle the dough with sesame seeds and cut into rounds, with a 5cm/2in pastry cutter. Lift on to a non-stick baking sheet.

5 Bake the crackers for about 10 minutes until lightly browned. Cool on a wire rack.

> **Variation**
> Sprinkle some poppy seeds on top of a few of the biscuits before baking.

Oatcakes

Old-fashioned they may be, but oatcakes are delicious, especially with cheese.

Makes 8
175g/6oz/1½ cups medium
 oatmeal, plus extra
 for sprinkling

2.5ml/½ tsp salt
pinch of bicarbonate of soda
15g/½oz/1 tbsp butter, plus
 extra for greasing
75ml/5 tbsp water

1 Preheat the oven to 150°C/300°F/Gas 2. Mix the oatmeal with the salt and bicarbonate of soda in a mixing bowl.

2 Melt the butter with the water in a small saucepan. Bring to the boil, then add to the oatmeal mixture and mix thoroughly to form a moist dough.

3 Turn the dough on to a surface sprinkled with oatmeal and knead to a smooth ball. Turn a large baking sheet upside-down, grease it, sprinkle it lightly with oatmeal and place the ball of dough on top. Sprinkle the dough with oatmeal, then roll out to a 25cm/10in round.

4 Cut the round into eight sections, ease them apart slightly and bake for 50–60 minutes until crisp. Leave to cool on the baking sheet, then remove the oatcakes with a palette knife.

Cook's Tips
• To achieve a neat round, place a 25cm/10in cake board or plate on top of the oatcake. Cut away any excess dough with a palette knife, then lift off the board or plate.
• Oatmeal is ground from the whole kernel of the cereal and is graded according to how finely it is ground. The largest and coarsest type is pinhead, then, in descending order of size, rough, medium, fine and superfine. Medium oatmeal is widely available, but fine is also suitable for oatcakes. Oat flakes, made from steamed rolled oats, are not suitable.

Rosemary Crackers

Rosemary is said to grow best for a strong-willed woman. If you have some in your garden, make these excellent crackers, and top them with cream cheese and rosemary flowers.

Makes about 25
225g/8oz/2 cups plain flour
2.5ml/½ tsp baking powder
a good pinch of salt

2.5ml/½ tsp curry powder
75g/3oz/6 tbsp butter, diced
30ml/2 tbsp finely chopped young
 rosemary leaves
1 egg yolk
30–45ml/2–3 tbsp water
milk, to glaze

To decorate
30ml/2 tbsp cream cheese
rosemary flowers

1 Put the flour, baking powder, salt and curry powder in a food processor. Add the butter and process until the mixture resembles fine breadcrumbs. Add the rosemary, egg yolk and 30ml/2 tbsp of the water. Process again, adding the remaining water, if needed, to make a firm dough. Wrap in clear film and chill in the fridge for 30 minutes.

2 Preheat the oven to 180°C/350°F/Gas 4. Roll out the dough thinly on a lightly floured surface and cut out the crackers using a 5cm/2in fluted cutter.

3 Transfer them to a large baking sheet and prick with a fork. Brush with milk to glaze and bake for about 10 minutes, until pale golden. Cool on a wire rack.

4 Spread a little cream cheese on to each biscuit and secure a few rosemary flowers on top, using tweezers to position the flowers, if this makes it easier.

Cook's Tip
If you do not have a food processor, simply rub the butter into the flour mixture in a bowl, then add the remaining ingredients and combine.

Index